CONTENTS

Classmates

volume three
sotsu gyo sei
- spring -

story and art
Asumiko Nakamura

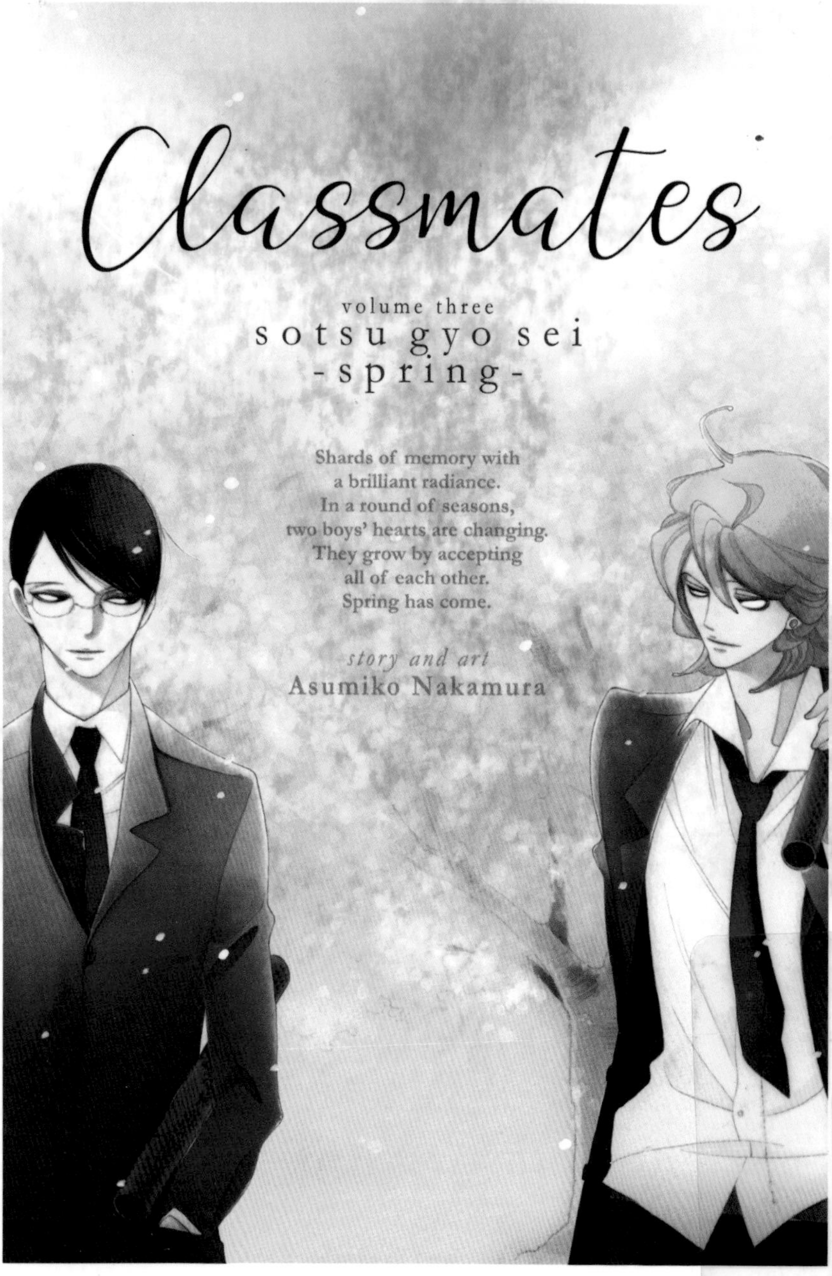

Classmates

volume three

sotsu gyo sei

-spring-

Shards of memory with
a brilliant radiance.
In a round of seasons,
two boys' hearts are changing.
They grow by accepting
all of each other.
Spring has come.

story and art
Asumiko Nakamura

[The Tears That Don't Spill Over]

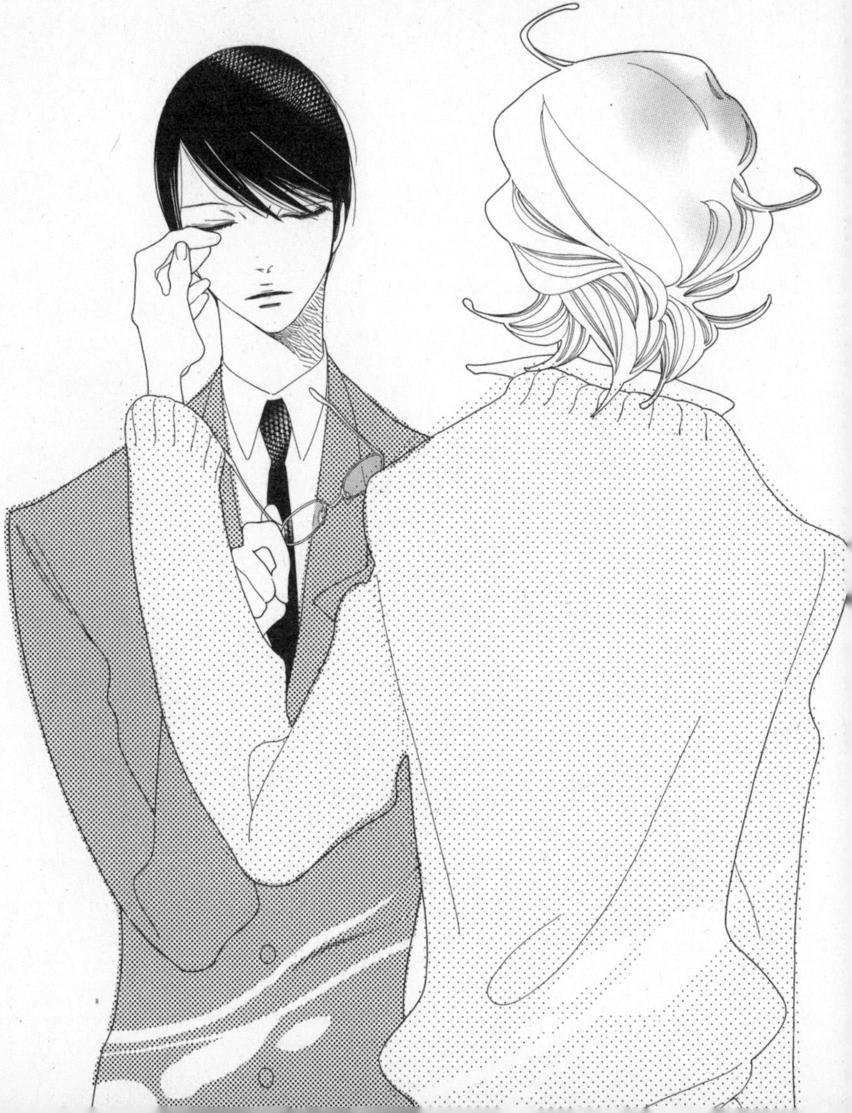

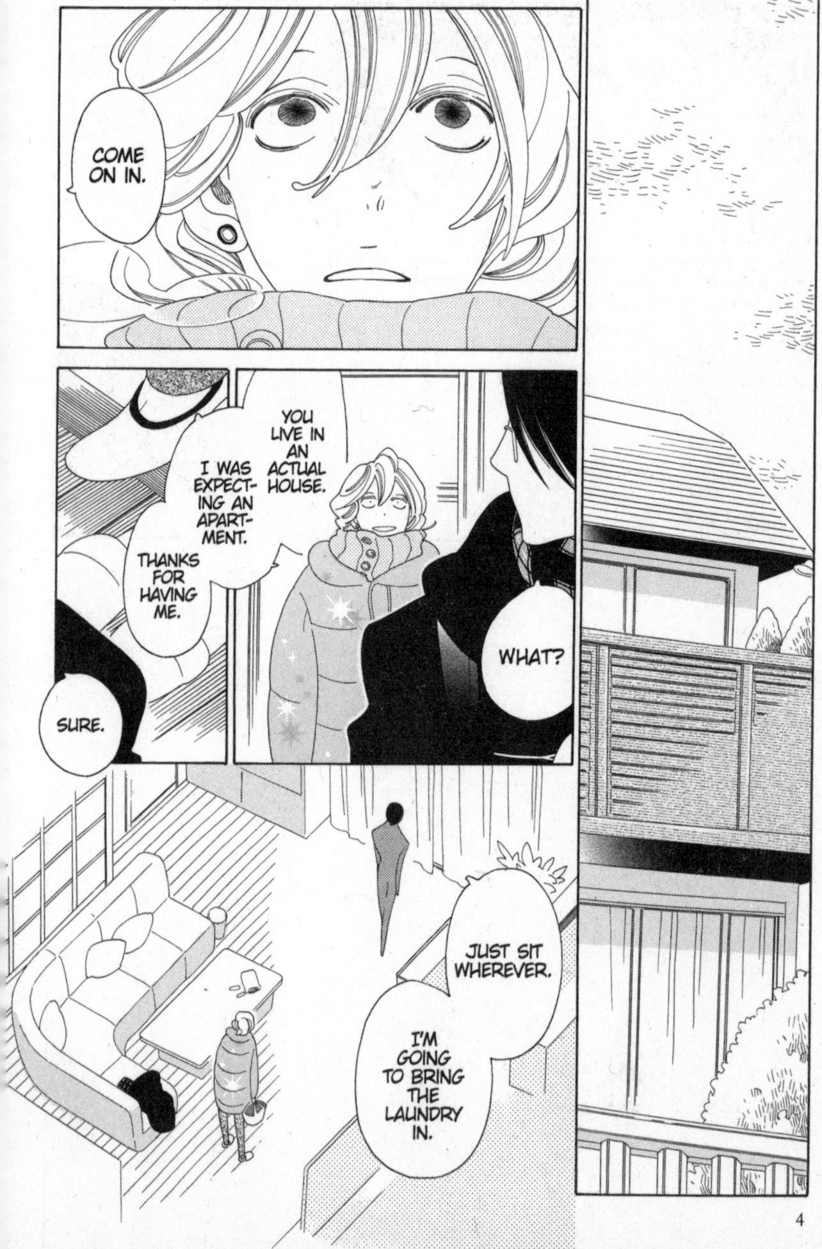
COME ON IN.
YOU LIVE IN AN ACTUAL HOUSE.
WHAT?
I WAS EXPECTING AN APARTMENT.
THANKS FOR HAVING ME.
SURE.
JUST SIT WHEREVER.
I'M GOING TO BRING THE LAUNDRY IN.

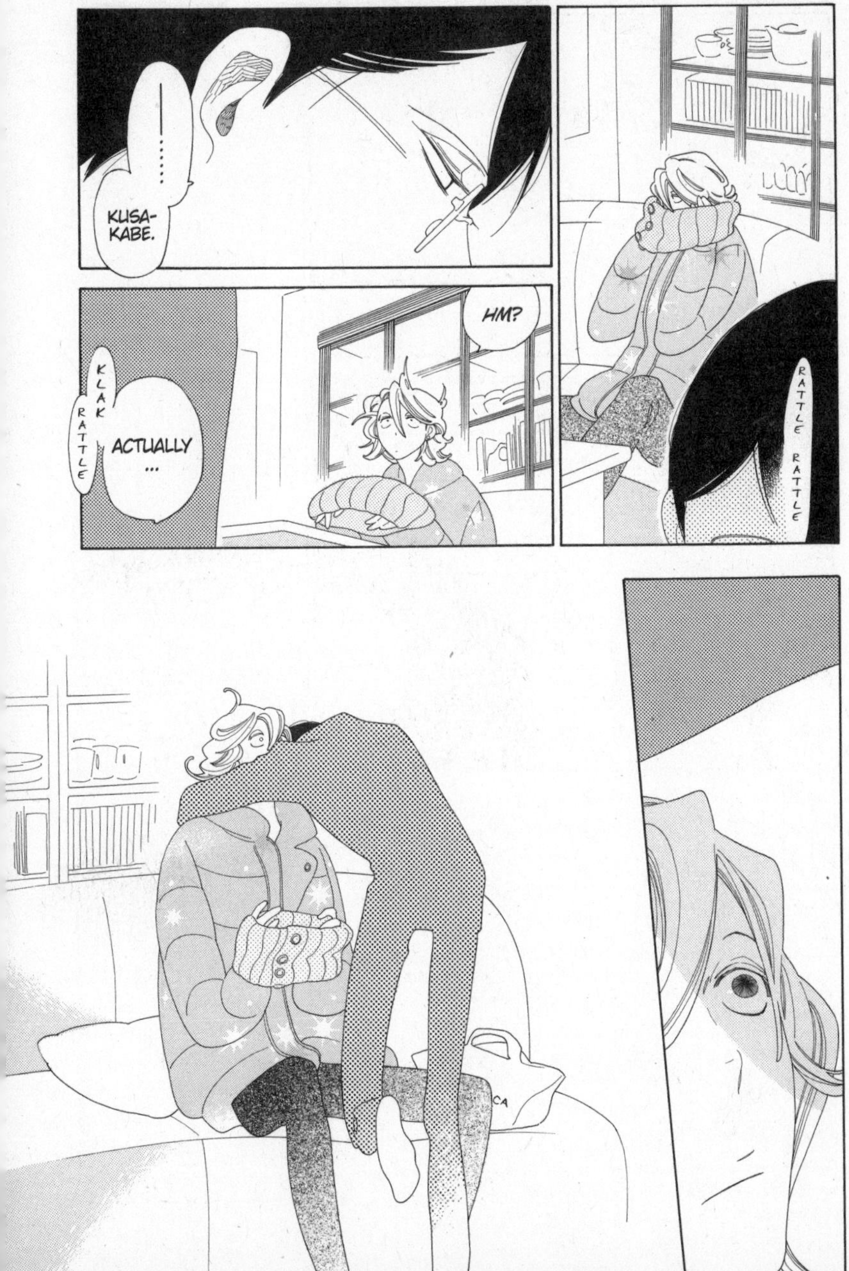
RATTLE RATTLE
......
KUSA-KABE.
HM?
ACTUALLY ...
KLAK
RATTLE
CA

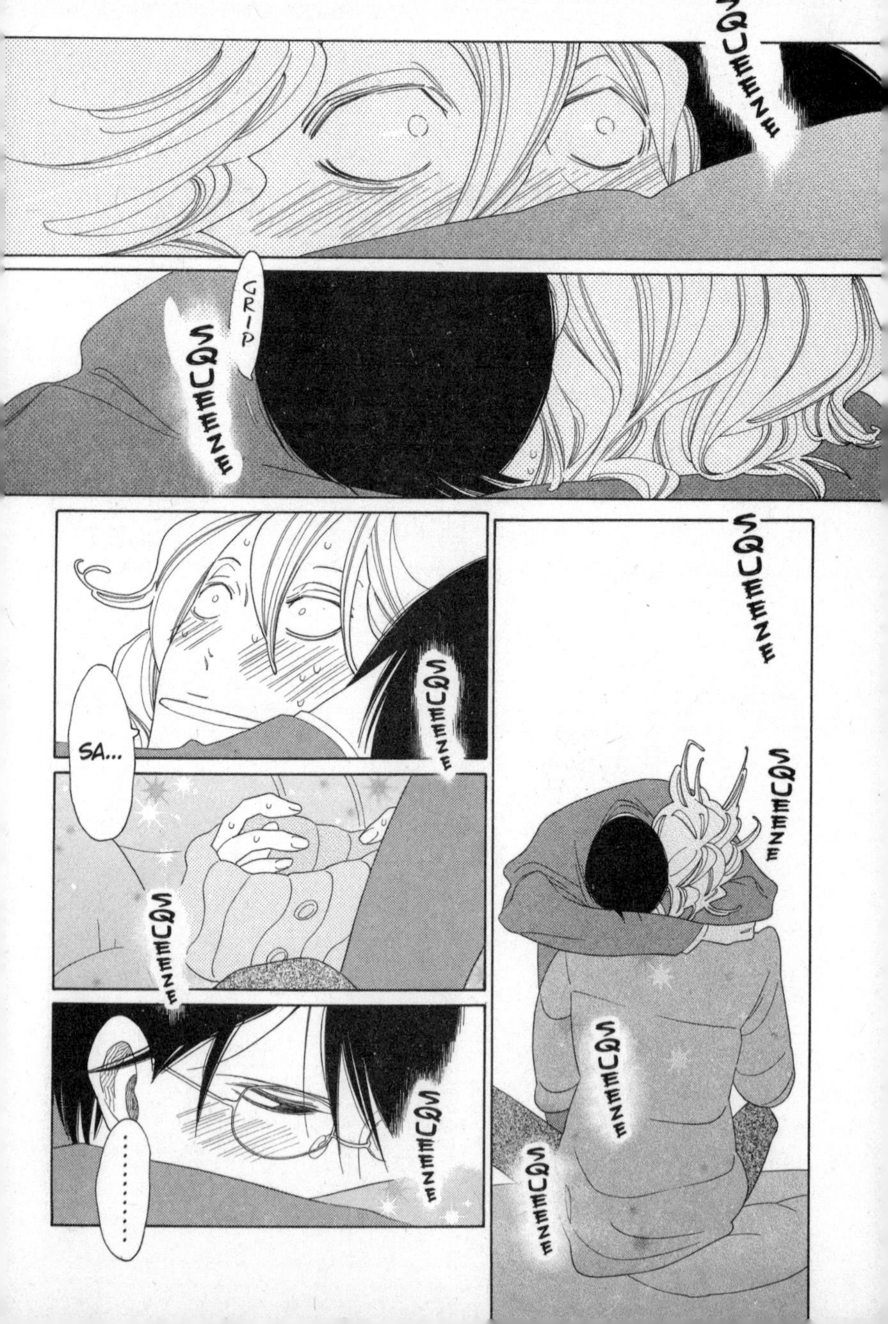
SQUEEZE
GRIP
SQUEEZE
SQUEEZE
SQUEEZE
SQUEEZE
SQUEEZE
SQUEEZE
SA...
SQUEEZE
SQUEEZE
....

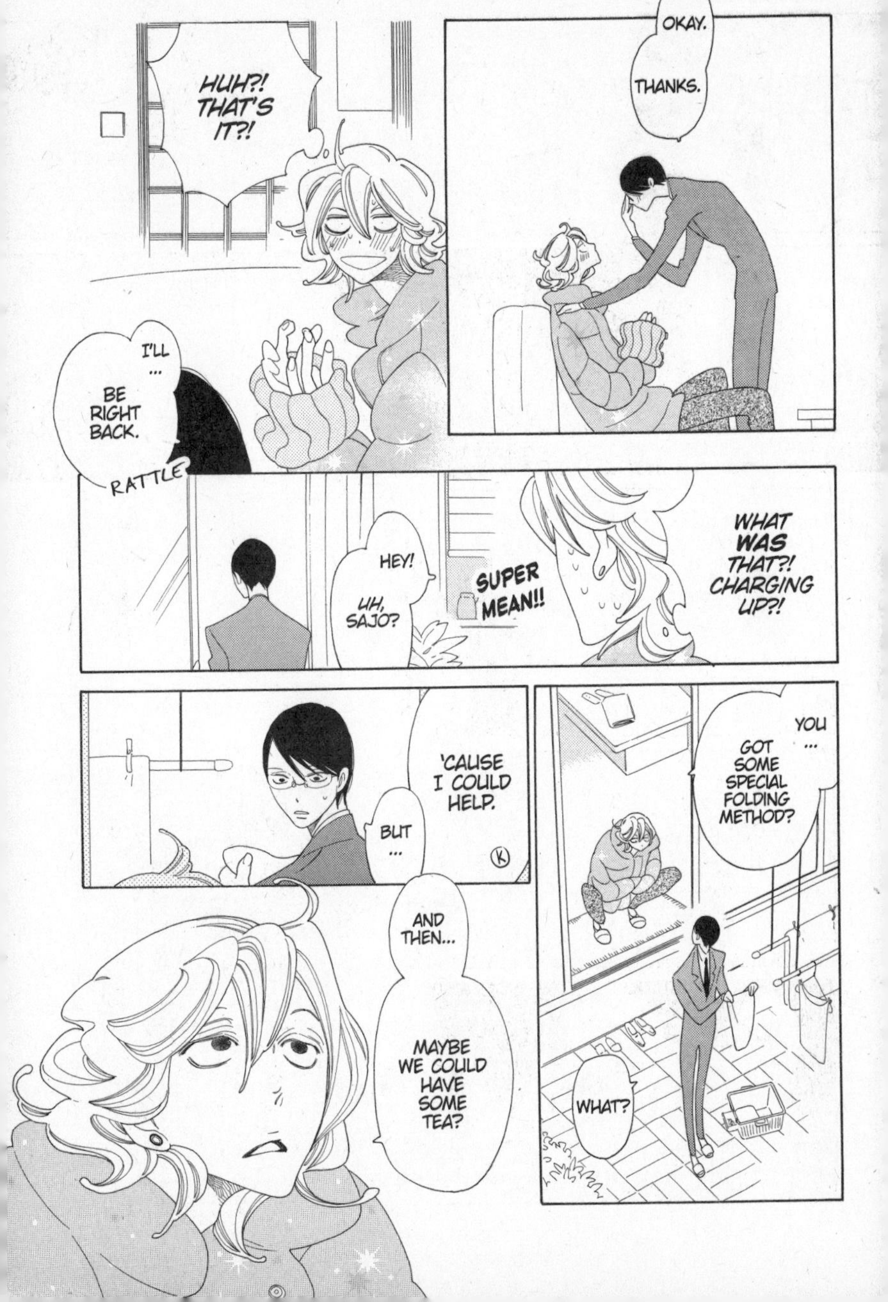

OKAY.
THANKS.
HUH?! THAT'S IT?!
I'LL ... BE RIGHT BACK.
RATTLE
WHAT WAS THAT?! CHARGING UP?!
SUPER MEAN!!
HEY!
UH, SAJO?
YOU ...
GOT SOME SPECIAL FOLDING METHOD?
WHAT?
'CAUSE I COULD HELP.
BUT ...
AND THEN...
MAYBE WE COULD HAVE SOME TEA?

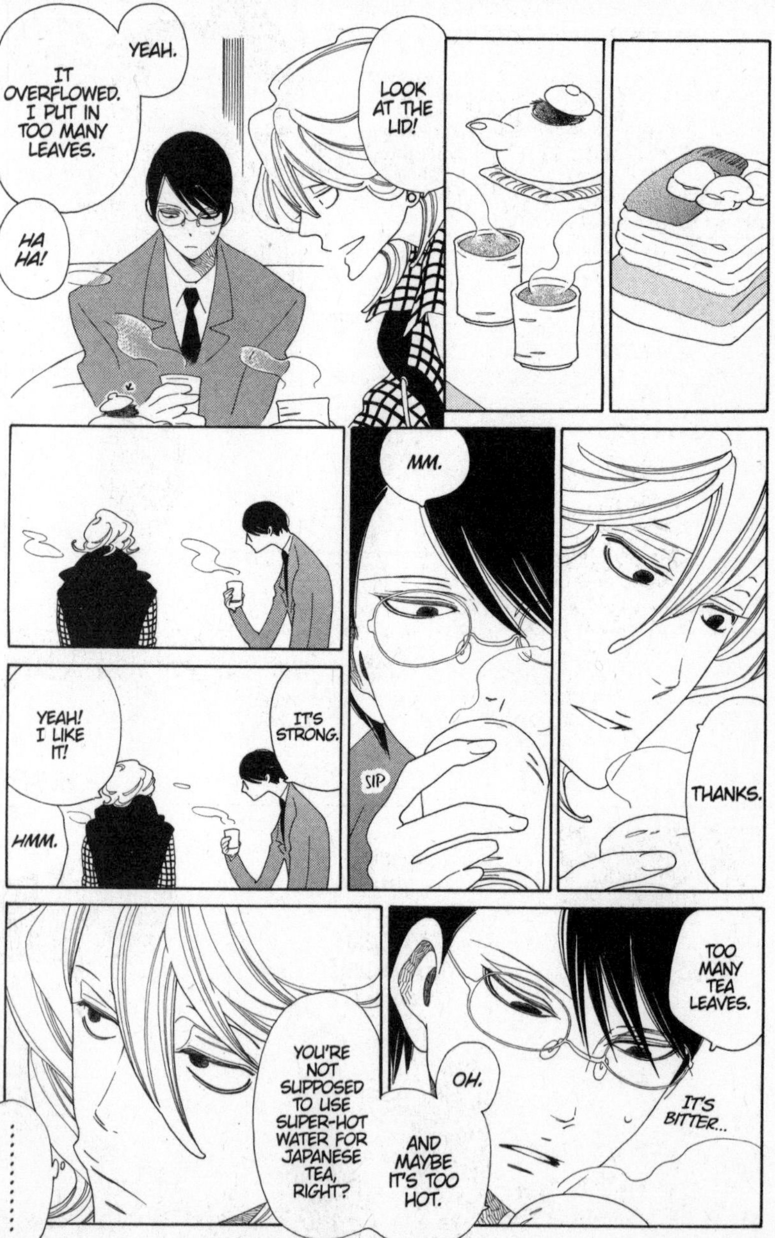
LOOK AT THE LID!
YEAH.
IT OVERFLOWED. I PUT IN TOO MANY LEAVES.
HA HA!
THANKS.
MM.
SIP
IT'S STRONG.
YEAH! I LIKE IT!
HMM.
TOO MANY TEA LEAVES.
IT'S BITTER...
OH.
AND MAYBE IT'S TOO HOT.
YOU'RE NOT SUPPOSED TO USE SUPER-HOT WATER FOR JAPANESE TEA, RIGHT?
......

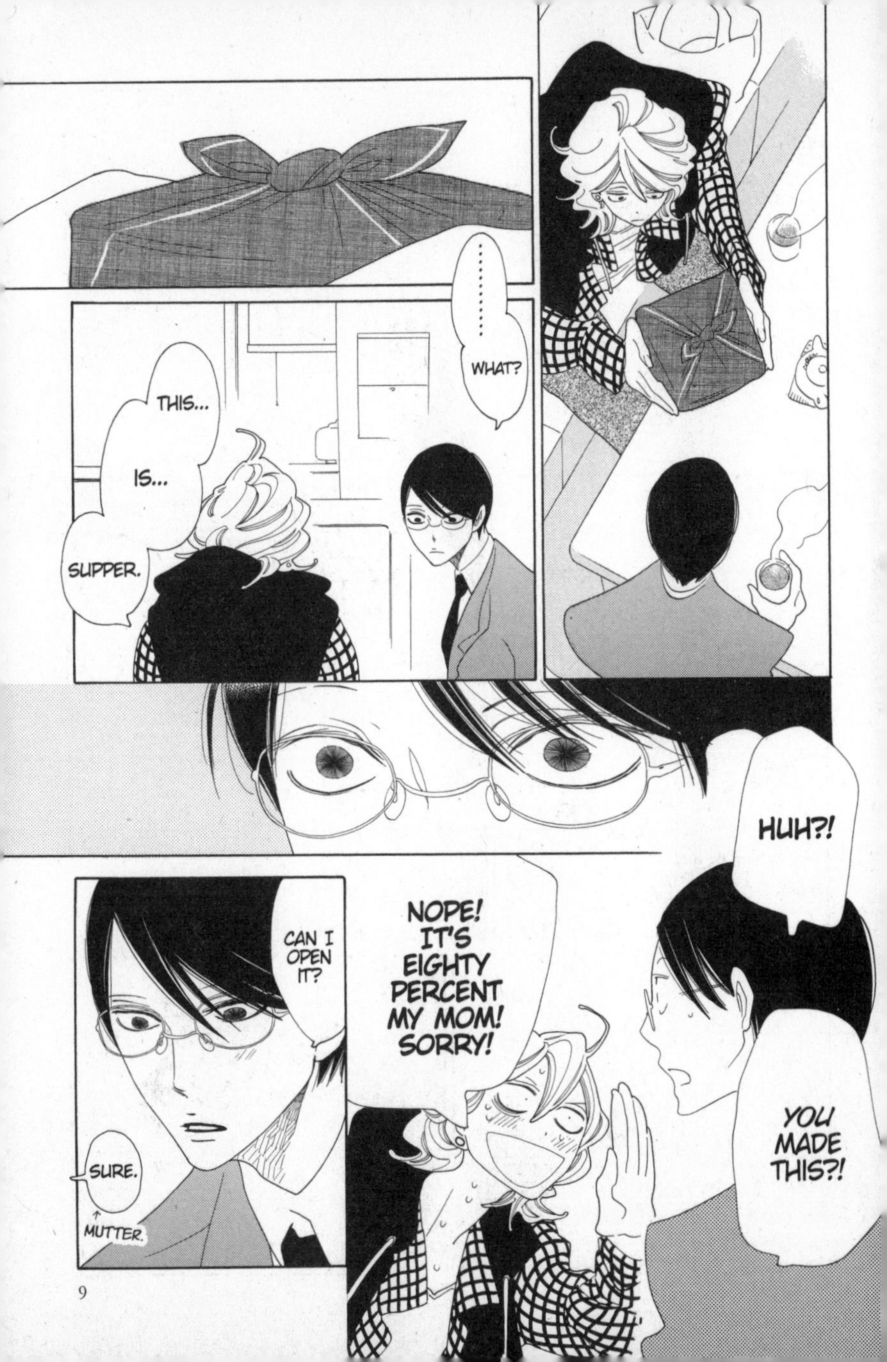

......
WHAT?
THIS...
IS...
SUPPER.
HUH?!
YOU MADE THIS?!
NOPE! IT'S EIGHTY PERCENT MY MOM! SORRY!
CAN I OPEN IT?
SURE.
MUTTER.

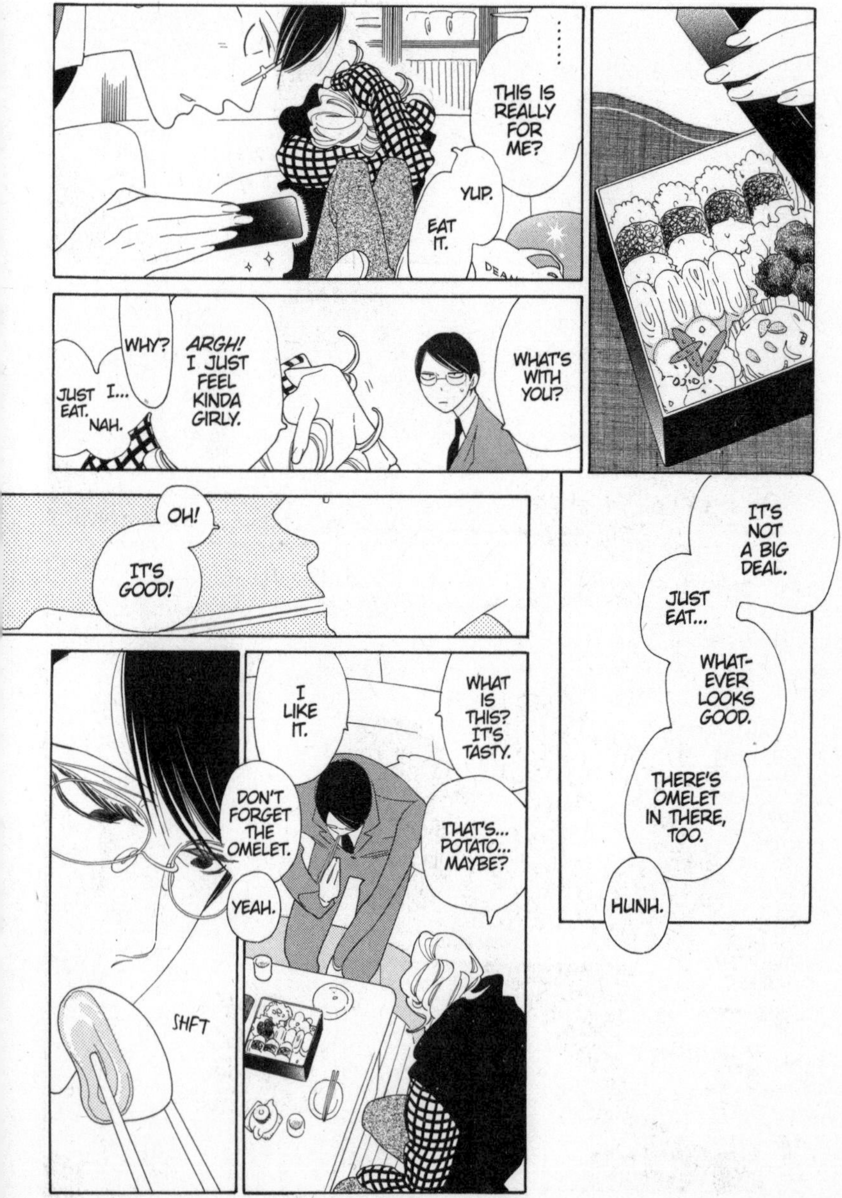
......
THIS IS REALLY FOR ME?
YUP.
EAT IT.
WHAT'S WITH YOU?
ARGH! I JUST FEEL KINDA GIRLY.
WHY?
I...
NAH.
JUST EAT.
IT'S NOT A BIG DEAL.
JUST EAT...
WHAT-EVER LOOKS GOOD.
THERE'S OMELET IN THERE, TOO.
HUNH.
OH!
IT'S GOOD!
WHAT IS THIS? IT'S TASTY.
I LIKE IT.
THAT'S... POTATO... MAYBE?
DON'T FORGET THE OMELET.
YEAH.
SHFT

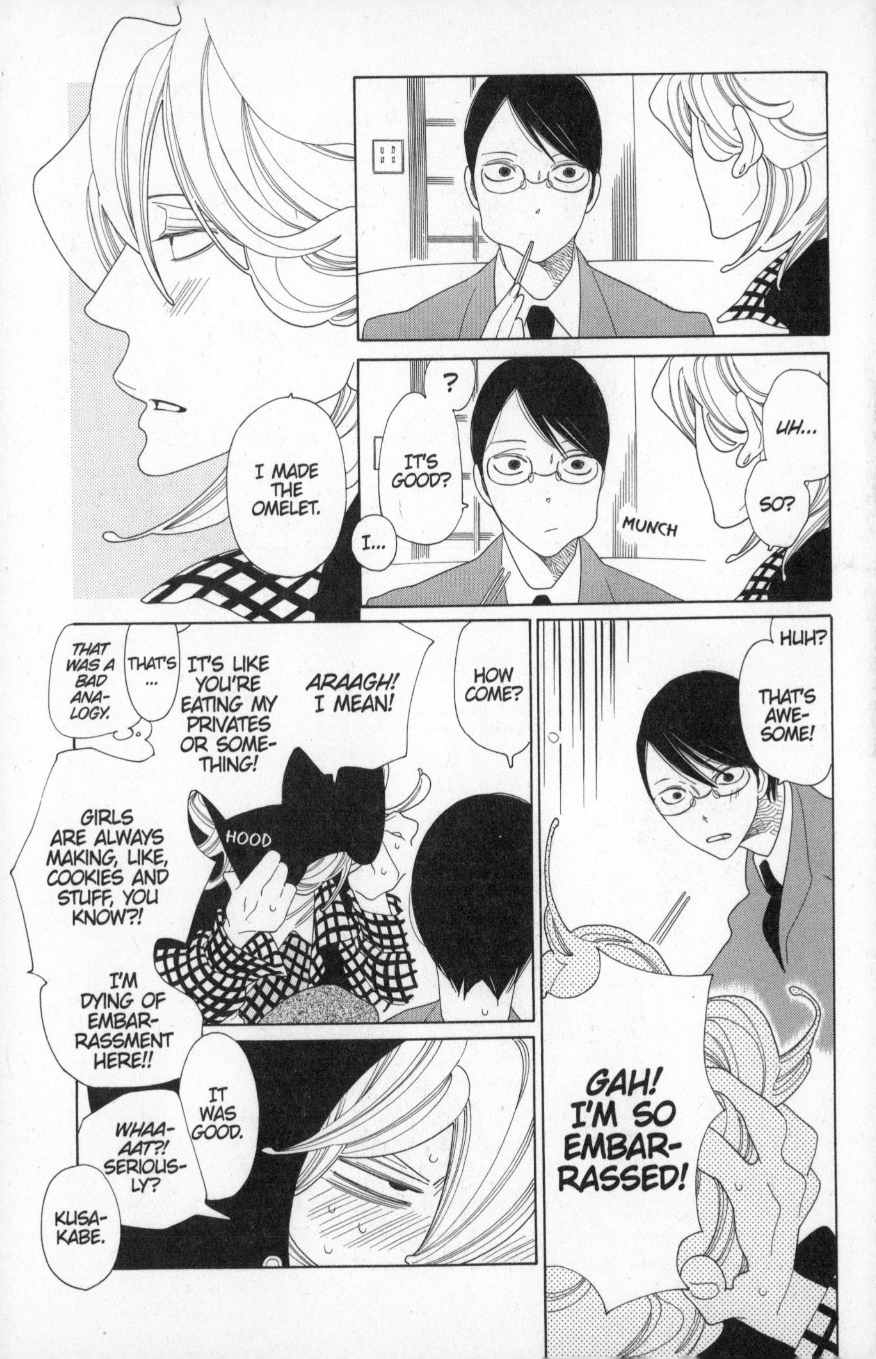
UH...
SO?
MUNCH
?
IT'S GOOD?
I...
I MADE THE OMELET.
HUH?
THAT'S AWE-SOME!
GAH! I'M SO EMBAR-RASSED!
HOW COME?
ARAAGH! I MEAN!
IT'S LIKE YOU'RE EATING MY PRIVATES OR SOME-THING!
THAT'S ...
THAT WAS A BAD ANA-LOGY.
HOOD
GIRLS ARE ALWAYS MAKING, LIKE, COOKIES AND STUFF, YOU KNOW?!
I'M DYING OF EMBAR-RASSMENT HERE!!
IT WAS GOOD.
WHAA-AAT?! SERIOUS-LY?
KUSA-KABE.

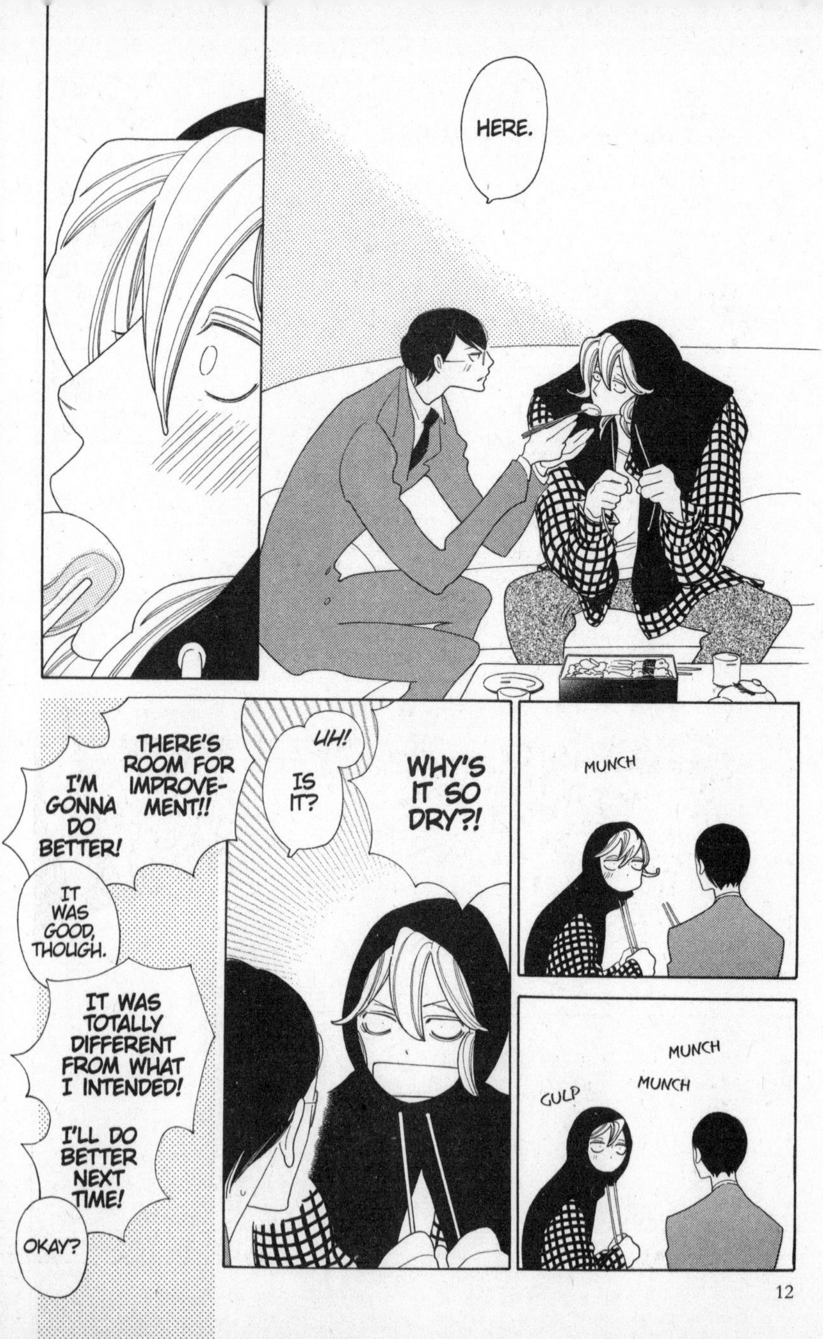
HERE.
MUNCH
MUNCH
MUNCH
GULP
WHY'S IT SO DRY?!
UH!
IS IT?
THERE'S ROOM FOR IMPROVEMENT!!
I'M GONNA DO BETTER!
IT WAS GOOD, THOUGH.
IT WAS TOTALLY DIFFERENT FROM WHAT I INTENDED!
I'LL DO BETTER NEXT TIME!
OKAY?

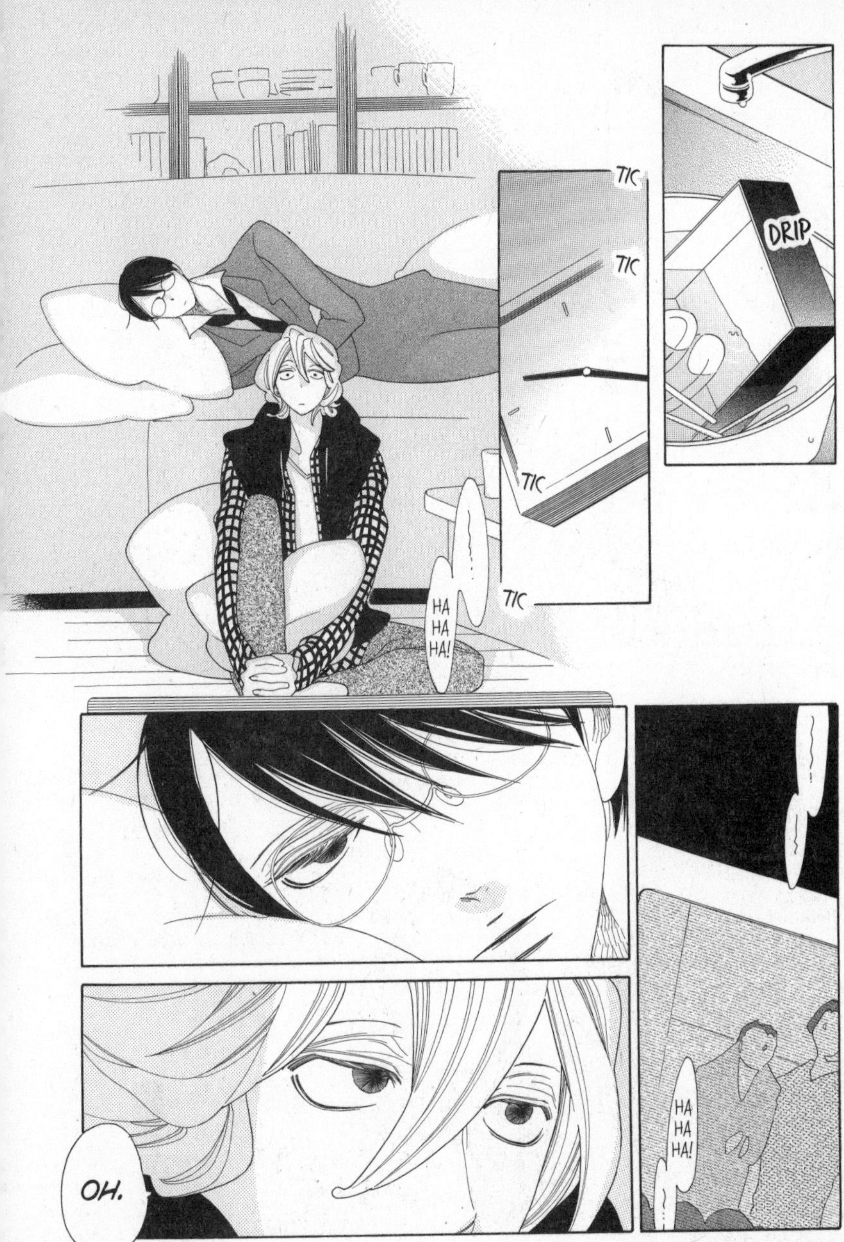

DRIP
TIC
TIC
TIC
TIC
...
HA HA HA!
...
...
HA HA HA!
...
OH.

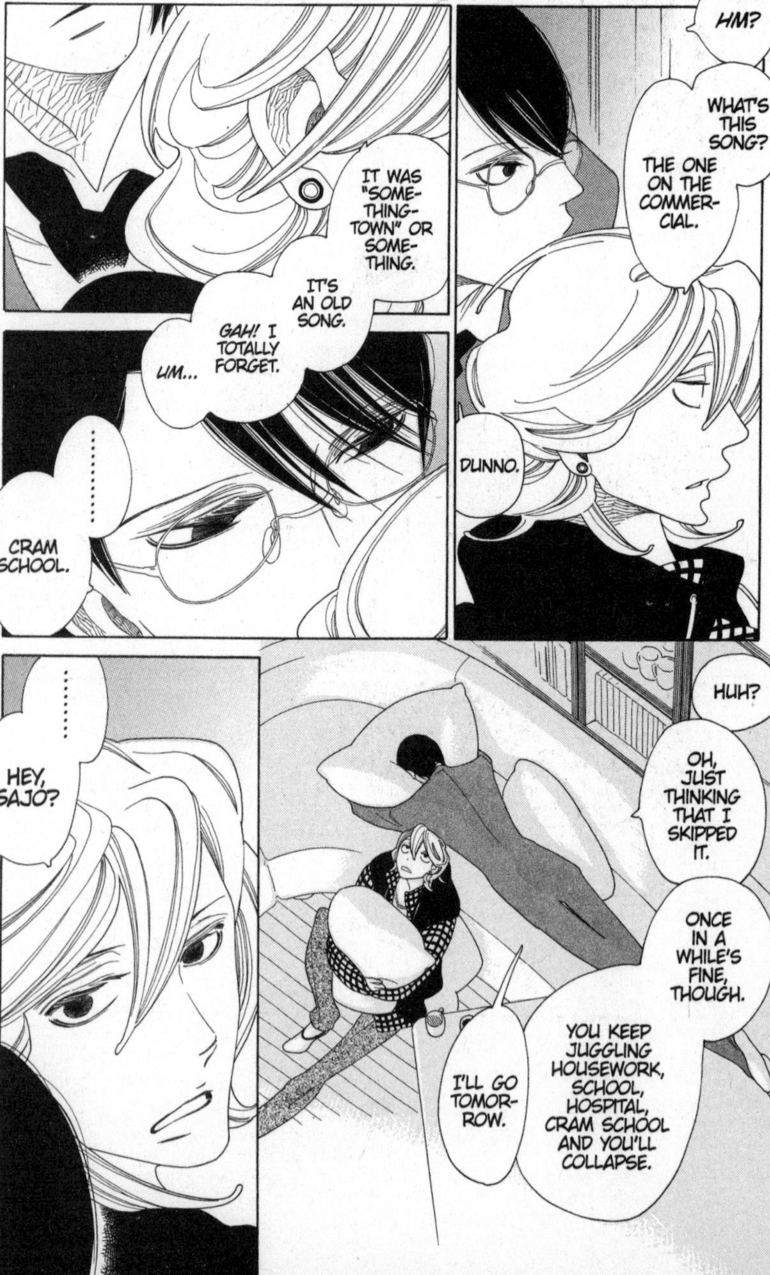
HM?
WHAT'S THIS SONG?
THE ONE ON THE COMMERCIAL.
DUNNO.
IT WAS "SOMETHING-TOWN" OR SOMETHING.
IT'S AN OLD SONG.
GAH! I TOTALLY FORGET.
UM...
......
CRAM SCHOOL.
HUH?
OH, JUST THINKING THAT I SKIPPED IT.
ONCE IN A WHILE'S FINE, THOUGH.
YOU KEEP JUGGLING HOUSEWORK, SCHOOL, HOSPITAL, CRAM SCHOOL AND YOU'LL COLLAPSE.
I'LL GO TOMORROW.
......
HEY, SAJO?

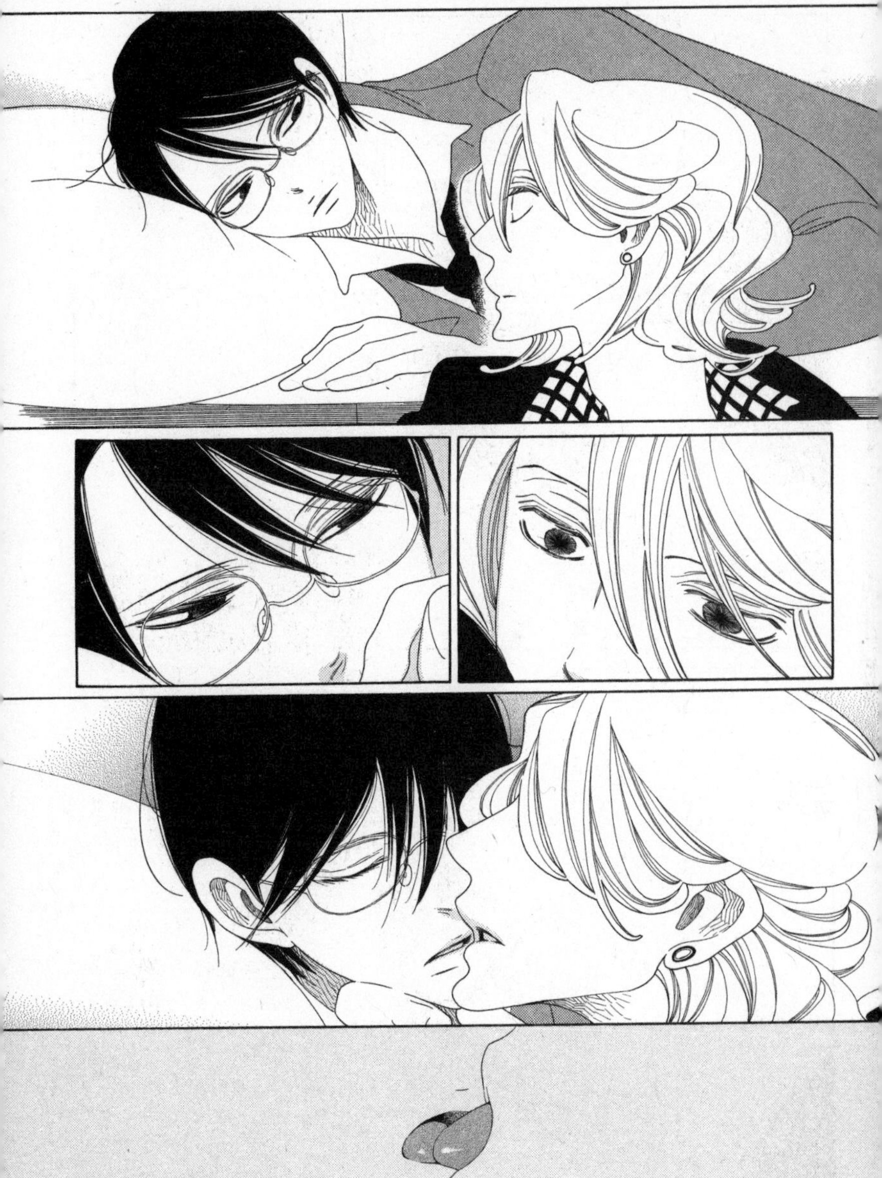

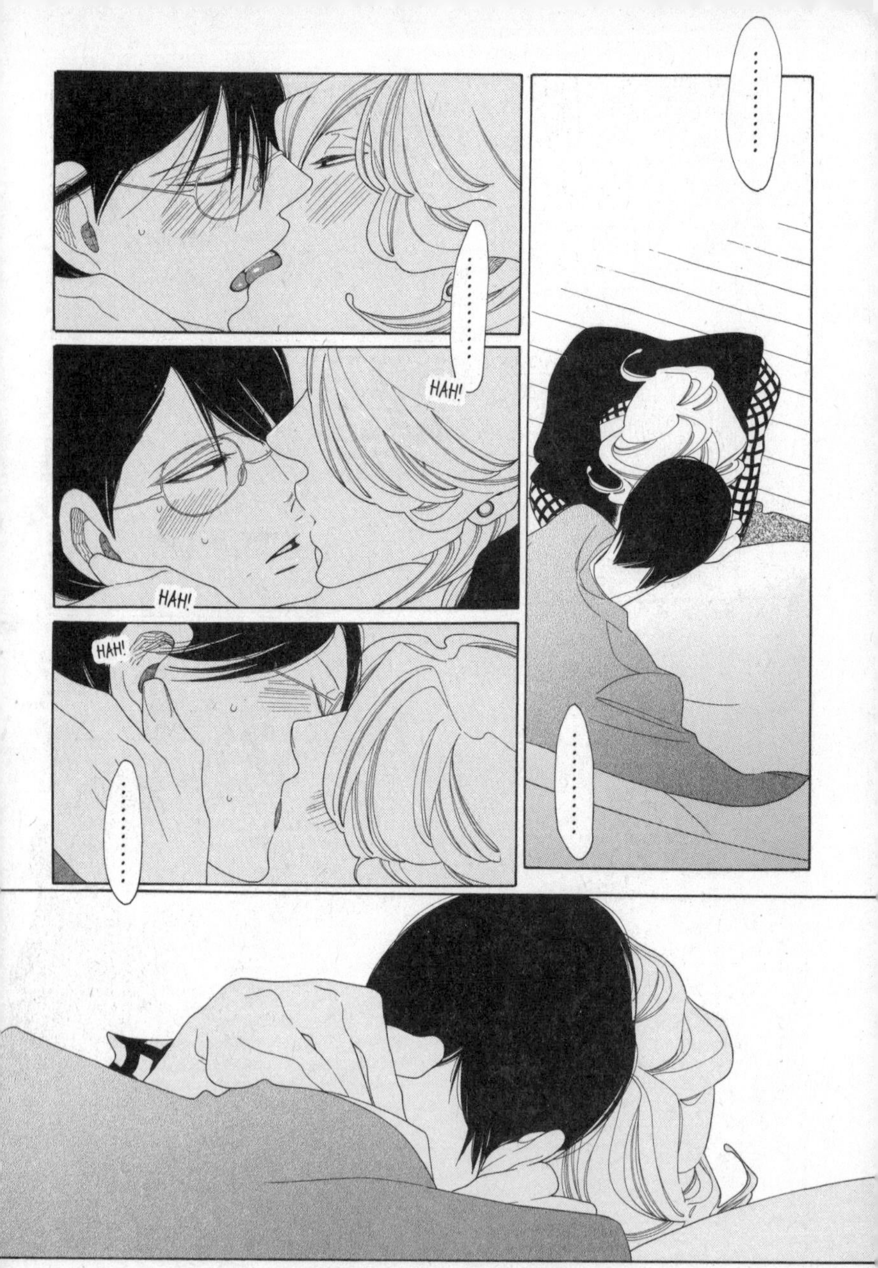
......
......
......
HAH!
HAH!
HAH!
......

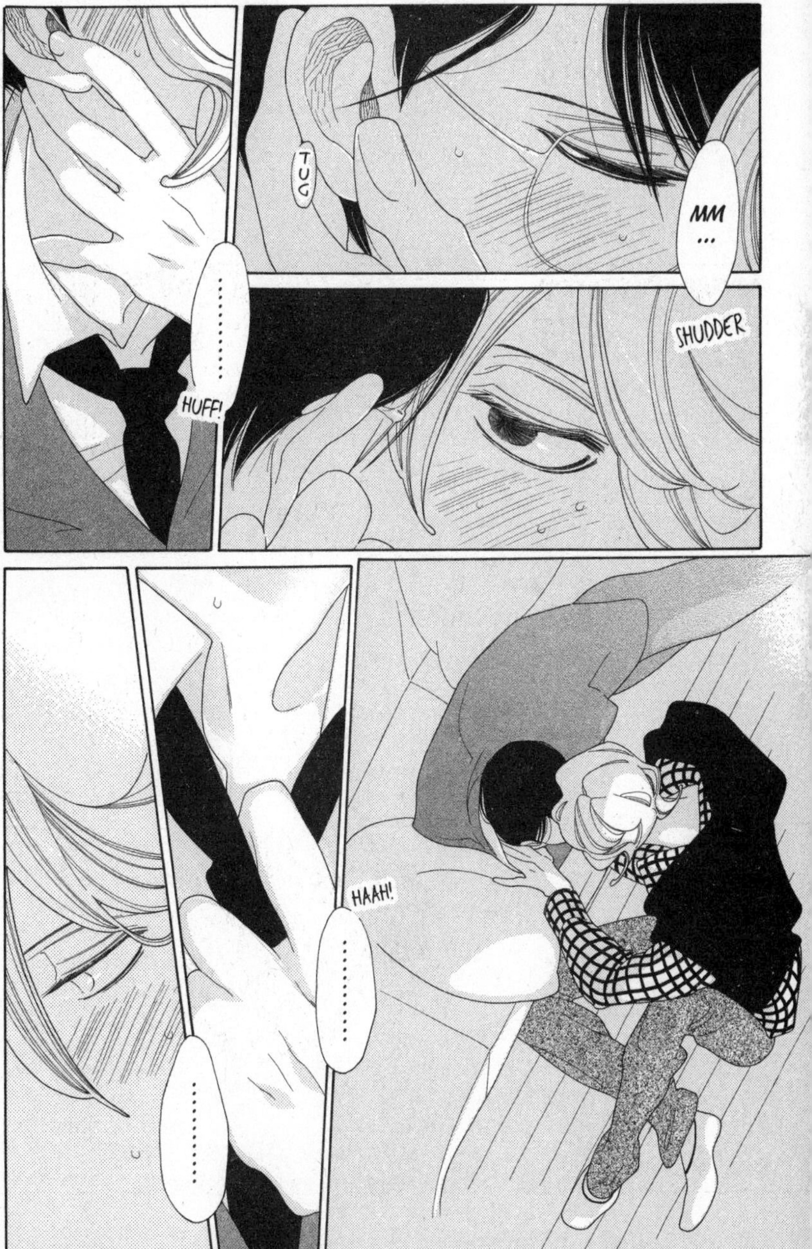
MM ...
TUG
SHUDDER
......
HUFF!
HAAH!
......
......

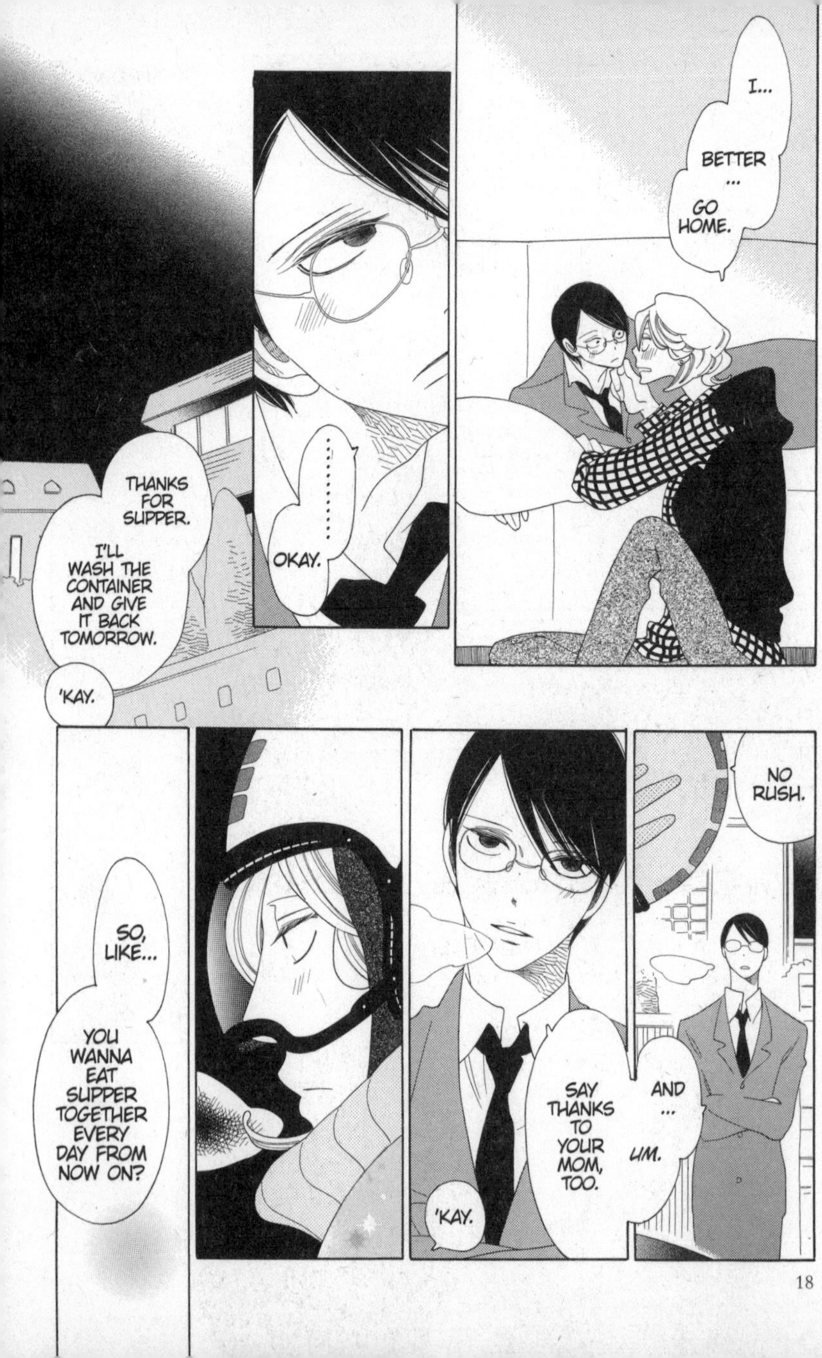
I... BETTER ... GO HOME.
......
OKAY.
THANKS FOR SUPPER.
I'LL WASH THE CONTAINER AND GIVE IT BACK TOMORROW.
'KAY.
NO RUSH.
AND ... UM.
SAY THANKS TO YOUR MOM, TOO.
'KAY.
SO, LIKE...
YOU WANNA EAT SUPPER TOGETHER EVERY DAY FROM NOW ON?

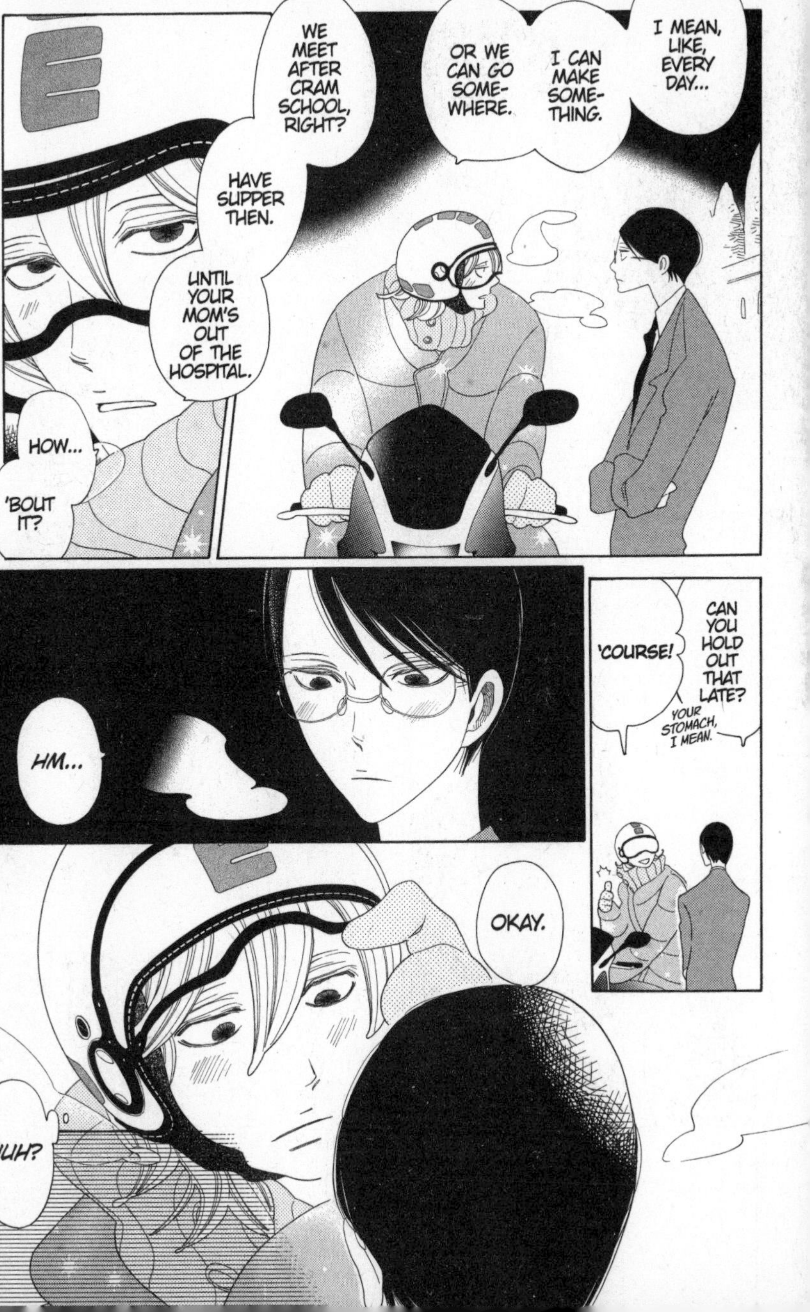
I MEAN, LIKE, EVERY DAY...
I CAN MAKE SOME-THING.
OR WE CAN GO SOME-WHERE.
WE MEET AFTER CRAM SCHOOL, RIGHT?
HAVE SUPPER THEN.
UNTIL YOUR MOM'S OUT OF THE HOSPITAL.
HOW...
'BOUT IT?
CAN YOU HOLD OUT THAT LATE?
YOUR STOMACH, I MEAN.
'COURSE!
HM...
OKAY.
HUH?

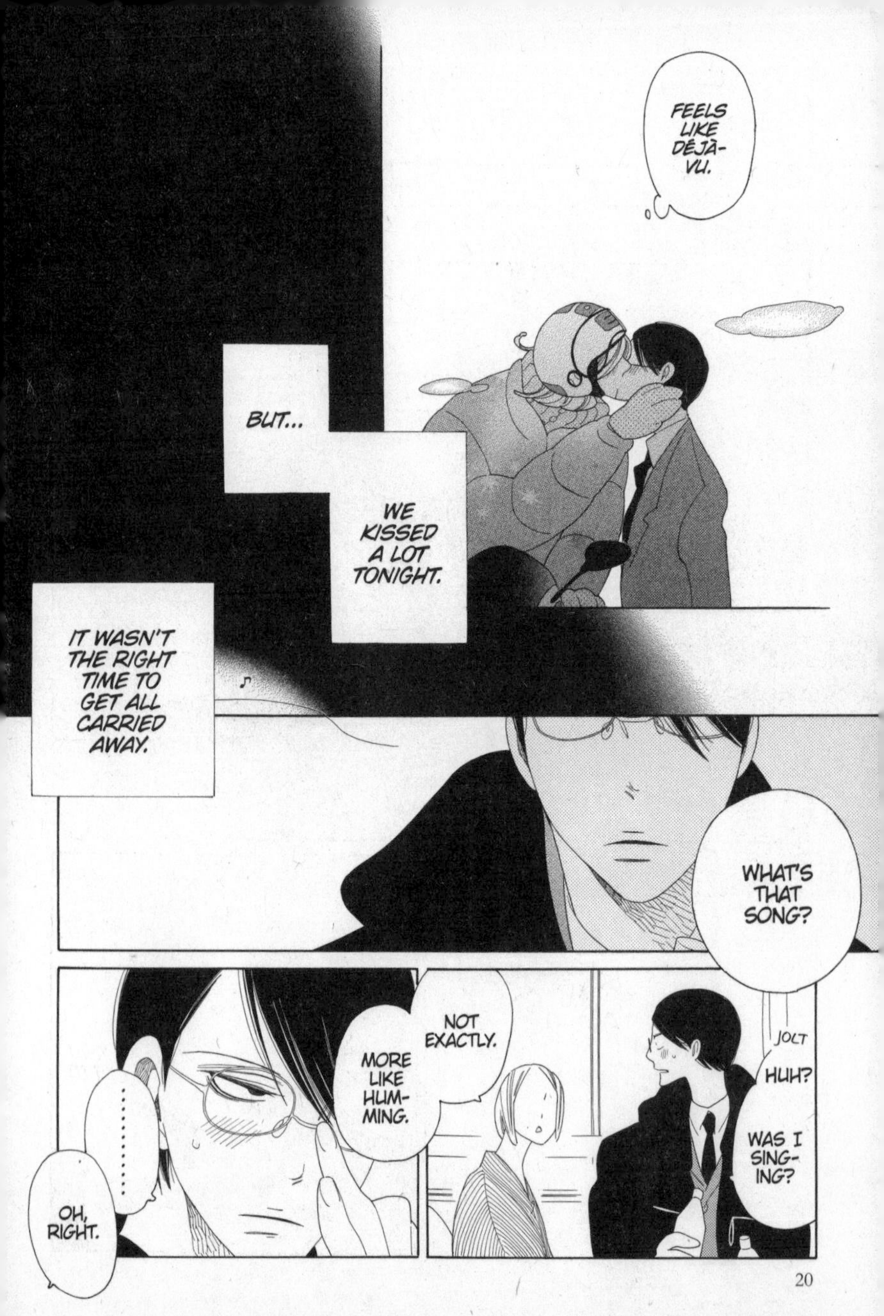
FEELS LIKE DÉJÀ-VU.
BUT...
WE KISSED A LOT TONIGHT.
IT WASN'T THE RIGHT TIME TO GET ALL CARRIED AWAY.
WHAT'S THAT SONG?
JOLT
HUH?
WAS I SING-ING?
NOT EXACTLY.
MORE LIKE HUM-MING.
......
OH, RIGHT.

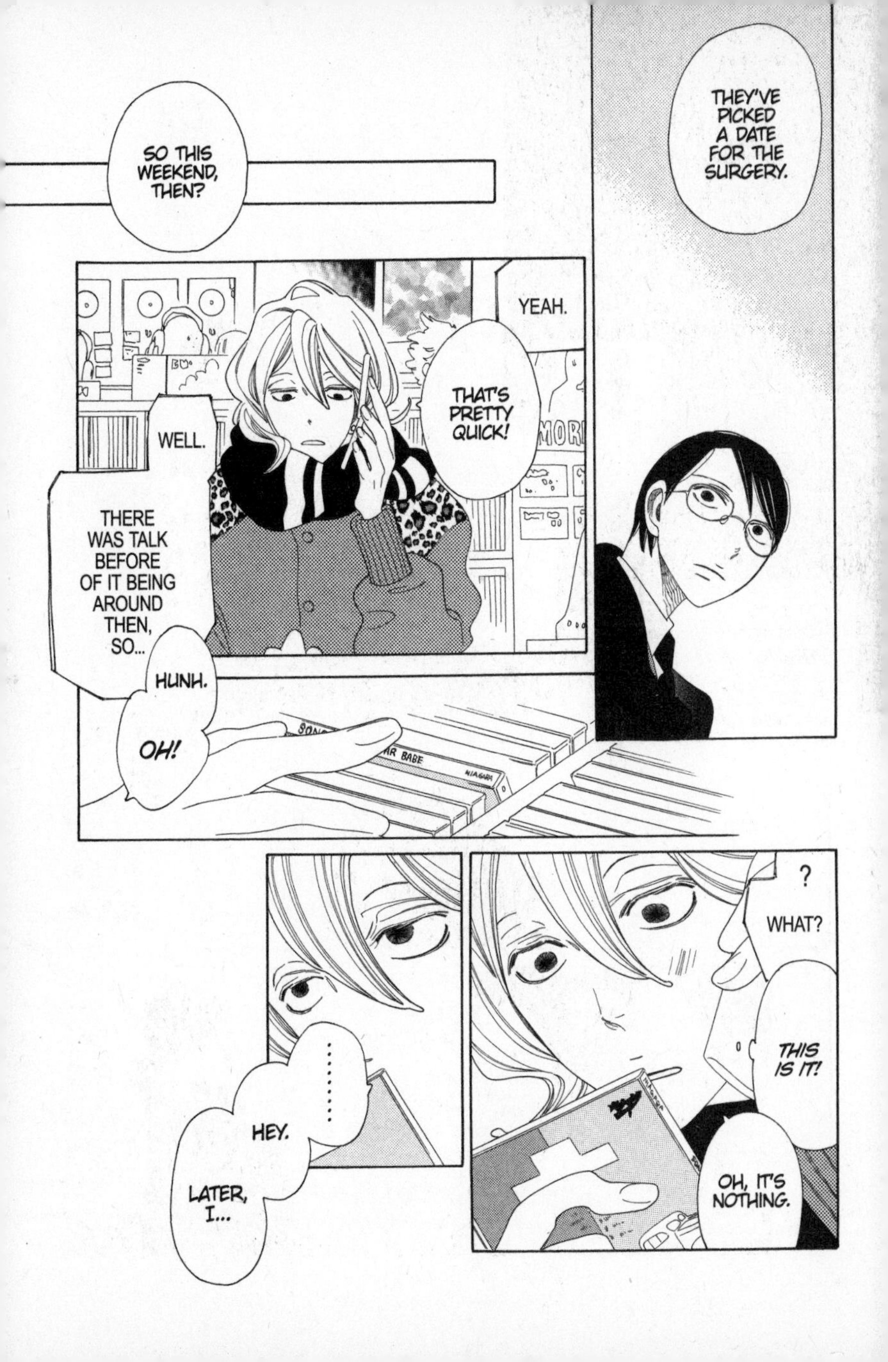
THEY'VE PICKED A DATE FOR THE SURGERY.
SO THIS WEEKEND, THEN?
YEAH.
THAT'S PRETTY QUICK!
WELL.
THERE WAS TALK BEFORE OF IT BEING AROUND THEN, SO...
HUNH.
OH!
?
WHAT?
THIS IS IT!
OH, IT'S NOTHING.
......
HEY.
LATER, I...

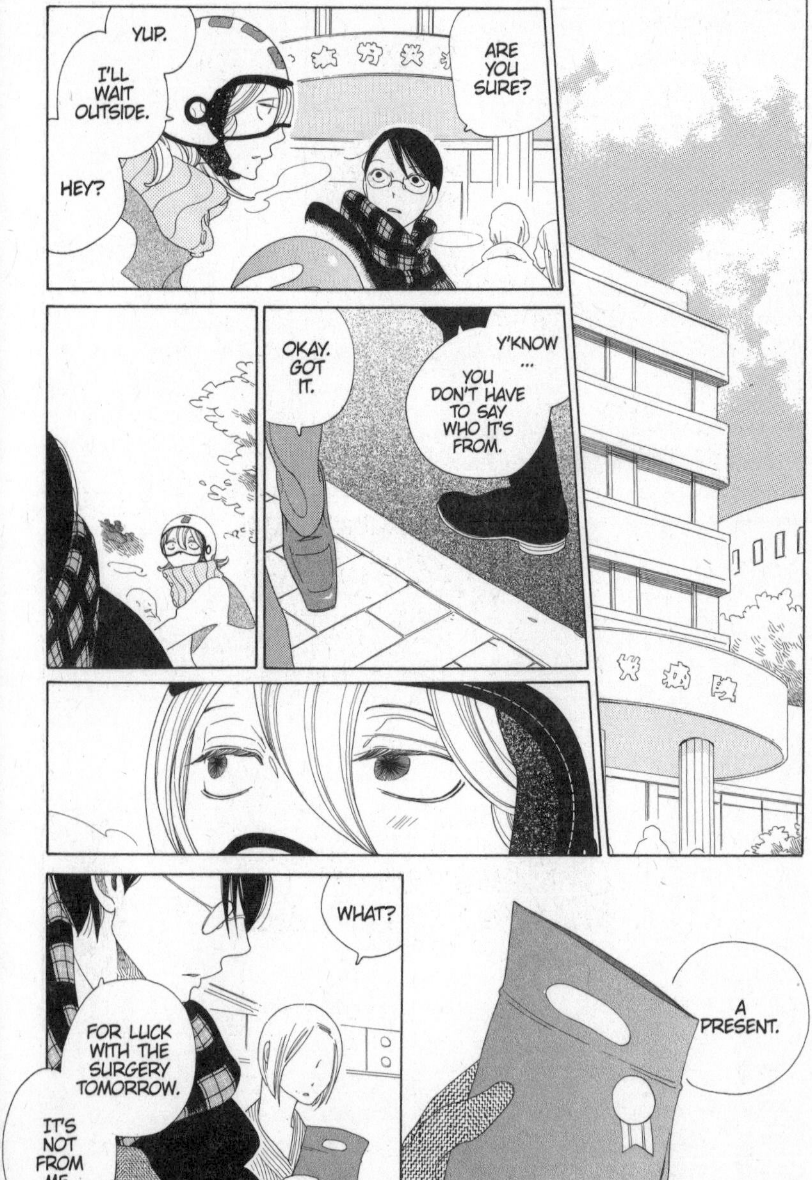
ARE YOU SURE?
YUP. I'LL WAIT OUTSIDE. HEY?
Y'KNOW ... YOU DON'T HAVE TO SAY WHO IT'S FROM.
OKAY. GOT IT.
A PRESENT.
WHAT?
FOR LUCK WITH THE SURGERY TOMORROW.
IT'S NOT FROM ME.

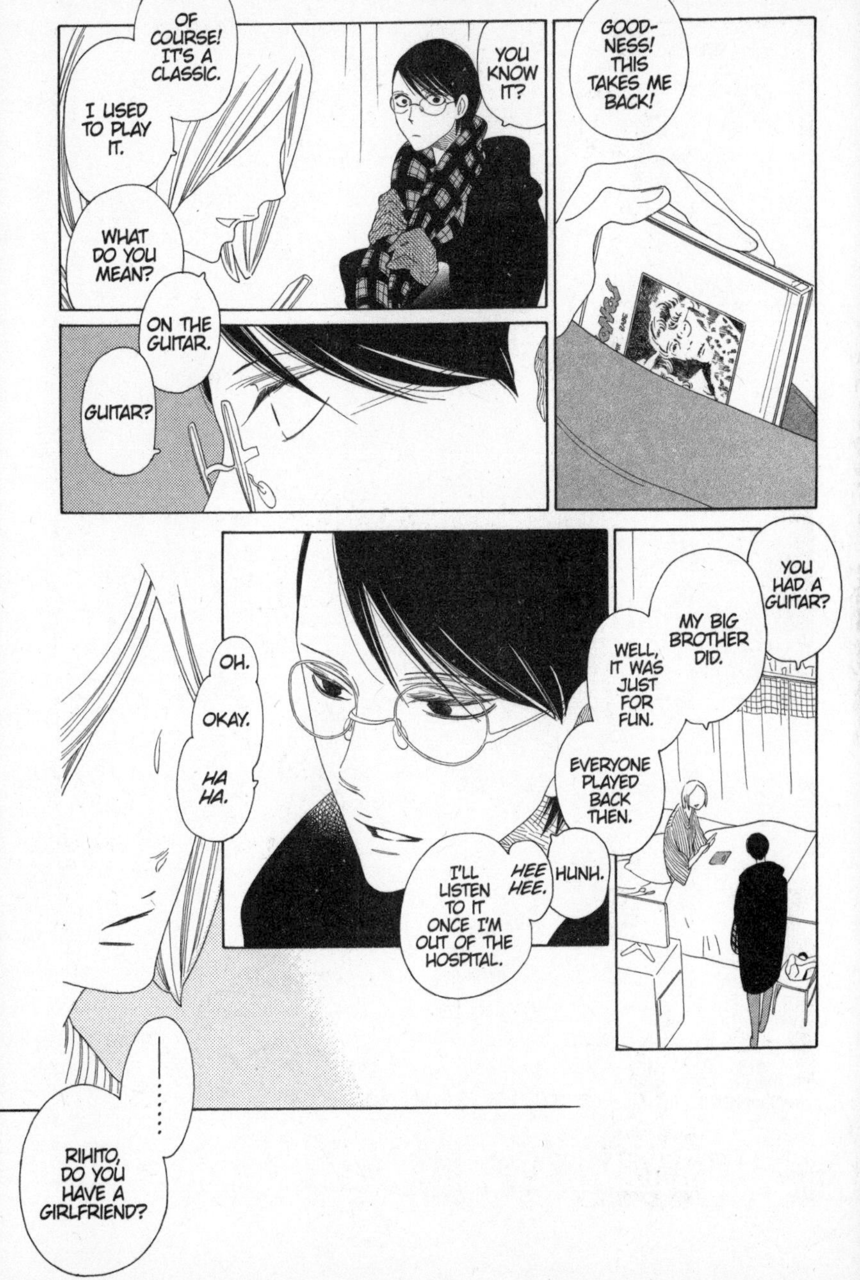
GOOD-NESS! THIS TAKES ME BACK!
YOU KNOW IT?
OF COURSE! IT'S A CLASSIC.
I USED TO PLAY IT.
WHAT DO YOU MEAN?
ON THE GUITAR.
GUITAR?
YOU HAD A GUITAR?
MY BIG BROTHER DID.
WELL, IT WAS JUST FOR FUN.
EVERYONE PLAYED BACK THEN.
HUNH.
HEE HEE.
I'LL LISTEN TO IT ONCE I'M OUT OF THE HOSPITAL.
OH.
OKAY.
HA HA.
......
RIHITO, DO YOU HAVE A GIRLFRIEND?

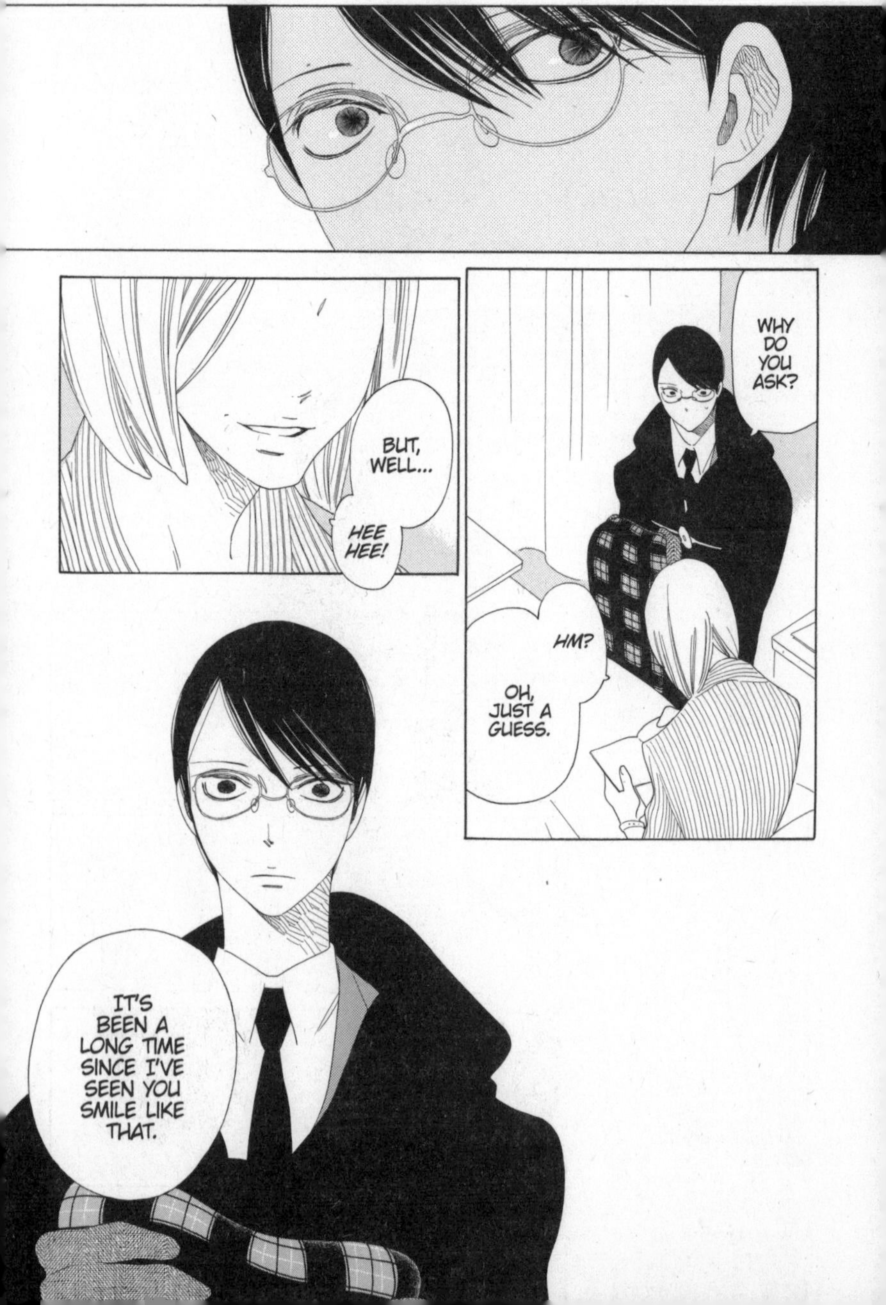
WHY DO YOU ASK?
HM?
OH, JUST A GUESS.
BUT, WELL...
HEE HEE!
IT'S BEEN A LONG TIME SINCE I'VE SEEN YOU SMILE LIKE THAT.

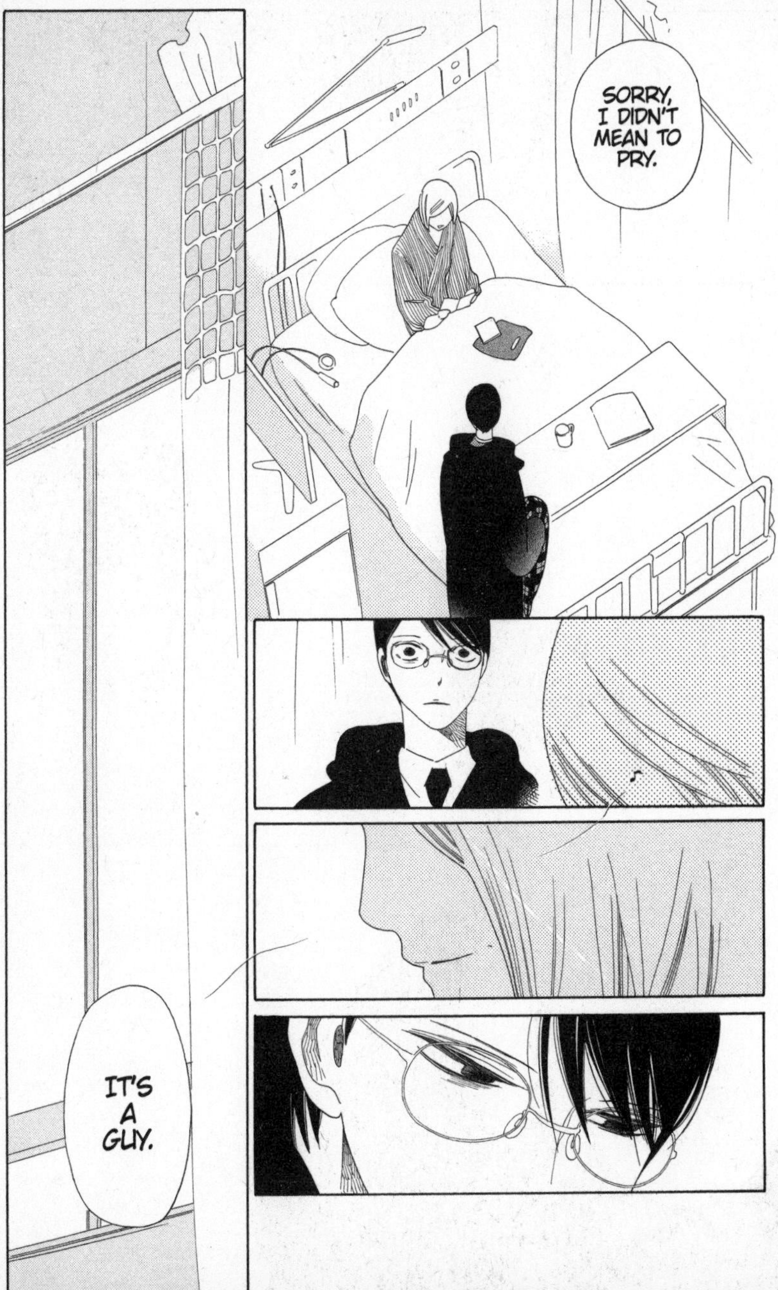
SORRY, I DIDN'T MEAN TO PRY.
IT'S A GUY.

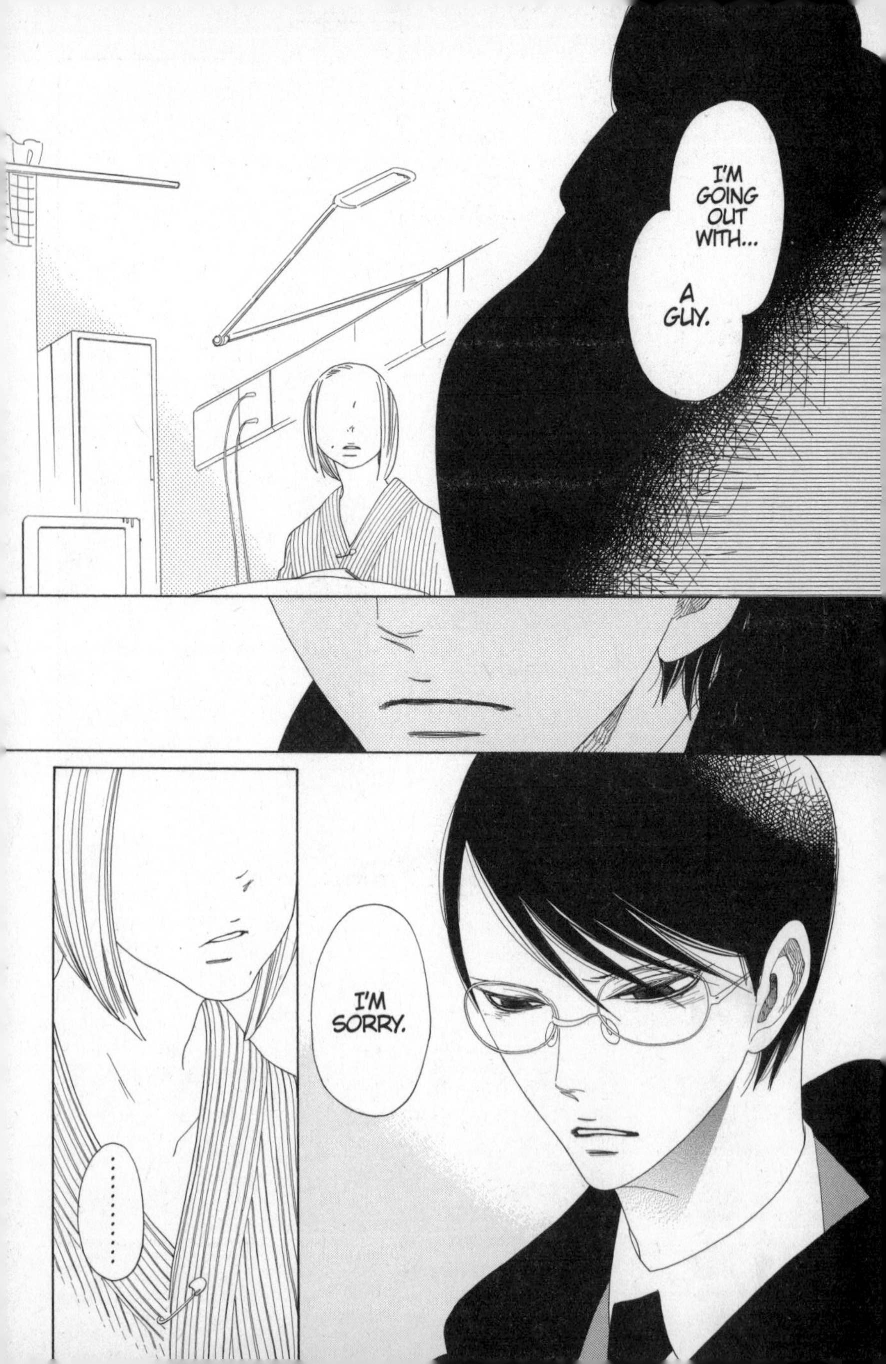
I'M GOING OUT WITH...
A GUY.
I'M SORRY.
....

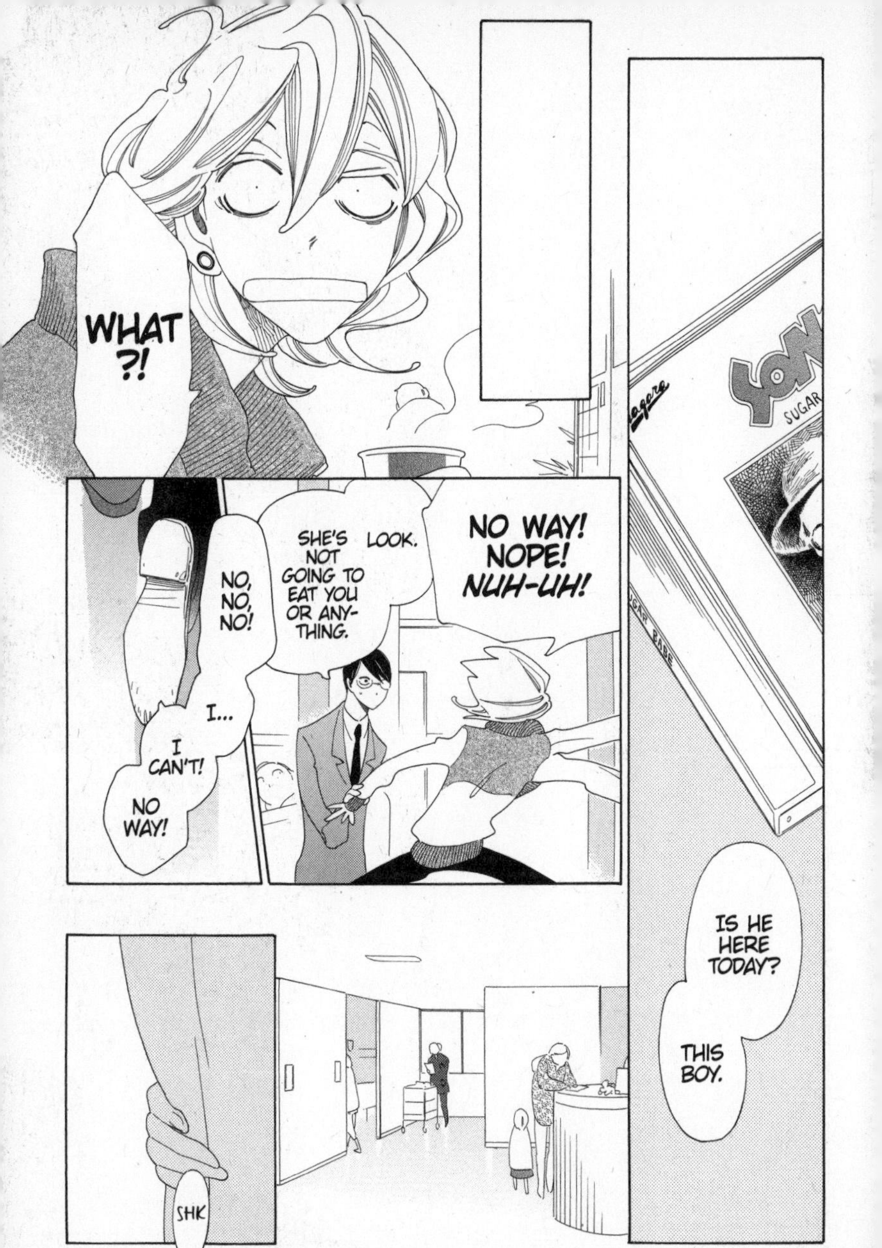
SUGAR
SUGAR BABE
IS HE HERE TODAY?
THIS BOY.
WHAT?!
NO WAY! NOPE! NUH-UH!
LOOK.
SHE'S NOT GOING TO EAT YOU OR ANYTHING.
NO, NO, NO!
I...
I CAN'T!
NO WAY!
SHK

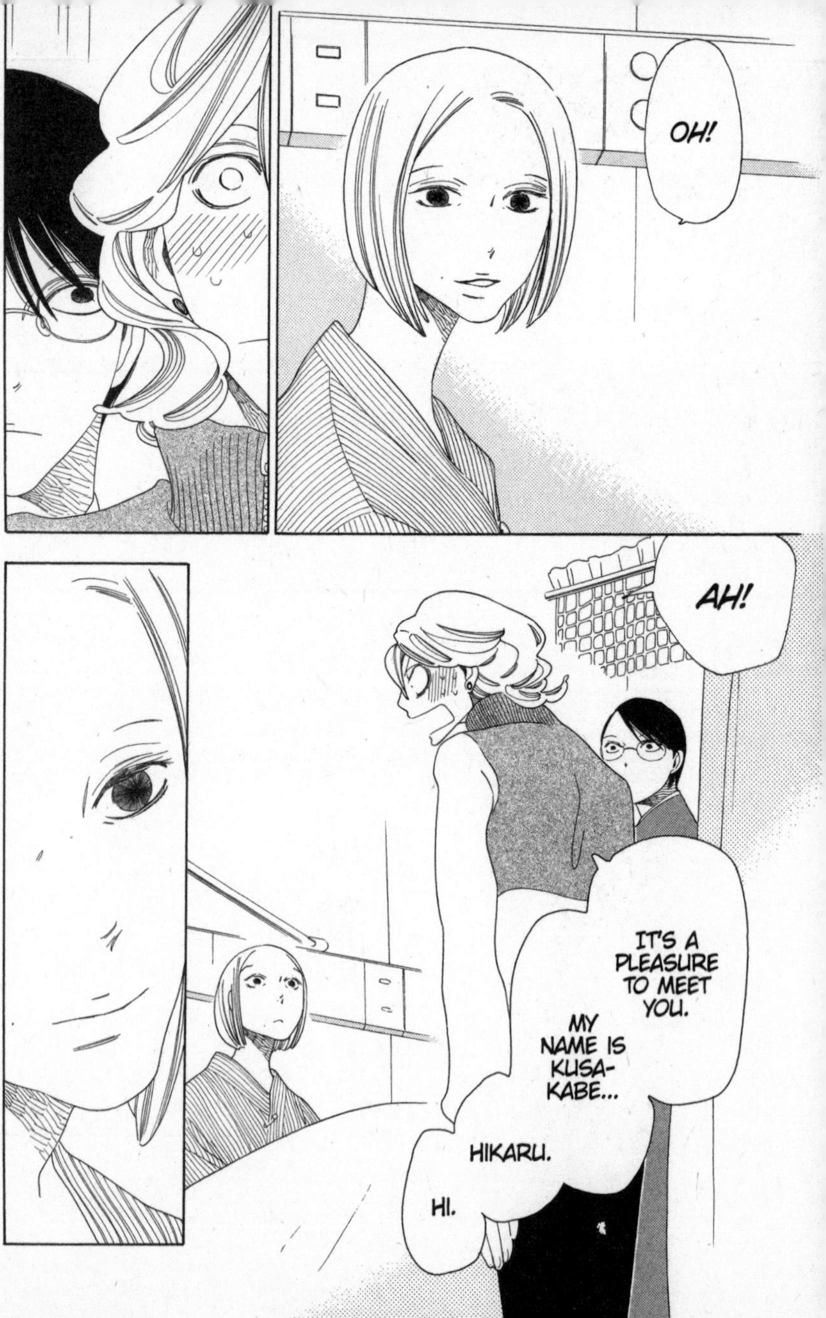
OH!
AH!
IT'S A PLEASURE TO MEET YOU.
MY NAME IS KUSA-KABE...
HIKARU.
HI.

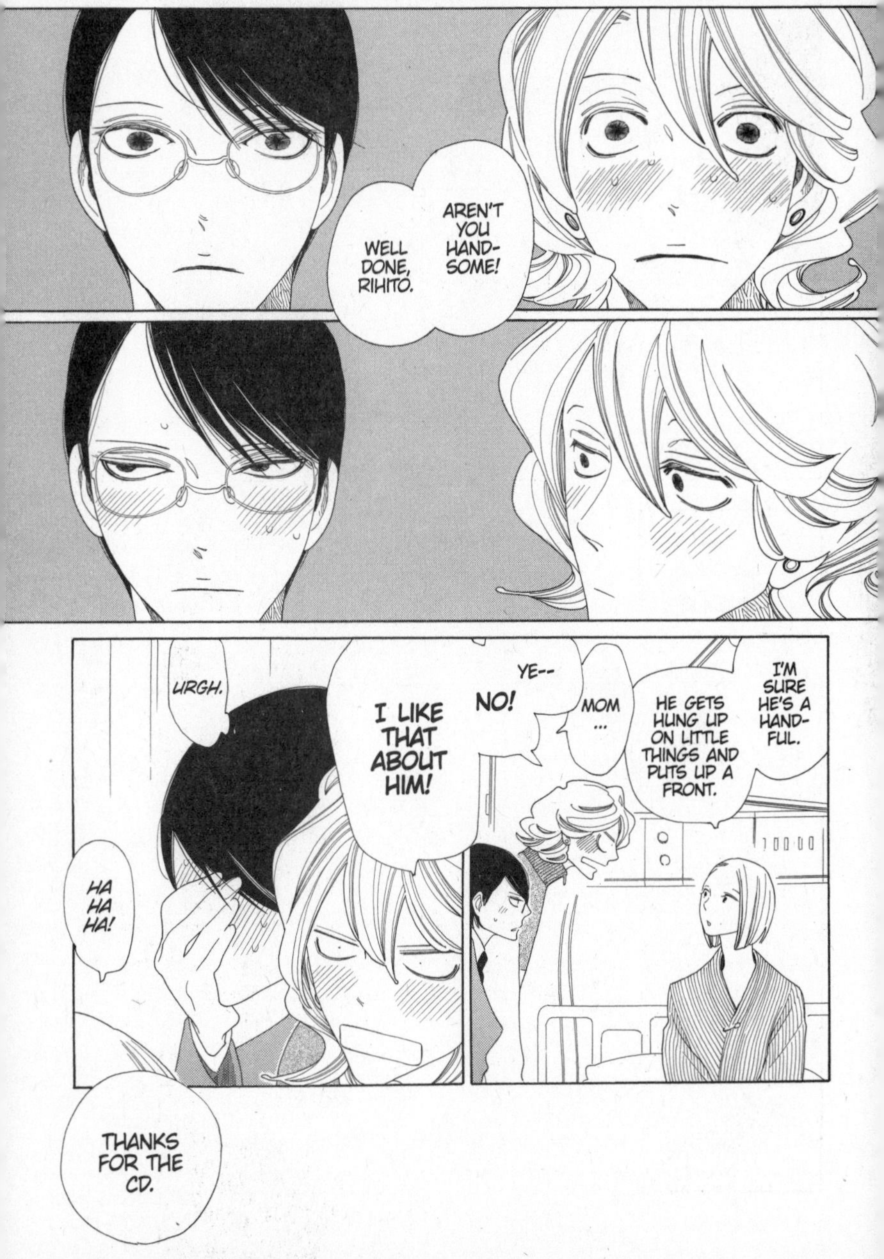
AREN'T YOU HANDSOME!
WELL DONE, RIHITO.
I'M SURE HE'S A HANDFUL.
HE GETS HUNG UP ON LITTLE THINGS AND PUTS UP A FRONT.
MOM ...
YE--
NO!
I LIKE THAT ABOUT HIM!
URGH.
HA HA HA!
THANKS FOR THE CD.

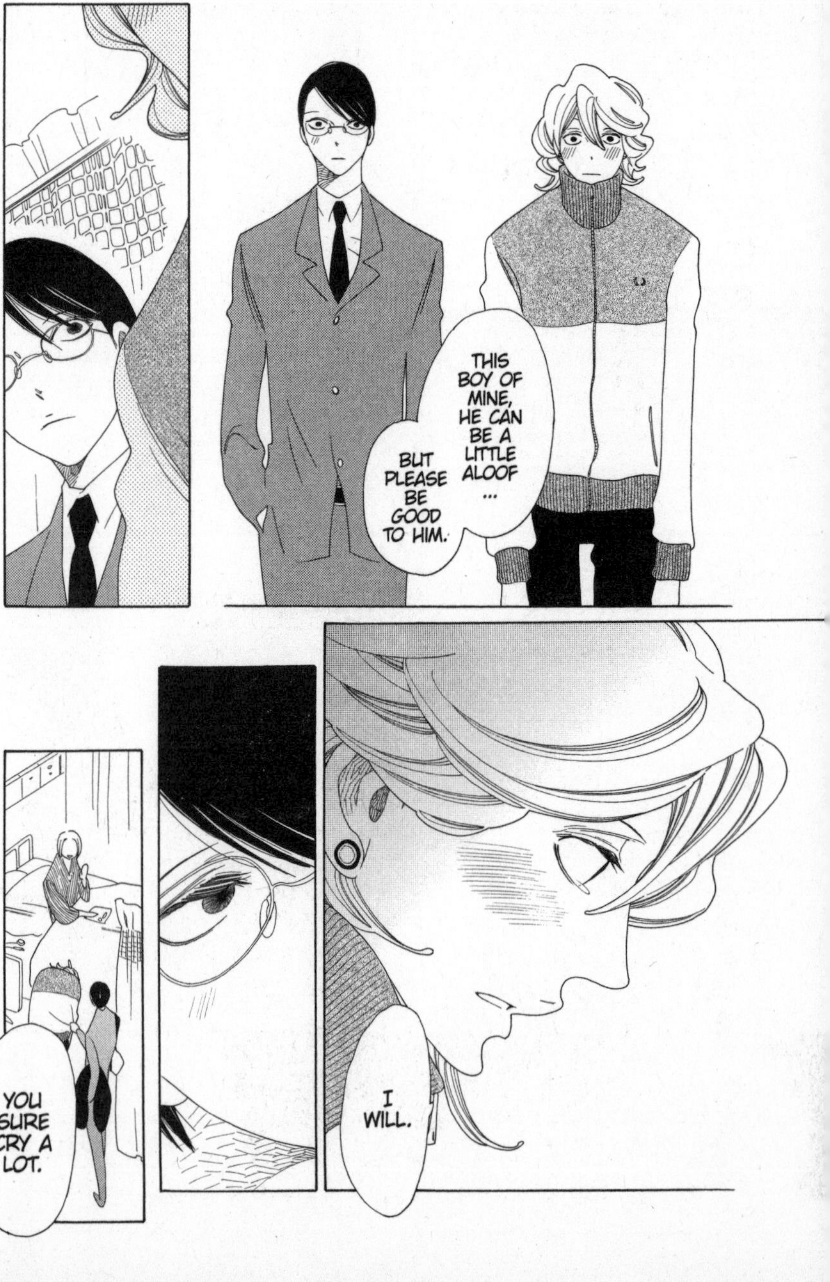
THIS BOY OF MINE, HE CAN BE A LITTLE ALOOF ...
BUT PLEASE BE GOOD TO HIM.
I WILL.
YOU SURE CRY A LOT.

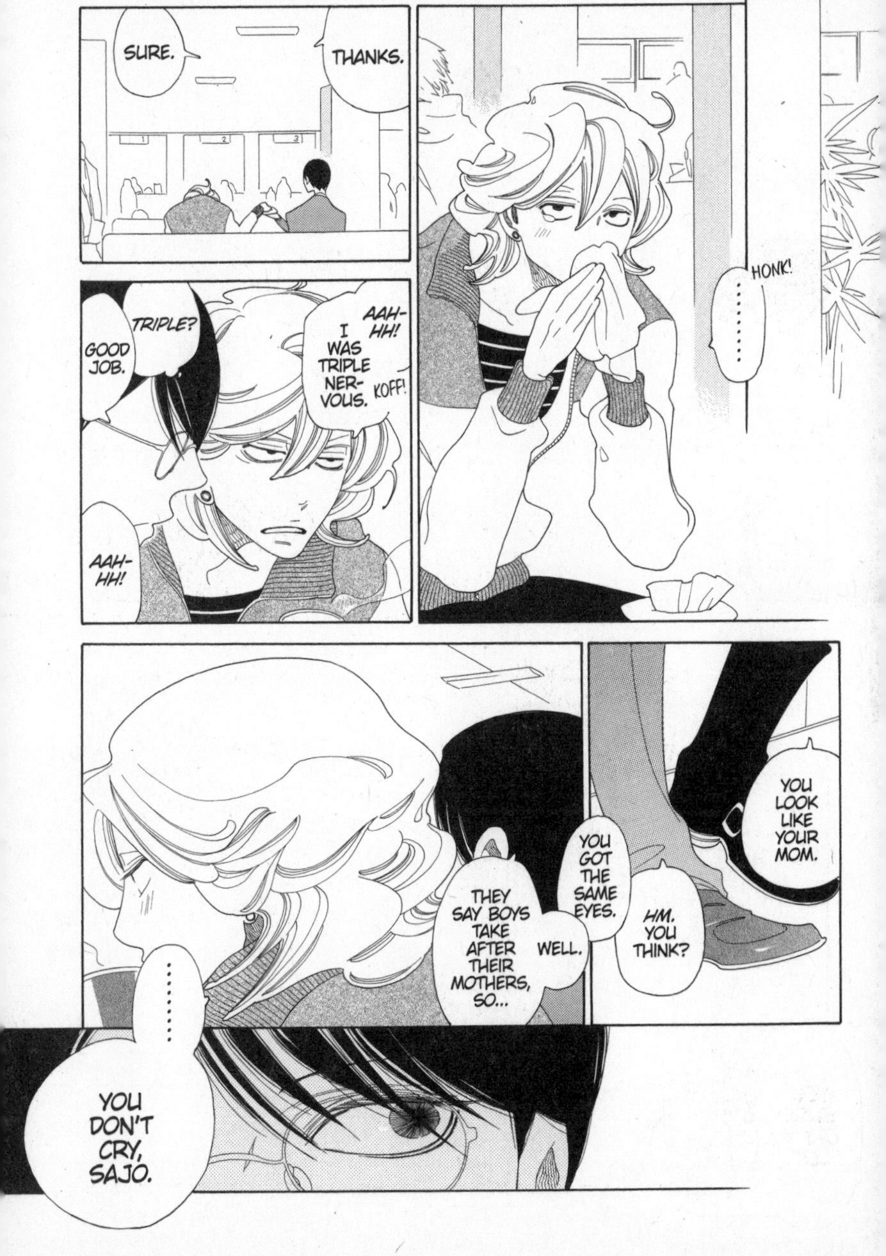
HONK!
......
THANKS.
SURE.
AAH-HH!
I WAS TRIPLE NERVOUS.
KOFF!
TRIPLE?
GOOD JOB.
AAH-HH!
YOU LOOK LIKE YOUR MOM.
HM. YOU THINK?
YOU GOT THE SAME EYES.
WELL.
THEY SAY BOYS TAKE AFTER THEIR MOTHERS, SO...
......
YOU DON'T CRY, SAJO.

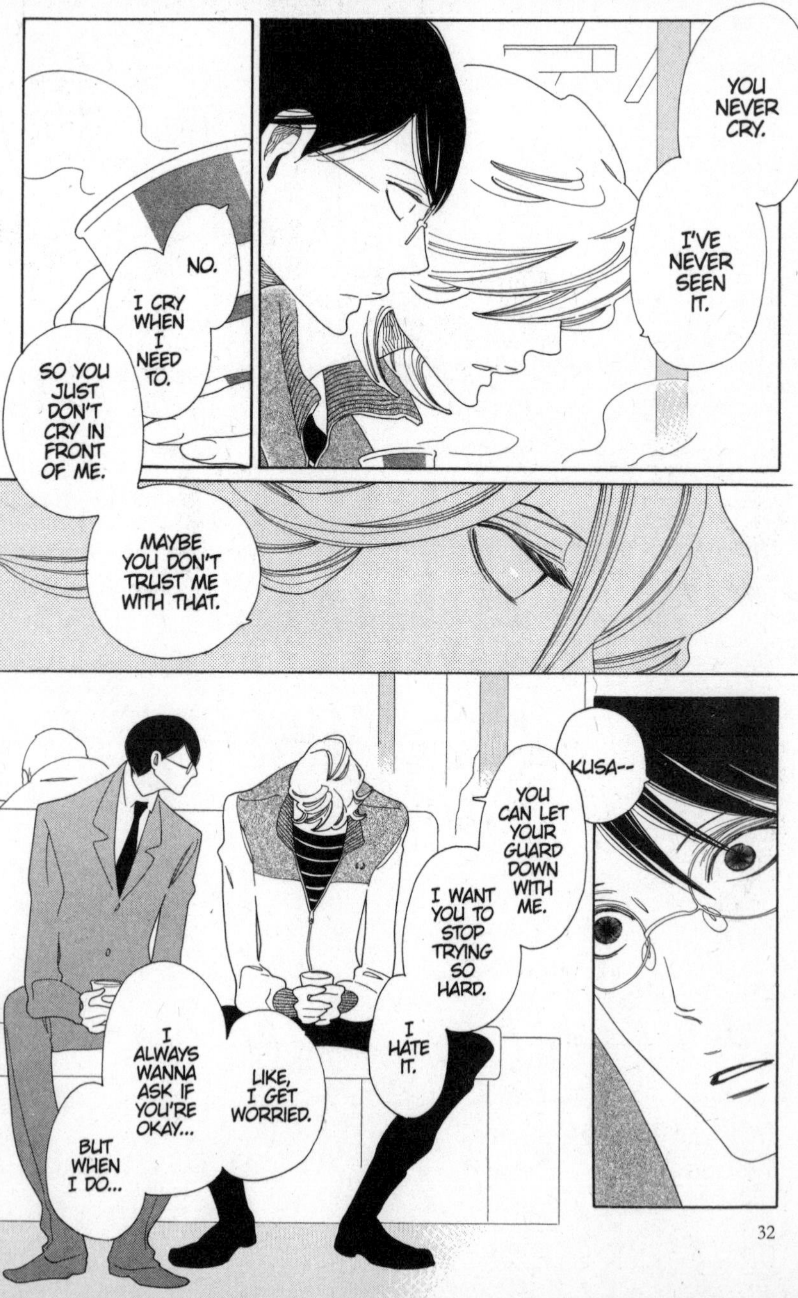
YOU NEVER CRY.
I'VE NEVER SEEN IT.
NO.
I CRY WHEN I NEED TO.
SO YOU JUST DON'T CRY IN FRONT OF ME.
MAYBE YOU DON'T TRUST ME WITH THAT.
KUSA--
YOU CAN LET YOUR GUARD DOWN WITH ME.
I WANT YOU TO STOP TRYING SO HARD.
I HATE IT.
LIKE, I GET WORRIED.
I ALWAYS WANNA ASK IF YOU'RE OKAY...
BUT WHEN I DO...

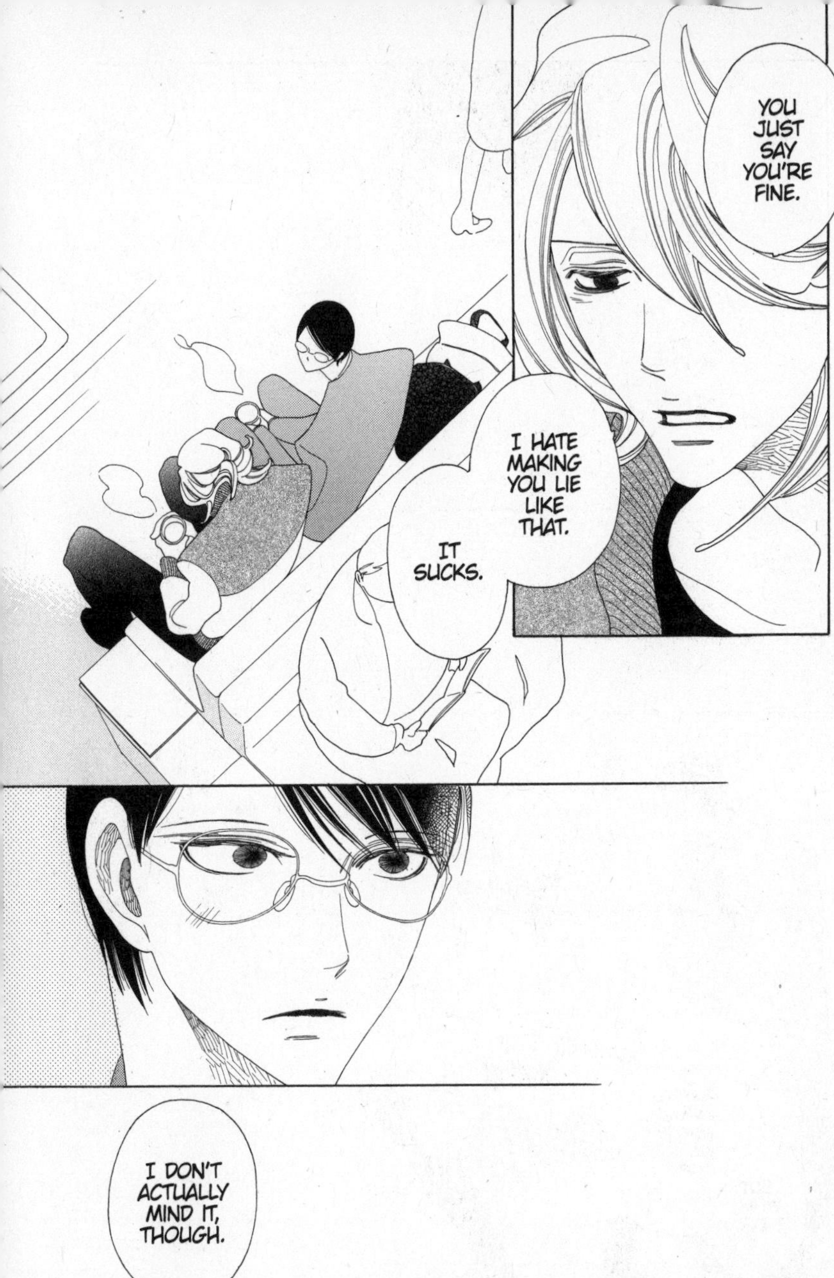
YOU JUST SAY YOU'RE FINE.
I HATE MAKING YOU LIE LIKE THAT.
IT SUCKS.
I DON'T ACTUALLY MIND IT, THOUGH.

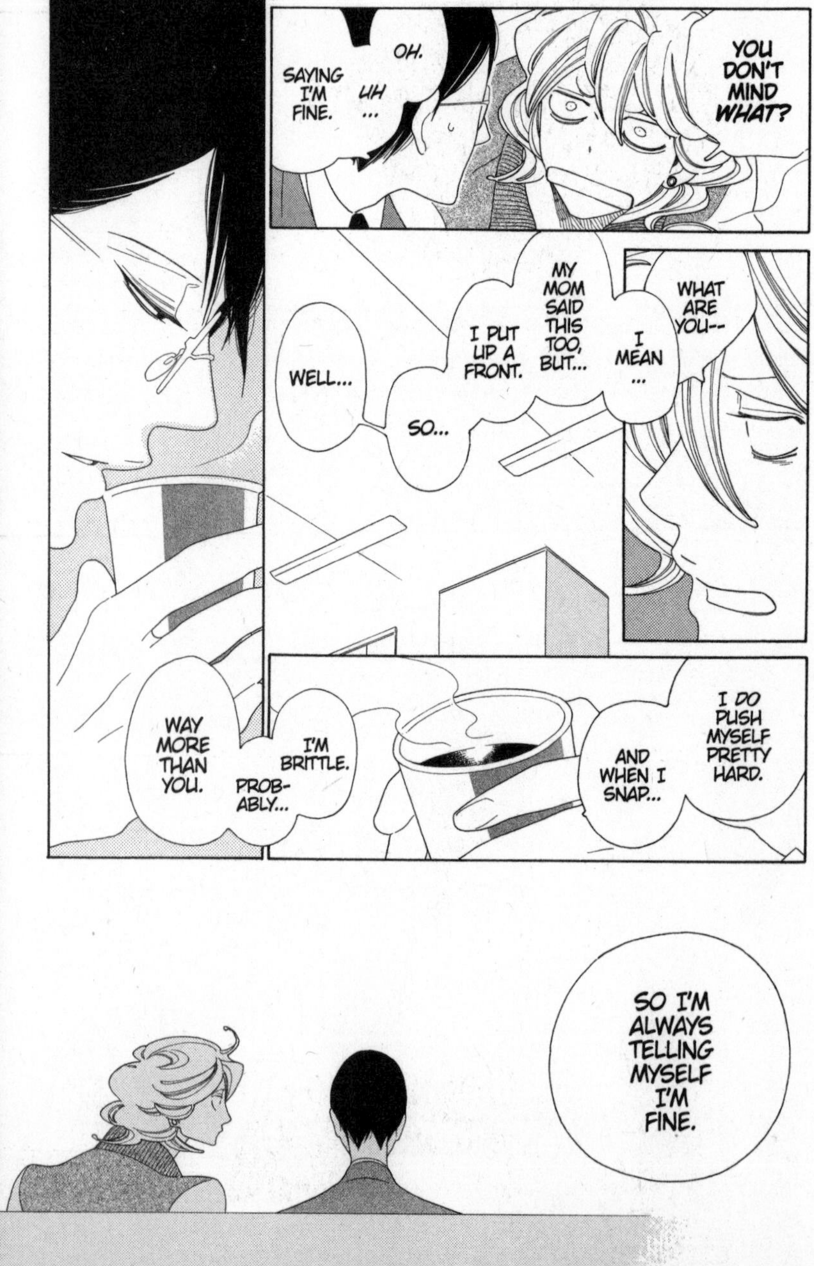
YOU DON'T MIND *WHAT?*
OH.
UH ...
SAYING I'M FINE.
WHAT ARE YOU--
I MEAN ...
MY MOM SAID THIS TOO, BUT...
I PUT UP A FRONT.
SO...
WELL...
I *DO* PUSH MYSELF PRETTY HARD.
AND WHEN I SNAP...
I'M BRITTLE.
PROBABLY...
WAY MORE THAN YOU.
SO I'M ALWAYS TELLING MYSELF I'M FINE.

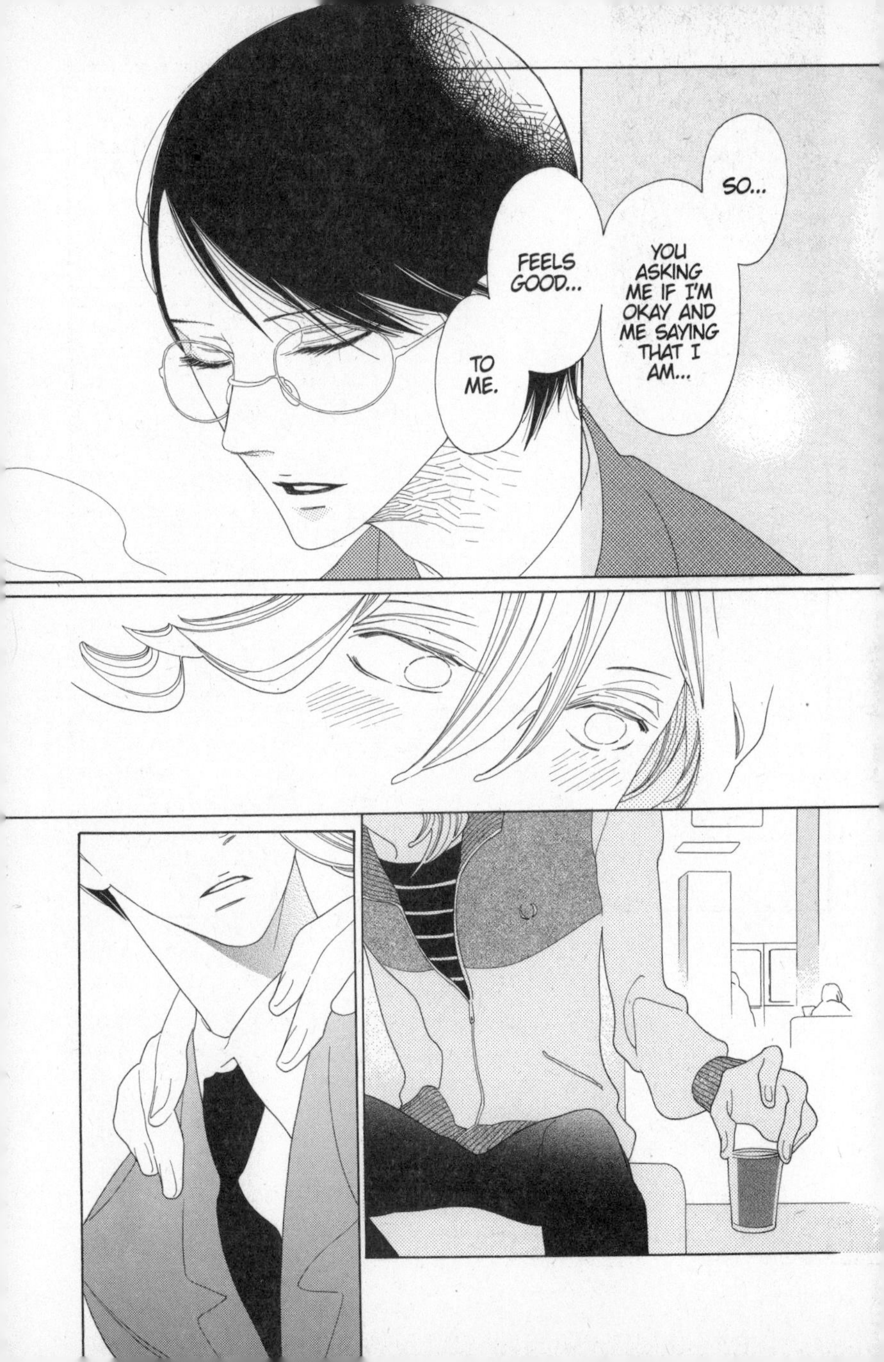
SO...
YOU ASKING ME IF I'M OKAY AND ME SAYING THAT I AM...
FEELS GOOD...
TO ME.

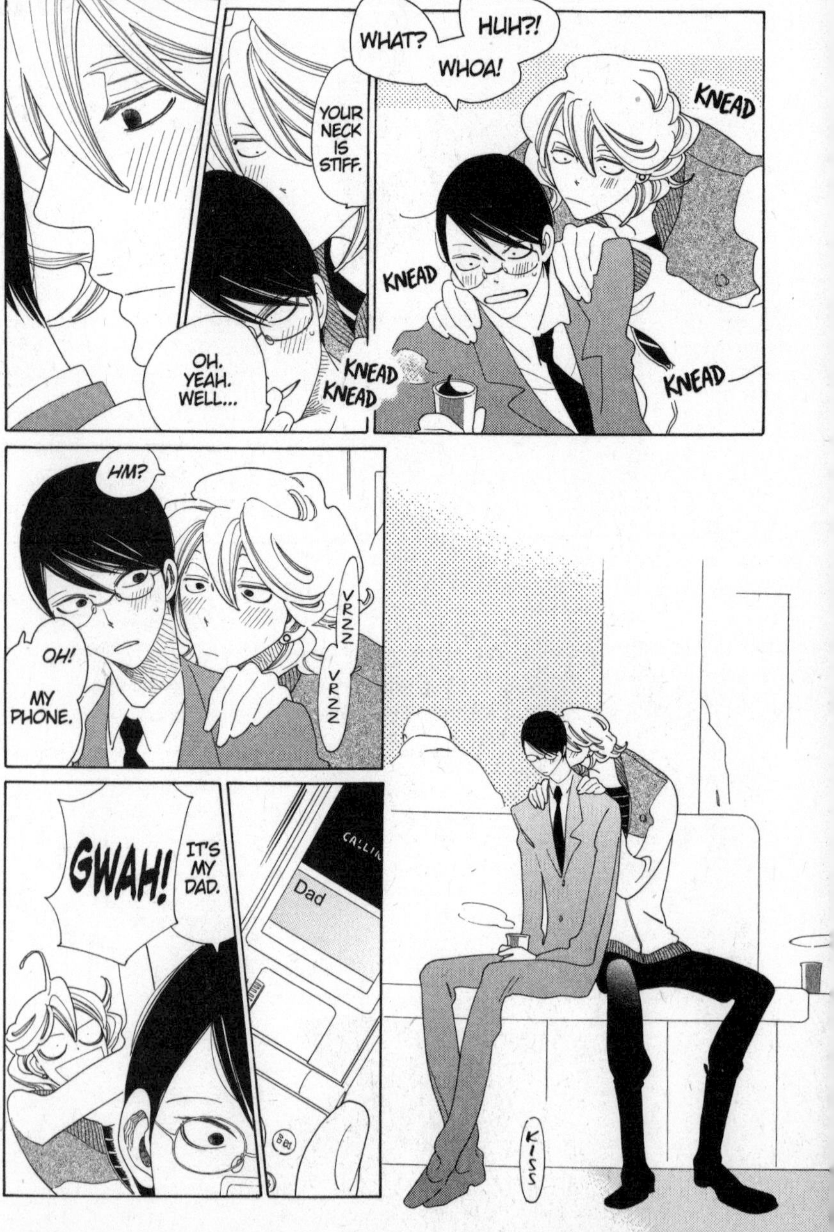
HUH?!
WHAT?
WHOA!
KNEAD
KNEAD
KNEAD
YOUR NECK IS STIFF.
OH. YEAH. WELL...
KNEAD KNEAD
KISS
HM?
VRZZ VRZZ
OH! MY PHONE.
Dad
IT'S MY DAD.
GWAH!

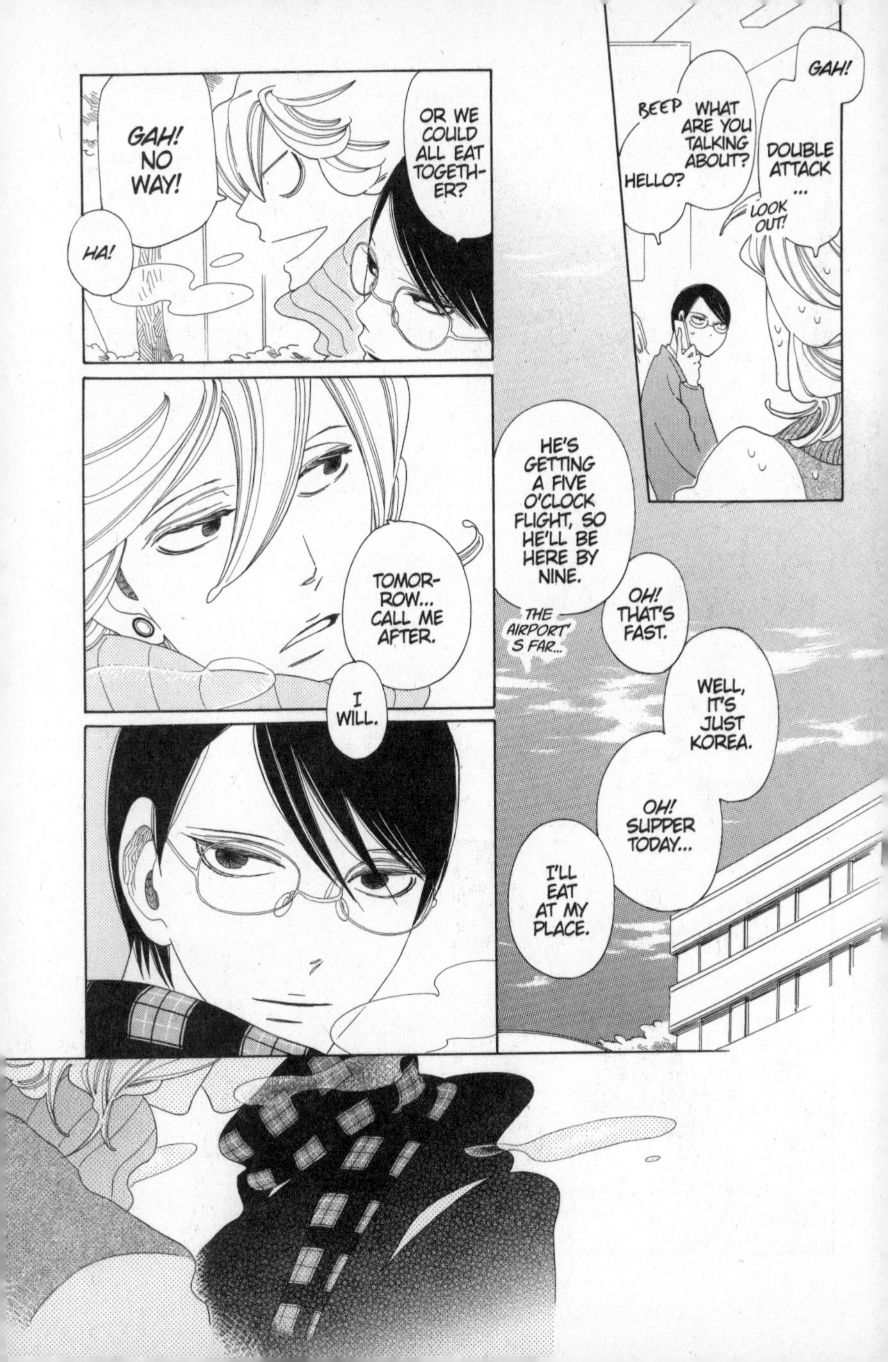
GAH!
DOUBLE ATTACK ...
LOOK OUT!
WHAT ARE YOU TALKING ABOUT?
BEEP
HELLO?
OR WE COULD ALL EAT TOGETH- ER?
GAH! NO WAY!
HA!
HE'S GETTING A FIVE O'CLOCK FLIGHT, SO HE'LL BE HERE BY NINE.
THE AIRPORT' S FAR...
OH! THAT'S FAST.
WELL, IT'S JUST KOREA.
OH! SUPPER TODAY...
I'LL EAT AT MY PLACE.
TOMOR- ROW... CALL ME AFTER.
I WILL.

FAMILY
WAITING
AREA

PLEAS
PATIEN

GRAND
MENU

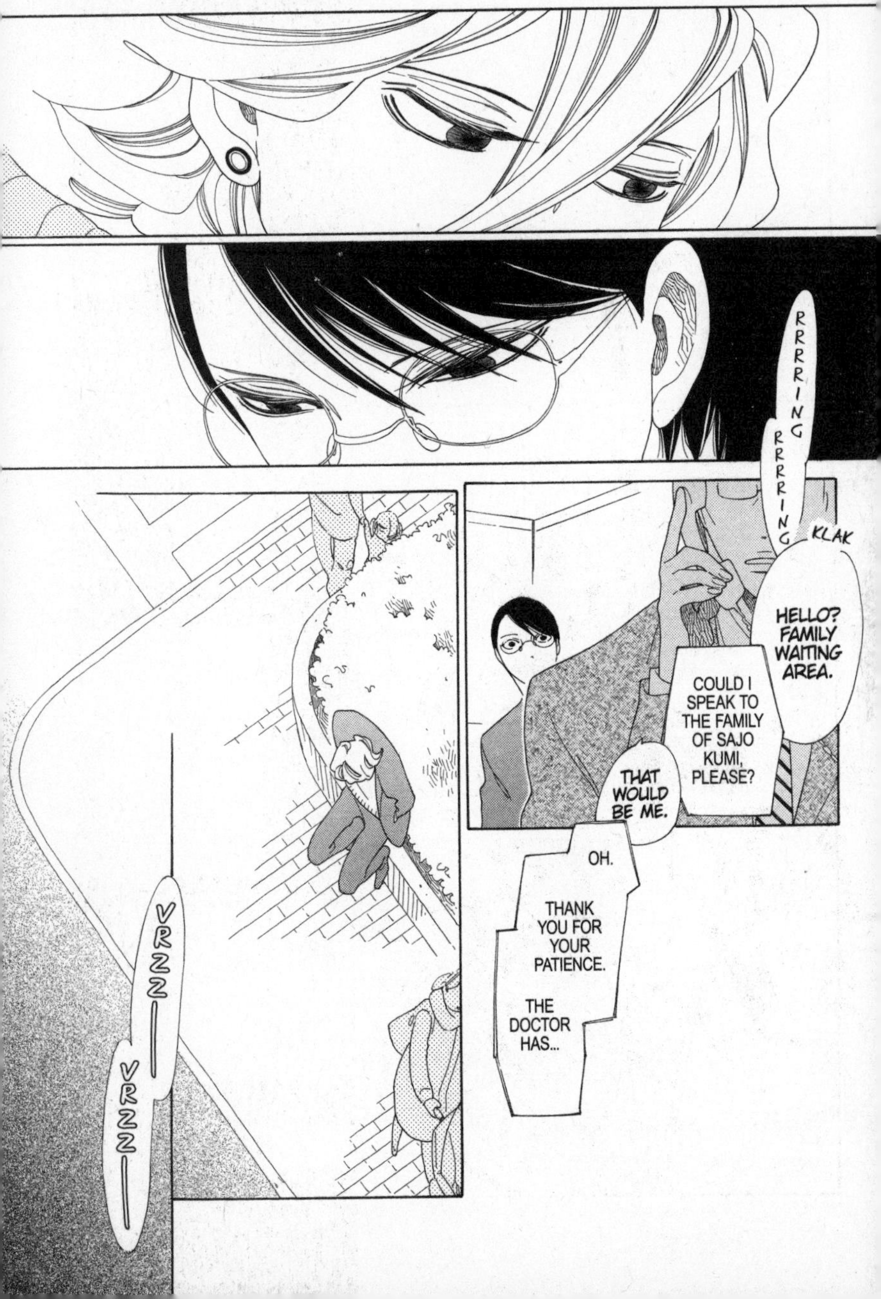
RRRRING
RRRRING
KLAK
HELLO? FAMILY WAITING AREA.
COULD I SPEAK TO THE FAMILY OF SAJO KUMI, PLEASE?
THAT WOULD BE ME.
OH.
THANK YOU FOR YOUR PATIENCE.
THE DOCTOR HAS...
VRZZ—
VRZZ—

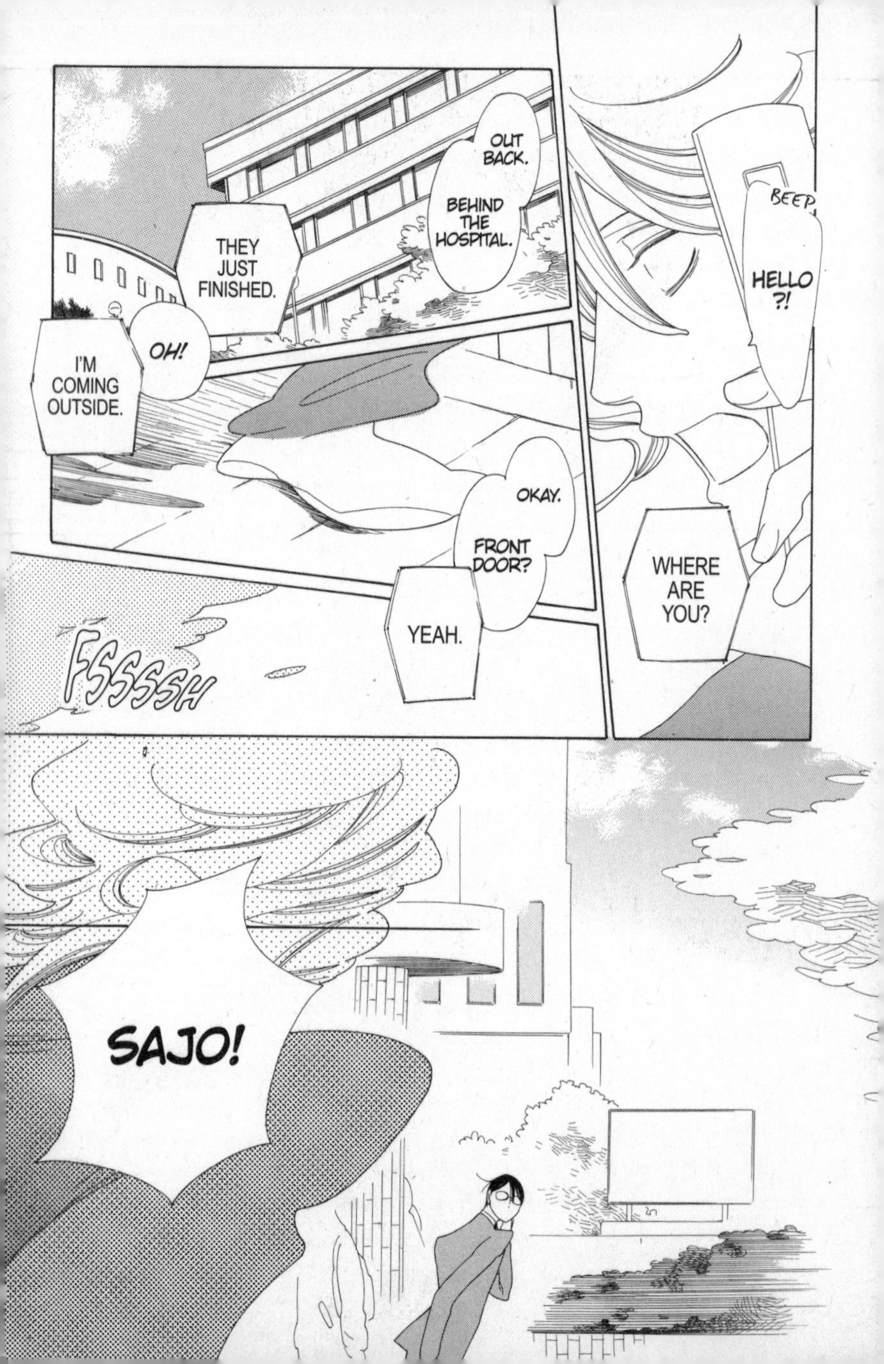
BEEP
HELLO ?!
WHERE ARE YOU?
OUT BACK.
BEHIND THE HOSPITAL.
THEY JUST FINISHED.
OH!
I'M COMING OUTSIDE.
OKAY.
FRONT DOOR?
YEAH.
FSSSSH
SAJO!

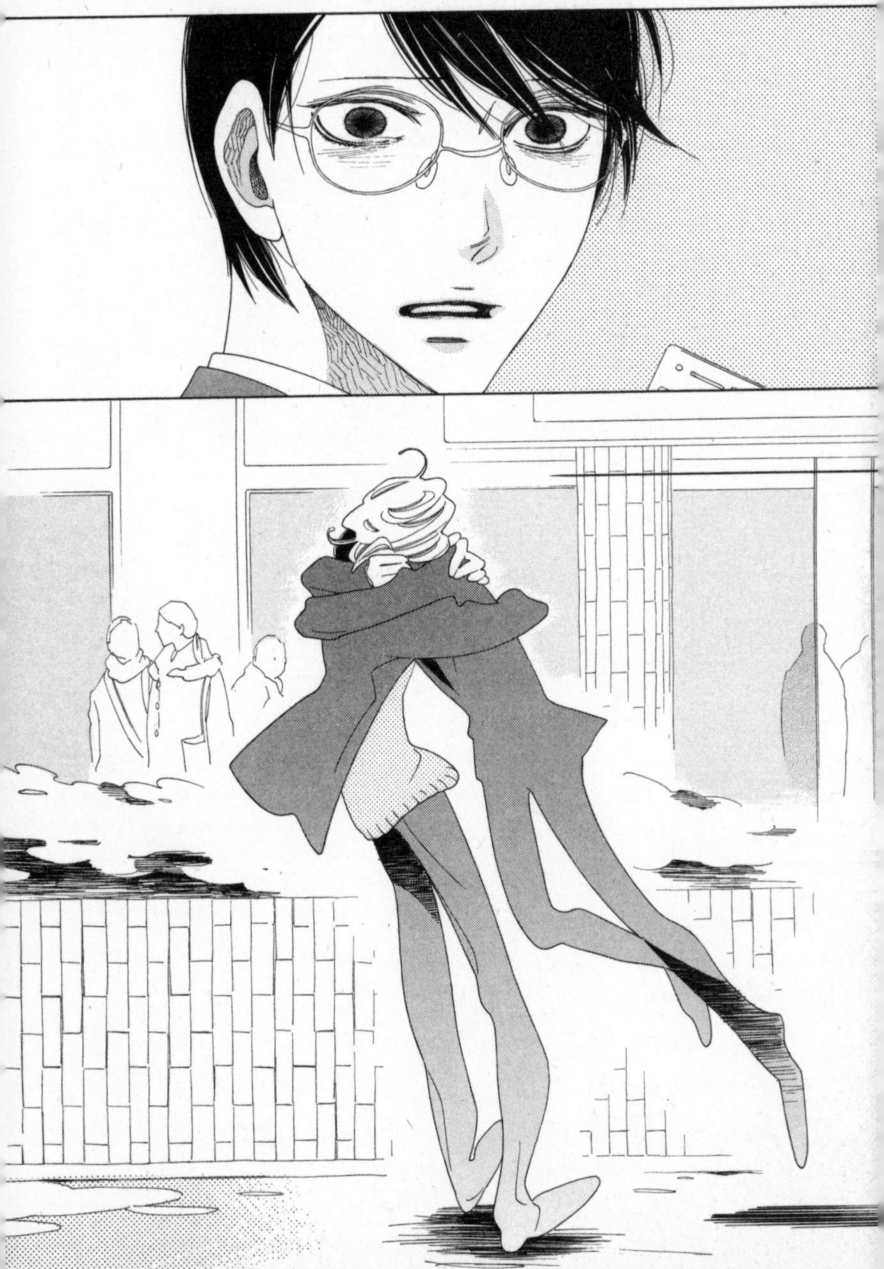

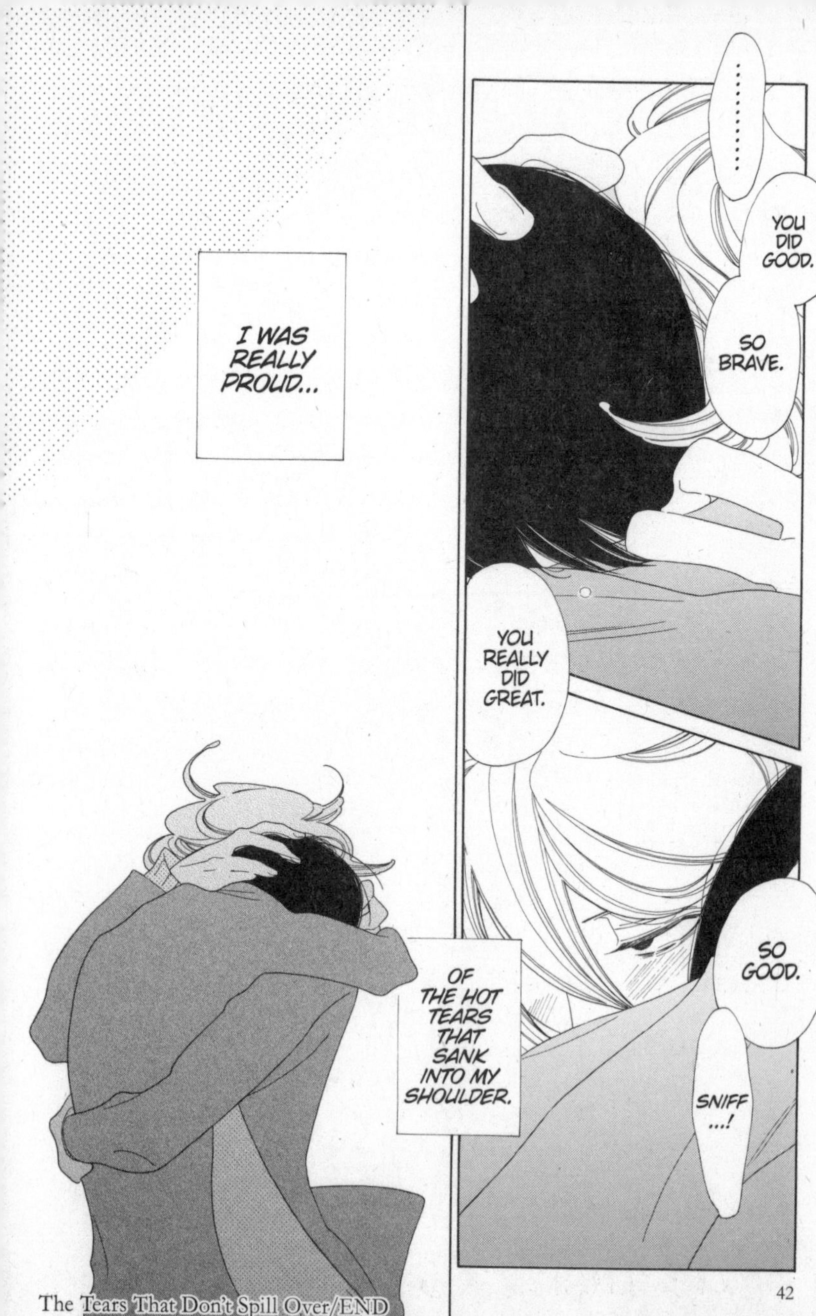
......
YOU DID GOOD.
SO BRAVE.
YOU REALLY DID GREAT.
SO GOOD.
SNIFF ...!
I WAS REALLY PROUD...
OF THE HOT TEARS THAT SANK INTO MY SHOULDER.

The Tears That Don't Spill Over/END

Classmates

Intermission

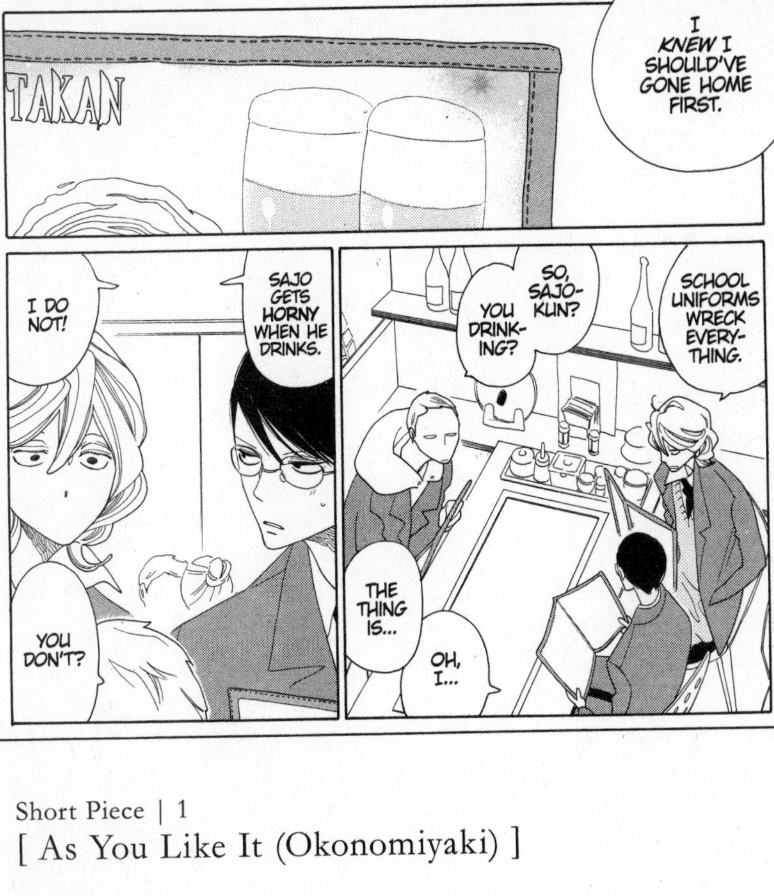
TAKAN
I KNEW I SHOULD'VE GONE HOME FIRST.
SCHOOL UNIFORMS WRECK EVERY-THING.
SO, SAJO-KUN?
YOU DRINK-ING?
THE THING IS...
OH, I...
SAJO GETS HORNY WHEN HE DRINKS.
I DO NOT!
YOU DON'T?

Short Piece | 1

[As You Like It (Okonomiyaki)]

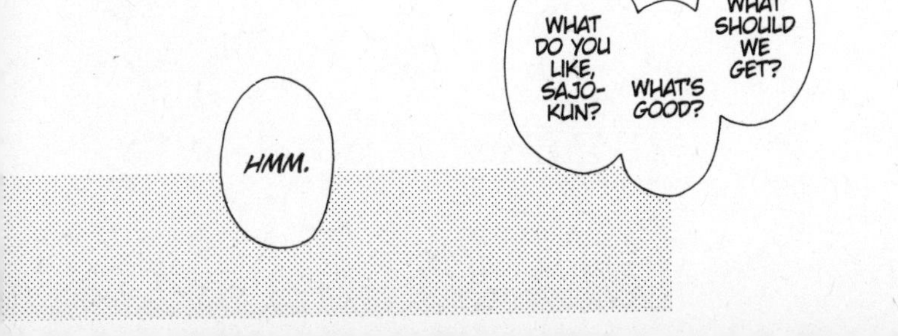
WHAT SHOULD WE GET?
WHAT'S GOOD?
WHAT DO YOU LIKE, SAJO-KUN?
HMM.

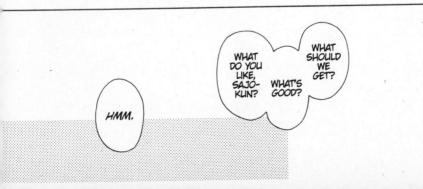

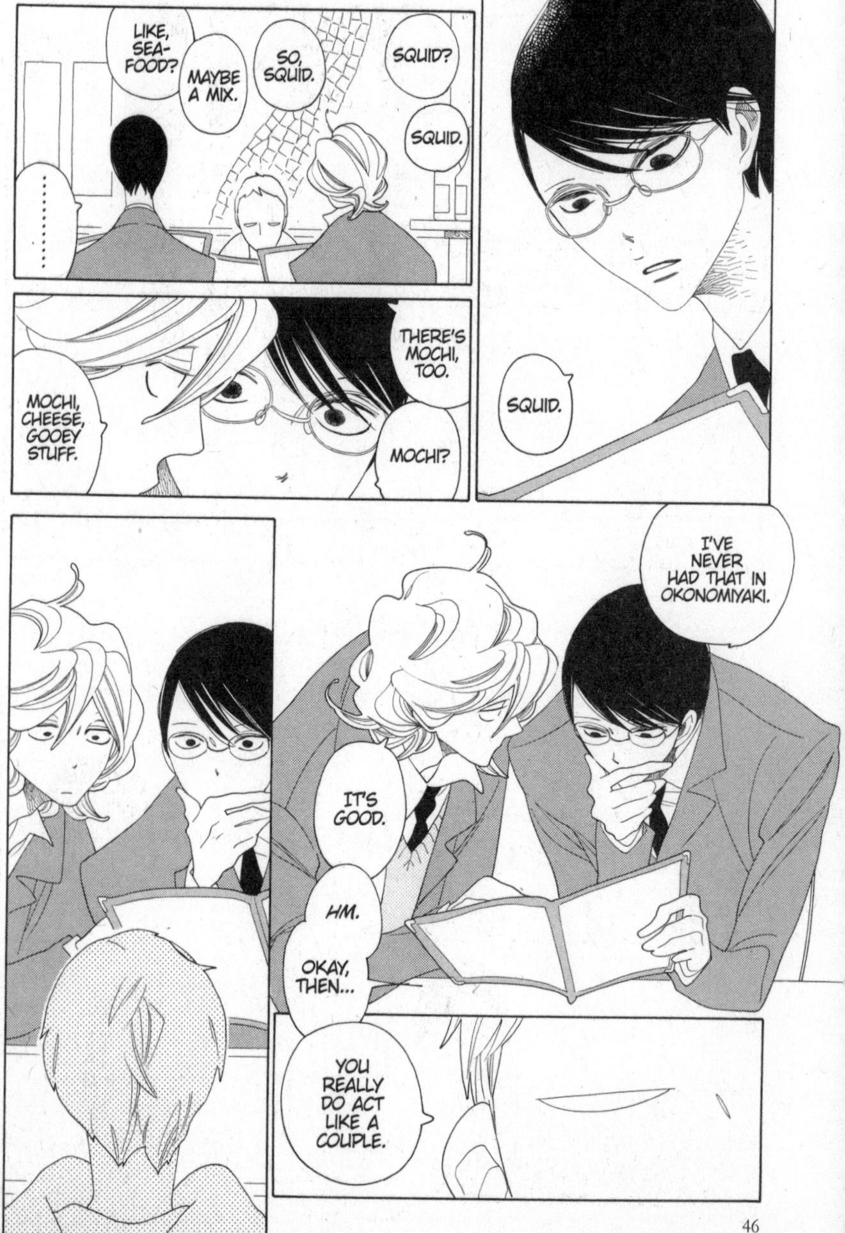
SQUID.
SQUID?
SO, SQUID.
SQUID.
LIKE, SEA-FOOD?
MAYBE A MIX.
......
THERE'S MOCHI, TOO.
MOCHI?
MOCHI, CHEESE, GOOEY STUFF.
I'VE NEVER HAD THAT IN OKONOMIYAKI.
IT'S GOOD.
HM.
OKAY, THEN...
YOU REALLY DO ACT LIKE A COUPLE.

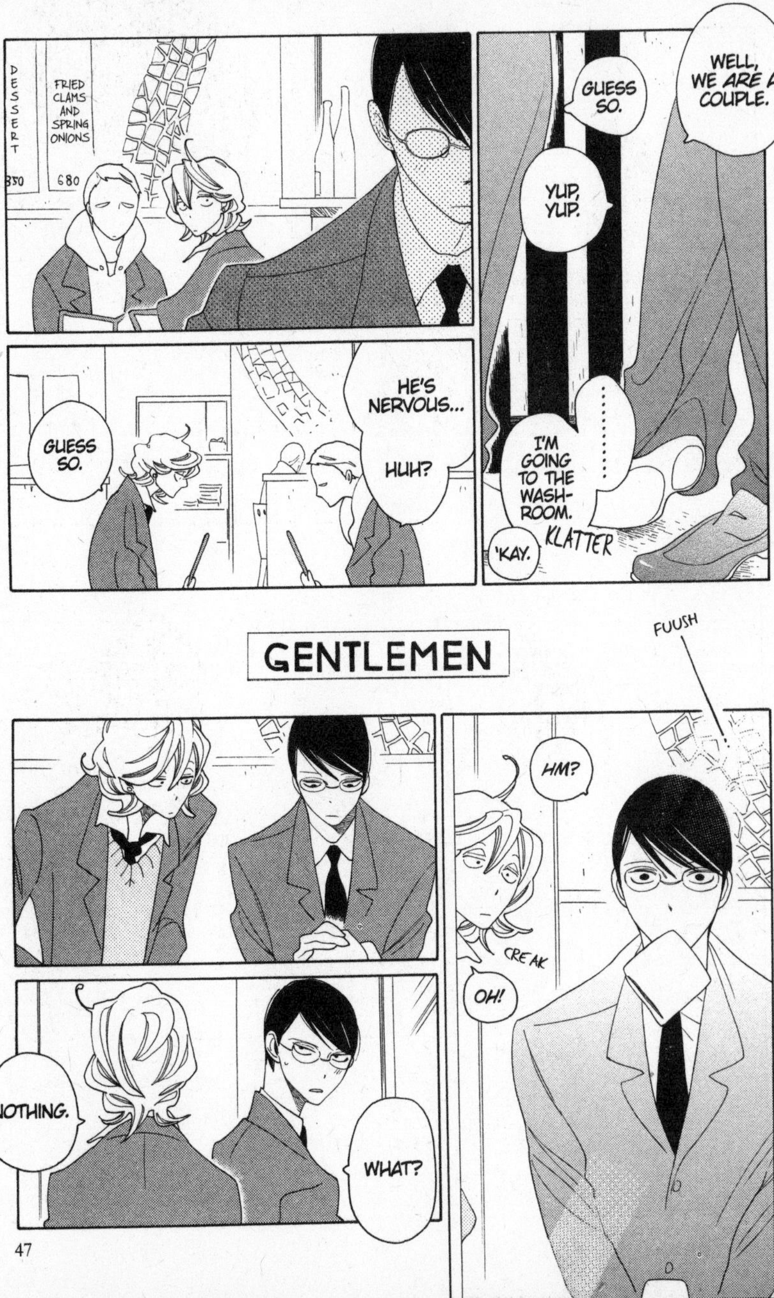
WELL, WE ARE A COUPLE.
GUESS SO.
YUP, YUP.
......
I'M GOING TO THE WASHROOM.
KLATTER
'KAY.
DESSERT
FRIED CLAMS AND SPRING ONIONS
350
680
HE'S NERVOUS...
HUH?
GUESS SO.
GENTLEMEN
FUUSH
HM?
CREAK
OH!
WHAT?
NOTHING.

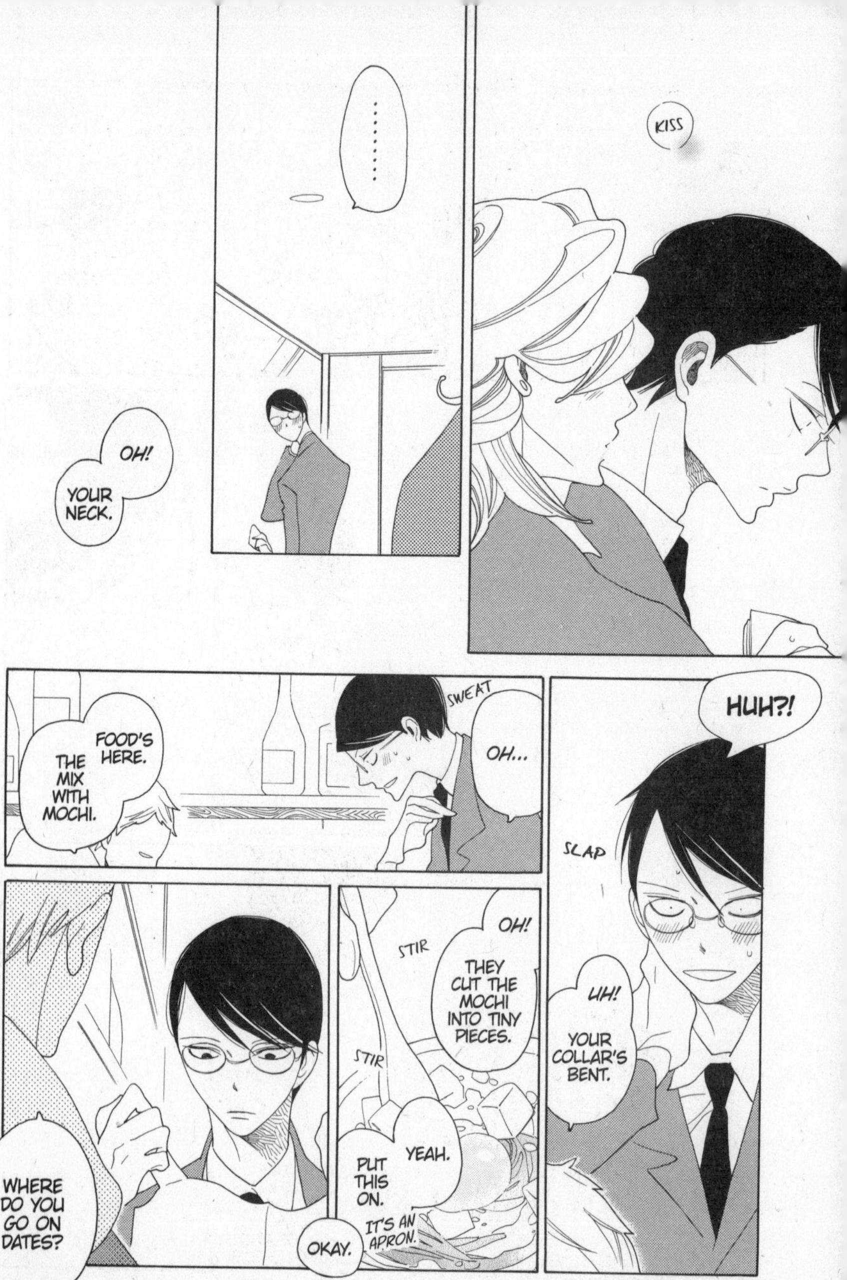
KISS
......
OH!
YOUR NECK.
HUH?!
SLAP
UH!
YOUR COLLAR'S BENT.
SWEAT
OH...
FOOD'S HERE.
THE MIX WITH MOCHI.
STIR
OH!
THEY CUT THE MOCHI INTO TINY PIECES.
STIR
YEAH.
PUT THIS ON.
IT'S AN APRON.
OKAY.
WHERE DO YOU GO ON DATES?

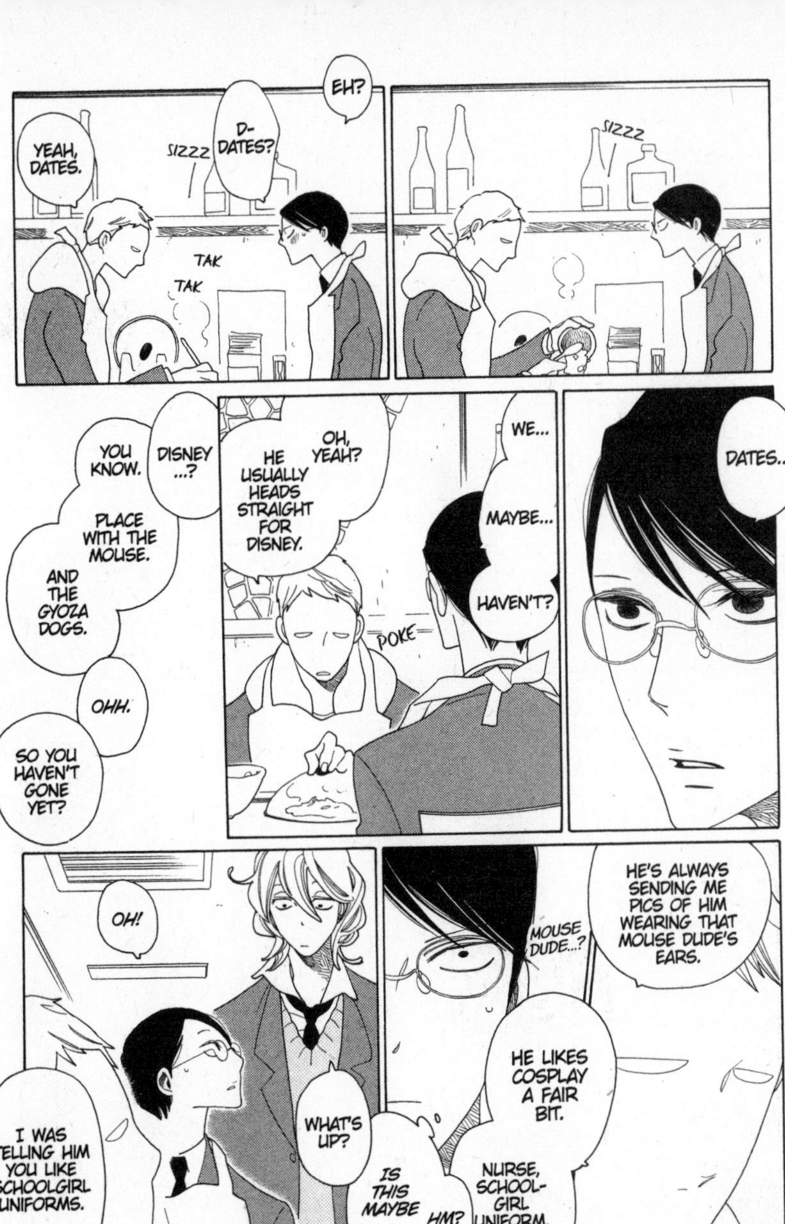
SIZZZ
EH?
D-DATES?
SIZZZ
YEAH, DATES.
TAK
TAK
DATES...
WE...
MAYBE...
HAVEN'T?
OH, YEAH?
HE USUALLY HEADS STRAIGHT FOR DISNEY.
POKE
DISNEY ...?
YOU KNOW.
PLACE WITH THE MOUSE.
AND THE GYOZA DOGS.
OHH.
SO YOU HAVEN'T GONE YET?
HE'S ALWAYS SENDING ME PICS OF HIM WEARING THAT MOUSE DUDE'S EARS.
MOUSE DUDE...?
HE LIKES COSPLAY A FAIR BIT.
NURSE, SCHOOL-GIRL UNIFORM, SHRINE PRIESTESS.
HM?
IS THIS MAYBE ...
OH!
WHAT'S UP?
I WAS TELLING HIM YOU LIKE SCHOOLGIRL UNIFORMS.

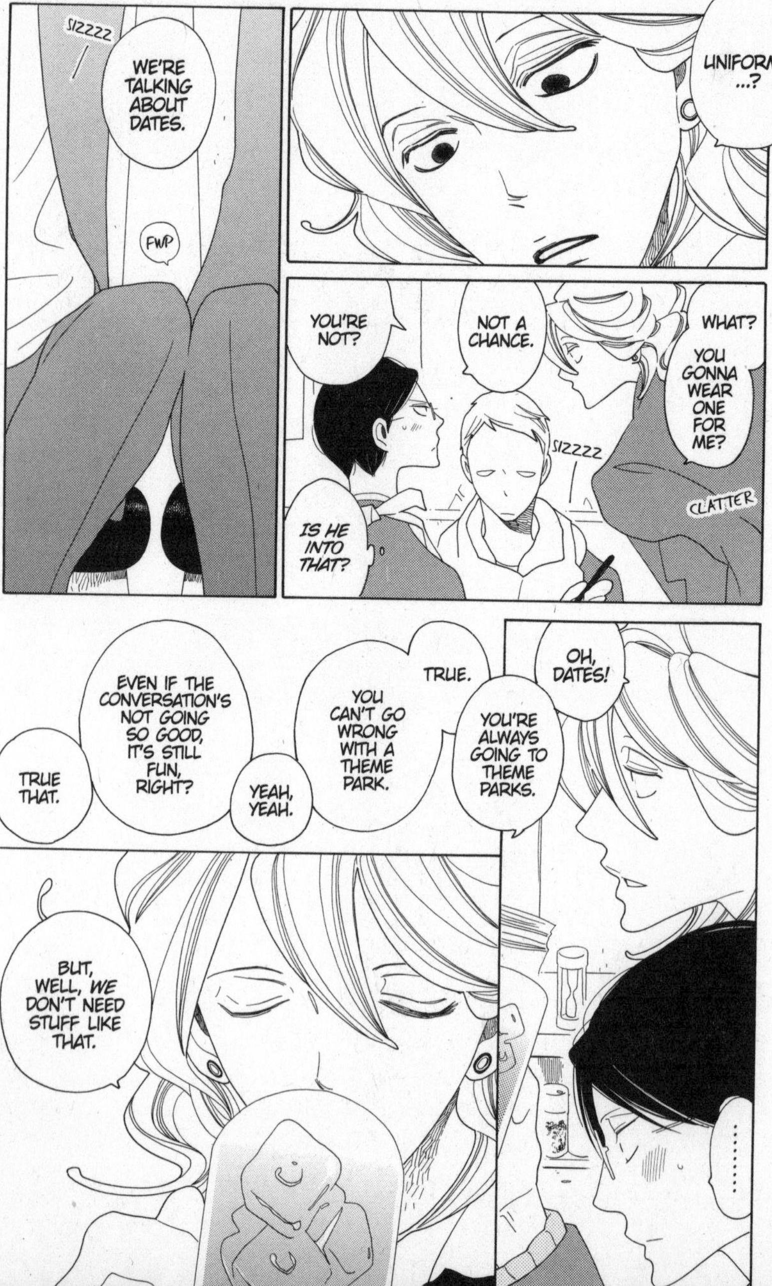
UNIFORMS ...?
WHAT? YOU GONNA WEAR ONE FOR ME?
NOT A CHANCE.
YOU'RE NOT?
SIZZZZ
CLATTER
IS HE INTO THAT?
SIZZZZ
WE'RE TALKING ABOUT DATES.
FWP
OH, DATES!
YOU'RE ALWAYS GOING TO THEME PARKS.
……
TRUE.
YOU CAN'T GO WRONG WITH A THEME PARK.
YEAH, YEAH.
EVEN IF THE CONVERSATION'S NOT GOING SO GOOD, IT'S STILL FUN, RIGHT?
TRUE THAT.
BUT, WELL, WE DON'T NEED STUFF LIKE THAT.

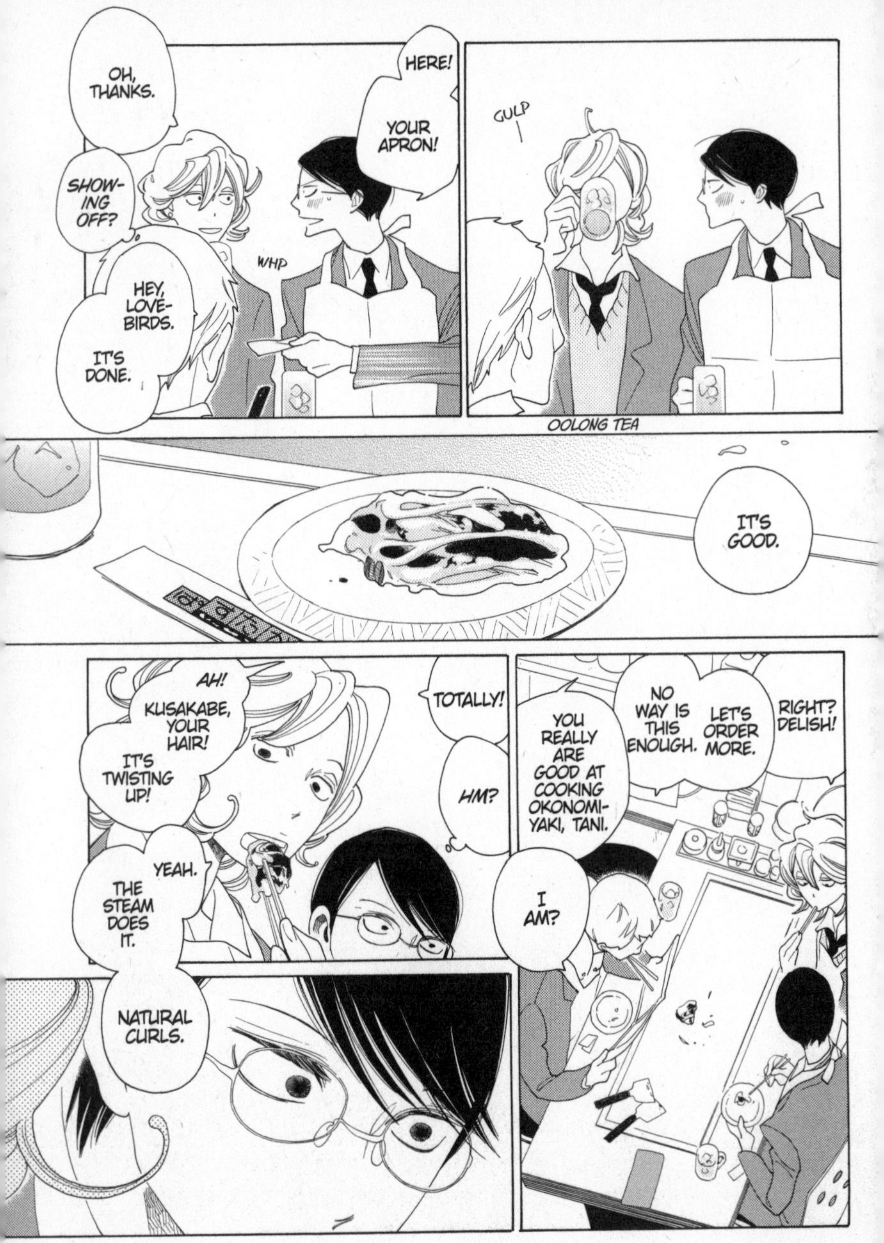
GULP
OOLONG TEA
HERE!
YOUR APRON!
OH, THANKS.
SHOW-ING OFF?
WHP
HEY, LOVE-BIRDS.
IT'S DONE.
IT'S GOOD.
RIGHT? DELISH!
LET'S ORDER MORE.
NO WAY IS THIS ENOUGH.
YOU REALLY ARE GOOD AT COOKING OKONOMI-YAKI, TANI.
I AM?
TOTALLY!
HM?
AH! KUSAKABE, YOUR HAIR!
IT'S TWISTING UP!
YEAH. THE STEAM DOES IT.
NATURAL CURLS.

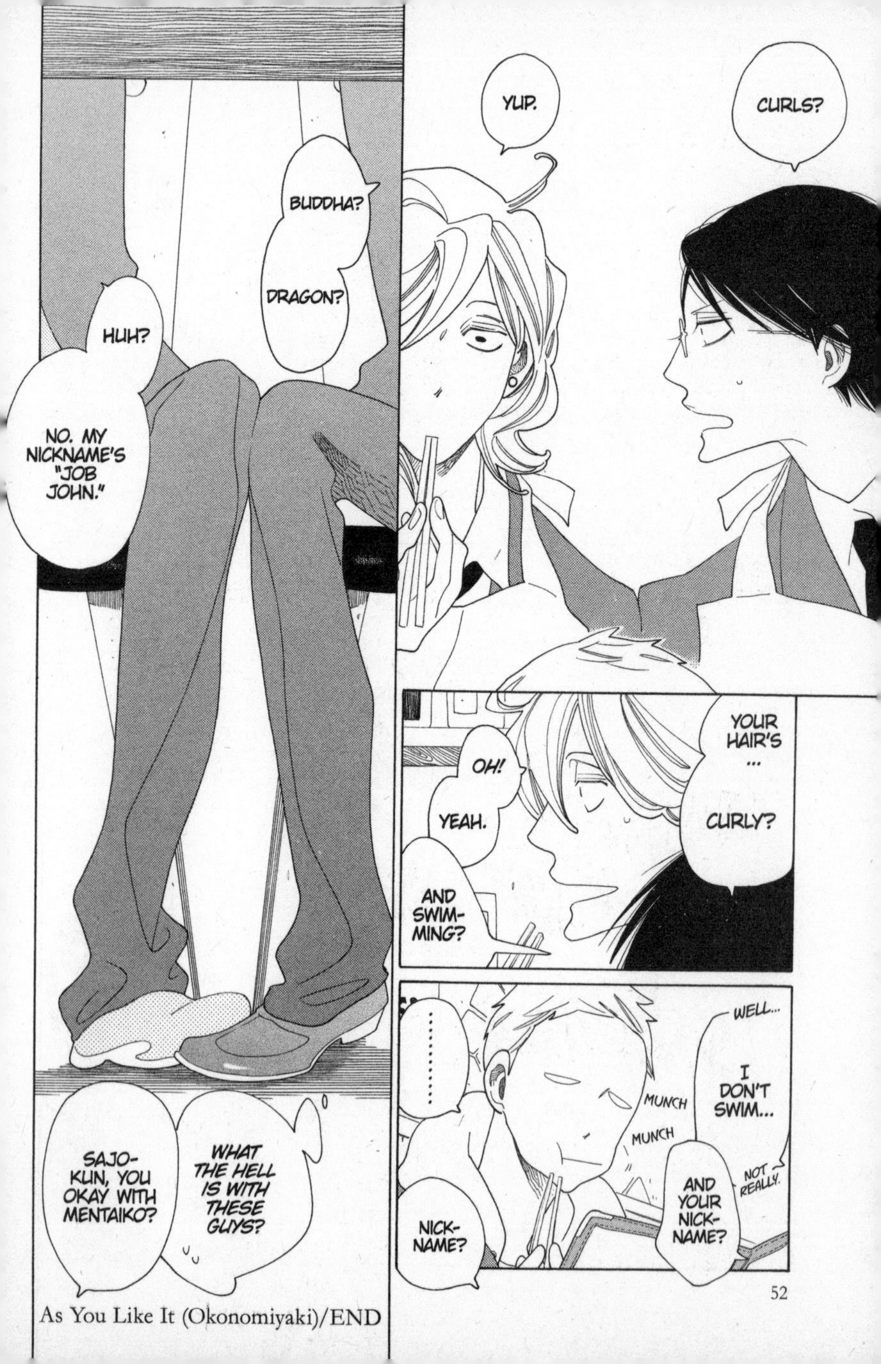
CURLS?
YUP.
YOUR HAIR'S ...
CURLY?
OH!
YEAH.
AND SWIMMING?
WELL...
I DON'T SWIM...
NOT REALLY.
AND YOUR NICKNAME?
MUNCH
MUNCH
......
NICKNAME?
BUDDHA?
DRAGON?
HUH?
NO. MY NICKNAME'S "JOB JOHN."
WHAT THE HELL IS WITH THESE GUYS?
SAJO-KUN, YOU OKAY WITH MENTAIKO?

As You Like It (Okonomiyaki)/END

Short Piece | 2

[Lost in a Wild Idea (Fried Egg)]

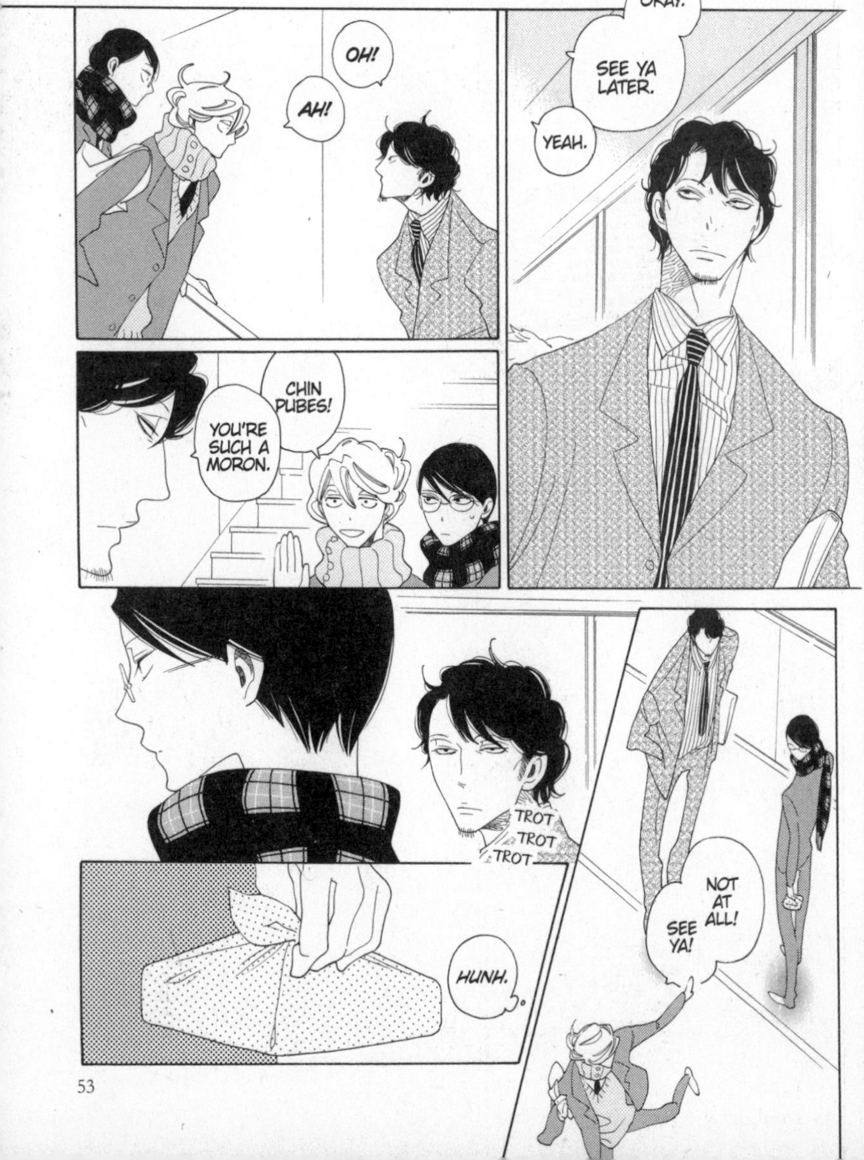
OKAY.
SEE YA LATER.
YEAH.
OH!
AH!
CHIN PUBES!
YOU'RE SUCH A MORON.
NOT AT ALL!
SEE YA!
TROT TROT TROT
HUNH.

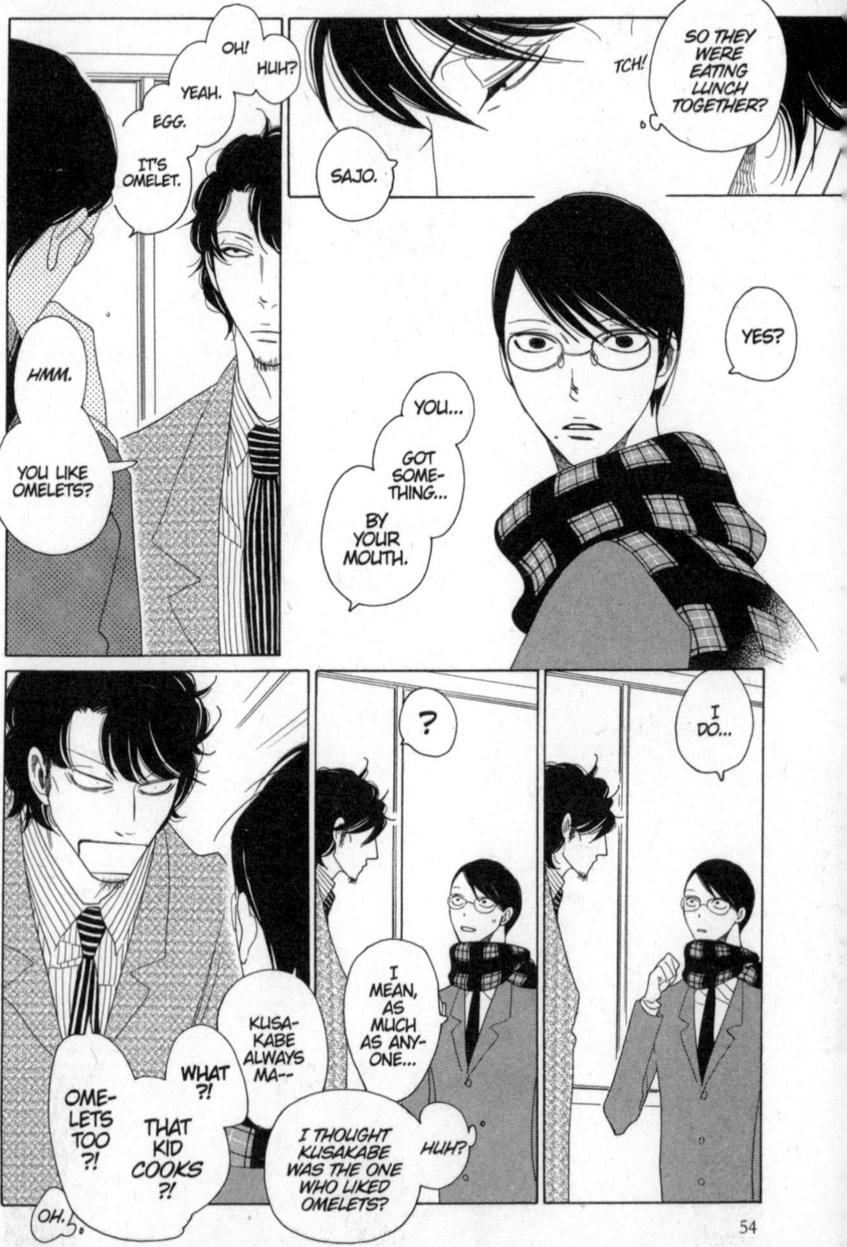
SO THEY WERE EATING LUNCH TOGETHER?
TCH!
SAJO.
YES?
YOU...
GOT SOMETHING...
BY YOUR MOUTH.
HUH?
OH!
YEAH.
EGG.
IT'S OMELET.
HMM.
YOU LIKE OMELETS?
I DO...
?
I MEAN, AS MUCH AS ANYONE...
HUH?
I THOUGHT KUSAKABE WAS THE ONE WHO LIKED OMELETS?
KUSAKABE ALWAYS MA--
WHAT?!
THAT KID COOKS?!
OMELETS TOO?!
OH.

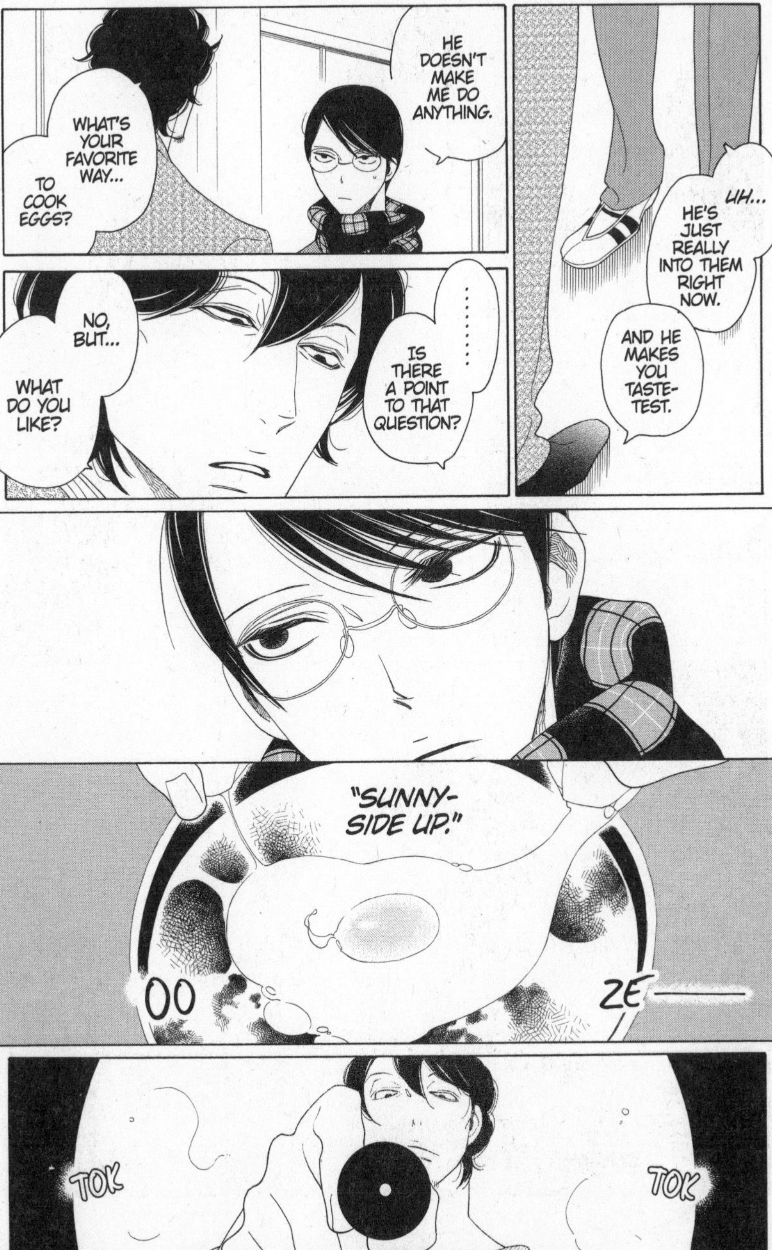
UH... HE'S JUST REALLY INTO THEM RIGHT NOW.
AND HE MAKES YOU TASTE-TEST.
HE DOESN'T MAKE ME DO ANYTHING.
WHAT'S YOUR FAVORITE WAY... TO COOK EGGS?
......
IS THERE A POINT TO THAT QUESTION?
NO, BUT... WHAT DO YOU LIKE?
"SUNNY-SIDE UP."
OO ZE——
TOK TOK

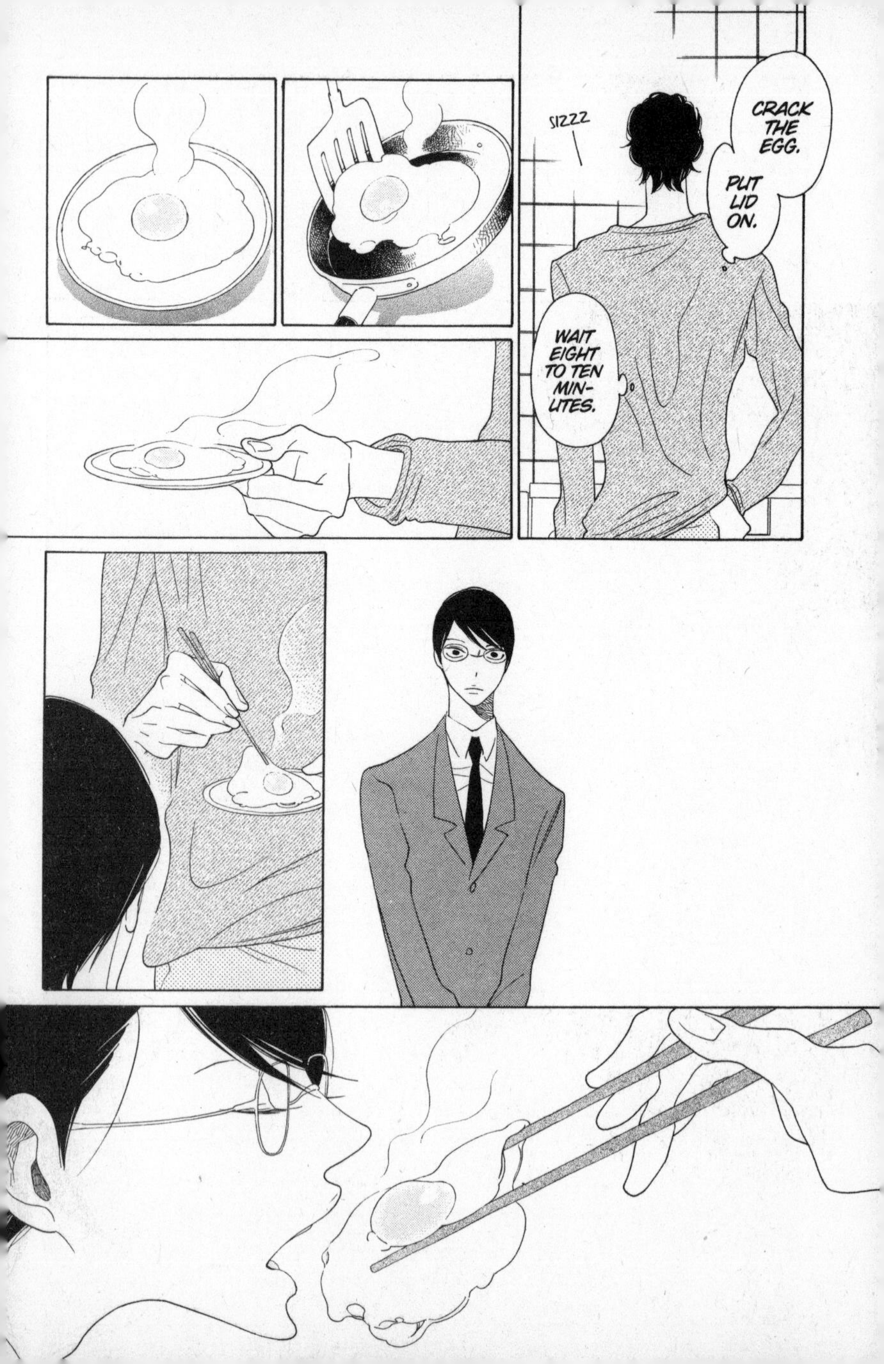
CRACK THE EGG.
PUT LID ON.
SIZZZ
WAIT EIGHT TO TEN MIN-UTES.

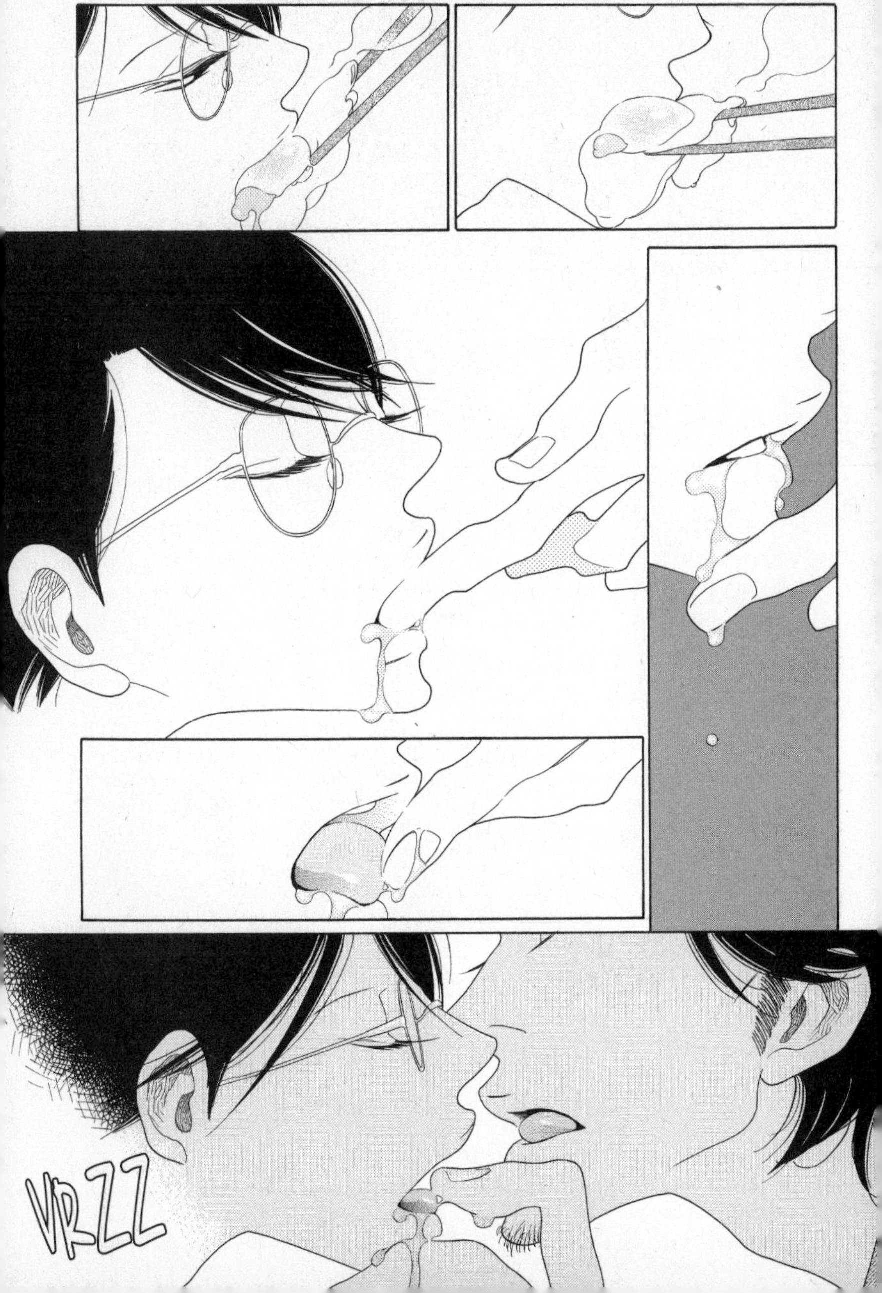
VRZZ

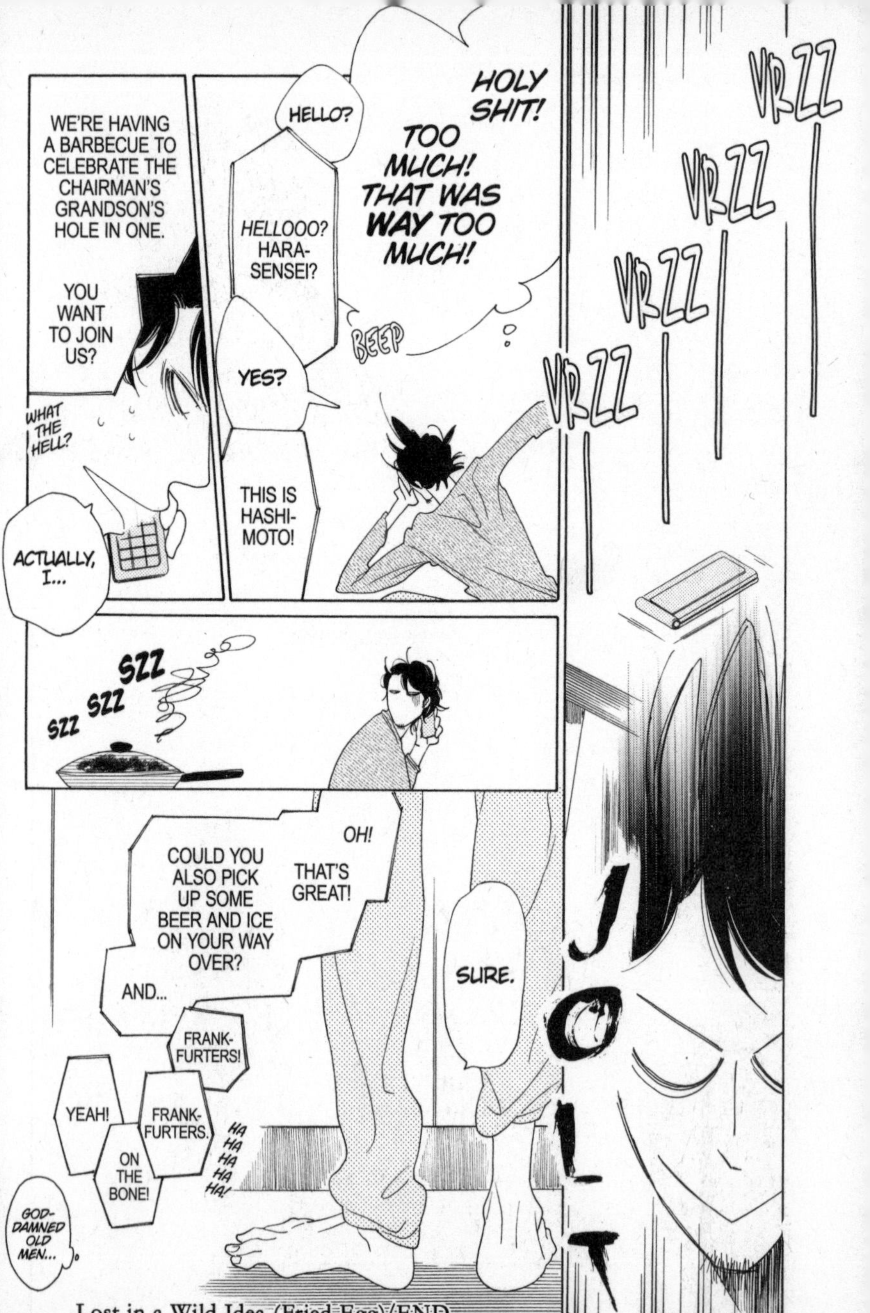

VRZZ
VRZZ
VRZZ
VRZZ
JOLT
HOLY SHIT!
TOO MUCH! THAT WAS WAY TOO MUCH!
BEEP
HELLO?
HELLOOO? HARA-SENSEI?
YES?
THIS IS HASHIMOTO!
WE'RE HAVING A BARBECUE TO CELEBRATE THE CHAIRMAN'S GRANDSON'S HOLE IN ONE.
YOU WANT TO JOIN US?
WHAT THE HELL?
ACTUALLY, I...
SZZ
SZZ
SZZ
OH!
THAT'S GREAT!
COULD YOU ALSO PICK UP SOME BEER AND ICE ON YOUR WAY OVER?
SURE.
AND...
FRANK-FURTERS!
FRANK-FURTERS.
YEAH!
ON THE BONE!
HA HA HA HA HA!
GOD-DAMNED OLD MEN...

Lost in a Wild Idea (Fried Egg)/END

Short Piece | 3

[Jealous (Grilled Mochi)]

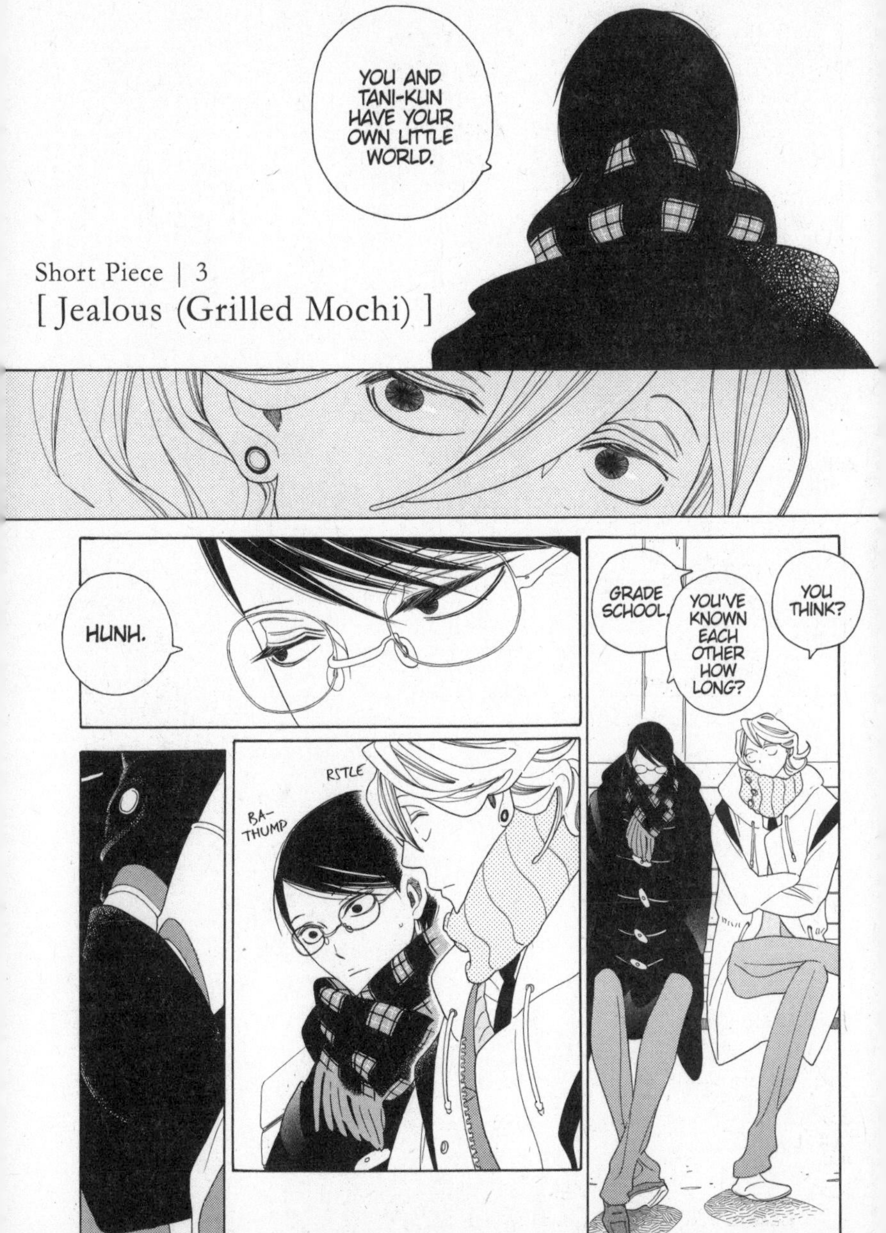
YOU AND TANI-KUN HAVE YOUR OWN LITTLE WORLD.
YOU THINK?
YOU'VE KNOWN EACH OTHER HOW LONG?
GRADE SCHOOL.
HUNH.
RSTLE
BA-THUMP

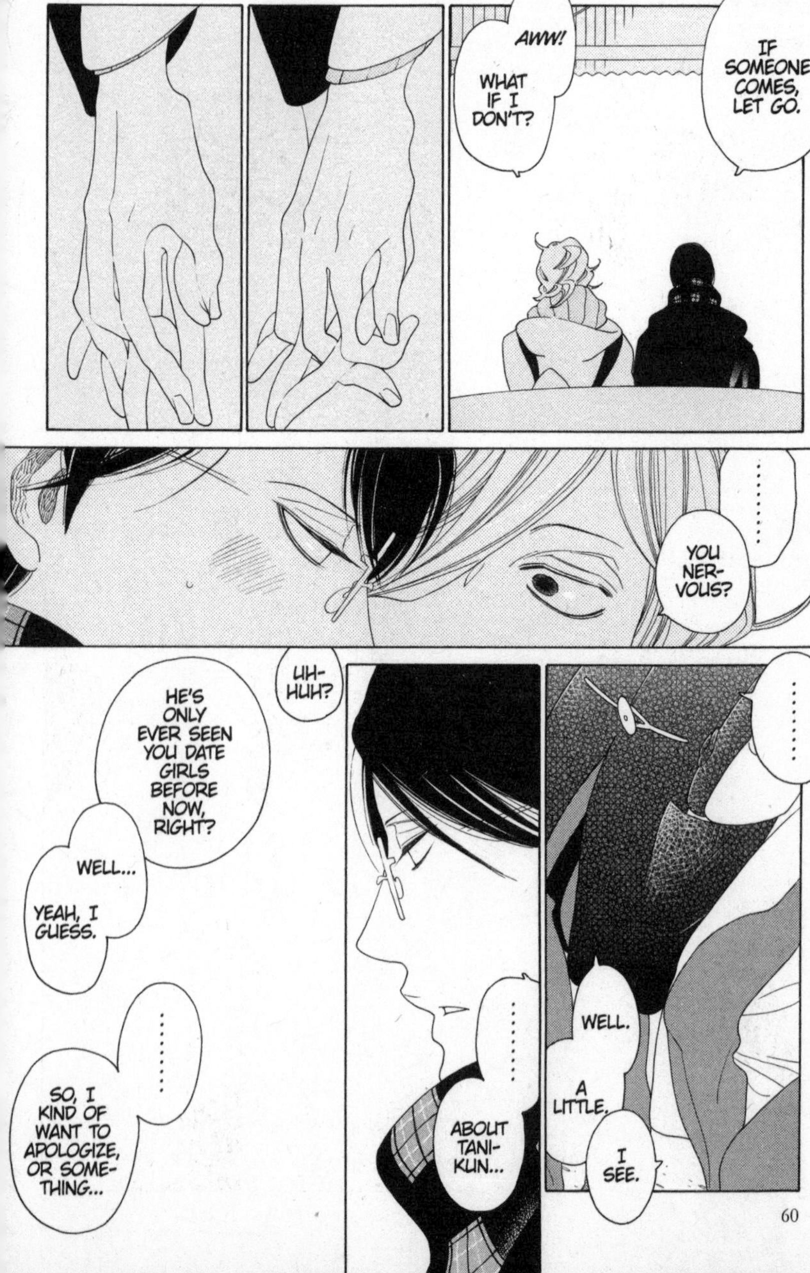
IF SOMEONE COMES, LET GO.
AWW! WHAT IF I DON'T?
......
YOU NERVOUS?
......
WELL.
A LITTLE.
I SEE.
......
ABOUT TANI-KUN...
UH-HUH?
HE'S ONLY EVER SEEN YOU DATE GIRLS BEFORE NOW, RIGHT?
WELL...
YEAH, I GUESS.
......
SO, I KIND OF WANT TO APOLOGIZE, OR SOMETHING...

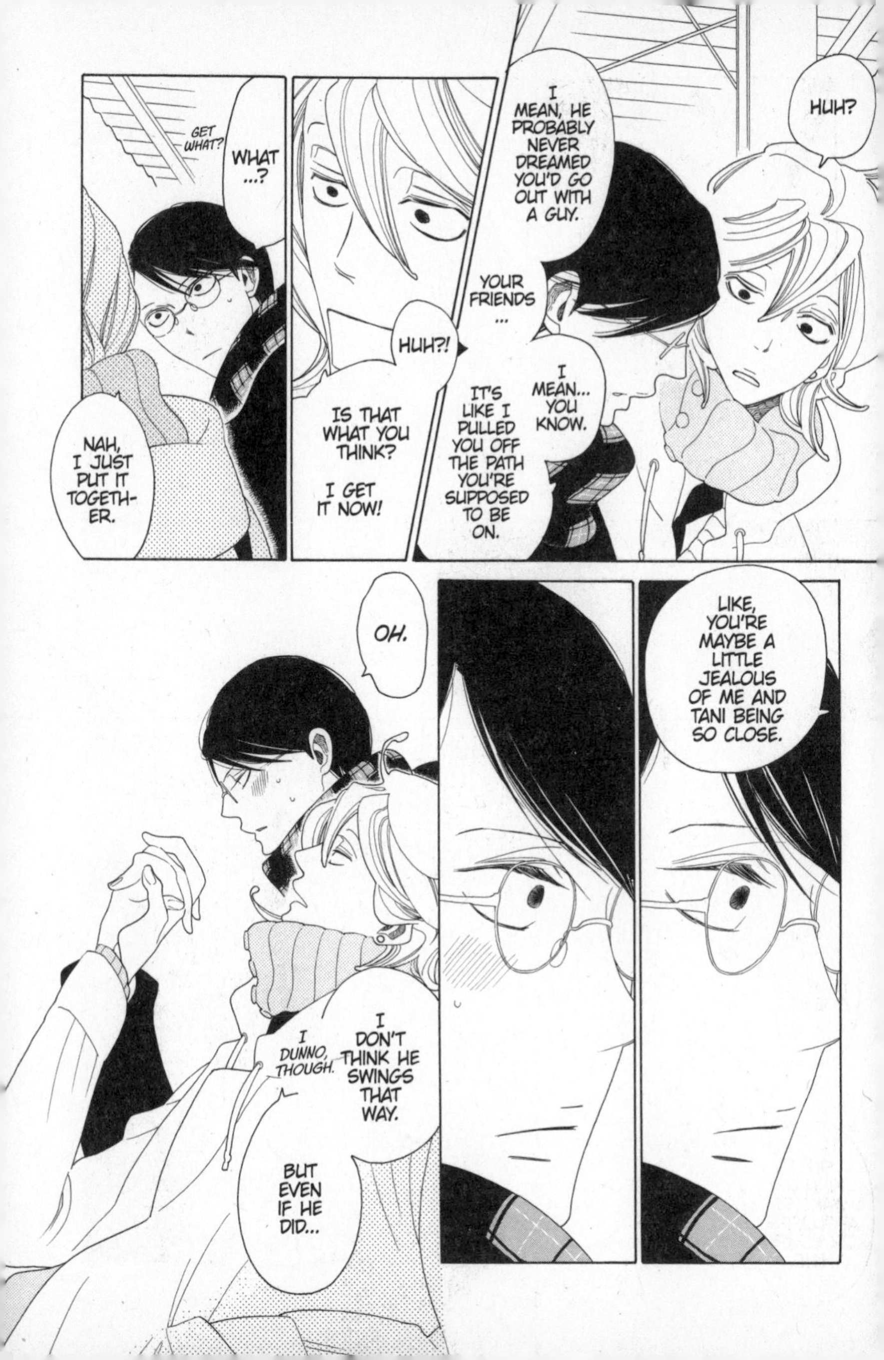
HUH?
I MEAN, HE PROBABLY NEVER DREAMED YOU'D GO OUT WITH A GUY.
I MEAN... YOU KNOW.
IT'S LIKE I PULLED YOU OFF THE PATH YOU'RE SUPPOSED TO BE ON.
YOUR FRIENDS ...
HUH?!
IS THAT WHAT YOU THINK?
I GET IT NOW!
WHAT ...?
GET WHAT?
NAH, I JUST PUT IT TOGETH-ER.
LIKE, YOU'RE MAYBE A LITTLE JEALOUS OF ME AND TANI BEING SO CLOSE.
OH.
I DON'T THINK HE SWINGS THAT WAY.
I DUNNO, THOUGH.
BUT EVEN IF HE DID...

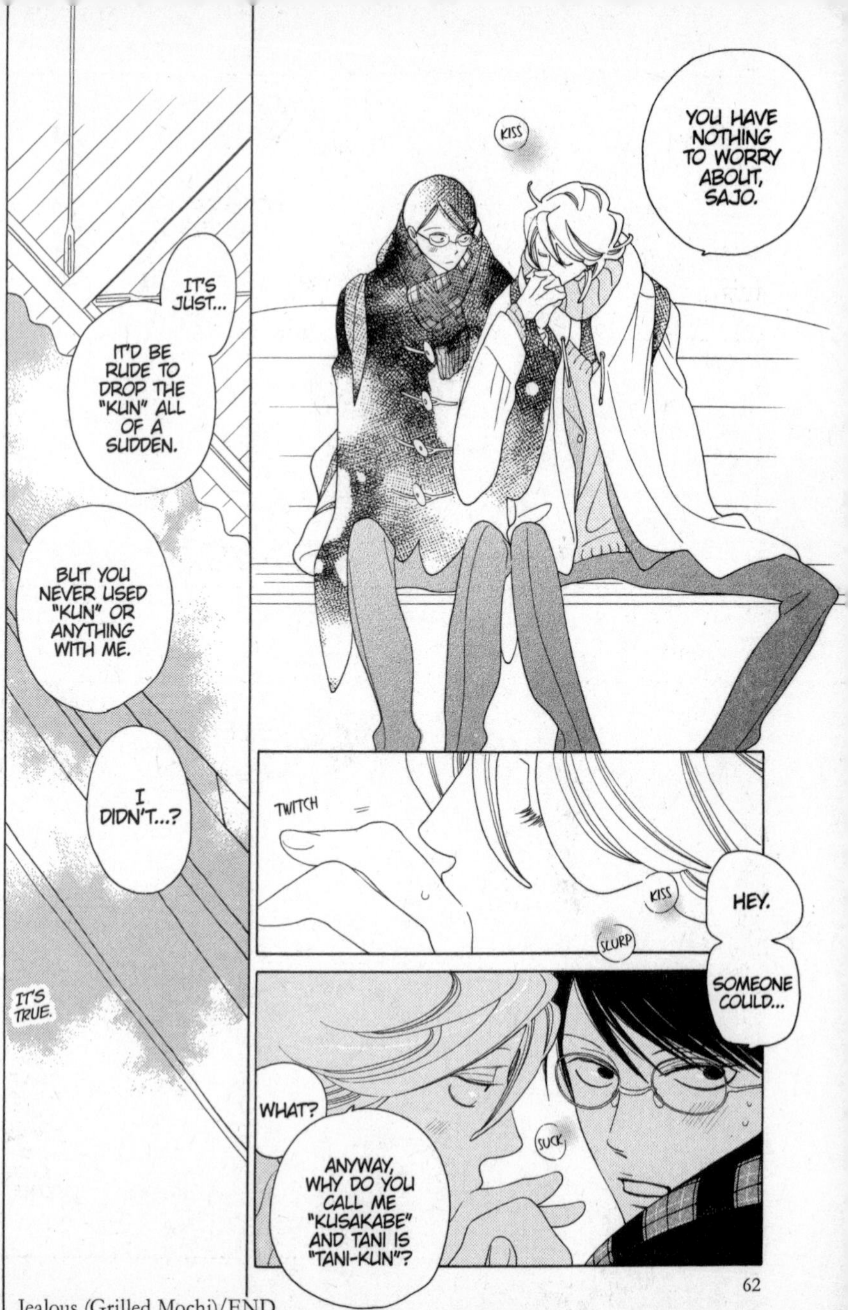
YOU HAVE NOTHING TO WORRY ABOUT, SAJO.
KISS
HEY.
KISS
TWITCH
SLURP
SOMEONE COULD...
WHAT?
SUCK
ANYWAY, WHY DO YOU CALL ME "KUSAKABE" AND TANI IS "TANI-KUN"?
IT'S JUST...
IT'D BE RUDE TO DROP THE "KUN" ALL OF A SUDDEN.
BUT YOU NEVER USED "KUN" OR ANYTHING WITH ME.
I DIDN'T...?
IT'S TRUE.

Jealous (Grilled Mochi)/END

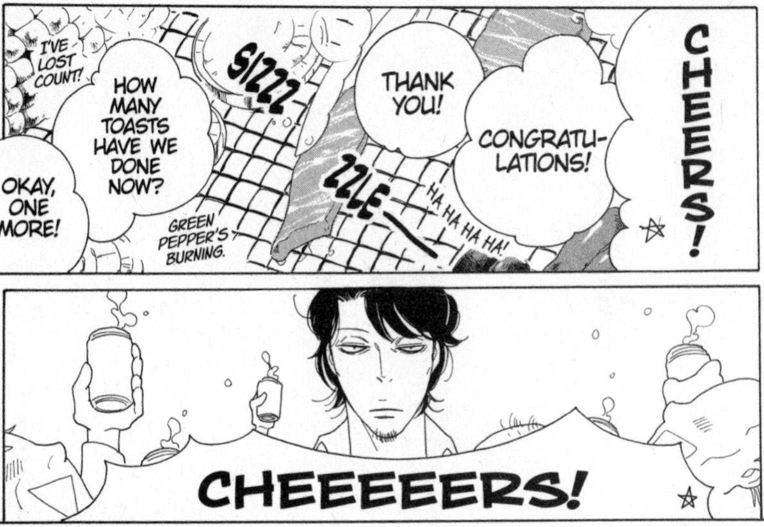
CHEERS!
CONGRATULATIONS!
THANK YOU!
HA HA HA HA!
SIZZZ ZZLE
HOW MANY TOASTS HAVE WE DONE NOW?
I'VE LOST COUNT!
GREEN PEPPER'S BURNING.
OKAY, ONE MORE!
CHEEEEEERS!

Short Piece | 4

[Bash (Barbecue)]

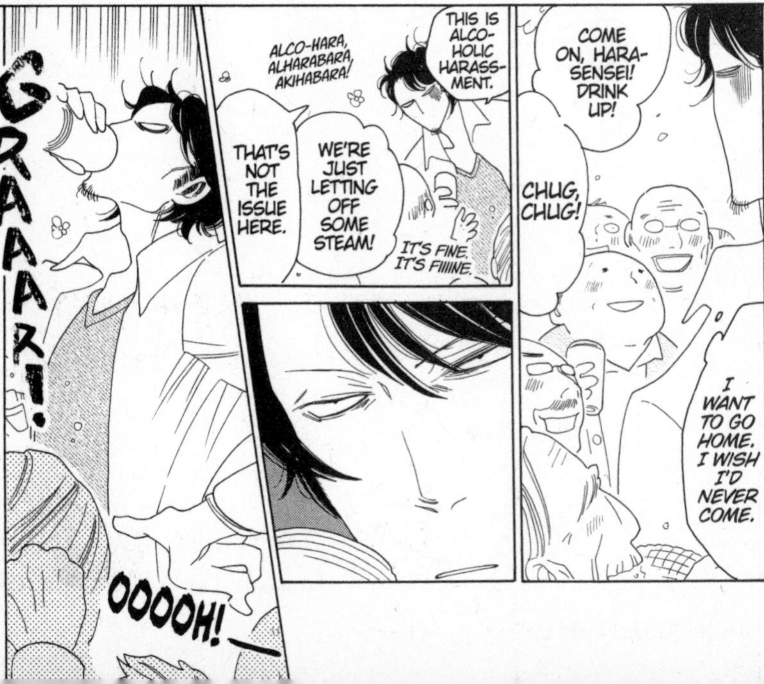
COME ON, HARA-SENSEI! DRINK UP!
CHUG, CHUG!
I WANT TO GO HOME. I WISH I'D NEVER COME.
THIS IS ALCOHOLIC HARASSMENT.
ALCO-HARA, ALHARABARA, AKIHABARA!
WE'RE JUST LETTING OFF SOME STEAM!
IT'S FINE. IT'S FIIIINE.
THAT'S NOT THE ISSUE HERE.
GRAAAR!
OOOOH!

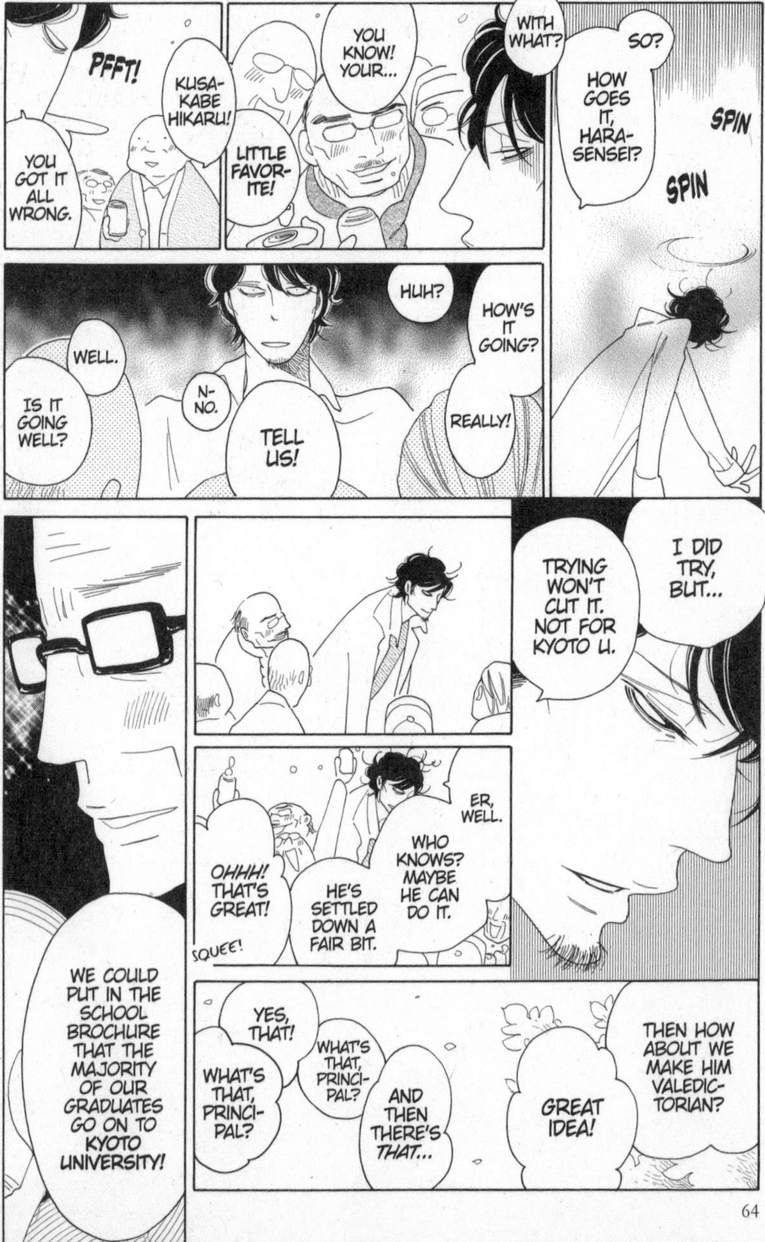
SO?
HOW GOES IT, HARA-SENSEI?
SPIN
SPIN
WITH WHAT?
YOU KNOW! YOUR...
LITTLE FAVOR-ITE!
KUSA-KABE HIKARU!
PFFT!
YOU GOT IT ALL WRONG.
HOW'S IT GOING?
REALLY!
HUH?
TELL US!
N-NO.
WELL.
IS IT GOING WELL?
I DID TRY, BUT...
TRYING WON'T CUT IT. NOT FOR KYOTO U.
ER, WELL.
WHO KNOWS? MAYBE HE CAN DO IT.
HE'S SETTLED DOWN A FAIR BIT.
OHHH! THAT'S GREAT!
SQUEE!
THEN HOW ABOUT WE MAKE HIM VALEDIC-TORIAN?
GREAT IDEA!
AND THEN THERE'S *THAT*...
WHAT'S THAT, PRINCI-PAL?
YES, THAT!
WHAT'S THAT, PRINCI-PAL?
WE COULD PUT IN THE SCHOOL BROCHURE THAT THE MAJORITY OF OUR GRADUATES GO ON TO KYOTO UNIVERSITY!

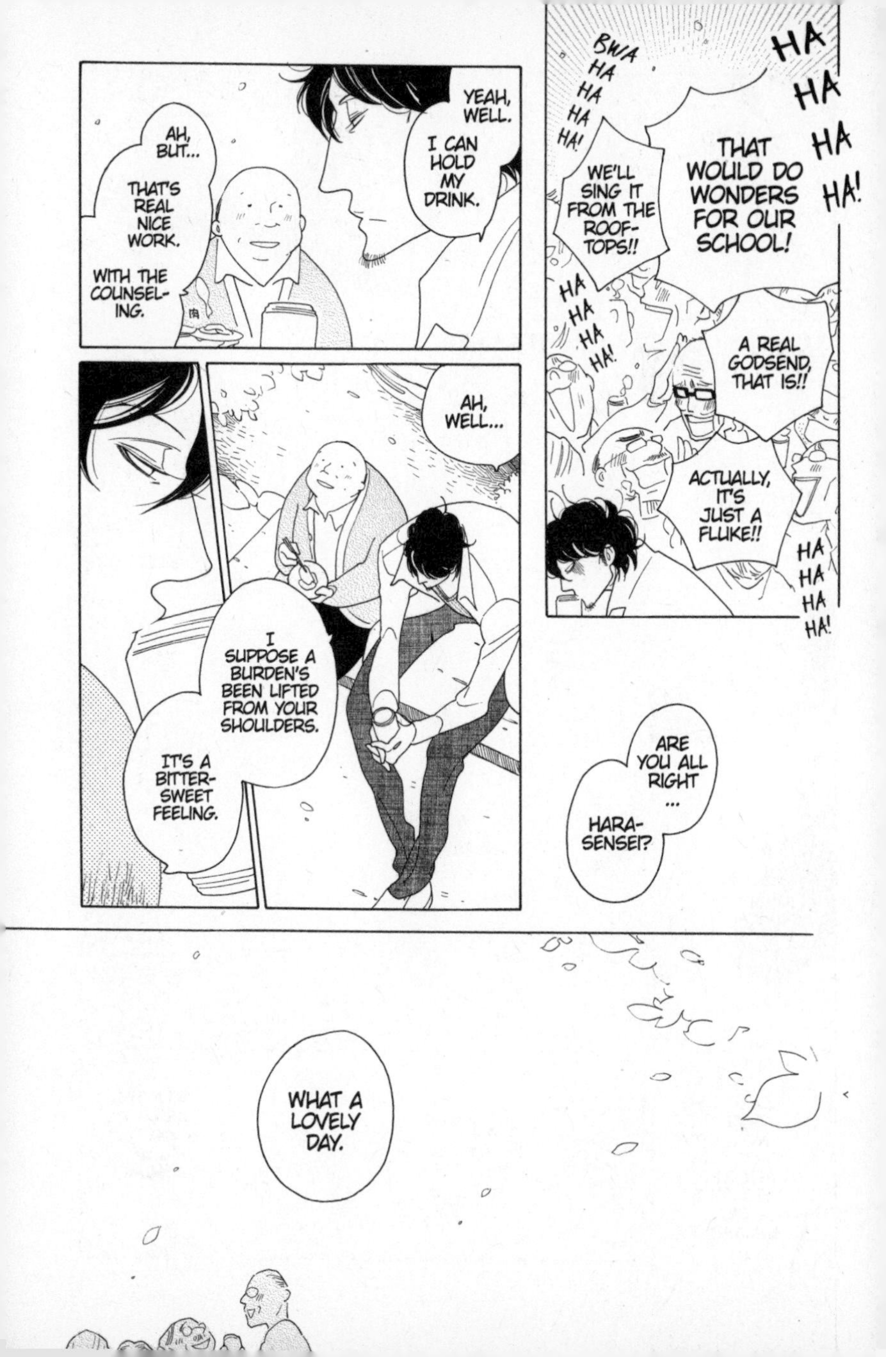
HA HA HA HA!
BWA HA HA HA HA!
THAT WOULD DO WONDERS FOR OUR SCHOOL!
WE'LL SING IT FROM THE ROOF-TOPS!!
HA HA HA HA!
A REAL GODSEND, THAT IS!!
ACTUALLY, IT'S JUST A FLUKE!!
HA HA HA HA!
ARE YOU ALL RIGHT ... HARA-SENSEI?
YEAH, WELL. I CAN HOLD MY DRINK.
AH, BUT... THAT'S REAL NICE WORK. WITH THE COUNSEL-ING.
AH, WELL...
I SUPPOSE A BURDEN'S BEEN LIFTED FROM YOUR SHOULDERS.
IT'S A BITTER-SWEET FEELING.
WHAT A LOVELY DAY.

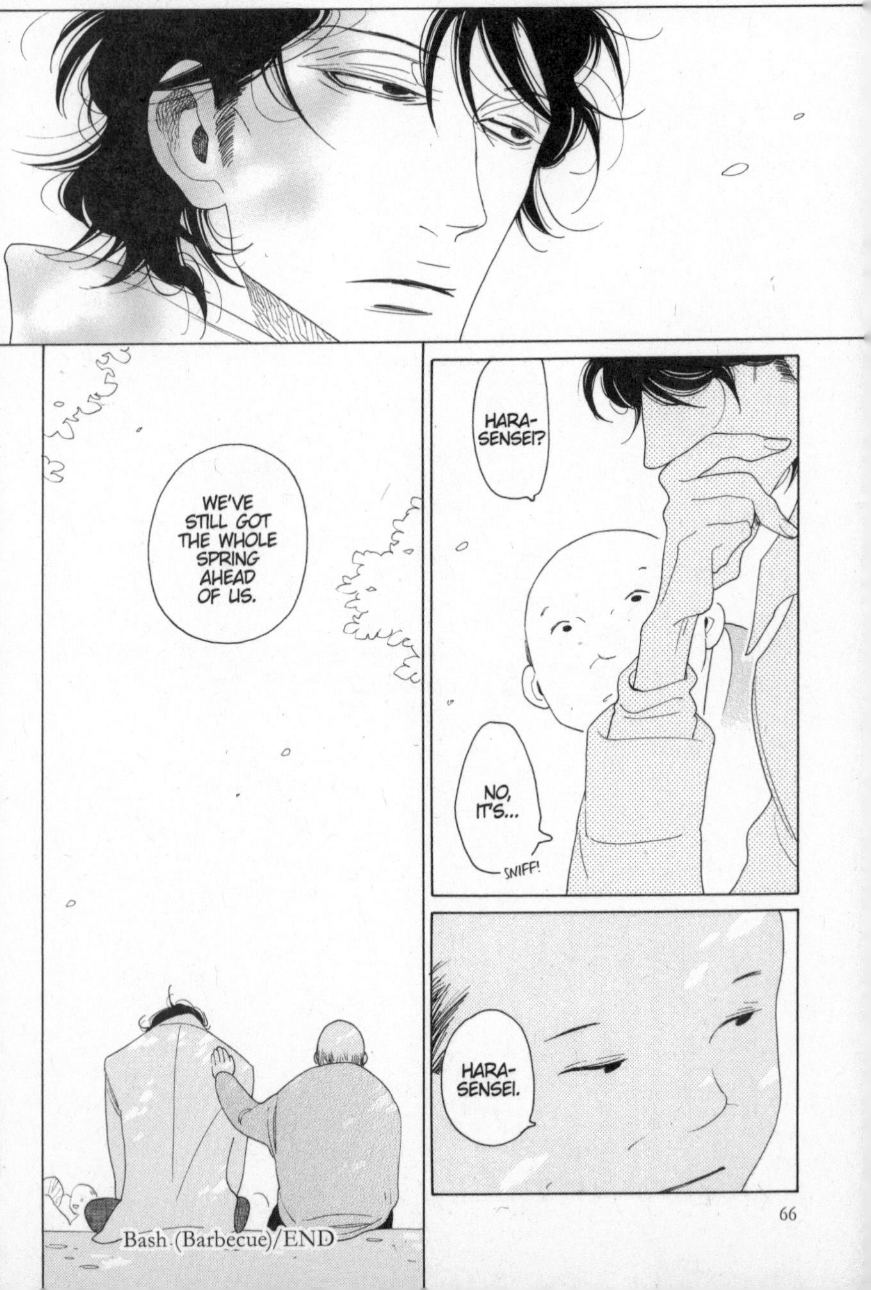
HARA-SENSEI?
NO, IT'S...
SNIFF!
HARA-SENSEI.
WE'VE STILL GOT THE WHOLE SPRING AHEAD OF US.
Bash (Barbecue)/END

Classmates

Intermission

GRAAARR!

GO FOR IT, HARA-SENSEI!

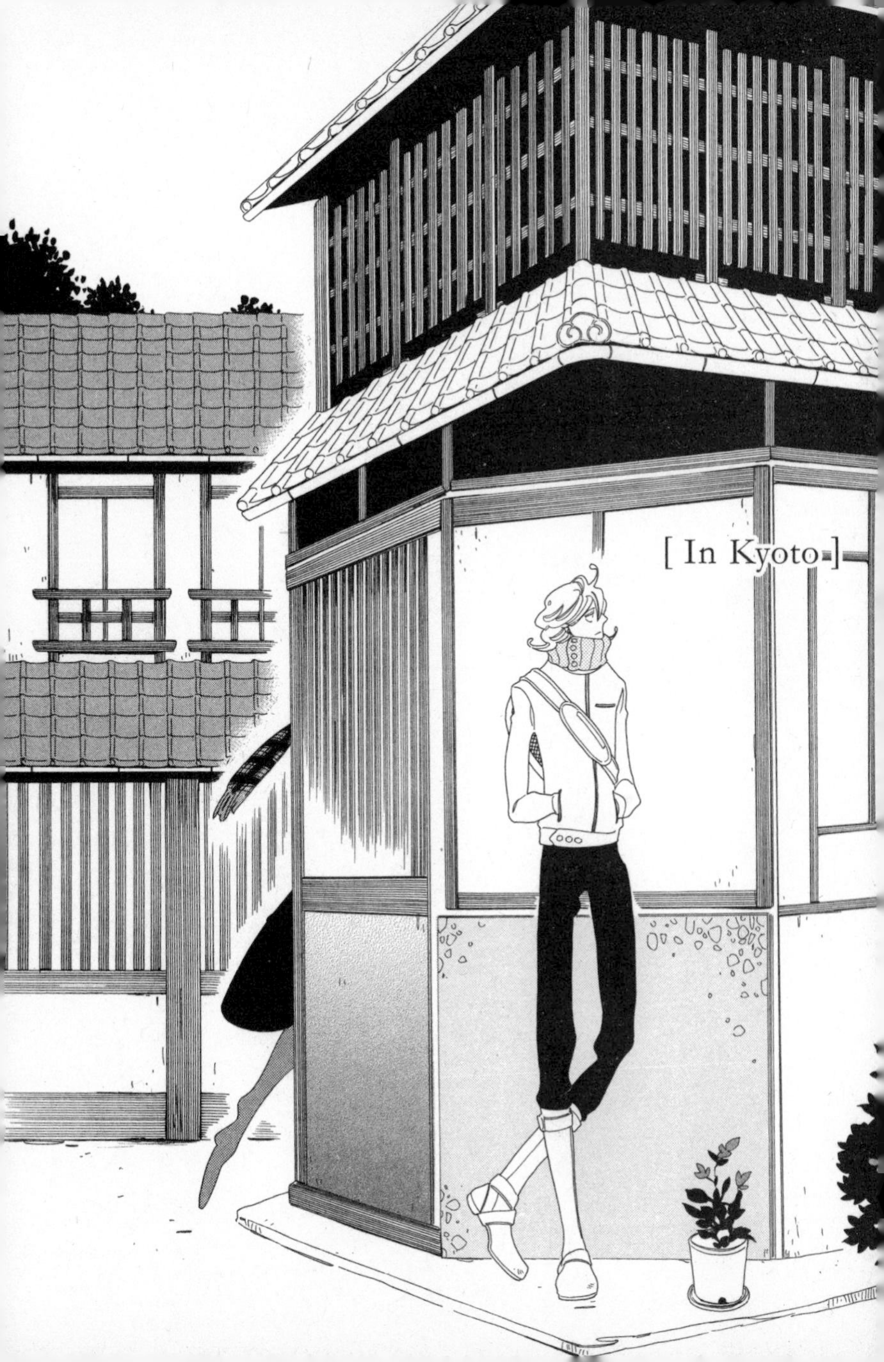
[In Kyoto]

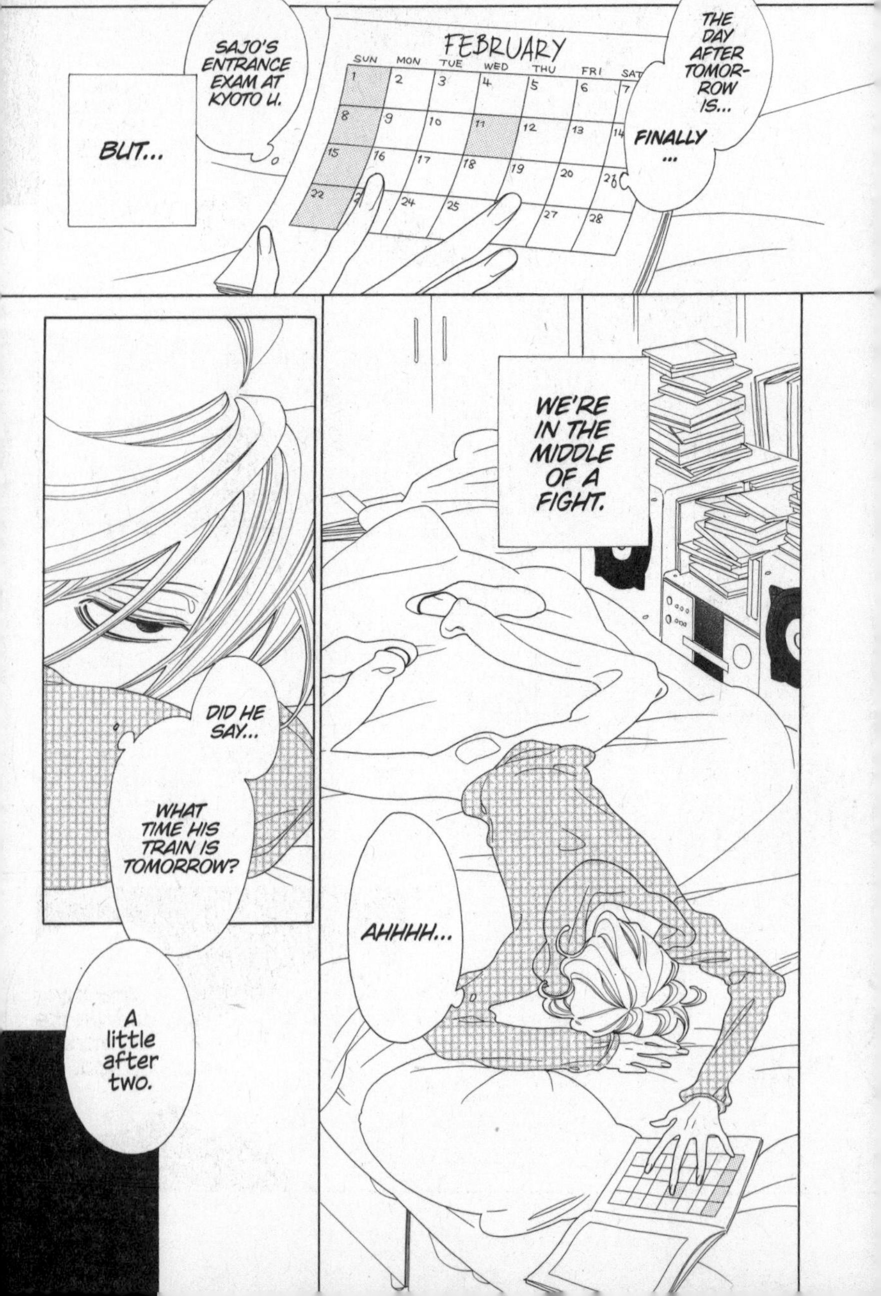
THE DAY AFTER TOMORROW IS...
FINALLY ...
FEBRUARY
SAJO'S ENTRANCE EXAM AT KYOTO U.
BUT...
WE'RE IN THE MIDDLE OF A FIGHT.
AHHHH...
DID HE SAY...
WHAT TIME HIS TRAIN IS TOMORROW?
A little after two.

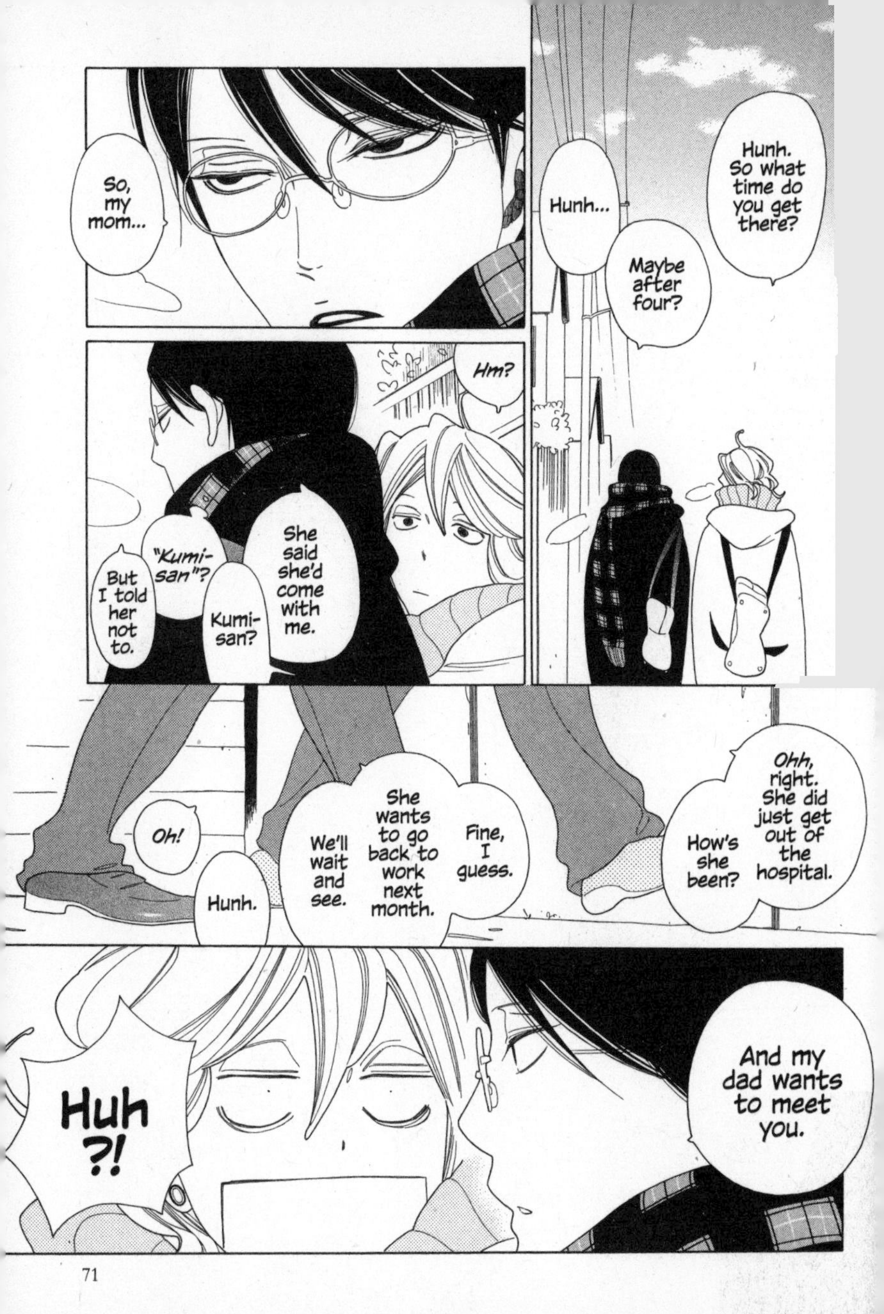

Hunh. So what time do you get there?
Hunh...
Maybe after four?
So, my mom...
Hm?
She said she'd come with me.
Kumi-san?
"Kumi-san"?
But I told her not to.
Ohh, right. She did just get out of the hospital.
How's she been?
Fine, I guess.
She wants to go back to work next month.
We'll wait and see.
Hunh.
Oh!
And my dad wants to meet you.
Huh ?!

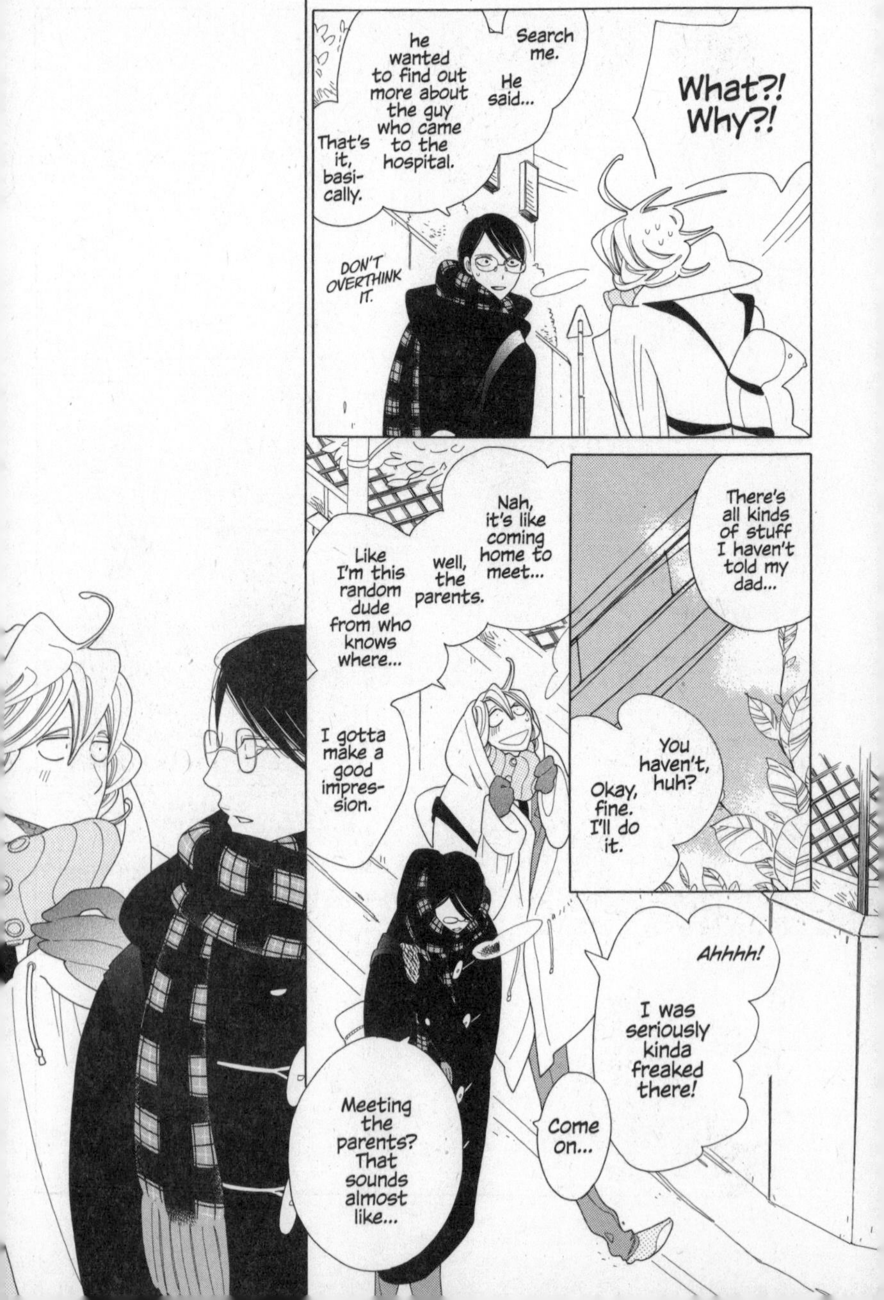
What?! Why?!
Search me.
He said...
he wanted to find out more about the guy who came to the hospital.
That's it, basically.
DON'T OVERTHINK IT.
There's all kinds of stuff I haven't told my dad...
You haven't, huh?
Okay, fine. I'll do it.
Nah, it's like coming home to meet...
well, the parents.
Like I'm this random dude from who knows where...
I gotta make a good impression.
Ahhhh!
I was seriously kinda freaked there!
Come on...
Meeting the parents? That sounds almost like...

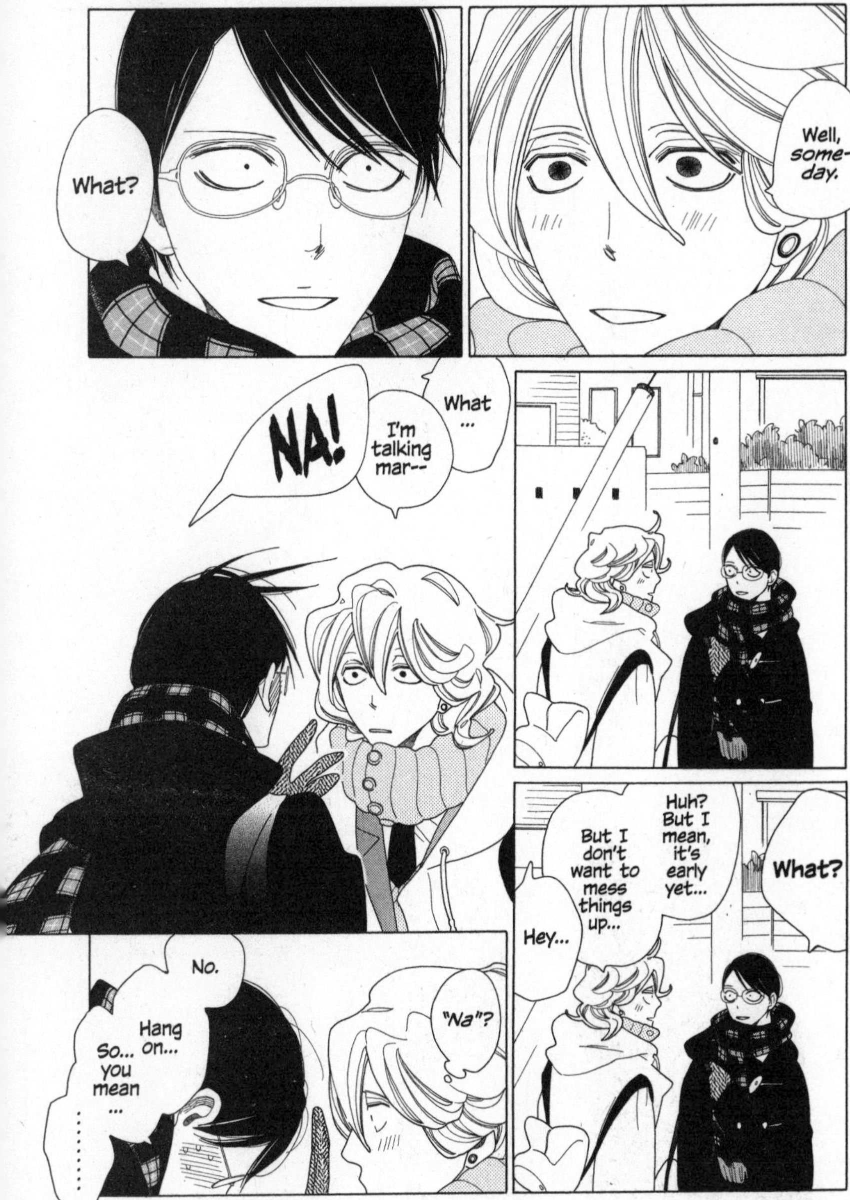
Well, someday.
What?
What?
Huh? But I mean, it's early yet...
But I don't want to mess things up...
Hey...
What ...
I'm talking mar--
NA!
"Na"?
No.
Hang on...
So... you mean ...
....

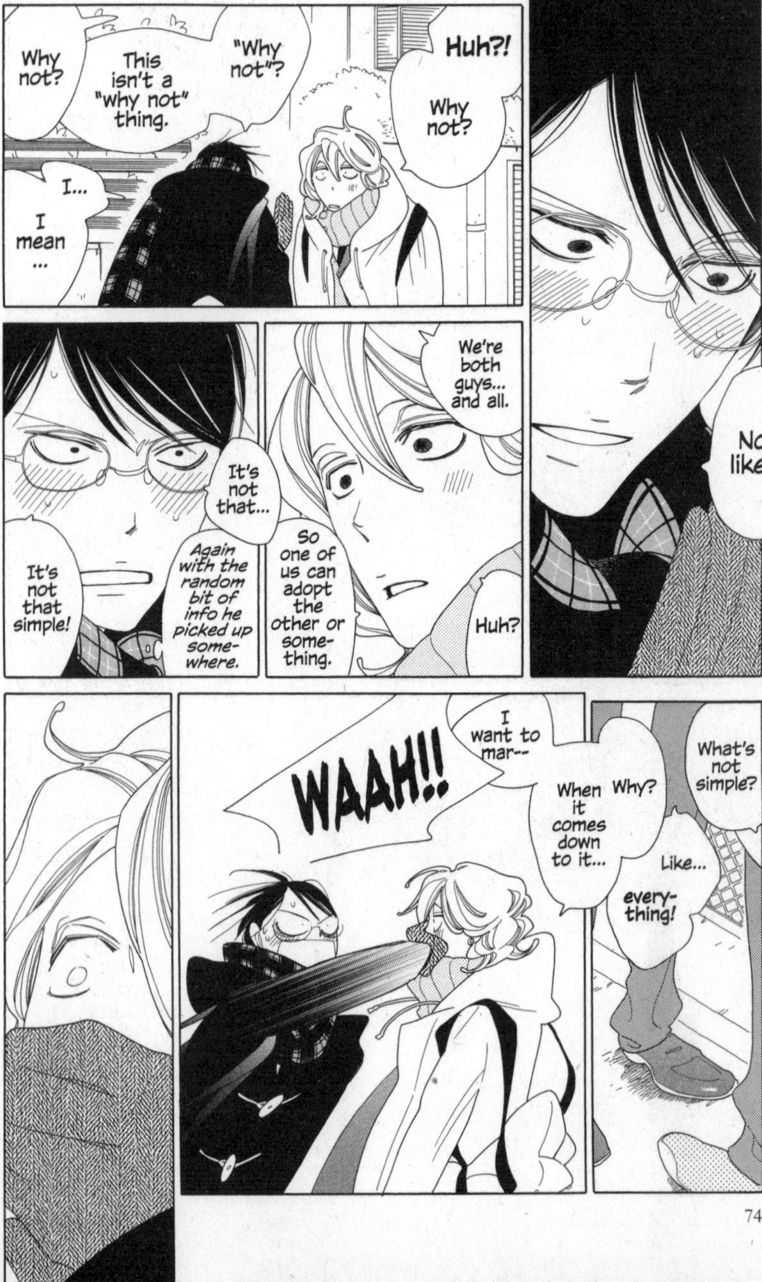
Not likely.
Huh?!
Why not?
"Why not"?
This isn't a "why not" thing.
Why not?
I...
I mean ...
We're both guys... and all.
Huh?
So one of us can adopt the other or some-thing.
It's not that...
Again with the random bit of info he picked up some-where.
It's not that simple!
What's not simple?
Why?
Like...
every-thing!
When it comes down to it...
I want to mar--
WAAH!!

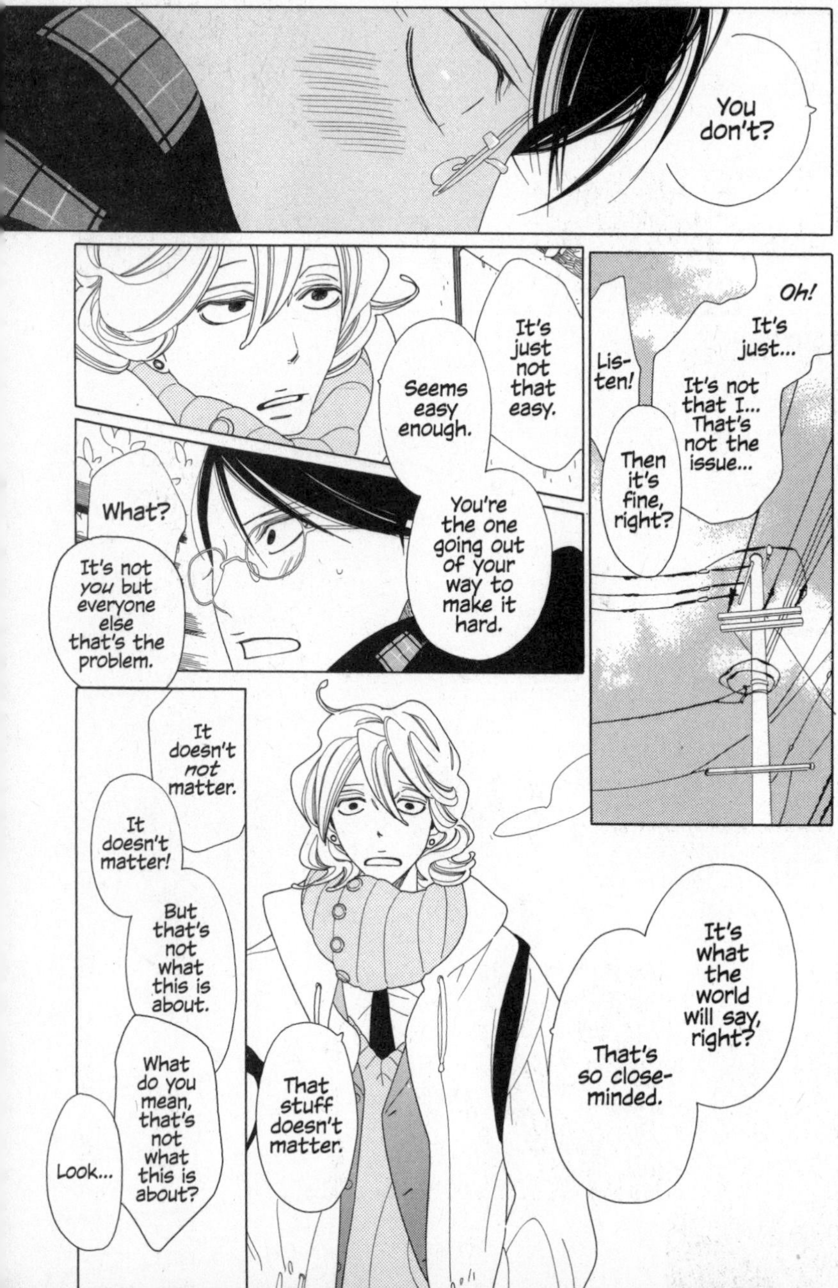
You don't?
Oh!
It's just...
It's not that I... That's not the issue...
Lis-ten!
Then it's fine, right?
It's just not that easy.
Seems easy enough.
You're the one going out of your way to make it hard.
What?
It's not *you* but everyone else that's the problem.
It's what the world will say, right?
That's so close-minded.
That stuff doesn't matter.
It doesn't *not* matter.
It doesn't matter!
But that's not what this is about.
What do you mean, that's not what this is about?
Look...

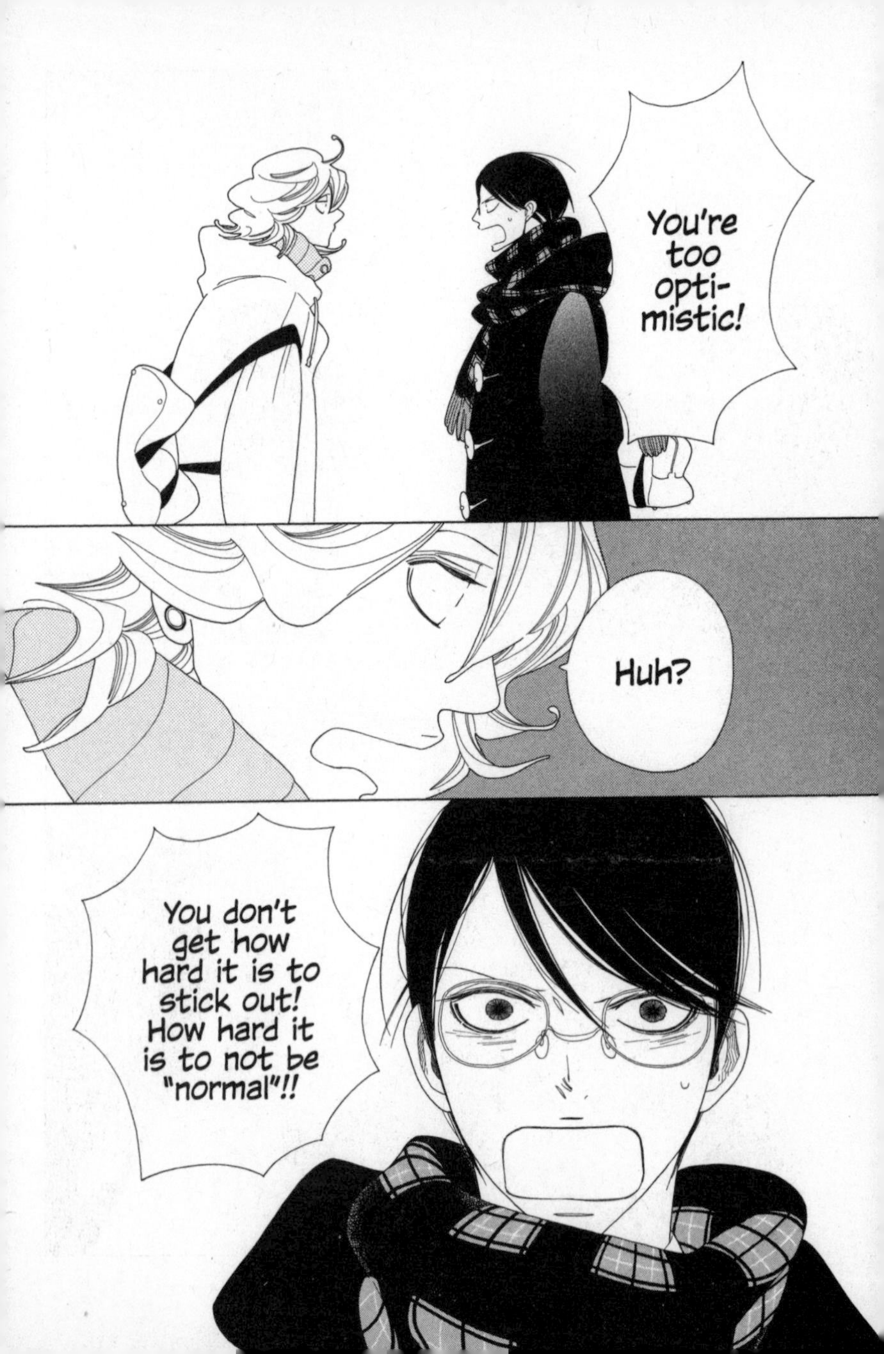
You're too opti-mistic!
Huh?
You don't get how hard it is to stick out! How hard it is to not be "normal"!!

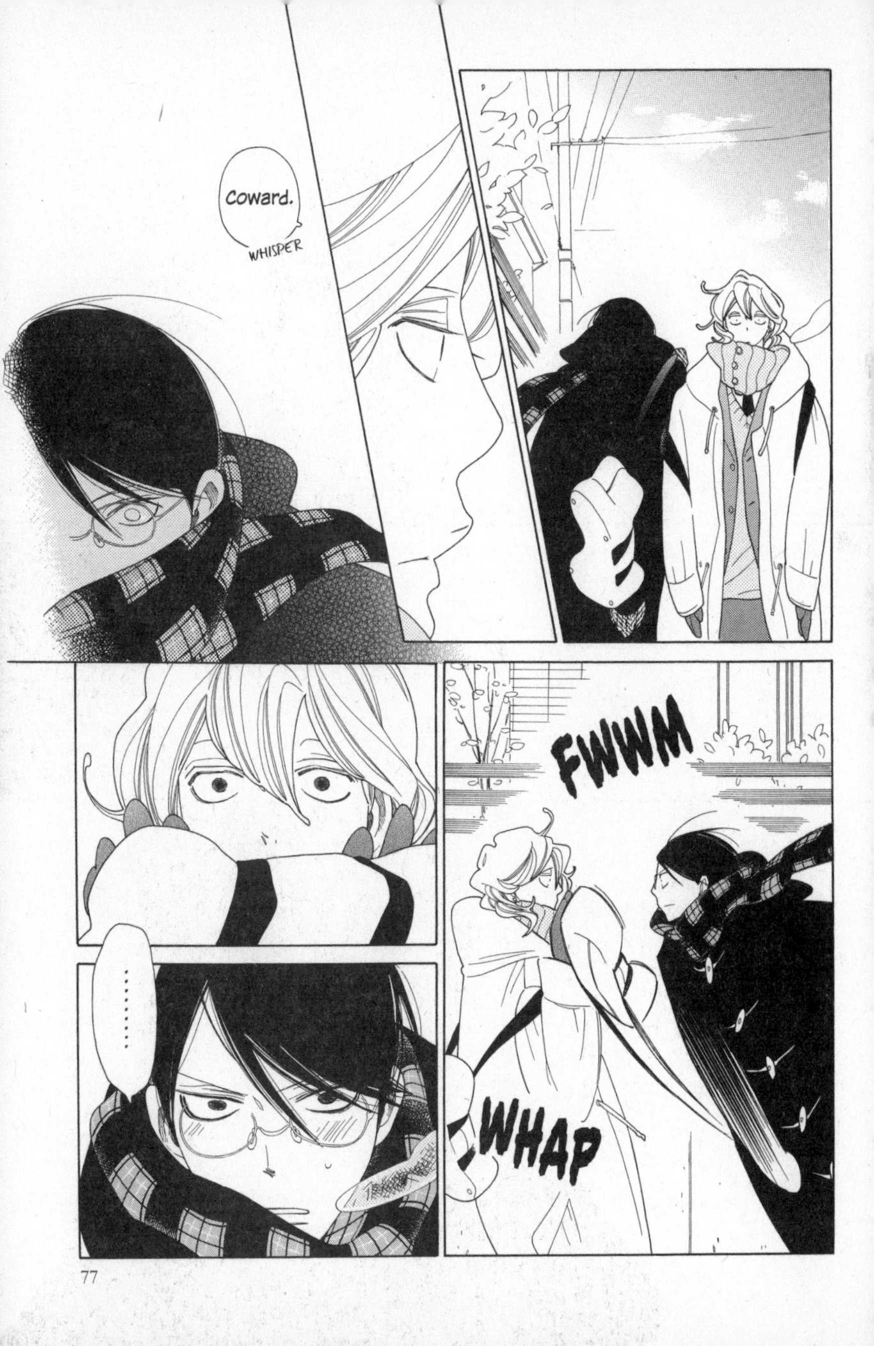
Coward.
WHISPER
FWWM
WHAP
......

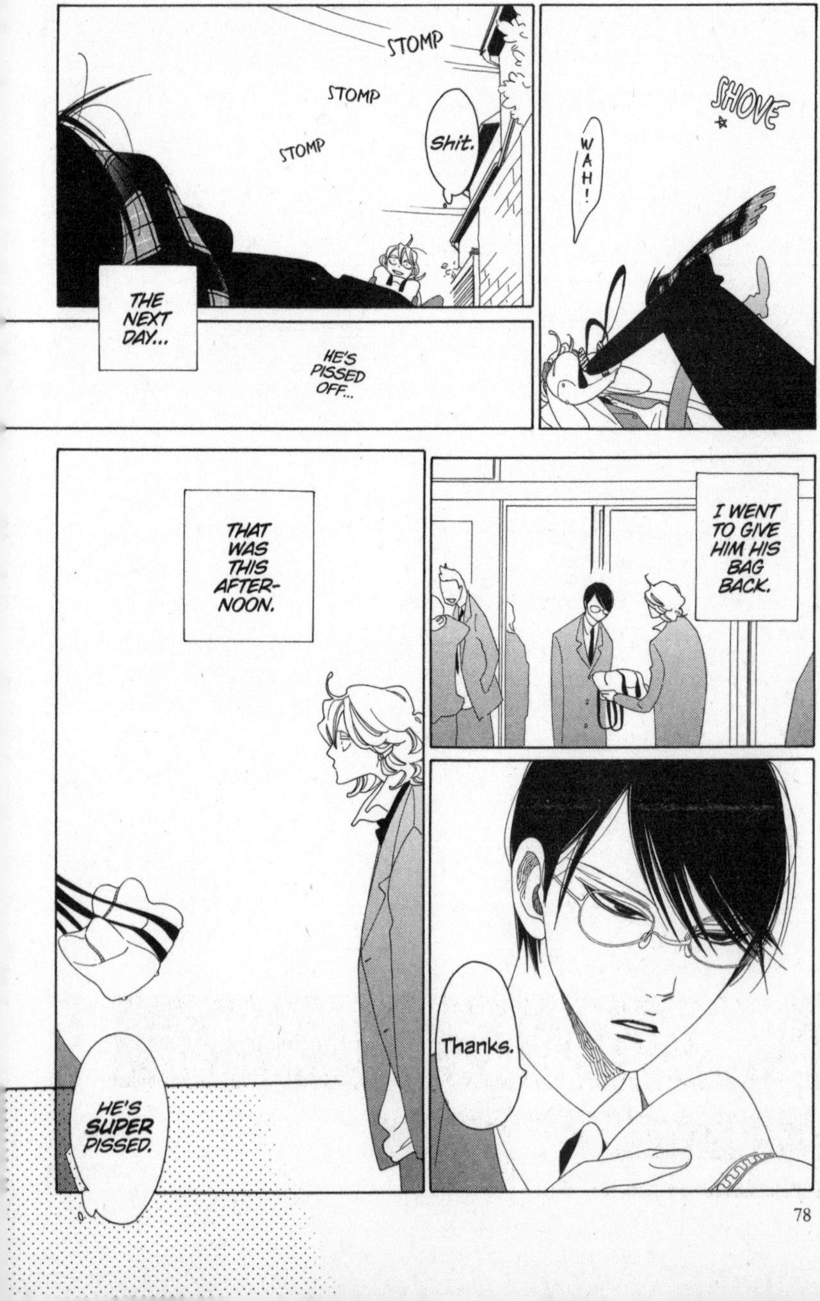
SHOVE
WAH!
STOMP
STOMP
STOMP
Shit.
THE NEXT DAY...
HE'S PISSED OFF...
I WENT TO GIVE HIM HIS BAG BACK.
Thanks.
THAT WAS THIS AFTER-NOON.
HE'S SUPER PISSED.

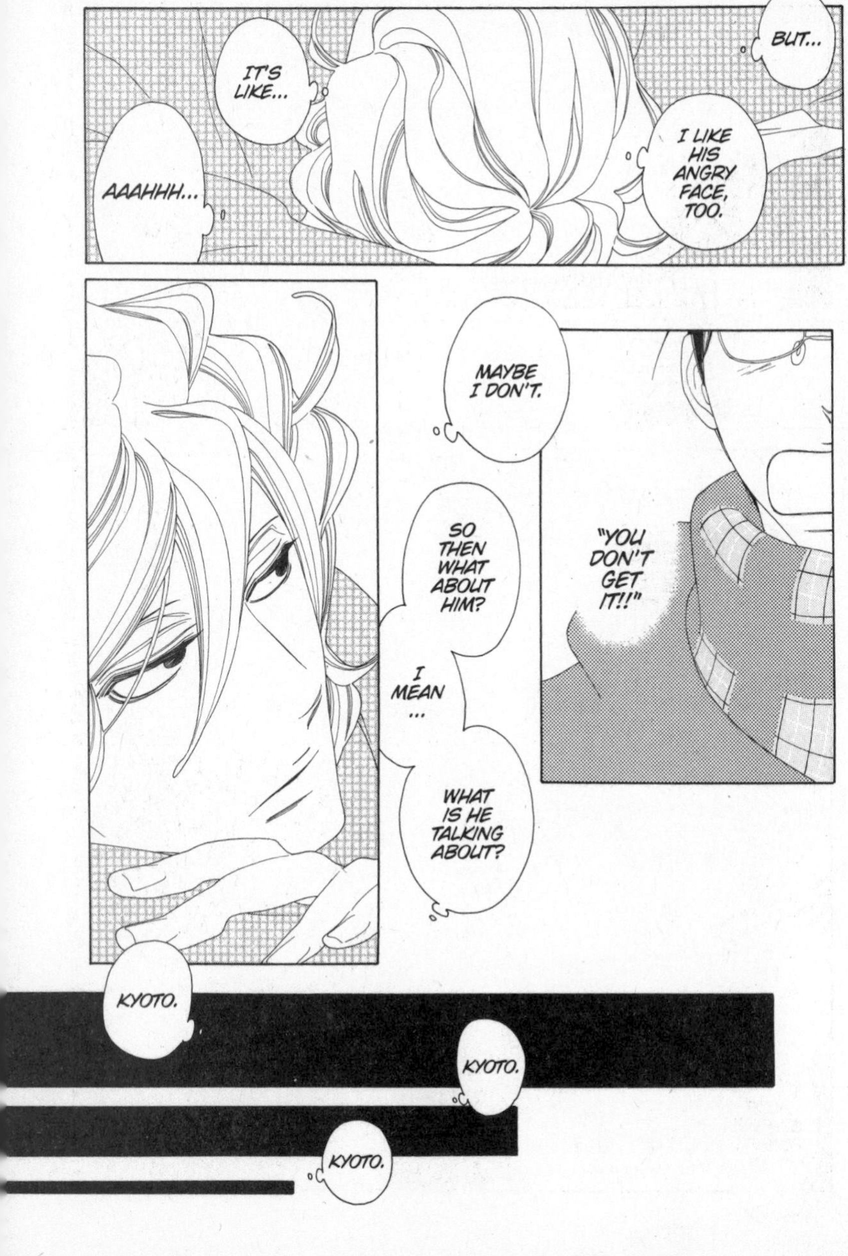
BUT...
I LIKE HIS ANGRY FACE, TOO.
IT'S LIKE...
AAAHHH...
"YOU DON'T GET IT!!"
MAYBE I DON'T.
SO THEN WHAT ABOUT HIM?
I MEAN ...
WHAT IS HE TALKING ABOUT?
KYOTO.
KYOTO.
KYOTO.

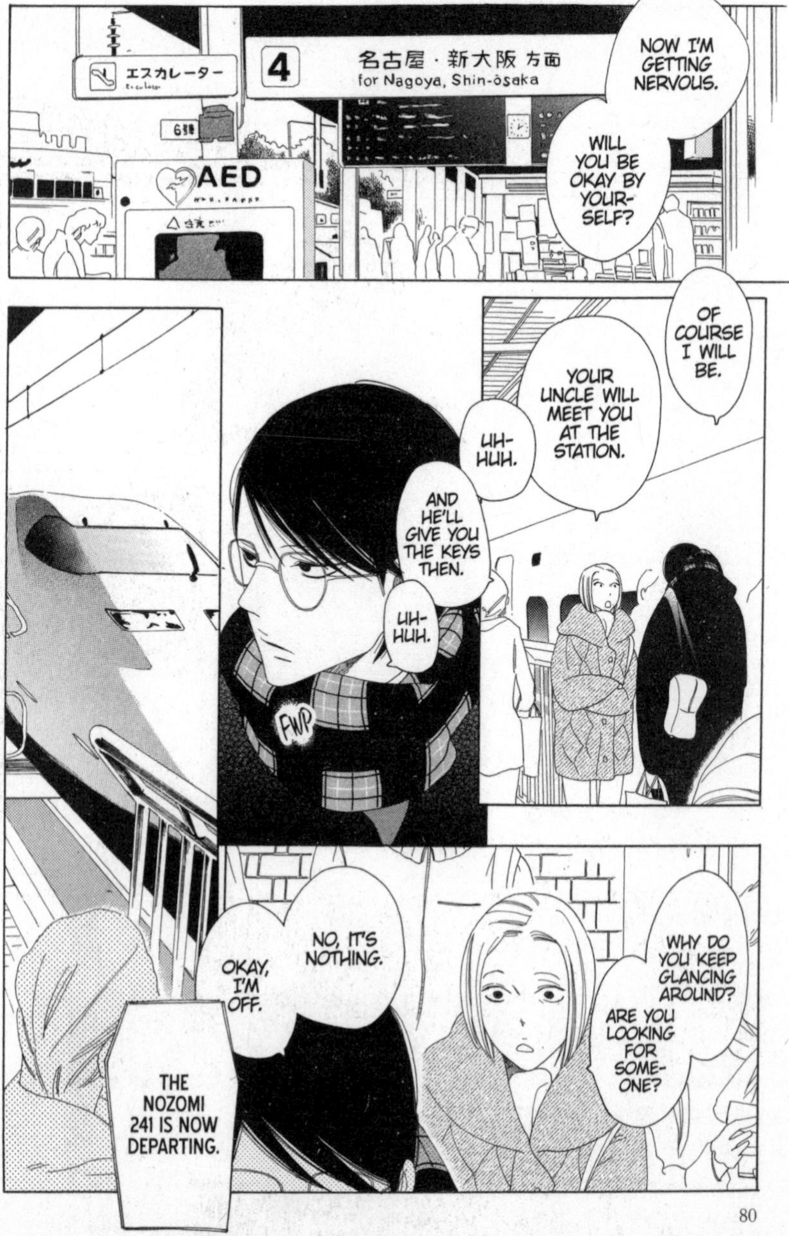
エスカレーター
4
名古屋・新大阪 方面
for Nagoya, Shin-ōsaka
AED
NOW I'M GETTING NERVOUS.
WILL YOU BE OKAY BY YOUR-SELF?
OF COURSE I WILL BE.
YOUR UNCLE WILL MEET YOU AT THE STATION.
UH-HUH.
AND HE'LL GIVE YOU THE KEYS THEN.
UH-HUH.
FWP
WHY DO YOU KEEP GLANCING AROUND?
ARE YOU LOOKING FOR SOME-ONE?
NO, IT'S NOTHING.
OKAY, I'M OFF.
THE NOZOMI 241 IS NOW DEPARTING.

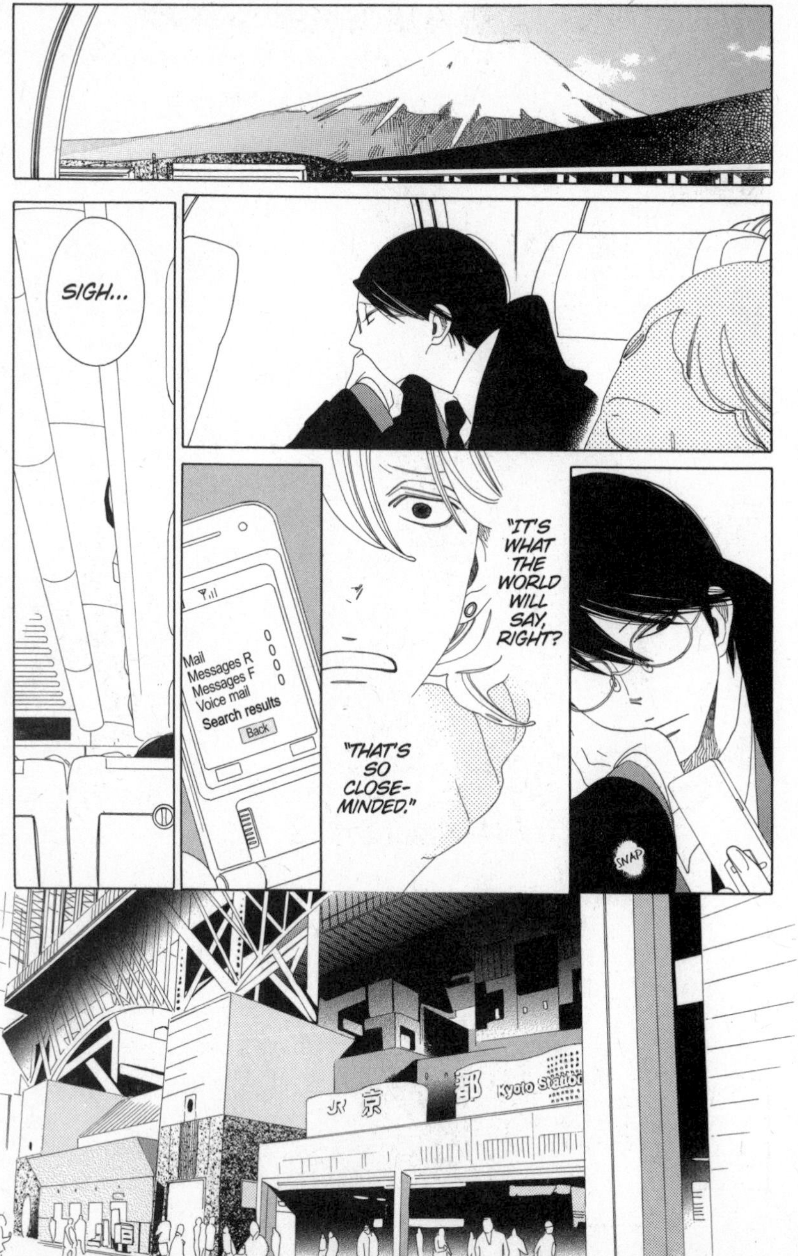
"IT'S WHAT THE WORLD WILL SAY, RIGHT?
SNAP
"THAT'S SO CLOSE-MINDED."
Mail
Messages R
Messages F
Voice mail
Search results
Back
SIGH...
JR 京 都

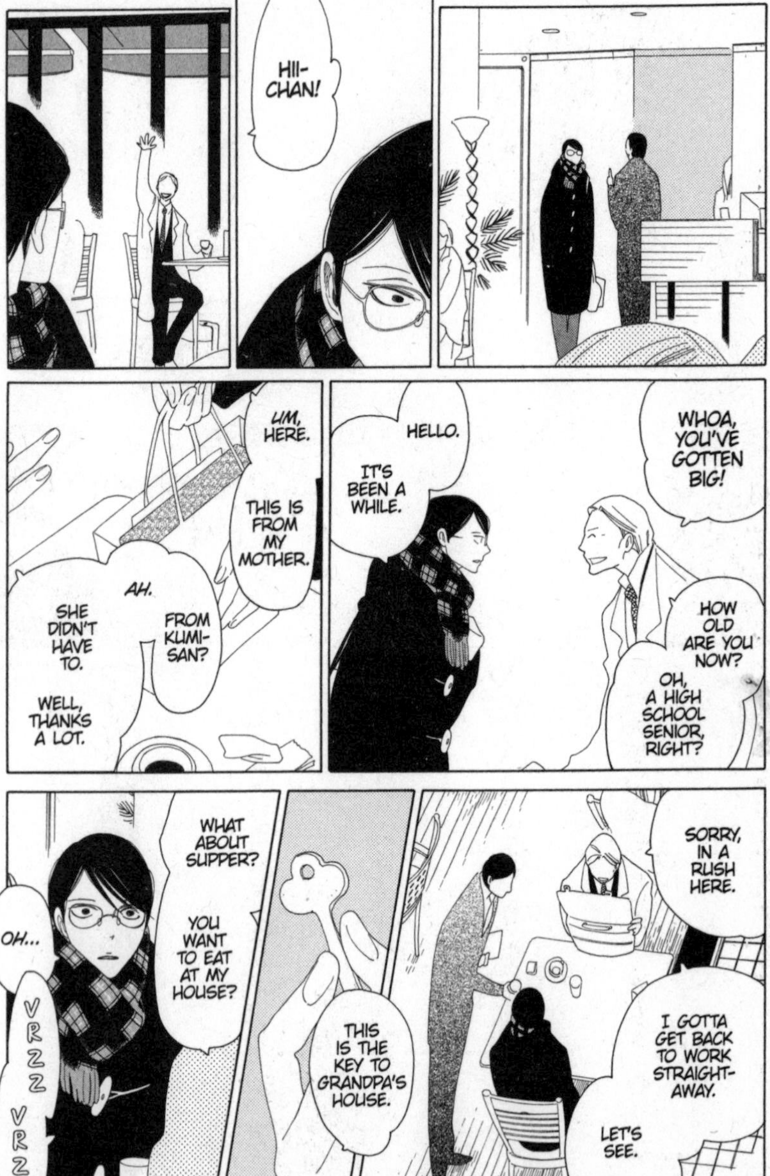
HII-CHAN!
WHOA, YOU'VE GOTTEN BIG!
HELLO.
IT'S BEEN A WHILE.
HOW OLD ARE YOU NOW?
OH, A HIGH SCHOOL SENIOR, RIGHT?
UM, HERE.
THIS IS FROM MY MOTHER.
AH.
FROM KUMI-SAN?
SHE DIDN'T HAVE TO.
WELL, THANKS A LOT.
SORRY, IN A RUSH HERE.
I GOTTA GET BACK TO WORK STRAIGHT-AWAY.
LET'S SEE.
THIS IS THE KEY TO GRANDPA'S HOUSE.
WHAT ABOUT SUPPER?
YOU WANT TO EAT AT MY HOUSE?
OH...
VRZZ VRZZ

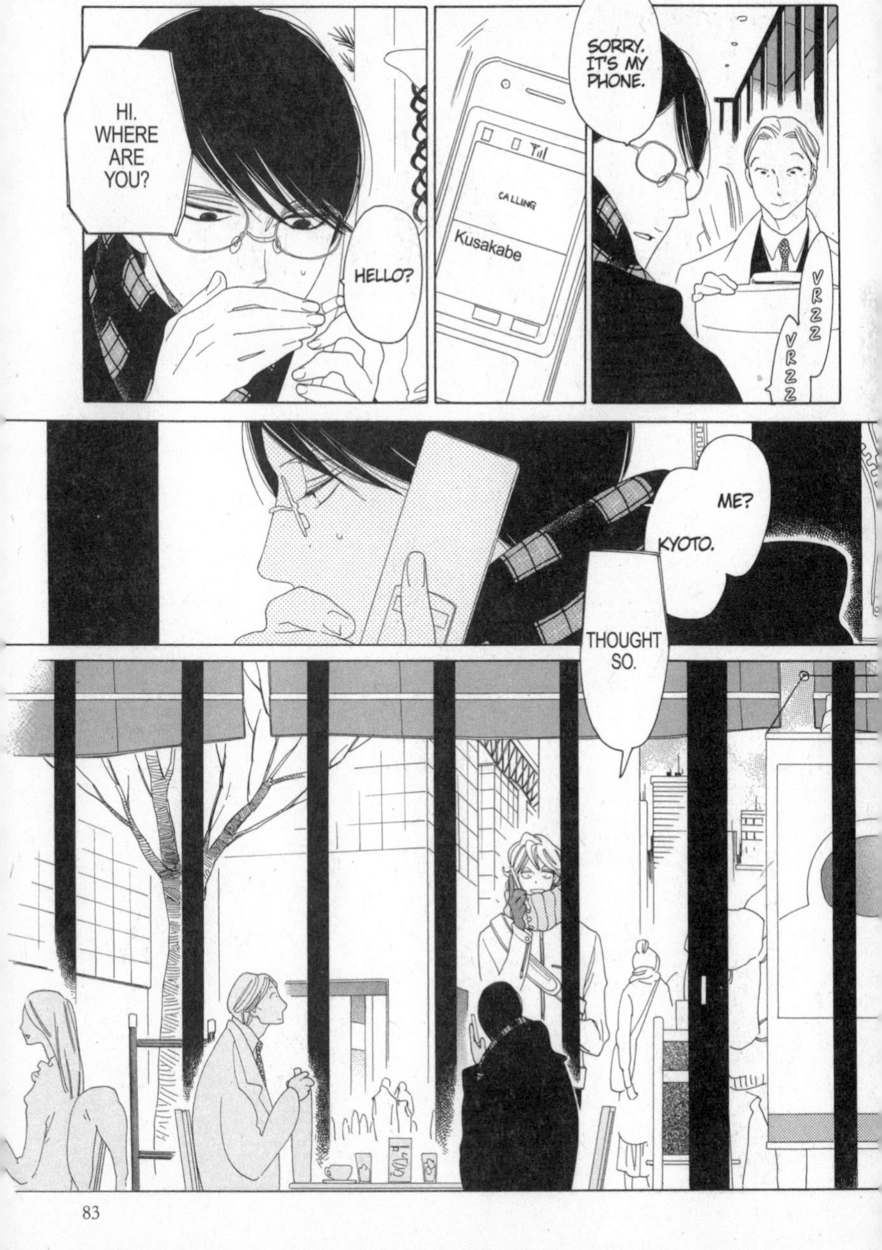
SORRY. IT'S MY PHONE.
VRZZ
VRZZ
CALLING
Kusakabe
HELLO?
HI. WHERE ARE YOU?
ME? KYOTO.
THOUGHT SO.

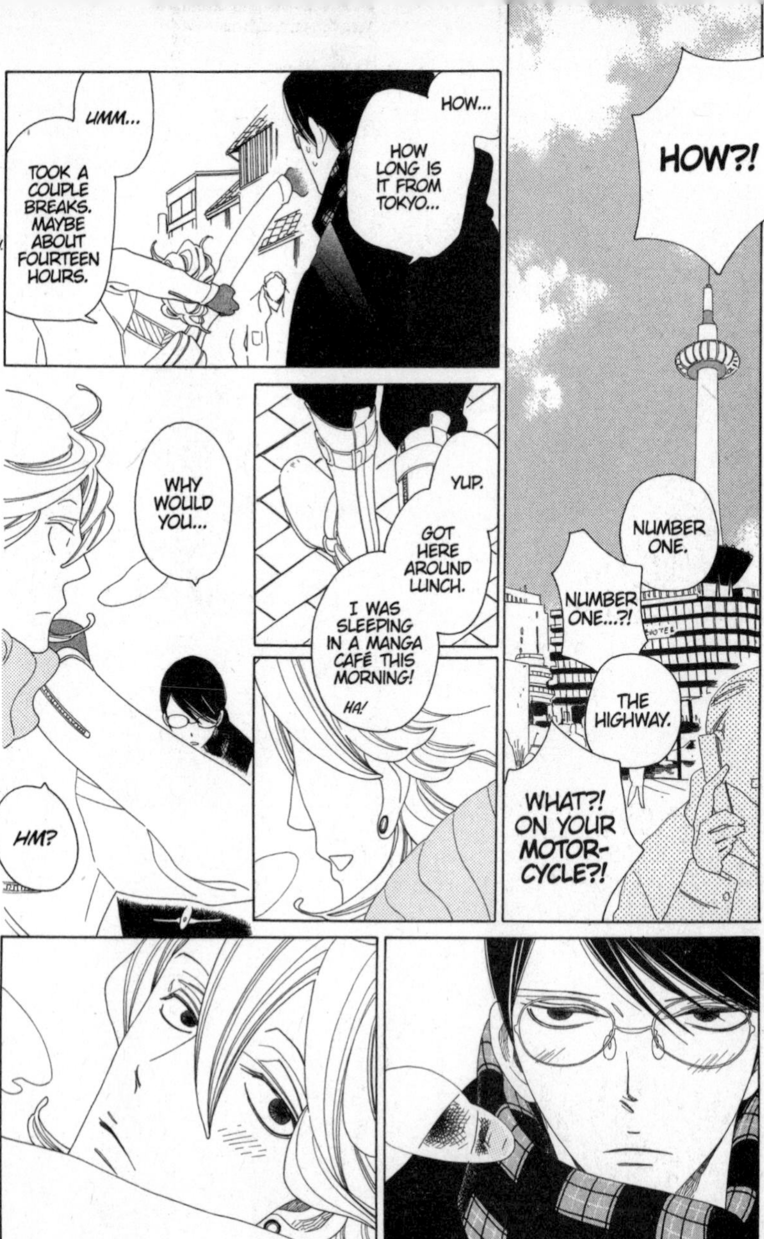
HOW?!
NUMBER ONE.
NUMBER ONE...?!
THE HIGHWAY.
WHAT?! ON YOUR MOTOR-CYCLE?!
HOW...
HOW LONG IS IT FROM TOKYO...
UMM...
TOOK A COUPLE BREAKS. MAYBE ABOUT FOURTEEN HOURS.
AH, YOUTH.
YUP.
GOT HERE AROUND LUNCH.
I WAS SLEEPING IN A MANGA CAFÉ THIS MORNING!
HA!
WHY WOULD YOU...
HM?

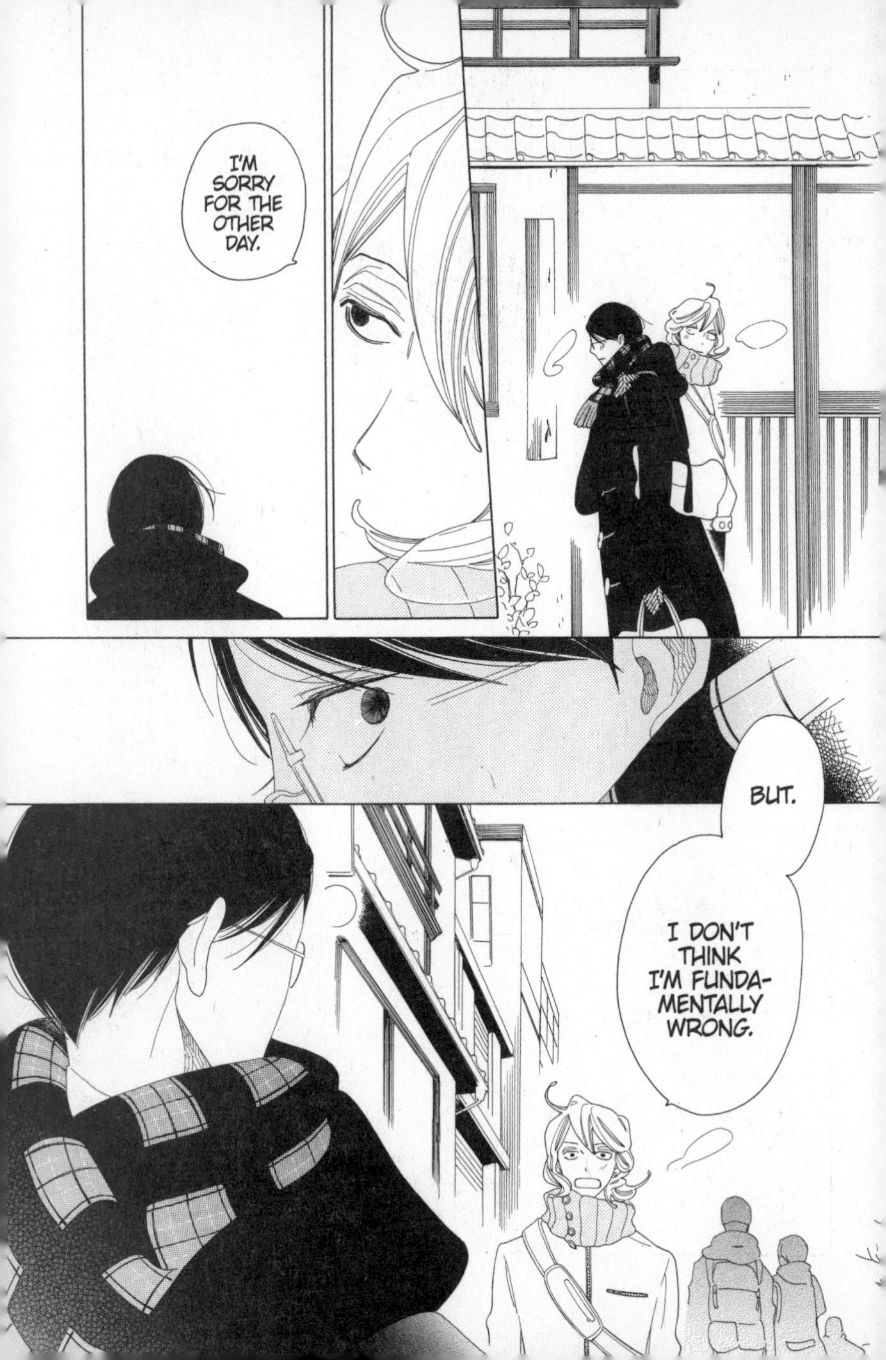
I'M SORRY FOR THE OTHER DAY.
BUT.
I DON'T THINK I'M FUNDA-MENTALLY WRONG.

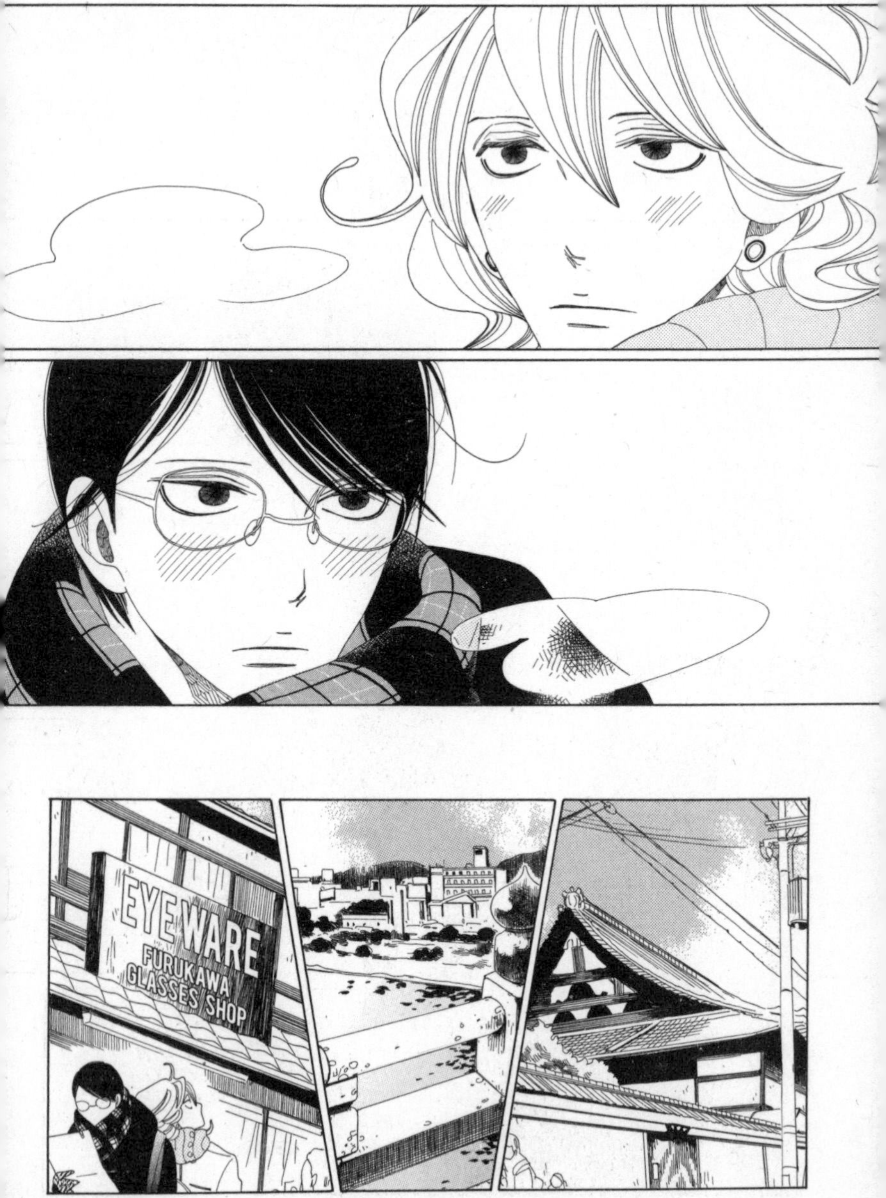
EYE WARE
FURUKAWA
GLASSES SHOP

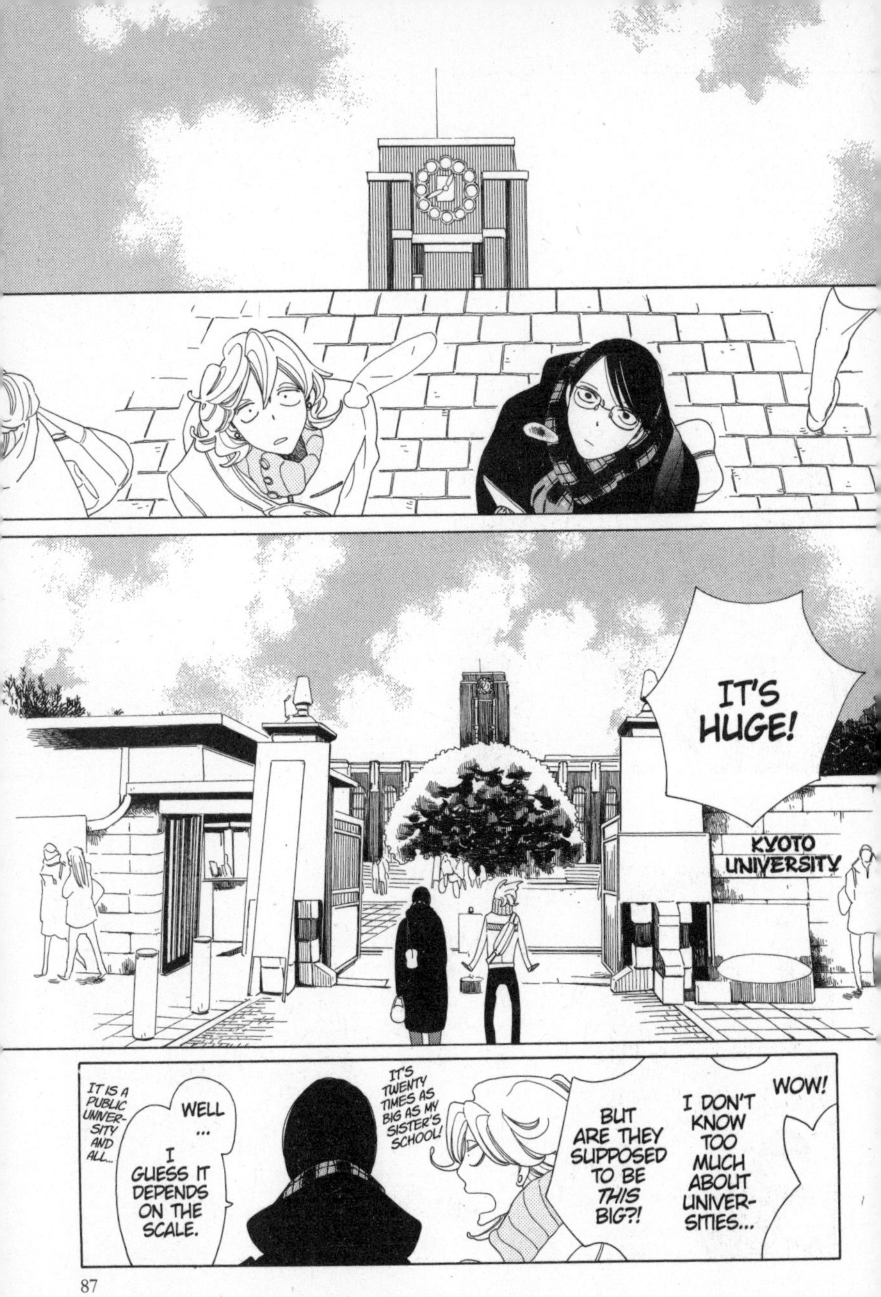
IT'S HUGE!
KYOTO UNIVERSITY
WOW!
I DON'T KNOW TOO MUCH ABOUT UNIVER-SITIES...
BUT ARE THEY SUPPOSED TO BE *THIS* BIG?!
IT'S TWENTY TIMES AS BIG AS MY SISTER'S SCHOOL!
WELL ... I GUESS IT DEPENDS ON THE SCALE.
IT IS A PUBLIC UNIVER-SITY AND ALL...

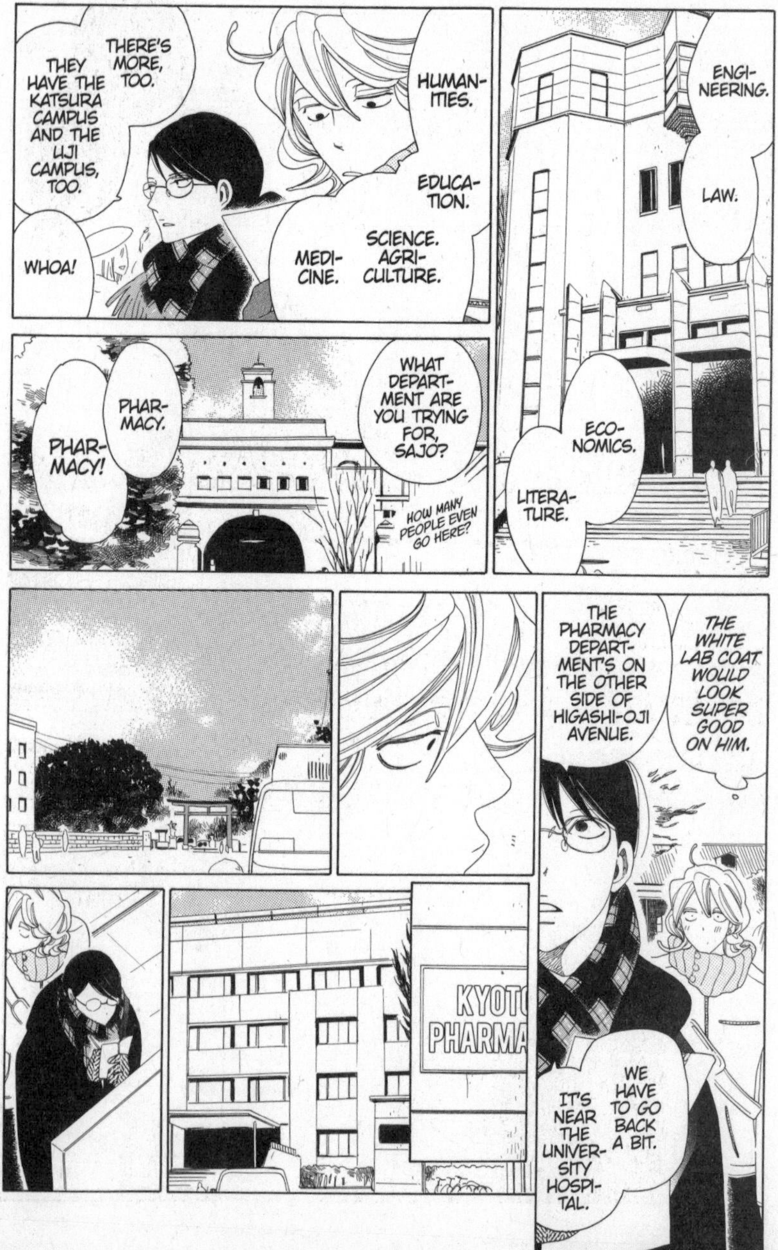
ENGI-NEERING.
LAW.
ECO-NOMICS.
LITERA-TURE.
HUMAN-ITIES.
EDUCA-TION.
SCIENCE. AGRI-CULTURE.
MEDI-CINE.
THERE'S MORE, TOO.
THEY HAVE THE KATSURA CAMPUS AND THE UJI CAMPUS, TOO.
WHOA!
WHAT DEPART-MENT ARE YOU TRYING FOR, SAJO?
HOW MANY PEOPLE EVEN GO HERE?
PHAR-MACY.
PHAR-MACY!
THE WHITE LAB COAT WOULD LOOK SUPER GOOD ON HIM.
THE PHARMACY DEPART-MENT'S ON THE OTHER SIDE OF HIGASHI-OJI AVENUE.
WE HAVE TO GO BACK A BIT.
IT'S NEAR THE UNIVER-SITY HOSPI-TAL.
KYOTO PHARMA

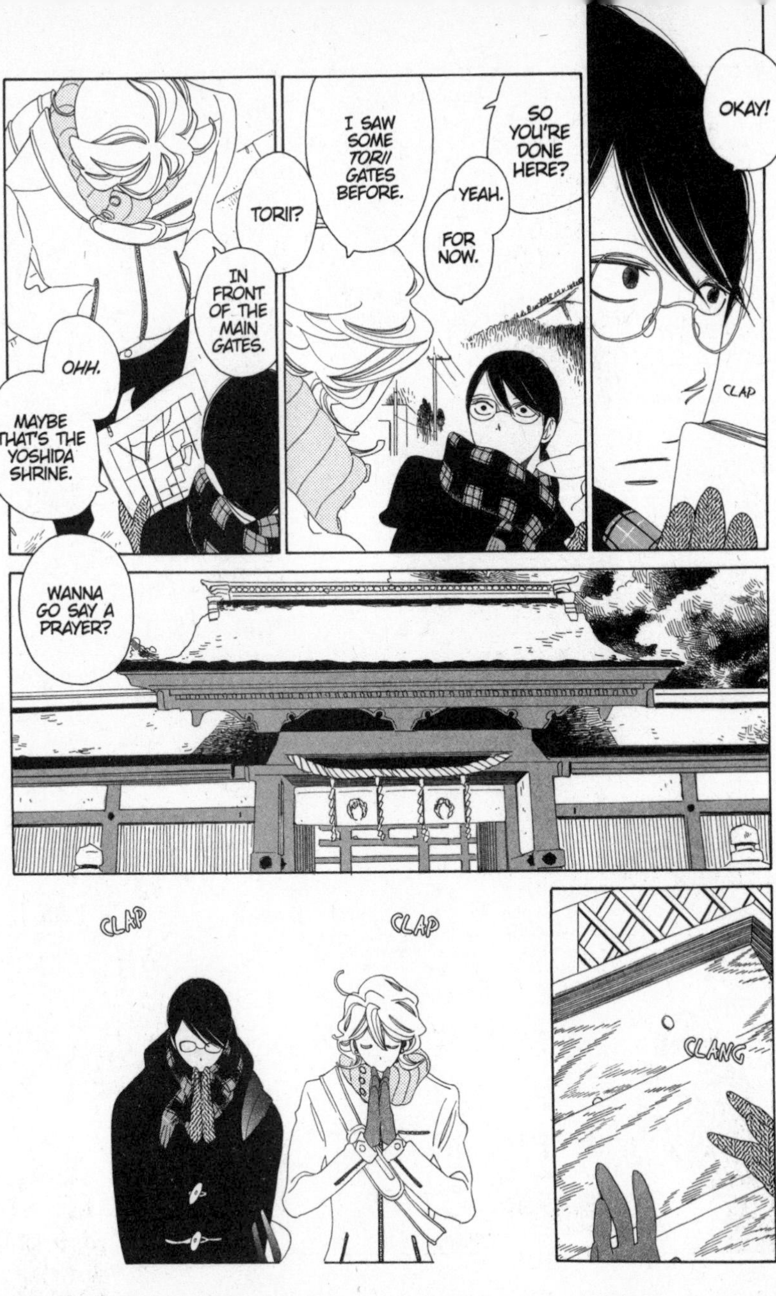
OKAY!
CLAP
SO YOU'RE DONE HERE?
YEAH.
FOR NOW.
I SAW SOME TORII GATES BEFORE.
TORII?
IN FRONT OF THE MAIN GATES.
OHH.
MAYBE THAT'S THE YOSHIDA SHRINE.
WANNA GO SAY A PRAYER?
CLANG
CLAP
CLAP

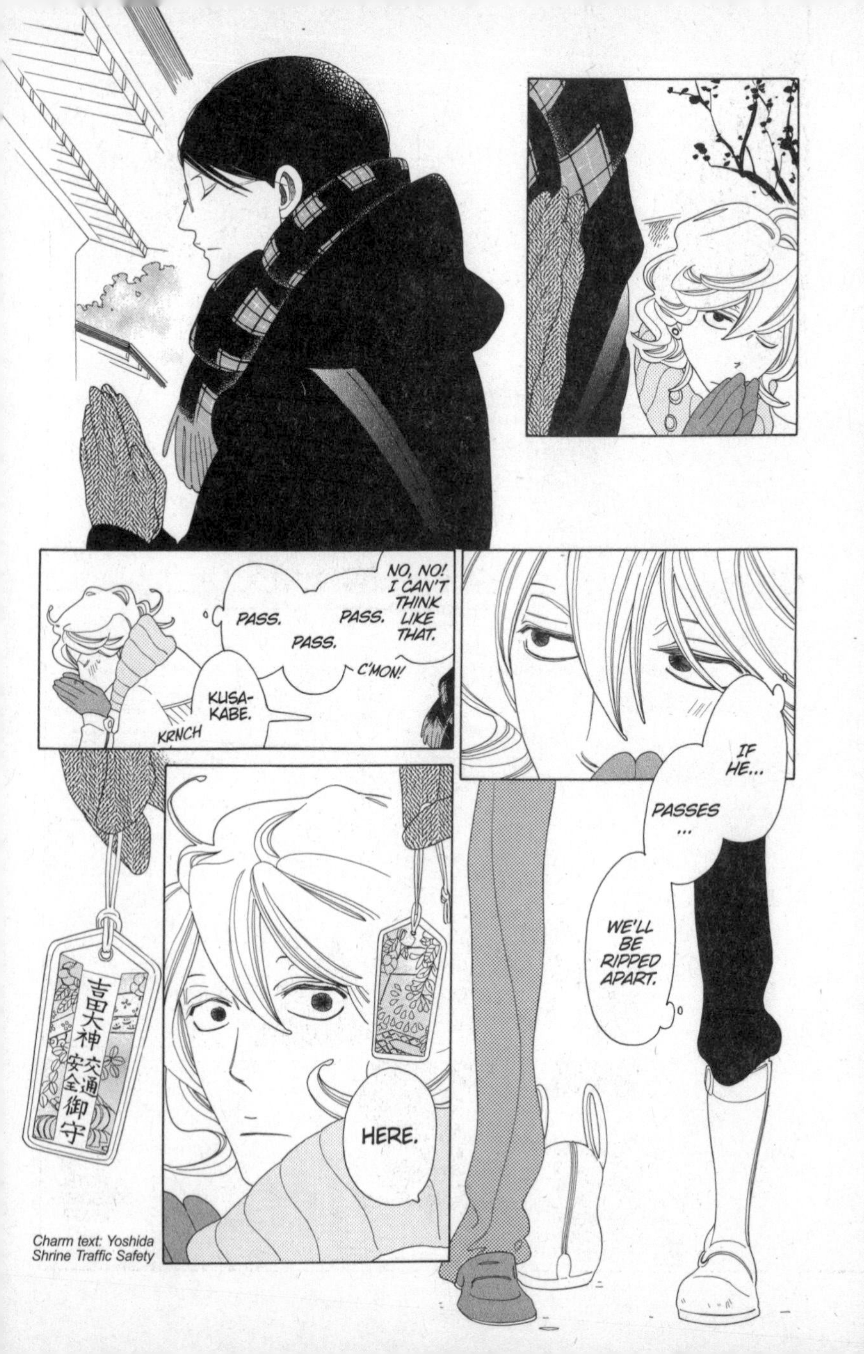
IF HE...
PASSES...
WE'LL BE RIPPED APART.
NO, NO! I CAN'T THINK LIKE THAT.
PASS.
PASS.
PASS.
C'MON!
KUSA-KABE.
KRNCH
HERE.
吉田大神
交通安全御守
Charm text: Yoshida Shrine Traffic Safety

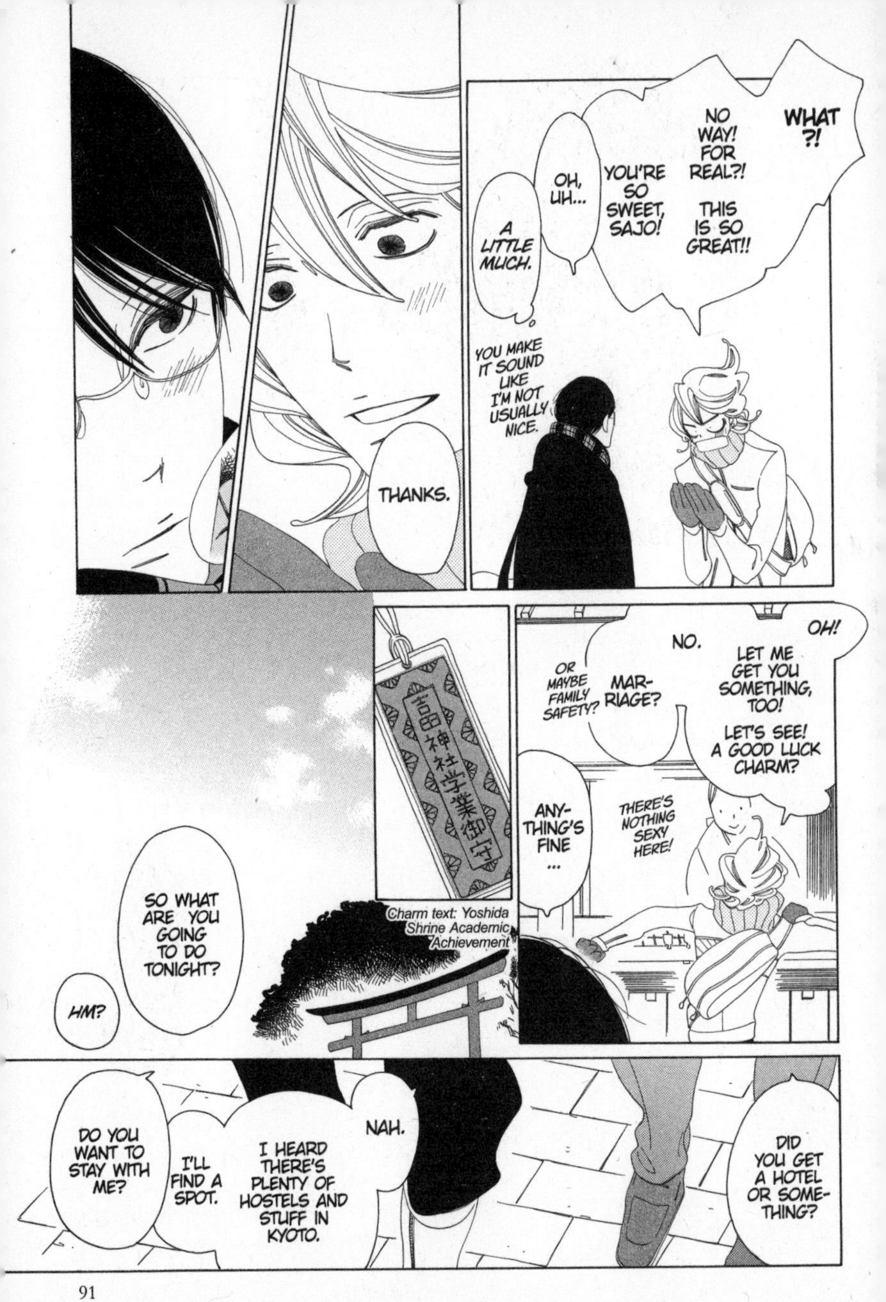
WHAT?!
NO WAY! FOR REAL?!
THIS IS SO GREAT!!
YOU'RE SO SWEET, SAJO!
OH, UH...
A LITTLE MUCH.
YOU MAKE IT SOUND LIKE I'M NOT USUALLY NICE.
THANKS.
OH!
LET ME GET YOU SOMETHING, TOO!
LET'S SEE! A GOOD LUCK CHARM?
NO.
MAR-RIAGE?
OR MAYBE FAMILY SAFETY?
THERE'S NOTHING SEXY HERE!
ANY-THING'S FINE...
吉田神社学業御守
Charm text: Yoshida Shrine Academic Achievement
SO WHAT ARE YOU GOING TO DO TONIGHT?
HM?
DID YOU GET A HOTEL OR SOME-THING?
NAH.
I HEARD THERE'S PLENTY OF HOSTELS AND STUFF IN KYOTO.
I'LL FIND A SPOT.
DO YOU WANT TO STAY WITH ME?

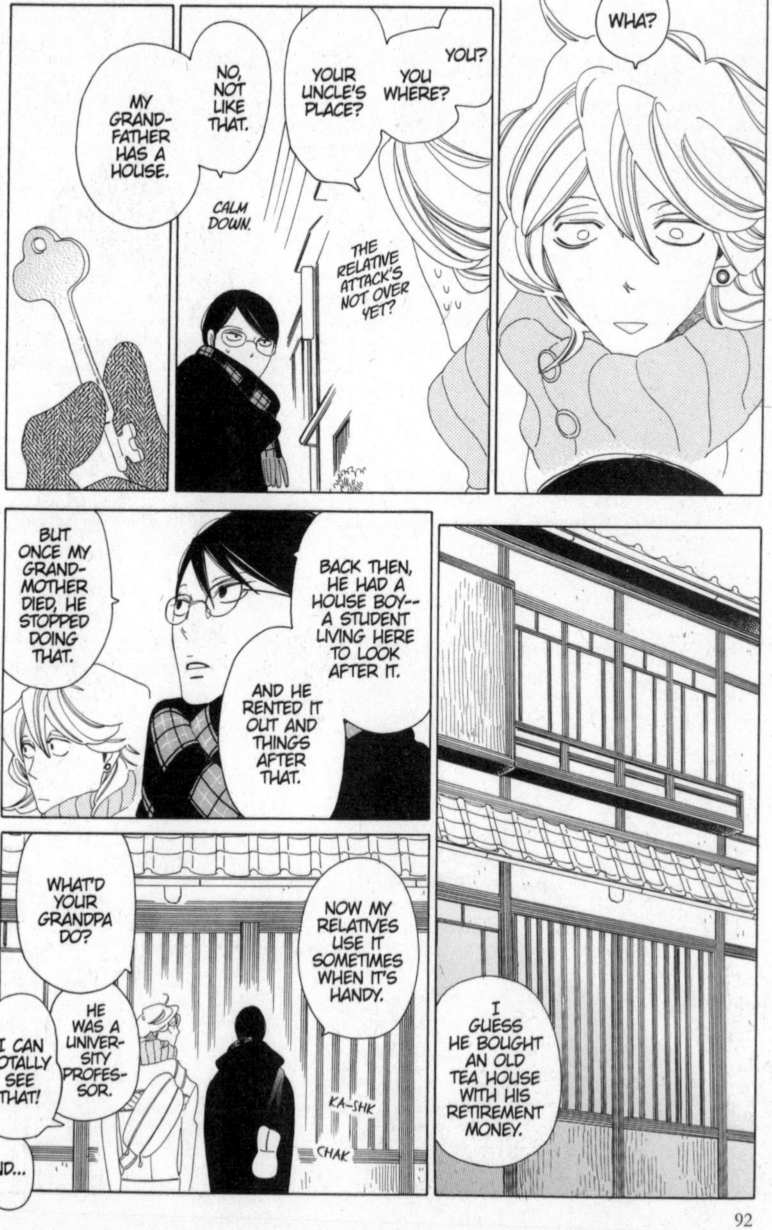
WHA?
YOU?
YOU WHERE?
YOUR UNCLE'S PLACE?
THE RELATIVE ATTACK'S NOT OVER YET?
NO, NOT LIKE THAT.
CALM DOWN.
MY GRANDFATHER HAS A HOUSE.
I GUESS HE BOUGHT AN OLD TEA HOUSE WITH HIS RETIREMENT MONEY.
BACK THEN, HE HAD A HOUSE BOY-- A STUDENT LIVING HERE TO LOOK AFTER IT.
AND HE RENTED IT OUT AND THINGS AFTER THAT.
BUT ONCE MY GRANDMOTHER DIED, HE STOPPED DOING THAT.
NOW MY RELATIVES USE IT SOMETIMES WHEN IT'S HANDY.
KA-SHK
CHAK
WHAT'D YOUR GRANDPA DO?
HE WAS A UNIVERSITY PROFESSOR.
I CAN TOTALLY SEE THAT!
AND...

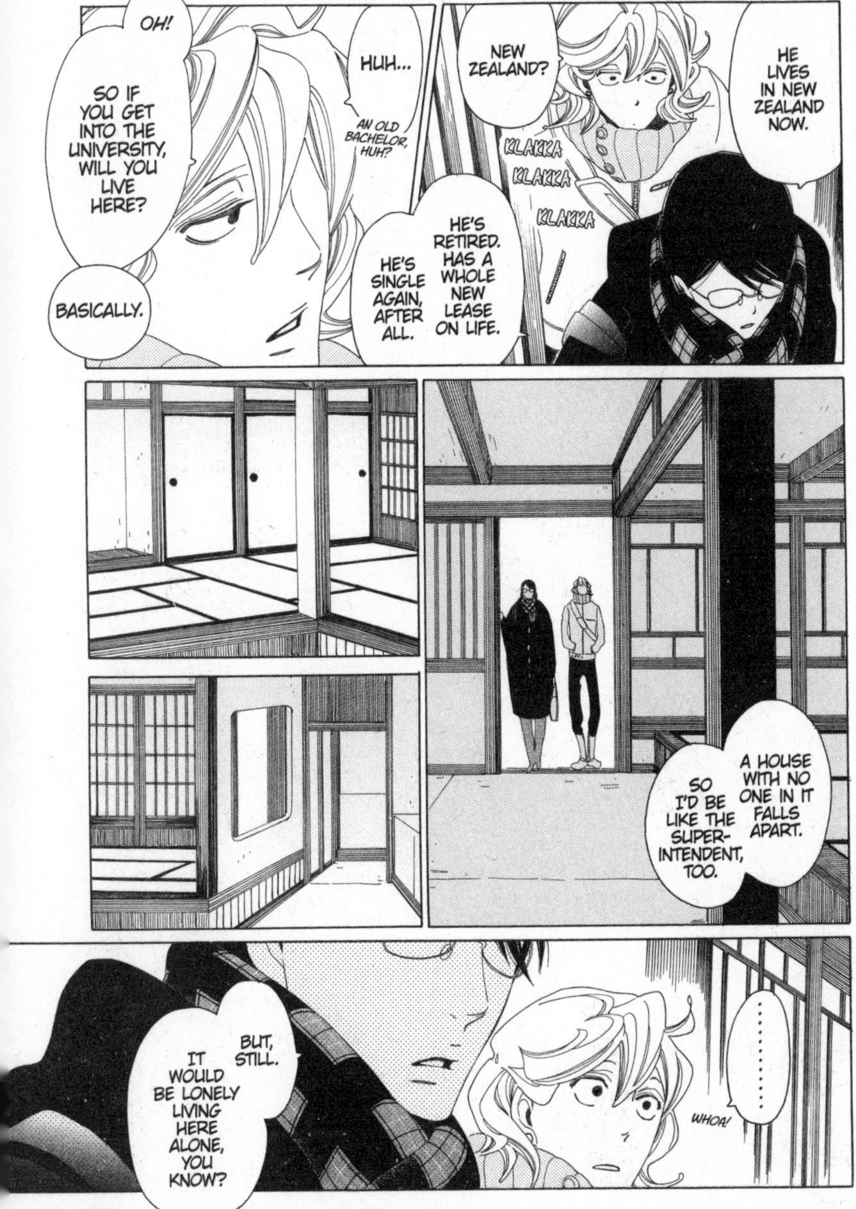
HE LIVES IN NEW ZEALAND NOW.
NEW ZEALAND?
KLAKKA
KLAKKA
KLAKKA
HE'S RETIRED. HAS A WHOLE NEW LEASE ON LIFE.
HE'S SINGLE AGAIN, AFTER ALL.
HUH...
AN OLD BACHELOR, HUH?
OH!
SO IF YOU GET INTO THE UNIVERSITY, WILL YOU LIVE HERE?
BASICALLY.
A HOUSE WITH NO ONE IN IT FALLS APART.
SO I'D BE LIKE THE SUPER-INTENDENT, TOO.
......
WHOA!
BUT, STILL.
IT WOULD BE LONELY LIVING HERE ALONE, YOU KNOW?

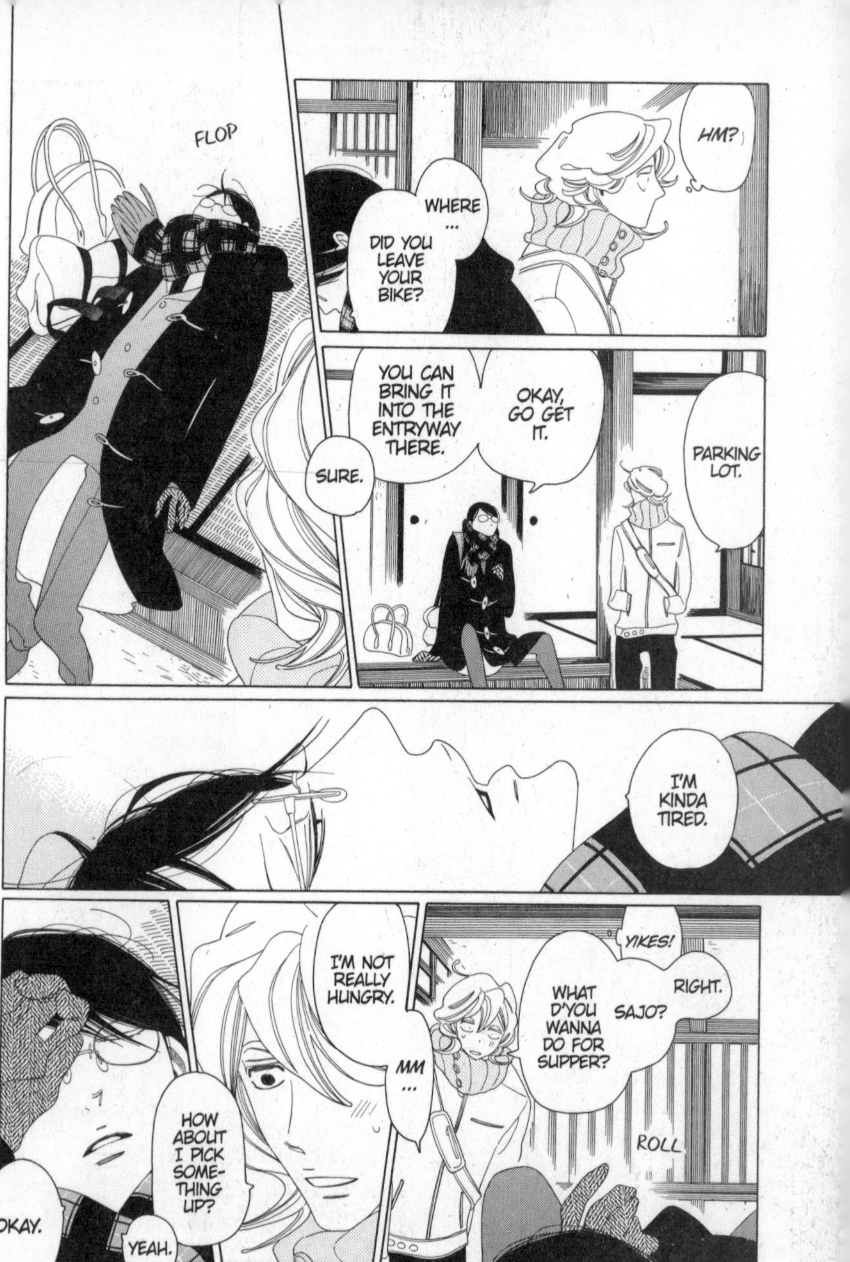
HM?
WHERE ... DID YOU LEAVE YOUR BIKE?
PARKING LOT.
OKAY, GO GET IT.
YOU CAN BRING IT INTO THE ENTRYWAY THERE.
SURE.
FLOP
I'M KINDA TIRED.
YIKES!
RIGHT.
SAJO?
WHAT D'YOU WANNA DO FOR SUPPER?
ROLL
I'M NOT REALLY HUNGRY.
MM ...
HOW ABOUT I PICK SOME-THING UP?
OKAY.
YEAH.

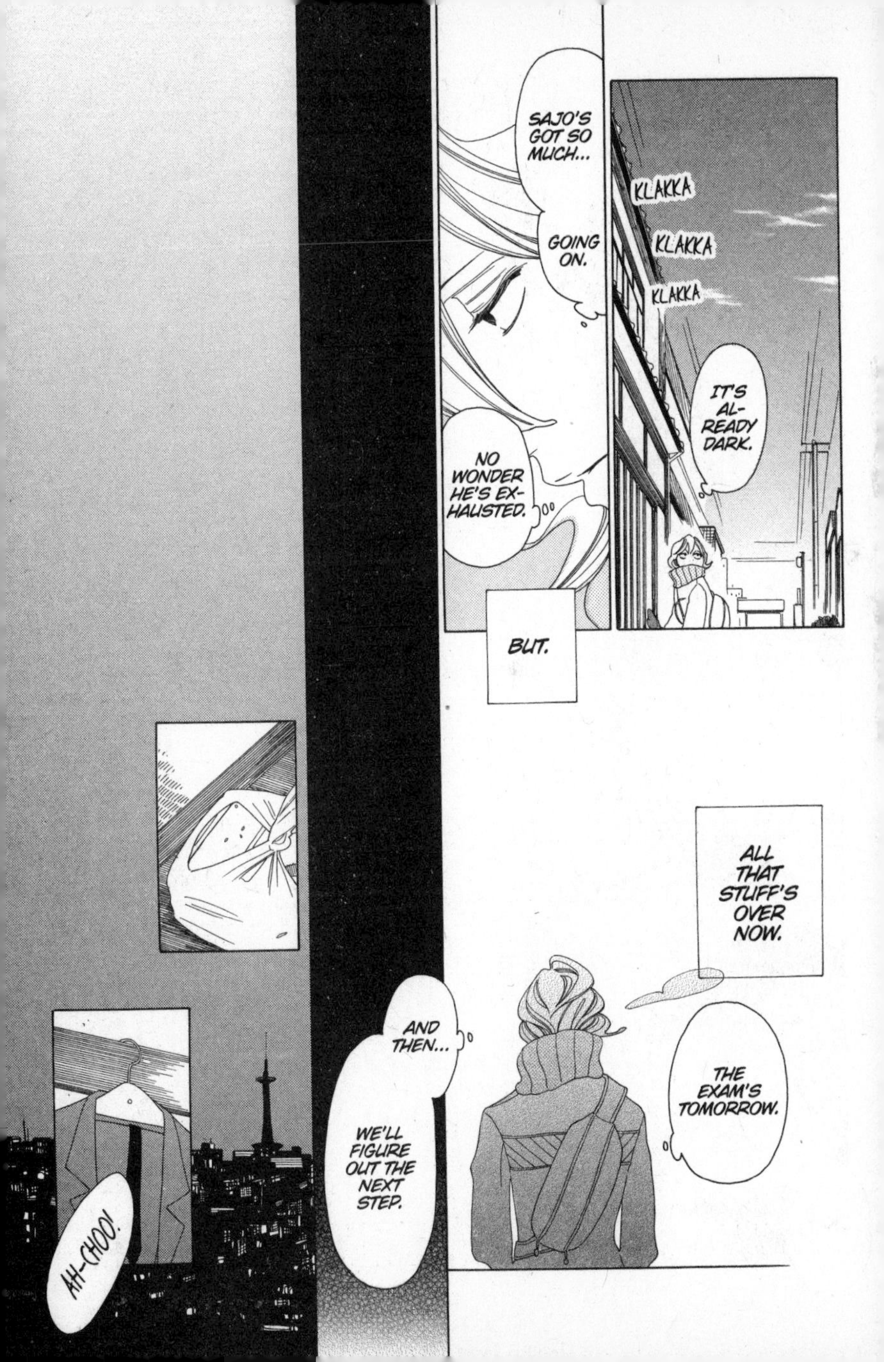
KLAKKA
KLAKKA
KLAKKA
IT'S AL-READY DARK.
SAJO'S GOT SO MUCH...
GOING ON.
NO WONDER HE'S EX-HAUSTED.
BUT.
ALL THAT STUFF'S OVER NOW.
THE EXAM'S TOMORROW.
AND THEN...
WE'LL FIGURE OUT THE NEXT STEP.
AH-CHOO!

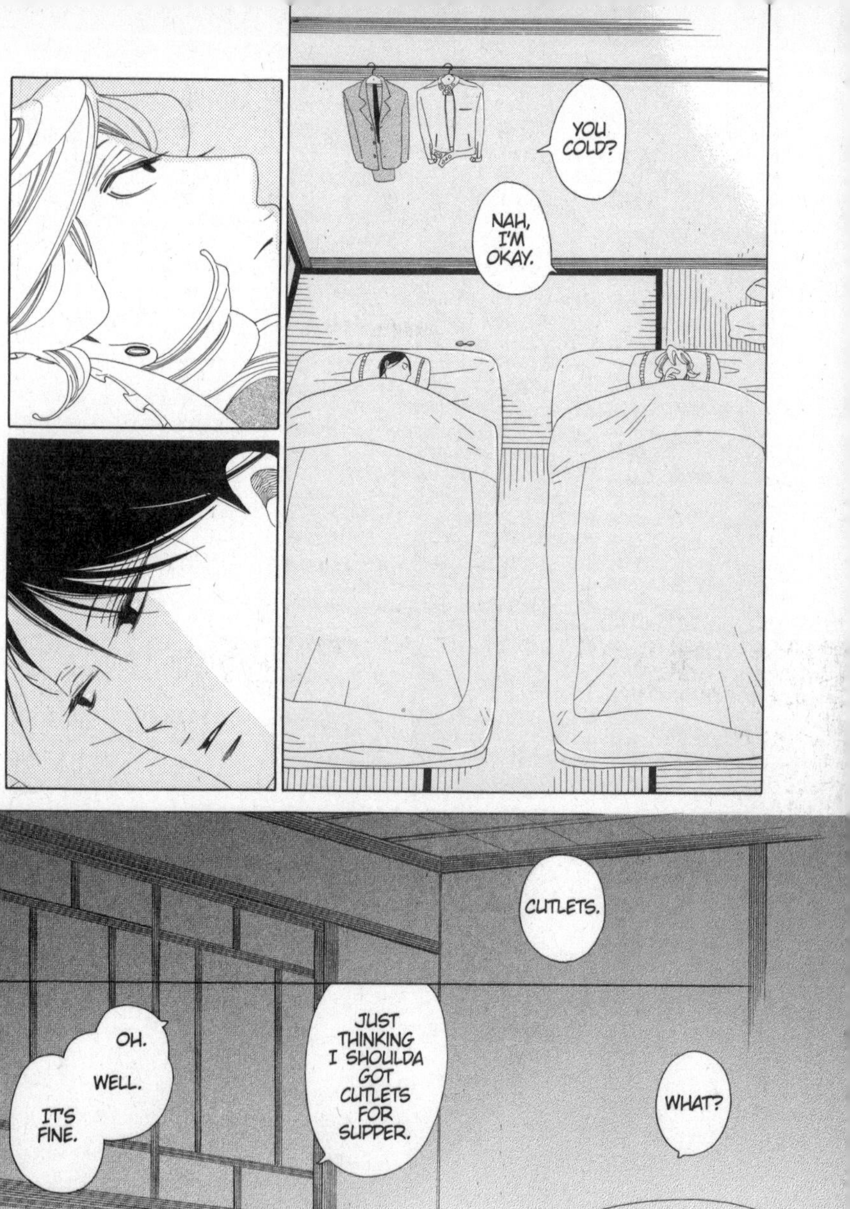
YOU COLD?
NAH, I'M OKAY.
CUTLETS.
WHAT?
JUST THINKING I SHOULDA GOT CUTLETS FOR SUPPER.
OH.
WELL.
IT'S FINE.

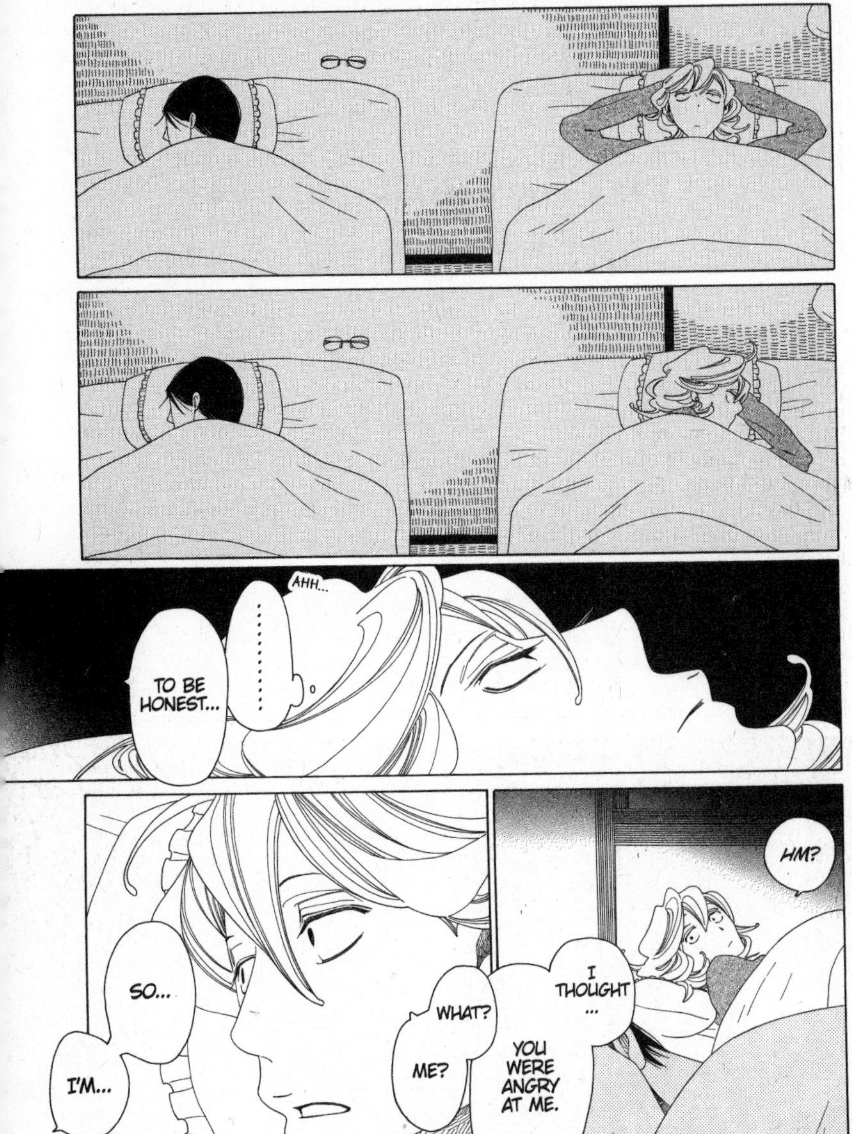
AHH...
......
TO BE HONEST...
HM?
I THOUGHT...
YOU WERE ANGRY AT ME.
WHAT?
ME?
SO...
I'M...

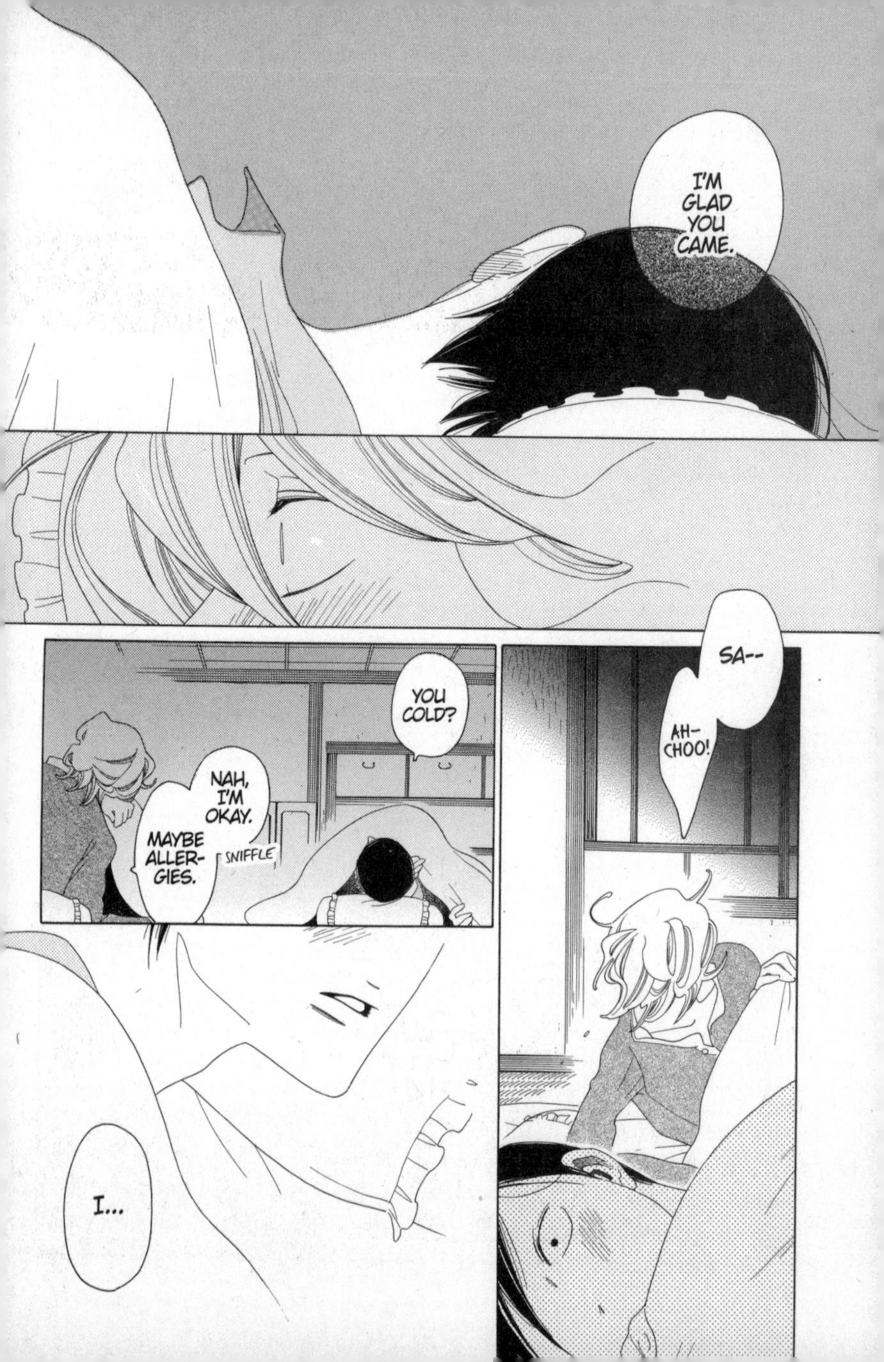
I'M GLAD YOU CAME.
SA--
AH-CHOO!
YOU COLD?
NAH, I'M OKAY.
MAYBE ALLER-GIES.
SNIFFLE
I...

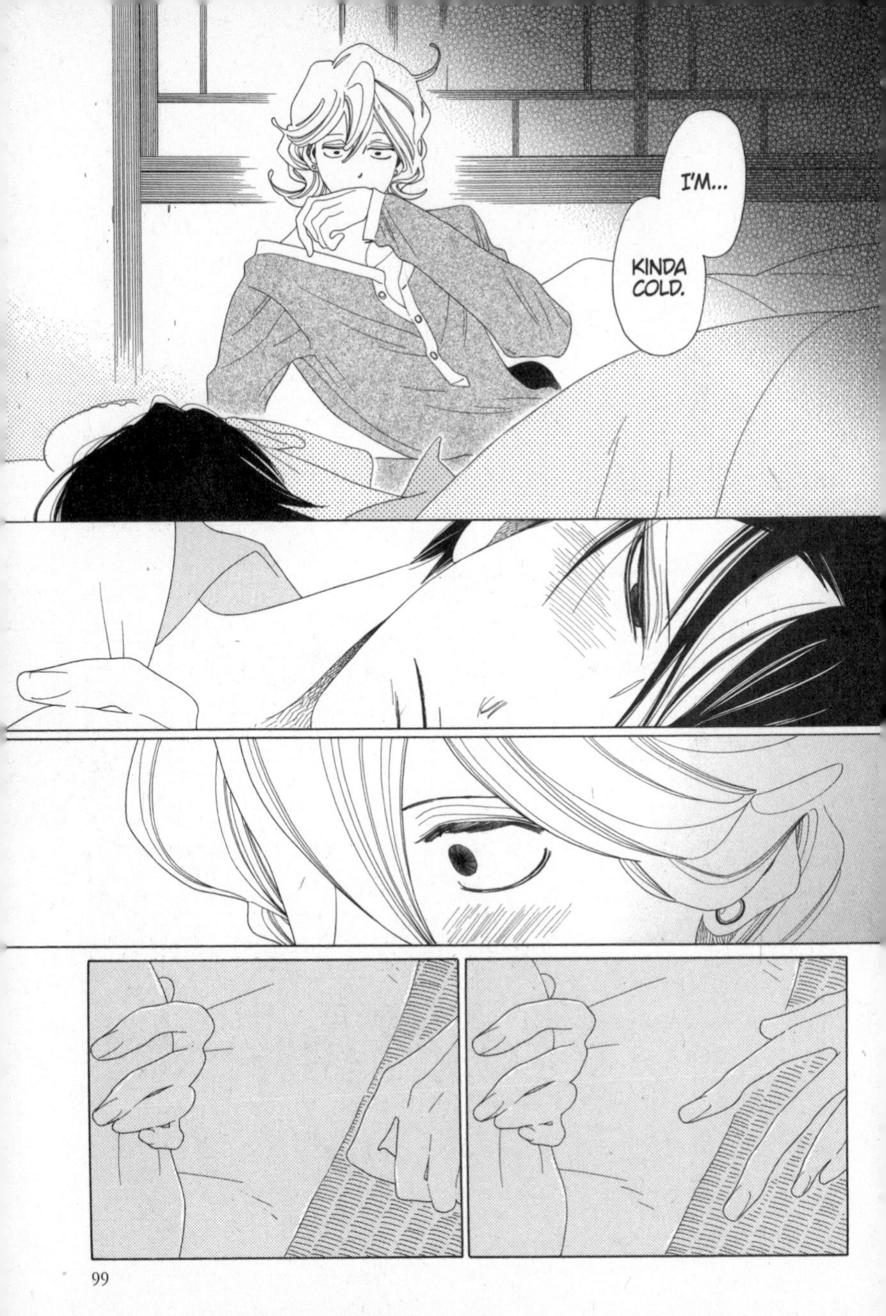
I'M...
KINDA COLD.

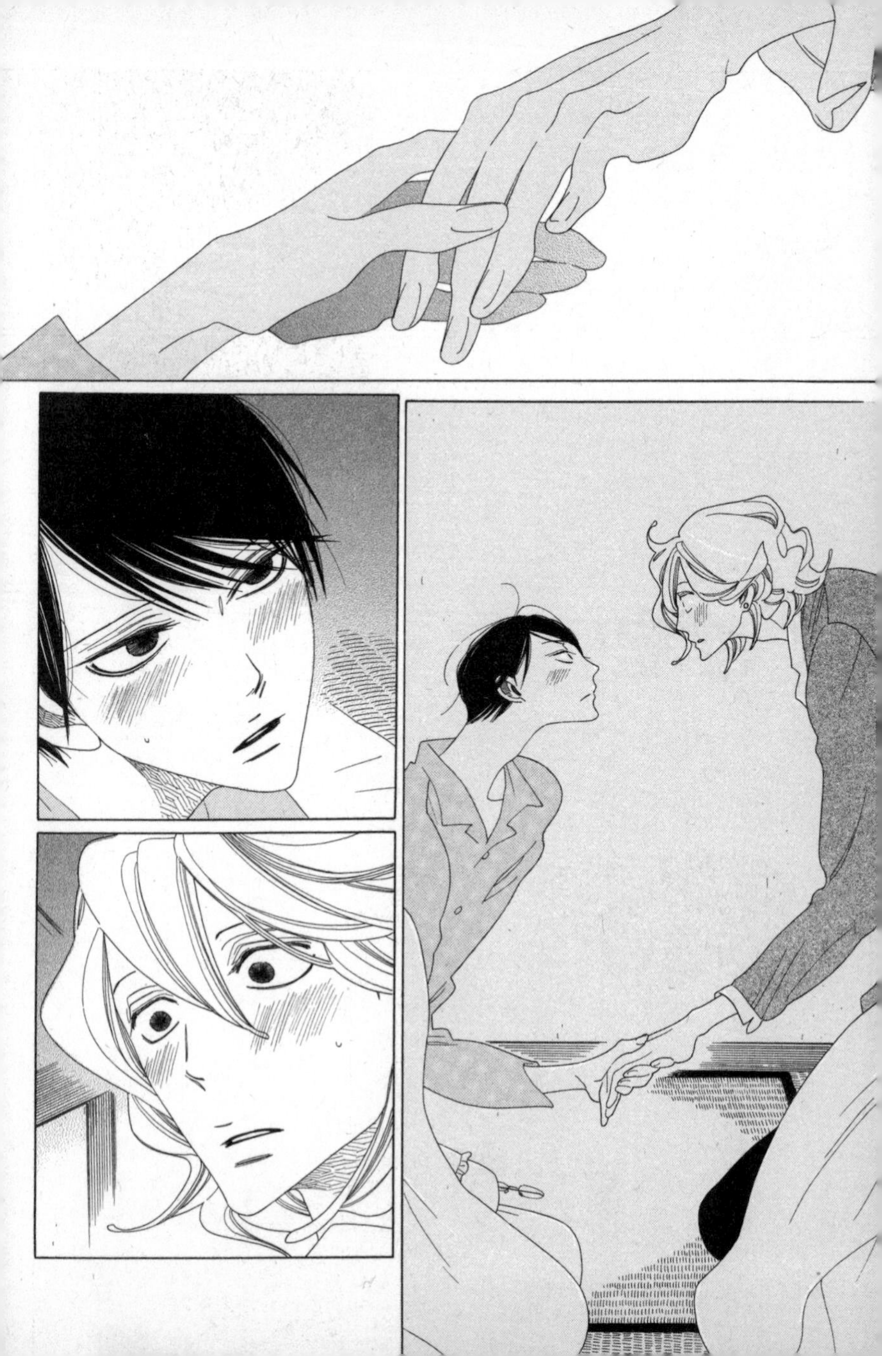

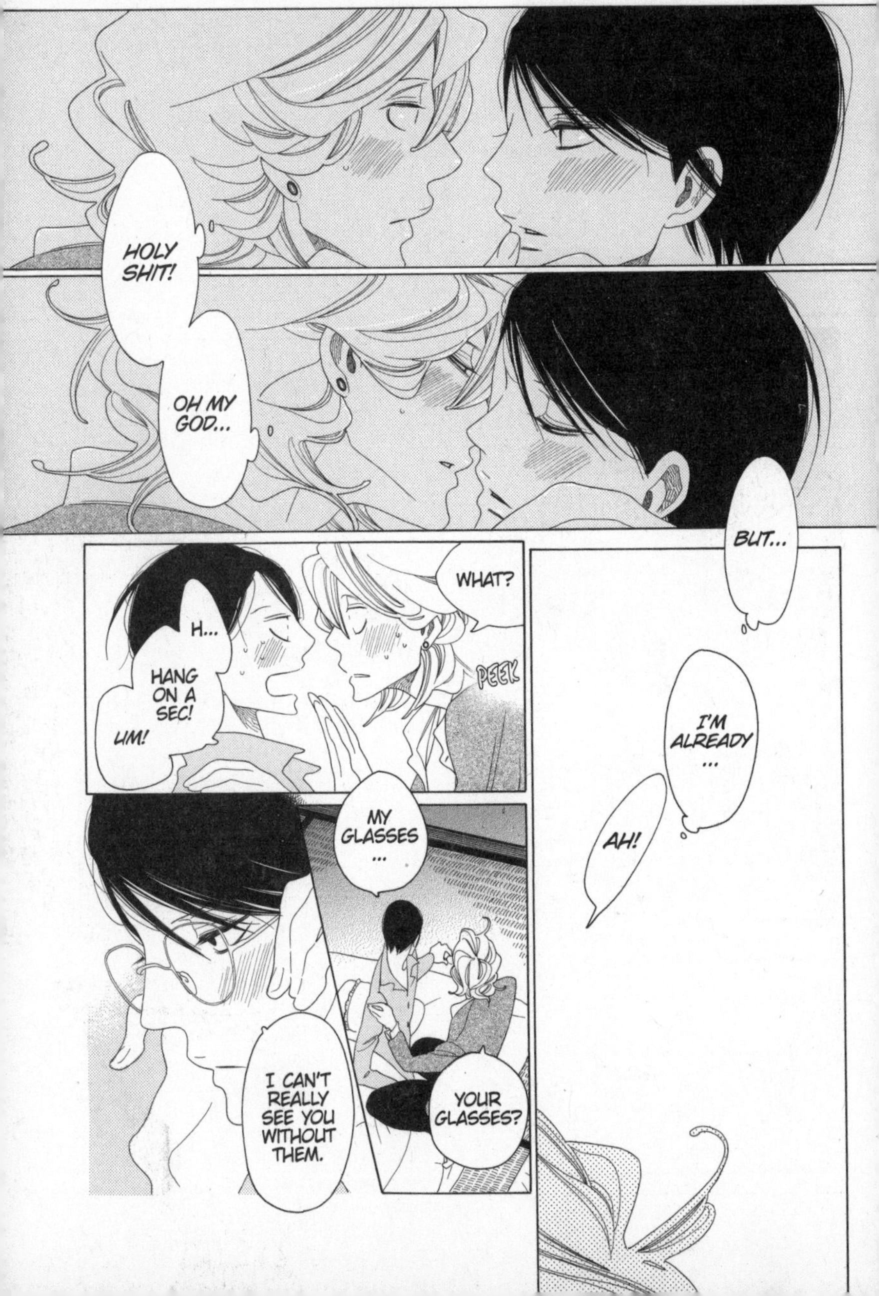
HOLY SHIT!
OH MY GOD...
BUT...
I'M ALREADY ...
AH!
WHAT?
PEEK
H...
HANG ON A SEC!
UM!
MY GLASSES ...
YOUR GLASSES?
I CAN'T REALLY SEE YOU WITHOUT THEM.

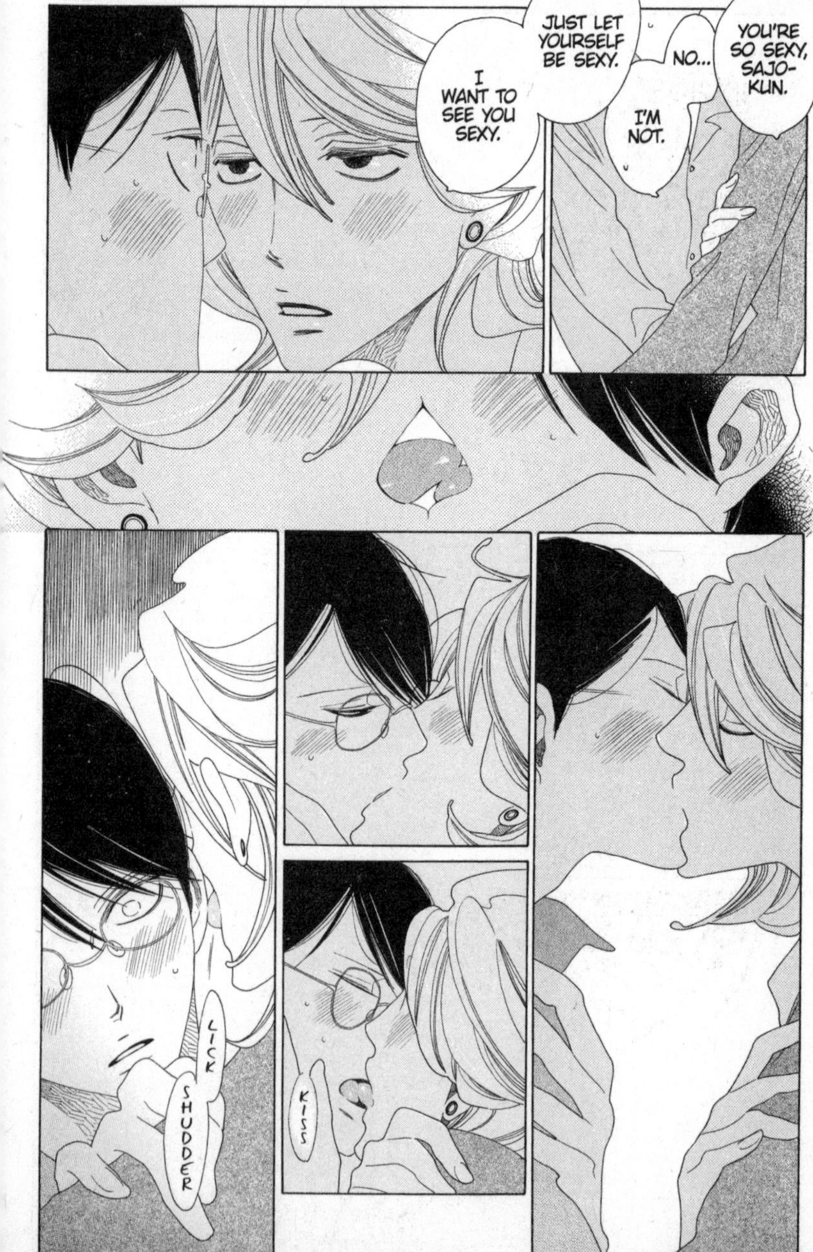
YOU'RE SO SEXY, SAJO-KUN.
NO...
I'M NOT.
JUST LET YOURSELF BE SEXY.
I WANT TO SEE YOU SEXY.
KISS
LICK
SHUDDER

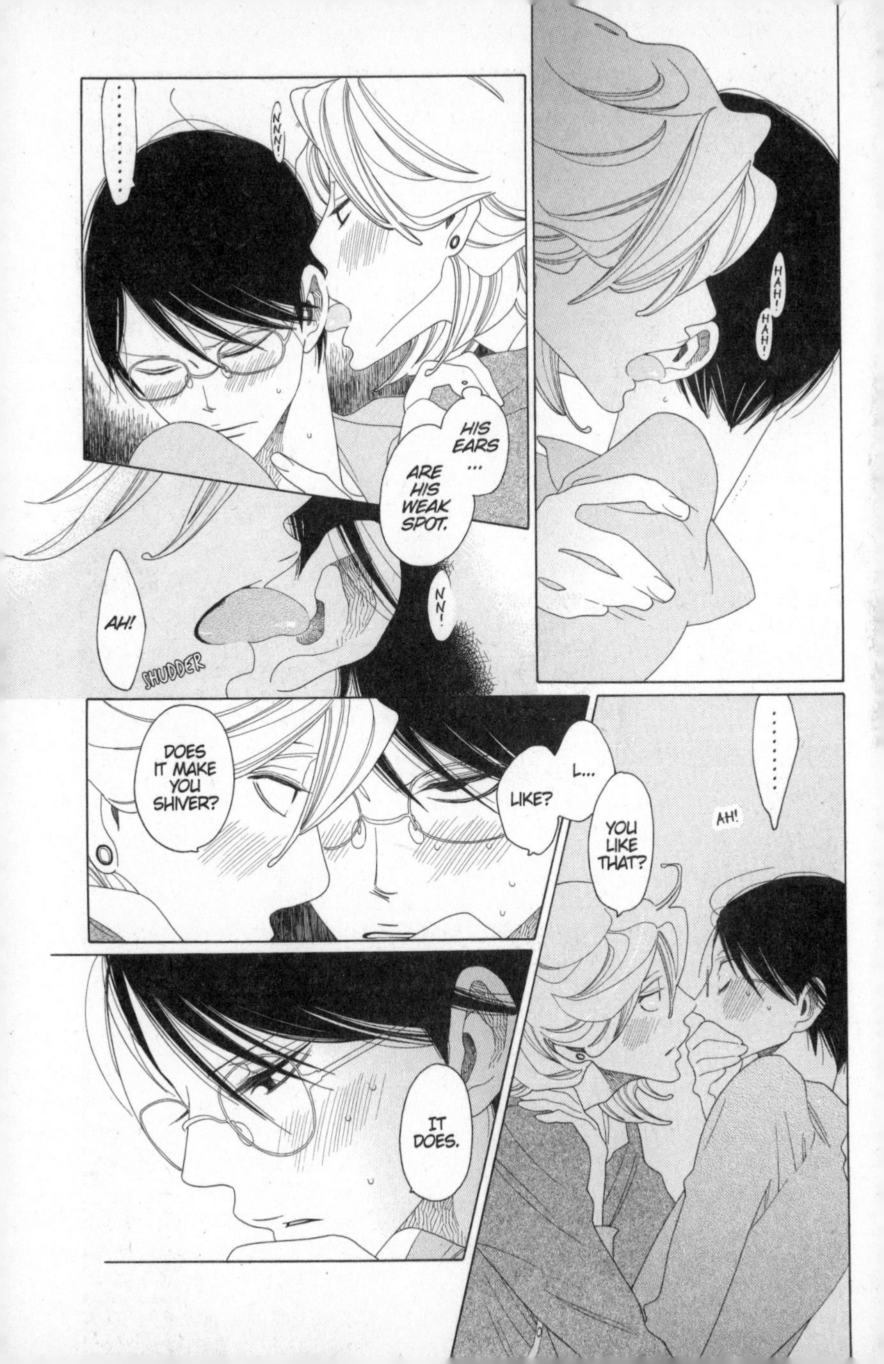
HAH!
HAH!
......
NNN!
HIS EARS ...
ARE HIS WEAK SPOT.
NN!
AH!
SHUDDER
......
AH!
YOU LIKE THAT?
L...
LIKE?
DOES IT MAKE YOU SHIVER?
IT DOES.

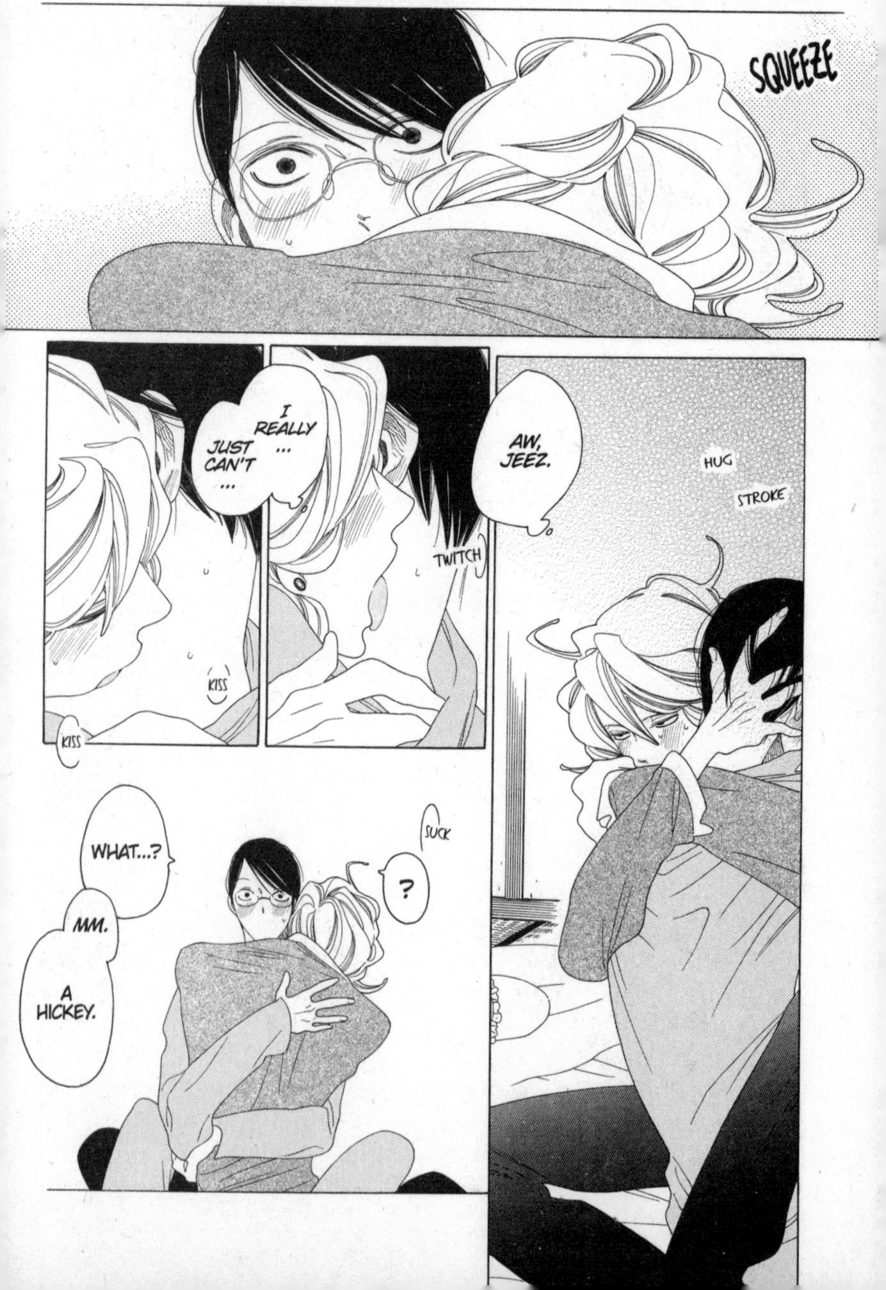
SQUEEZE
AW, JEEZ.
HUG
STROKE
I REALLY... JUST CAN'T...
TWITCH
KISS
KISS
SUCK
?
WHAT...?
MM.
A HICKEY.

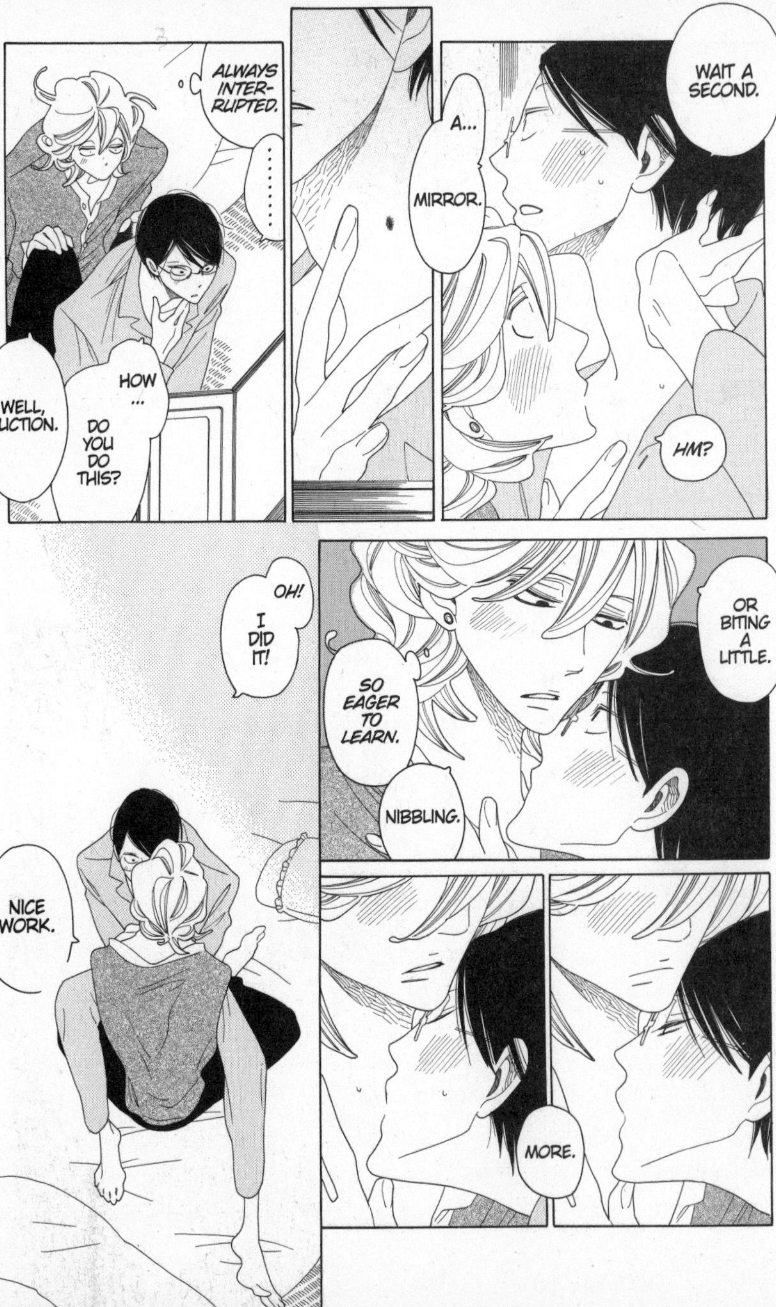
WAIT A SECOND.
A... MIRROR.
HM?
ALWAYS INTER-RUPTED.
......
HOW... DO YOU DO THIS?
WELL, SUCTION.
OR BITING A LITTLE.
SO EAGER TO LEARN.
NIBBLING.
MORE.
OH! I DID IT!
NICE WORK.

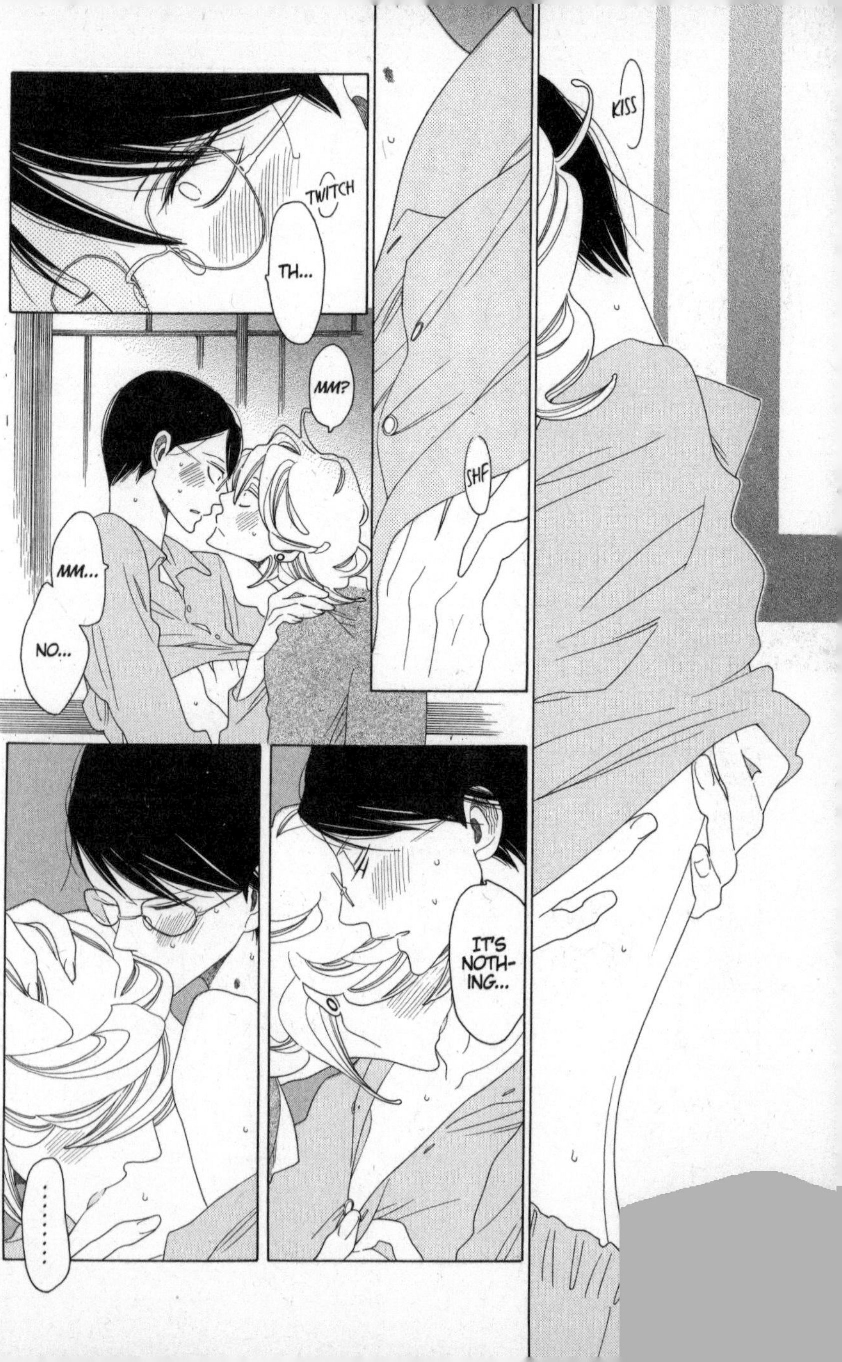
KISS
SHF
TWITCH
TH...
MM?
MM...
NO...
IT'S NOTHING-ING...
....

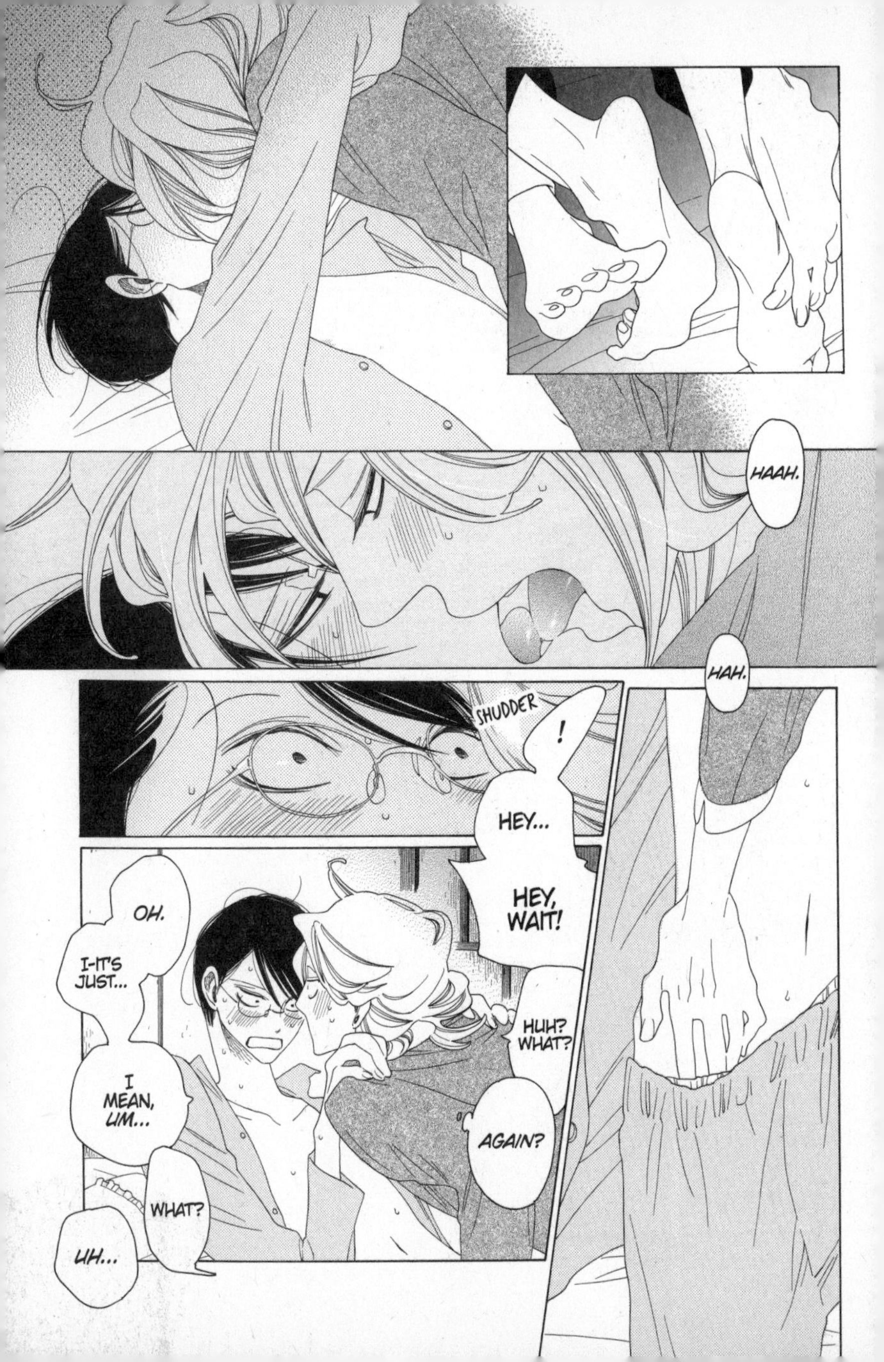
HAAH.
HAH.
SHUDDER
!
HEY...
HEY, WAIT!
HUH? WHAT?
AGAIN?
OH.
I-IT'S JUST...
I MEAN, UM...
WHAT?
UH...

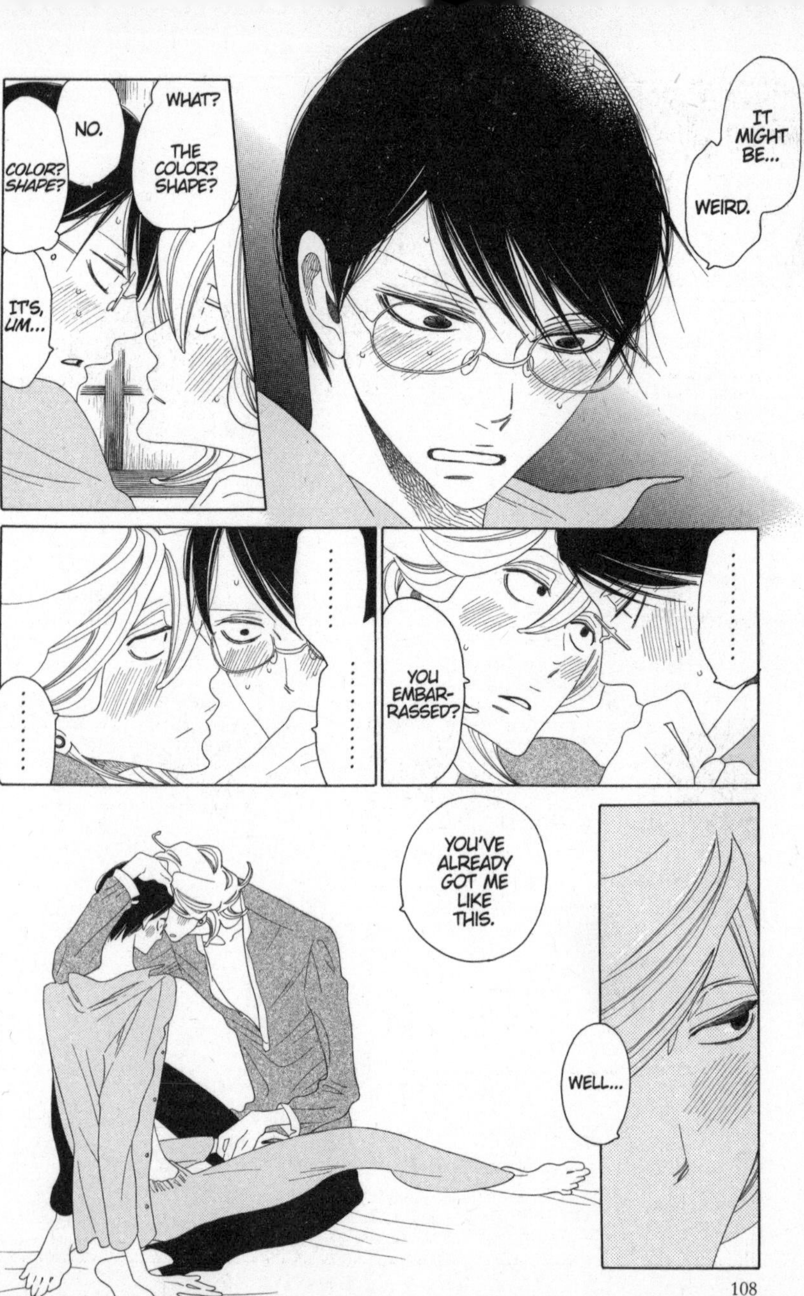
IT MIGHT BE...
WEIRD.
WHAT?
NO.
THE COLOR? SHAPE?
COLOR? SHAPE?
IT'S, UM...
......
YOU EMBARRASSED?
......
......
......
WELL...
YOU'VE ALREADY GOT ME LIKE THIS.

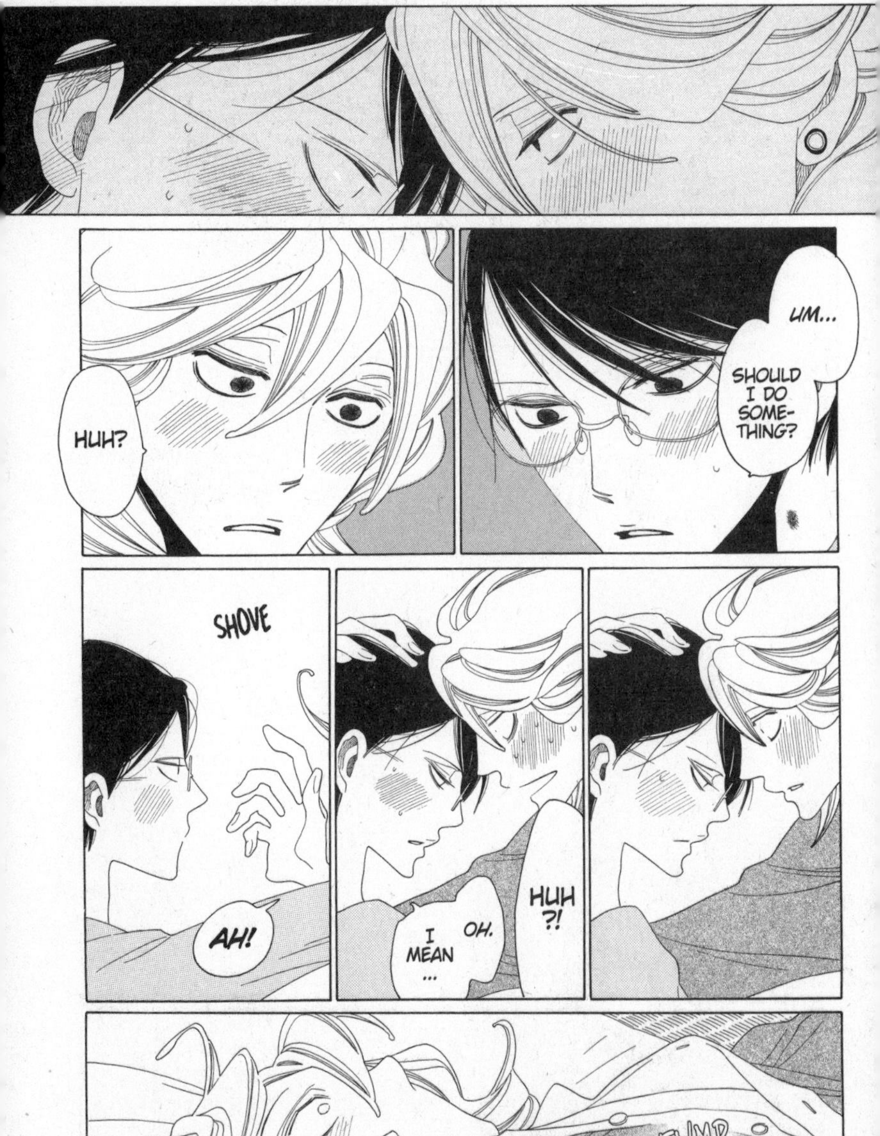
UM...
SHOULD I DO SOMETHING?
HUH?
HUH?!
OH. I MEAN...
SHOVE
AH!
FWMP

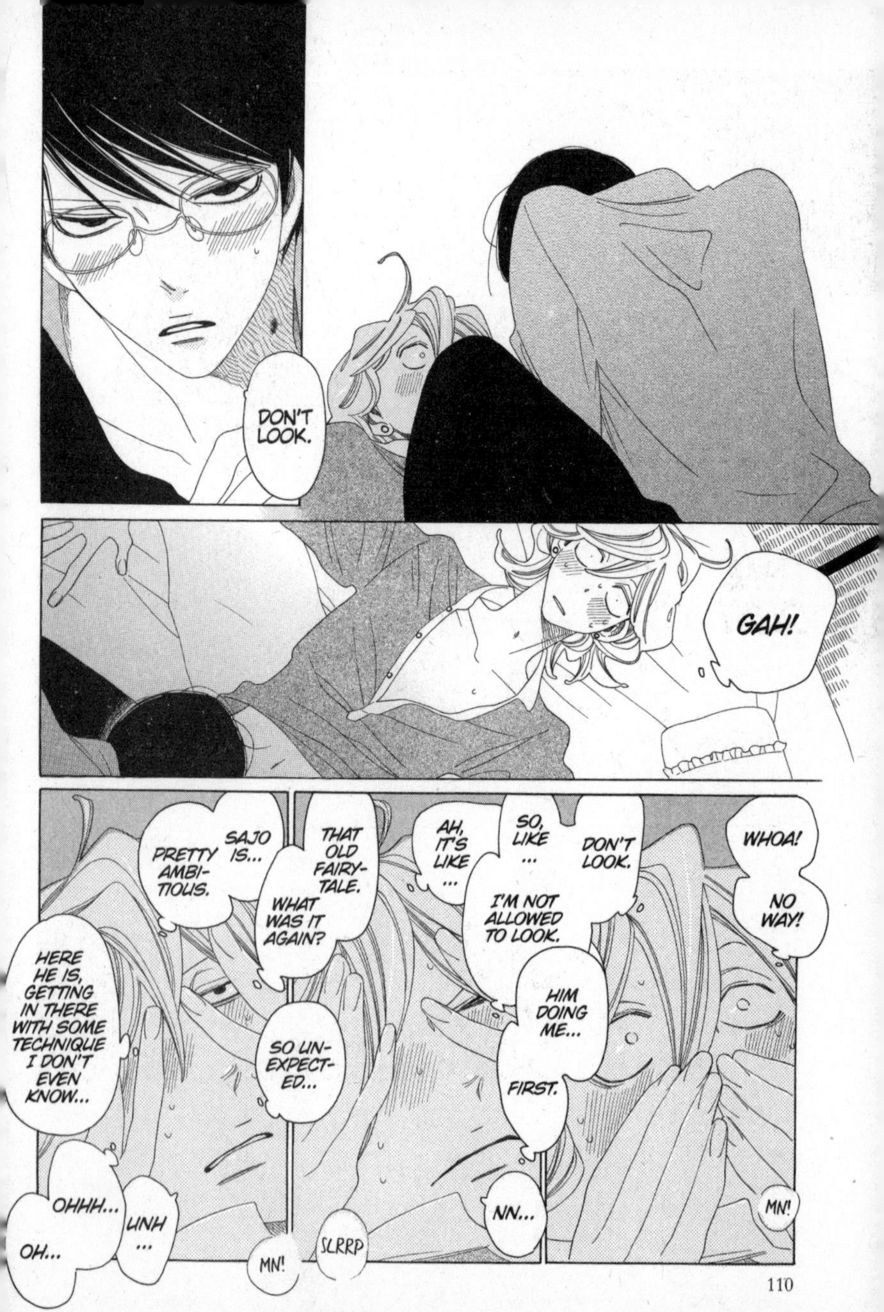
DON'T LOOK.
GAH!
WHOA!
NO WAY!
MN!
DON'T LOOK.
I'M NOT ALLOWED TO LOOK.
HIM DOING ME... FIRST.
SO, LIKE ...
AH, IT'S LIKE ...
THAT OLD FAIRY-TALE.
WHAT WAS IT AGAIN?
SO UN-EXPECT-ED...
NN...
SLRRP
SAJO IS...
PRETTY AMBI-TIOUS.
HERE HE IS, GETTING IN THERE WITH SOME TECHNIQUE I DON'T EVEN KNOW...
MN!
UNH ...
OHHH...
OH...

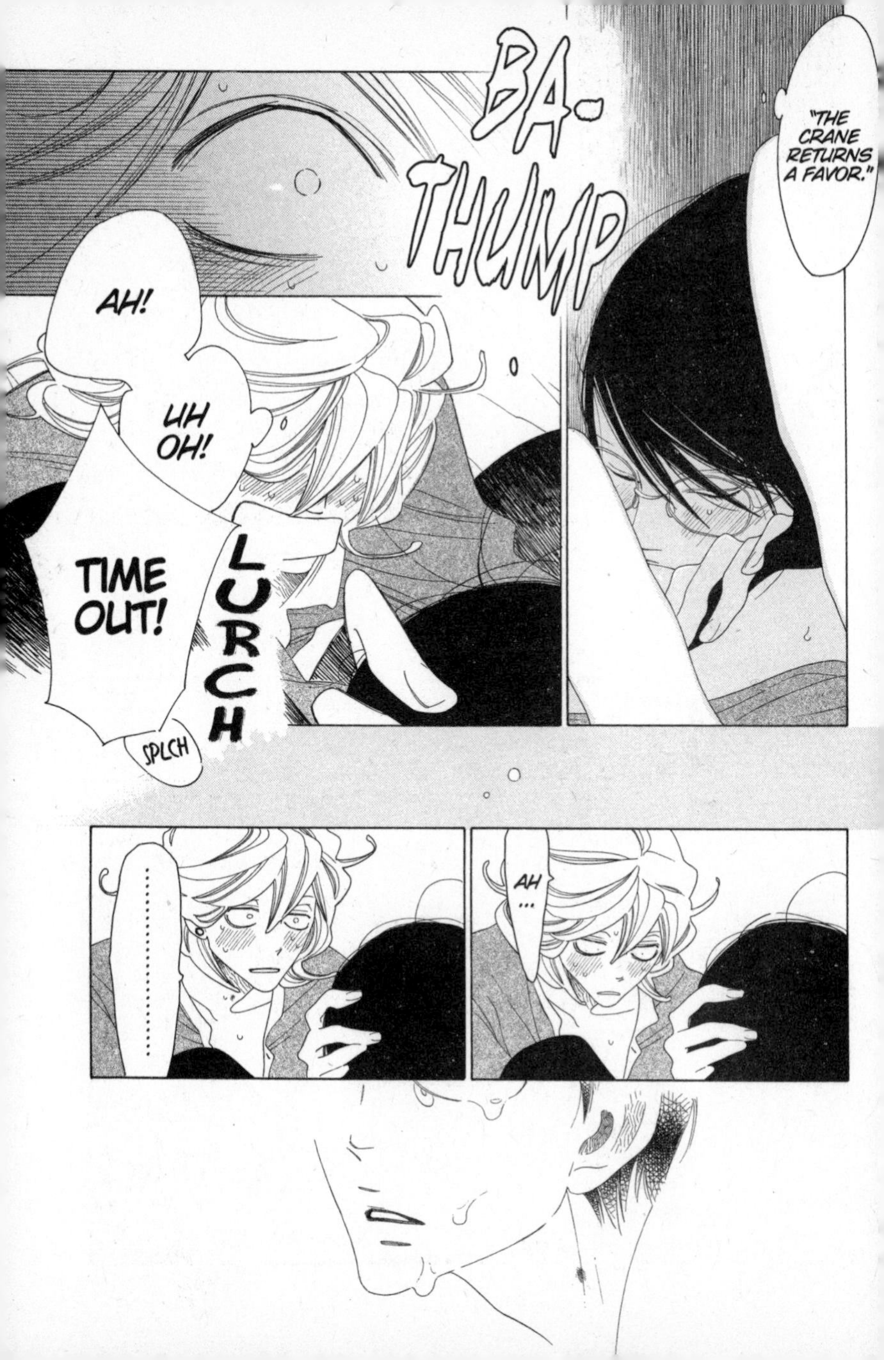
"THE CRANE RETURNS A FAVOR."
BA-THUMP
AH!
UH OH!
TIME OUT!
LURCH
SPLCH
AH ...
....

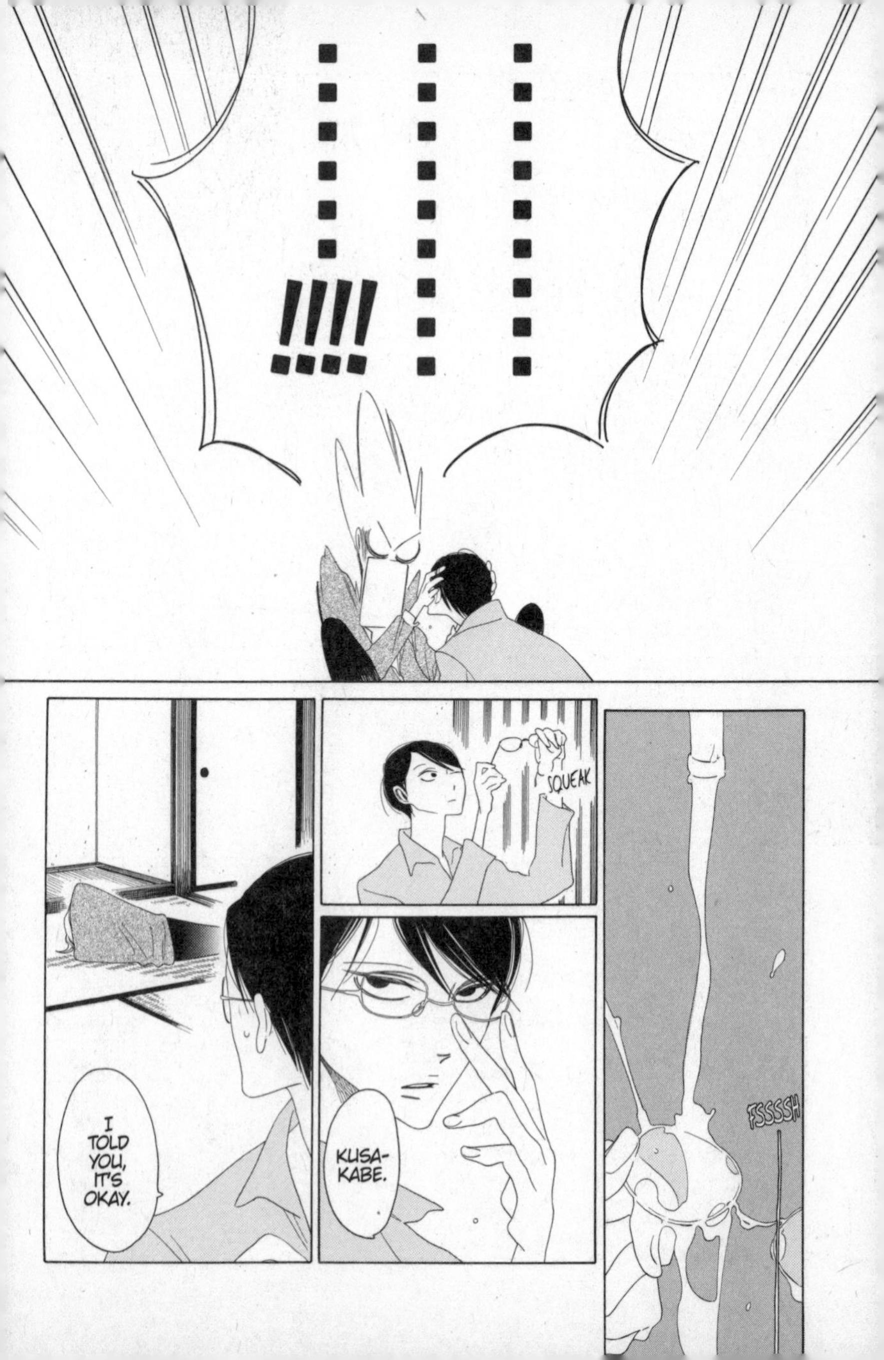
......!!!!
FSSSSH
SQUEAK
KUSA-KABE.
I TOLD YOU, IT'S OKAY.

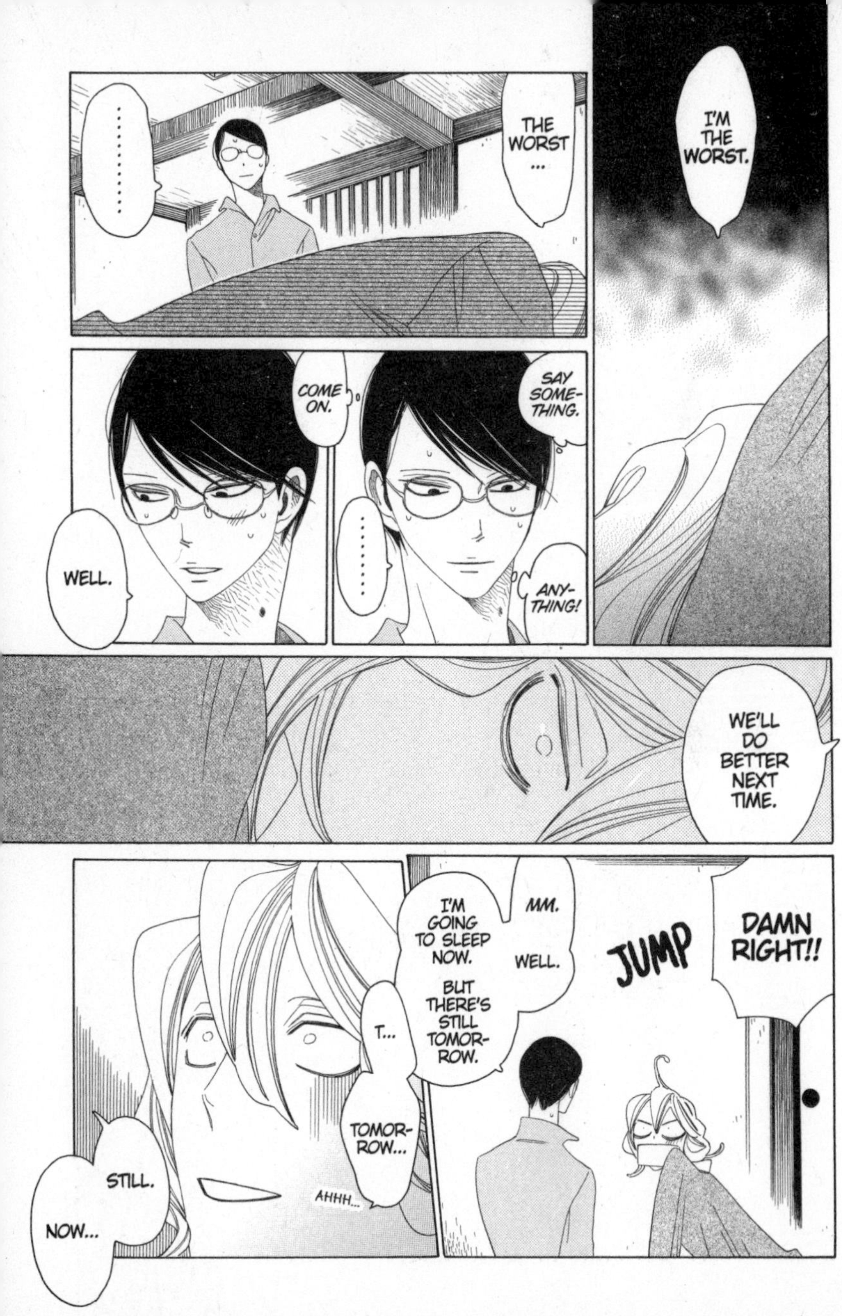
I'M THE WORST.
THE WORST...
......
SAY SOMETHING.
ANYTHING!
......
COME ON.
WELL.
WE'LL DO BETTER NEXT TIME.
DAMN RIGHT!!
JUMP
MM.
WELL.
I'M GOING TO SLEEP NOW.
BUT THERE'S STILL TOMORROW.
T...
TOMORROW...
AHHH...
STILL.
NOW...

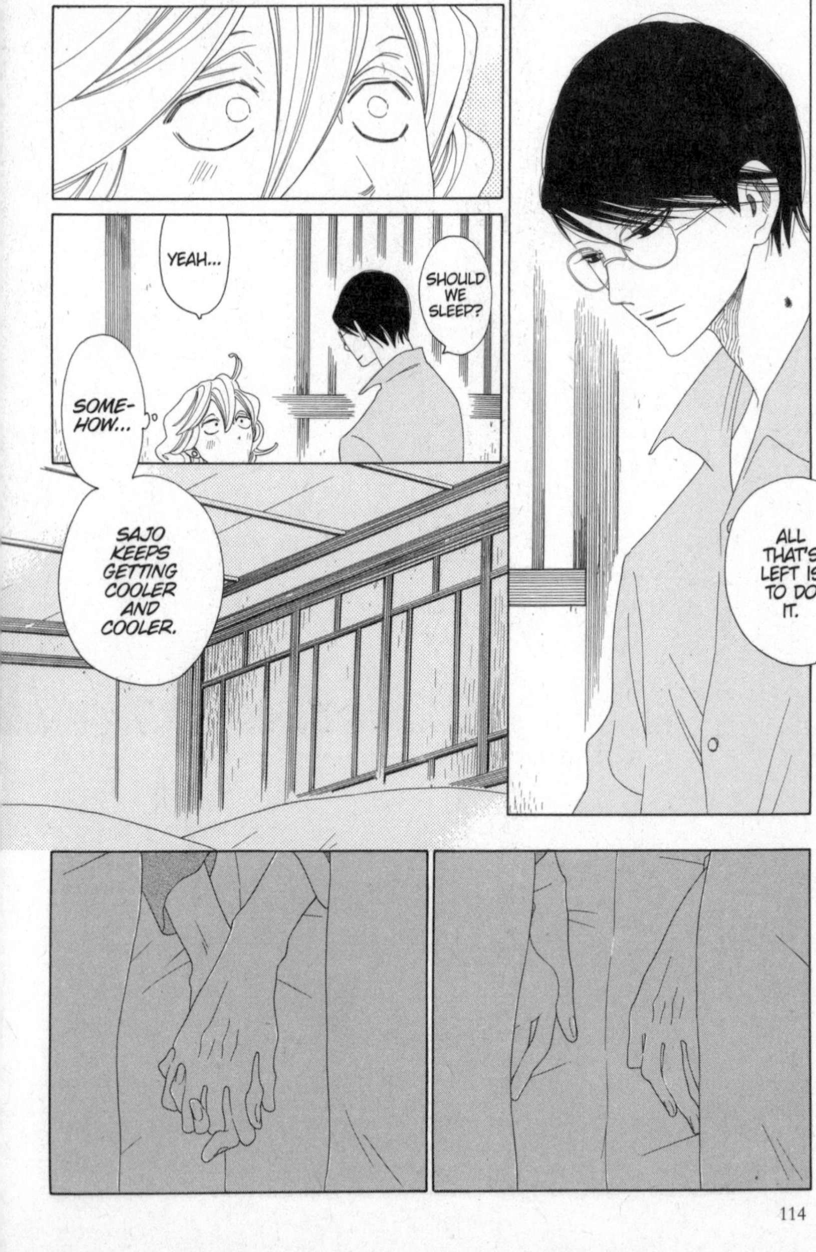
ALL THAT'S LEFT IS TO DO IT.
SHOULD WE SLEEP?
YEAH...
SOME-HOW...
SAJO KEEPS GETTING COOLER AND COOLER.

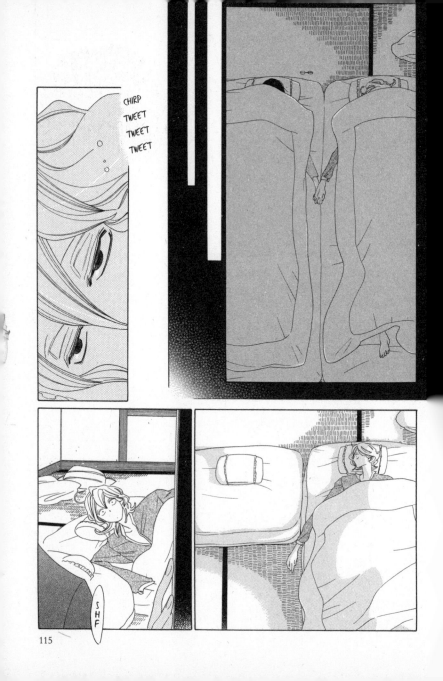

CHIRP
TWEET
TWEET
TWEET

SHF

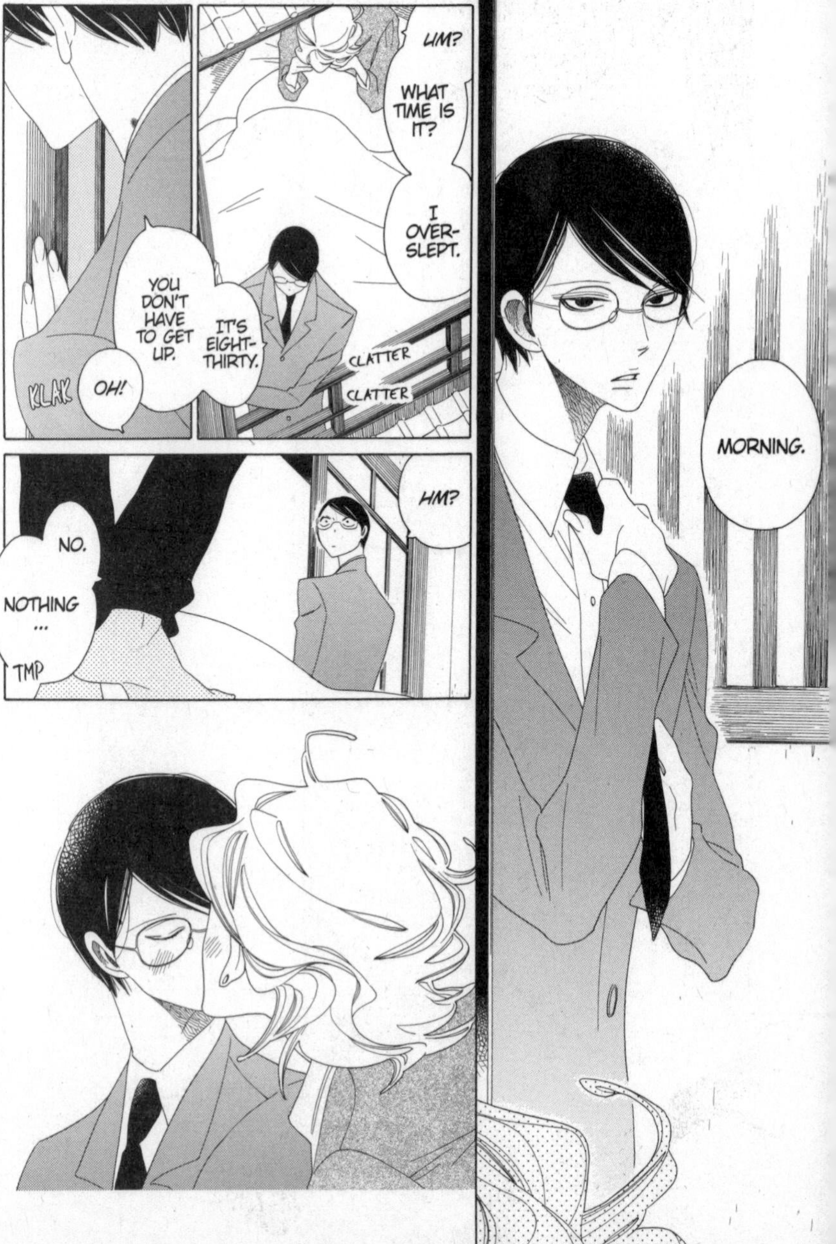
MORNING.
UM?
WHAT TIME IS IT?
I OVERSLEPT.
CLATTER
CLATTER
IT'S EIGHT-THIRTY.
YOU DON'T HAVE TO GET UP.
OH!
KLAK
HM?
NO.
NOTHING...
TMP

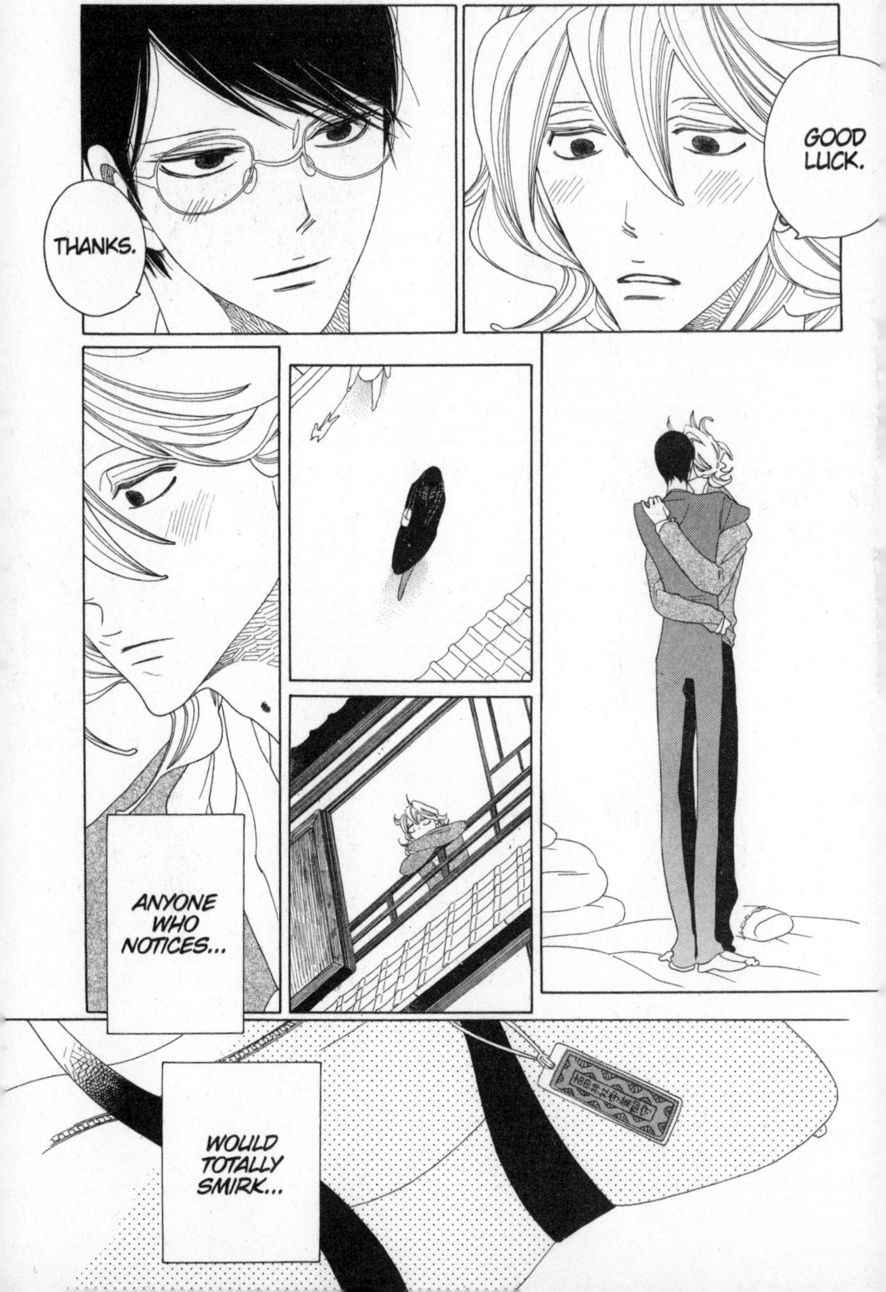
GOOD LUCK.
THANKS.
ANYONE WHO NOTICES...
WOULD TOTALLY SMIRK...

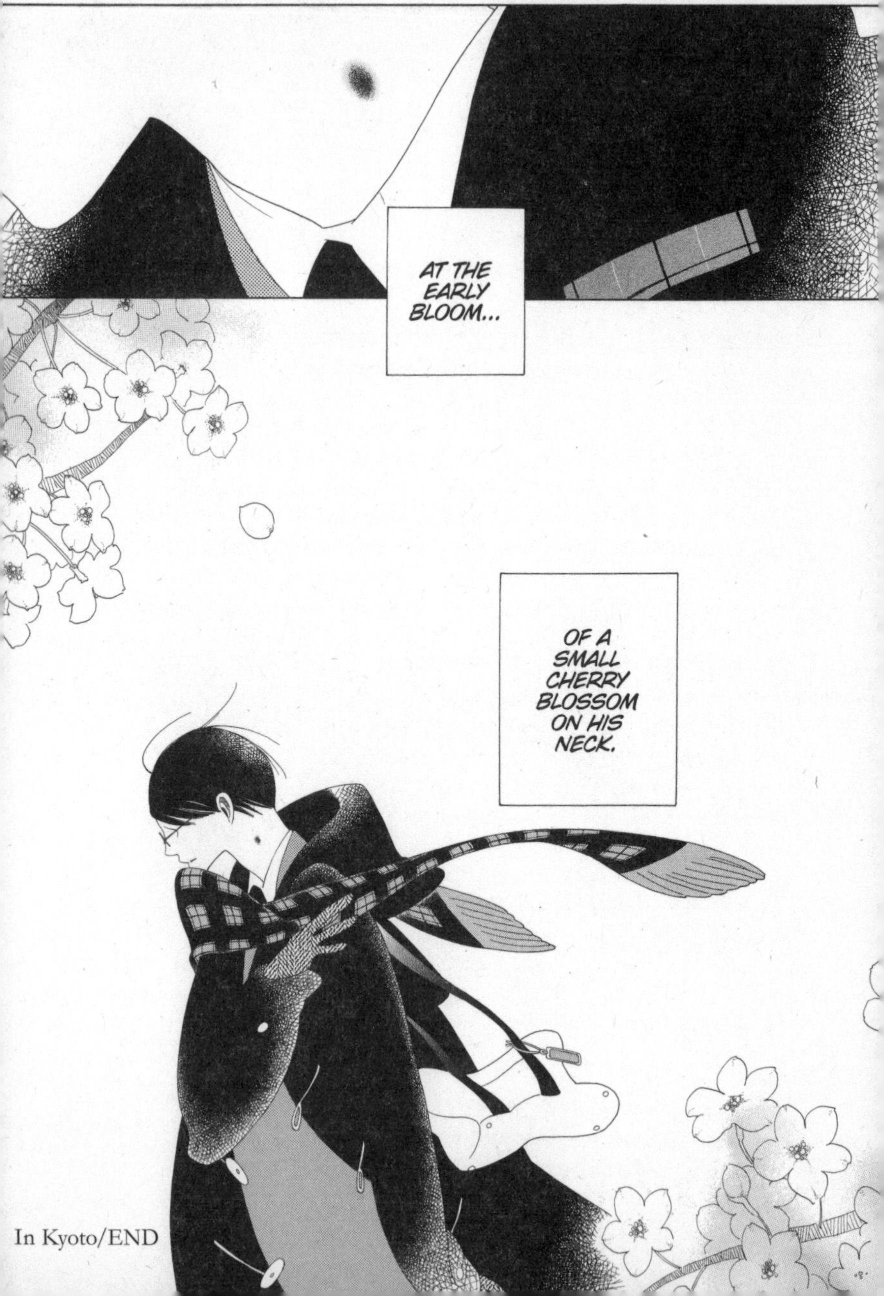
AT THE EARLY BLOOM...
OF A SMALL CHERRY BLOSSOM ON HIS NECK.
In Kyoto/END

Classmates

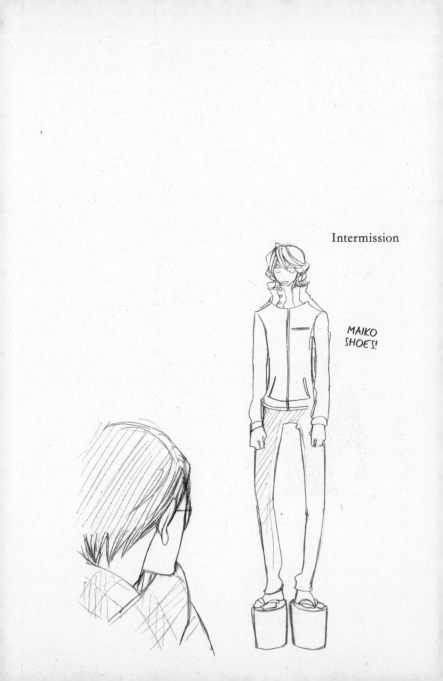

Intermission

MAIKO
SHOES!

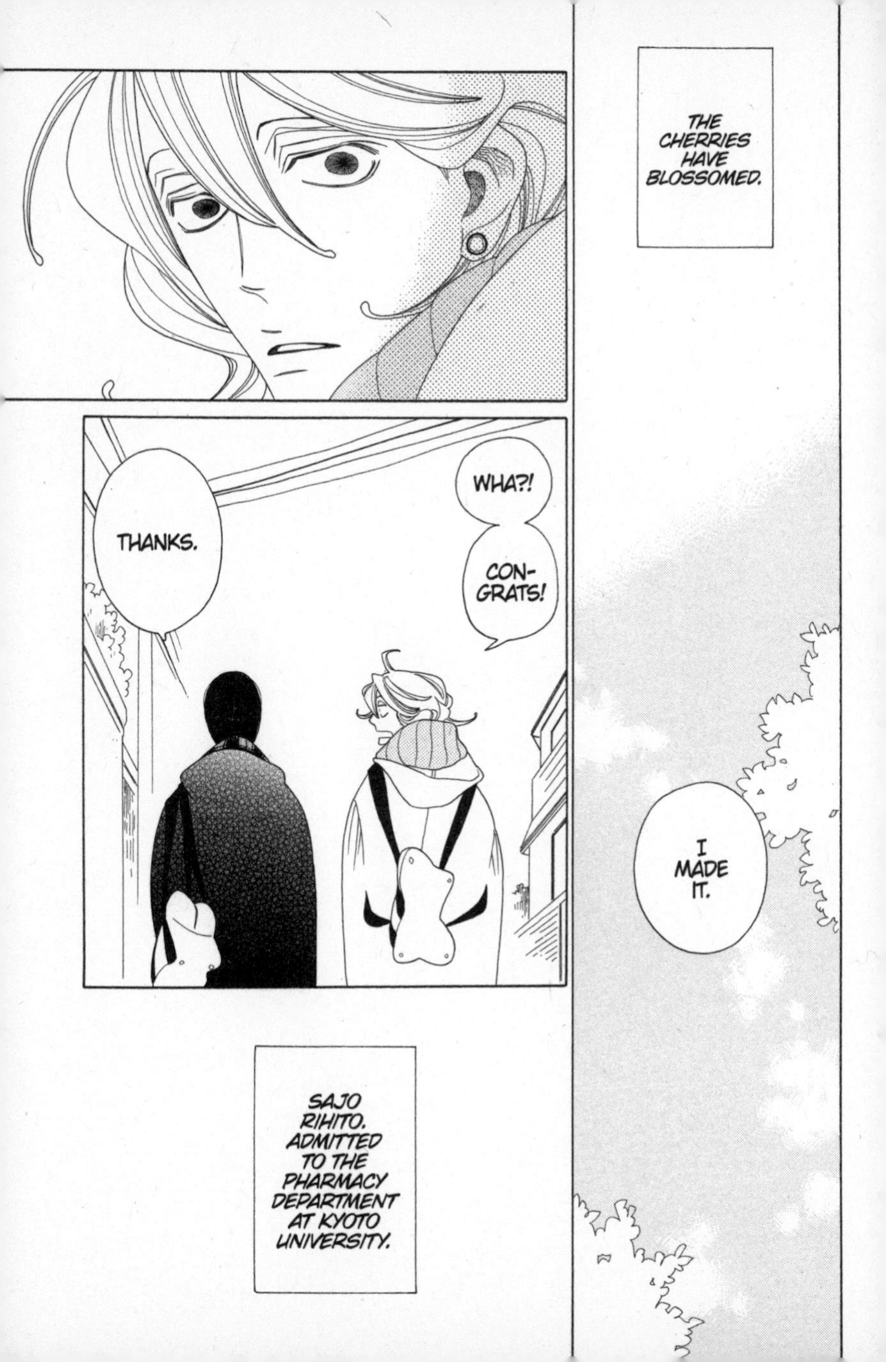
THE CHERRIES HAVE BLOSSOMED.
I MADE IT.
WHA?!
CON-GRATS!
THANKS.
SAJO RIHITO. ADMITTED TO THE PHARMACY DEPARTMENT AT KYOTO UNIVERSITY.

[Graduation]

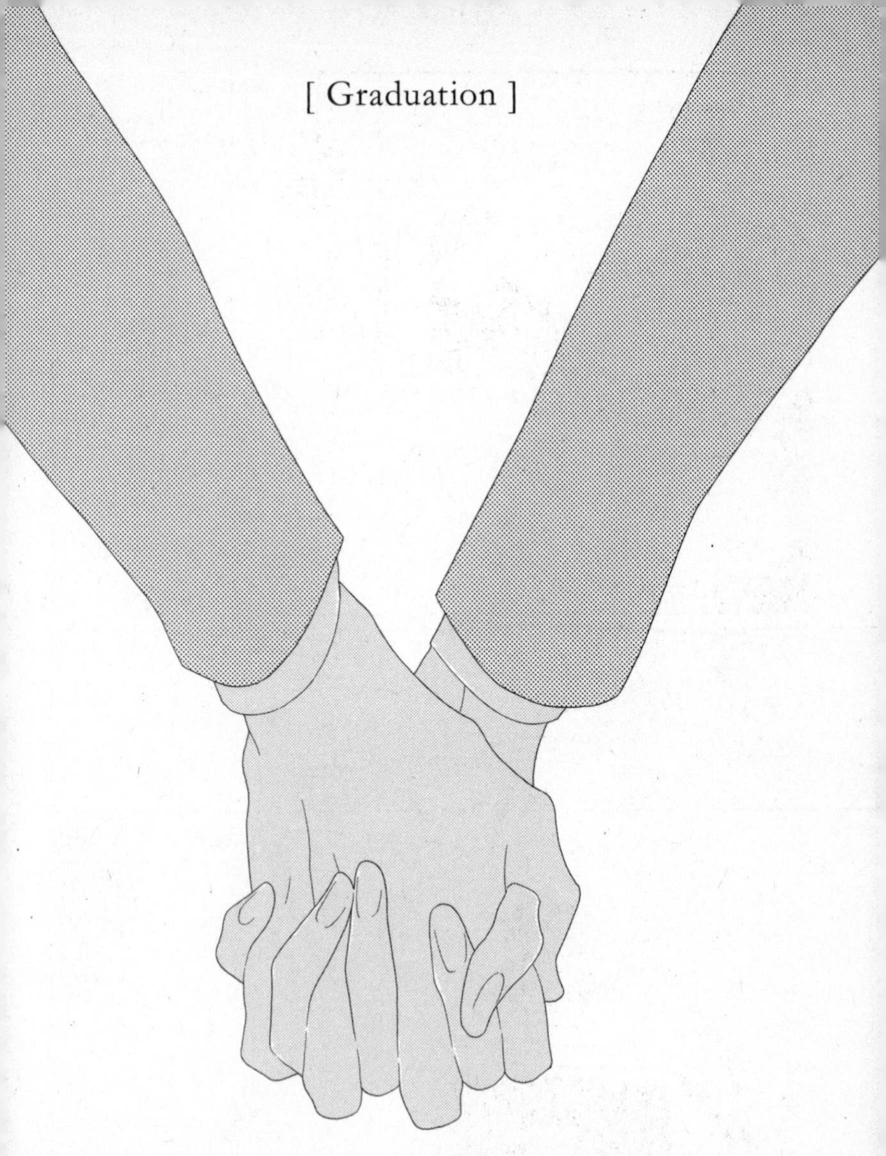

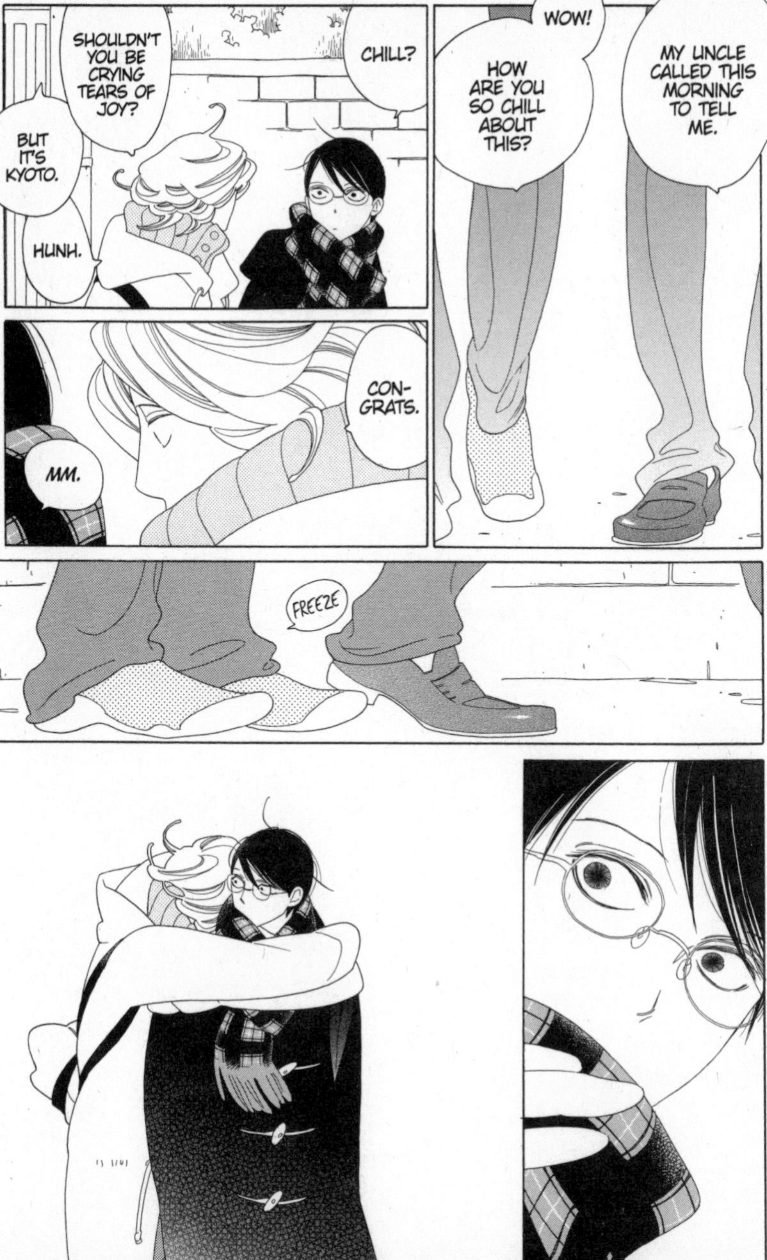
MY UNCLE CALLED THIS MORNING TO TELL ME.
WOW!
HOW ARE YOU SO CHILL ABOUT THIS?
CHILL?
SHOULDN'T YOU BE CRYING TEARS OF JOY?
BUT IT'S KYOTO.
HUNH.
CON-GRATS.
MM.
FREEZE

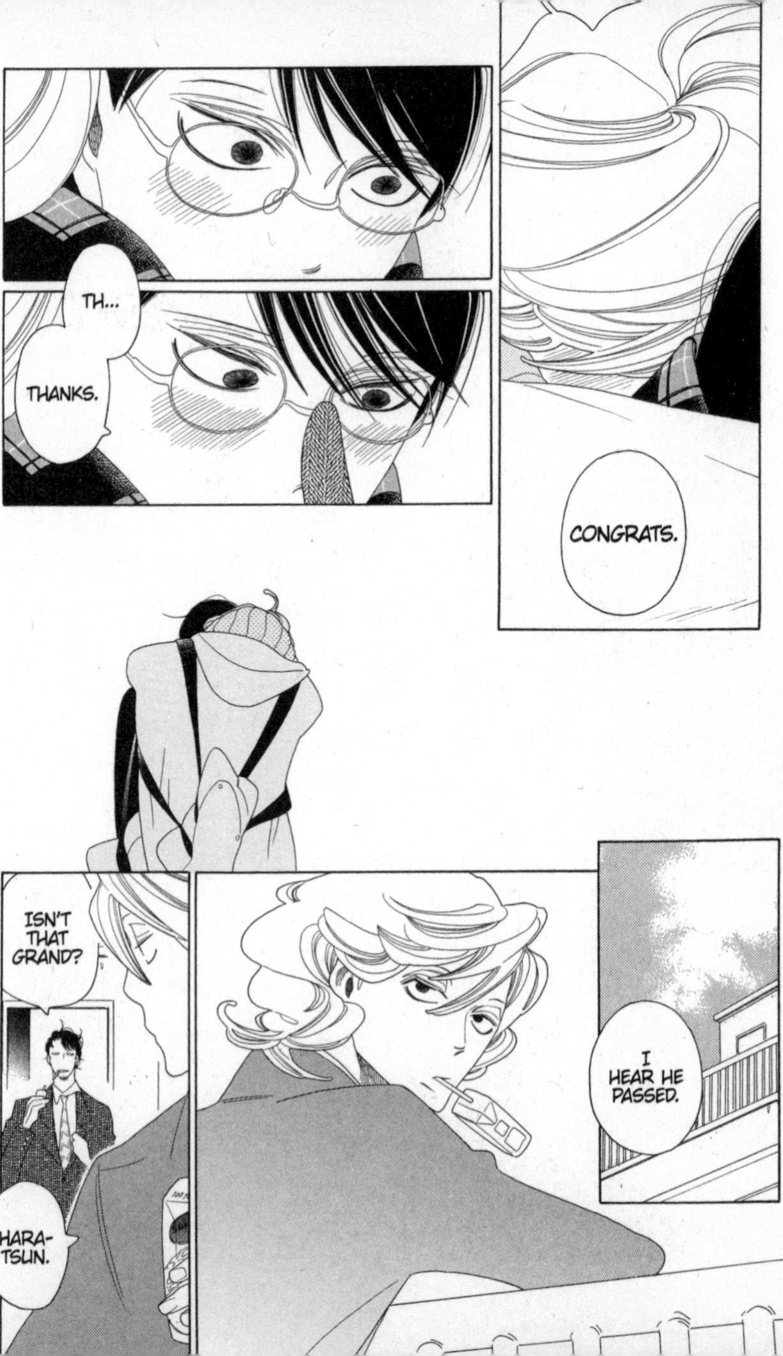
CONGRATS.
TH...
THANKS.
I HEAR HE PASSED.
ISN'T THAT GRAND?
HARA-TSUN.

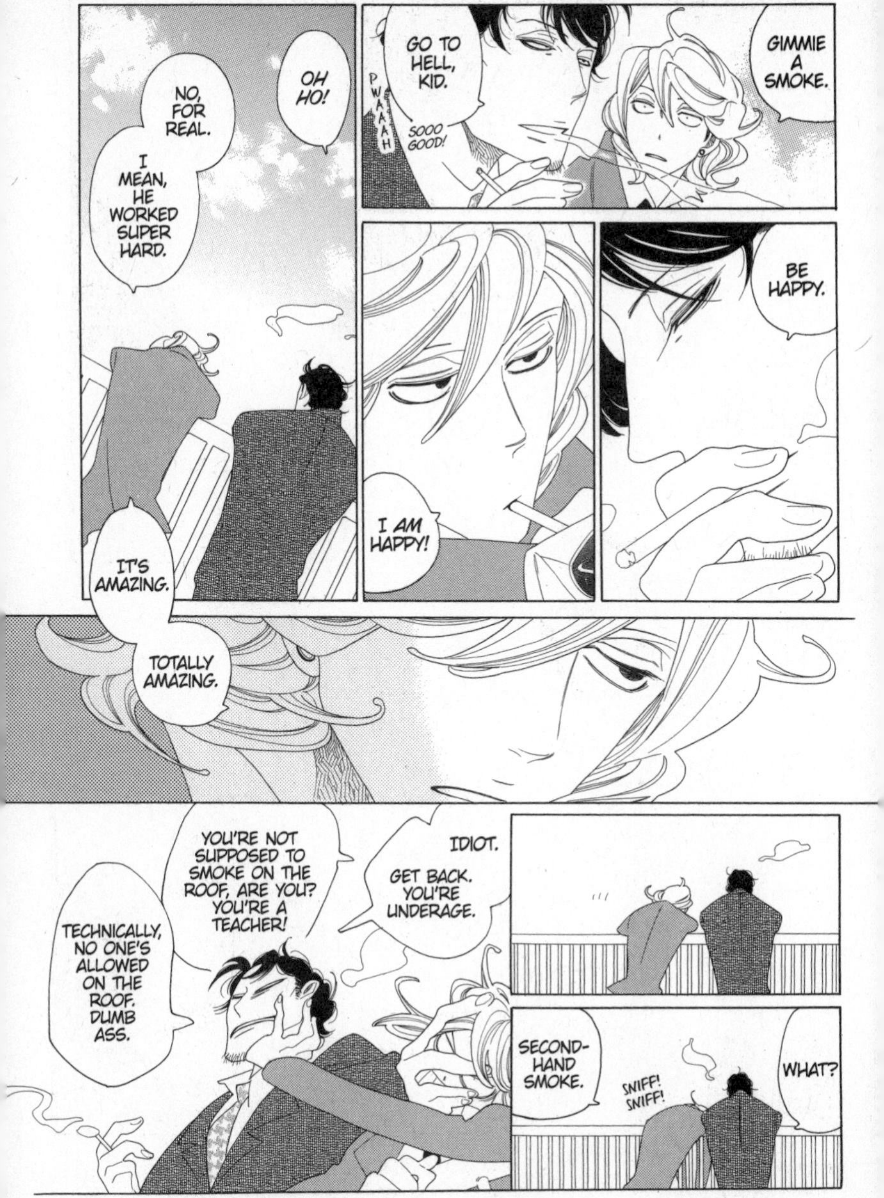
GIMMIE A SMOKE.
GO TO HELL, KID.
PWAAAH
SOOO GOOD!
BE HAPPY.
I AM HAPPY!
OH HO!
NO, FOR REAL.
I MEAN, HE WORKED SUPER HARD.
IT'S AMAZING.
TOTALLY AMAZING.
WHAT?
SECOND-HAND SMOKE.
SNIFF! SNIFF!
IDIOT.
GET BACK. YOU'RE UNDERAGE.
YOU'RE NOT SUPPOSED TO SMOKE ON THE ROOF, ARE YOU? YOU'RE A TEACHER!
TECHNICALLY, NO ONE'S ALLOWED ON THE ROOF. DUMB ASS.

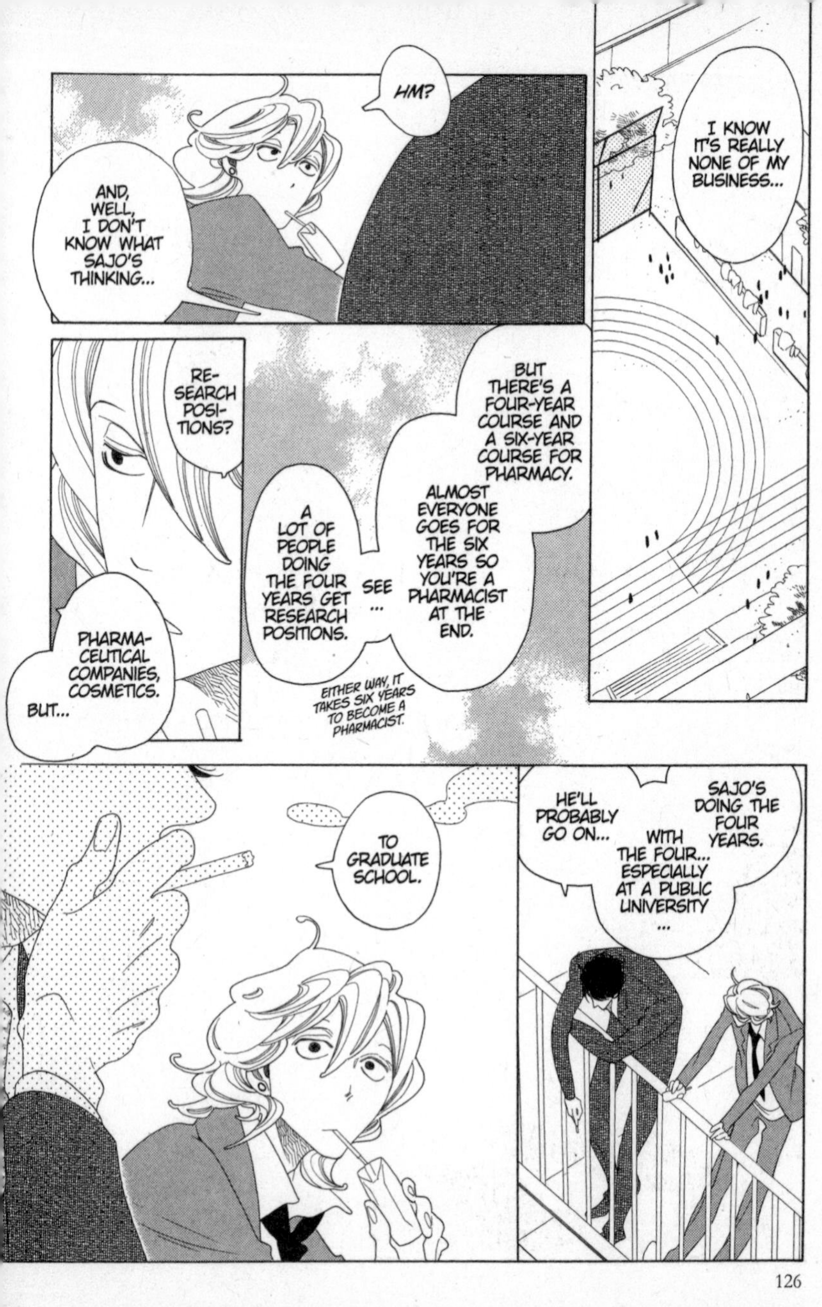
I KNOW IT'S REALLY NONE OF MY BUSINESS...
HM?
AND, WELL, I DON'T KNOW WHAT SAJO'S THINKING...
BUT THERE'S A FOUR-YEAR COURSE AND A SIX-YEAR COURSE FOR PHARMACY.
ALMOST EVERYONE GOES FOR THE SIX YEARS SO YOU'RE A PHARMACIST AT THE END.
SEE...
A LOT OF PEOPLE DOING THE FOUR YEARS GET RESEARCH POSITIONS.
RE-SEARCH POSI-TIONS?
EITHER WAY, IT TAKES SIX YEARS TO BECOME A PHARMACIST.
PHARMA-CEUTICAL COMPANIES, COSMETICS. BUT...
SAJO'S DOING THE FOUR YEARS.
WITH THE FOUR... ESPECIALLY AT A PUBLIC UNIVERSITY...
HE'LL PROBABLY GO ON...
TO GRADUATE SCHOOL.

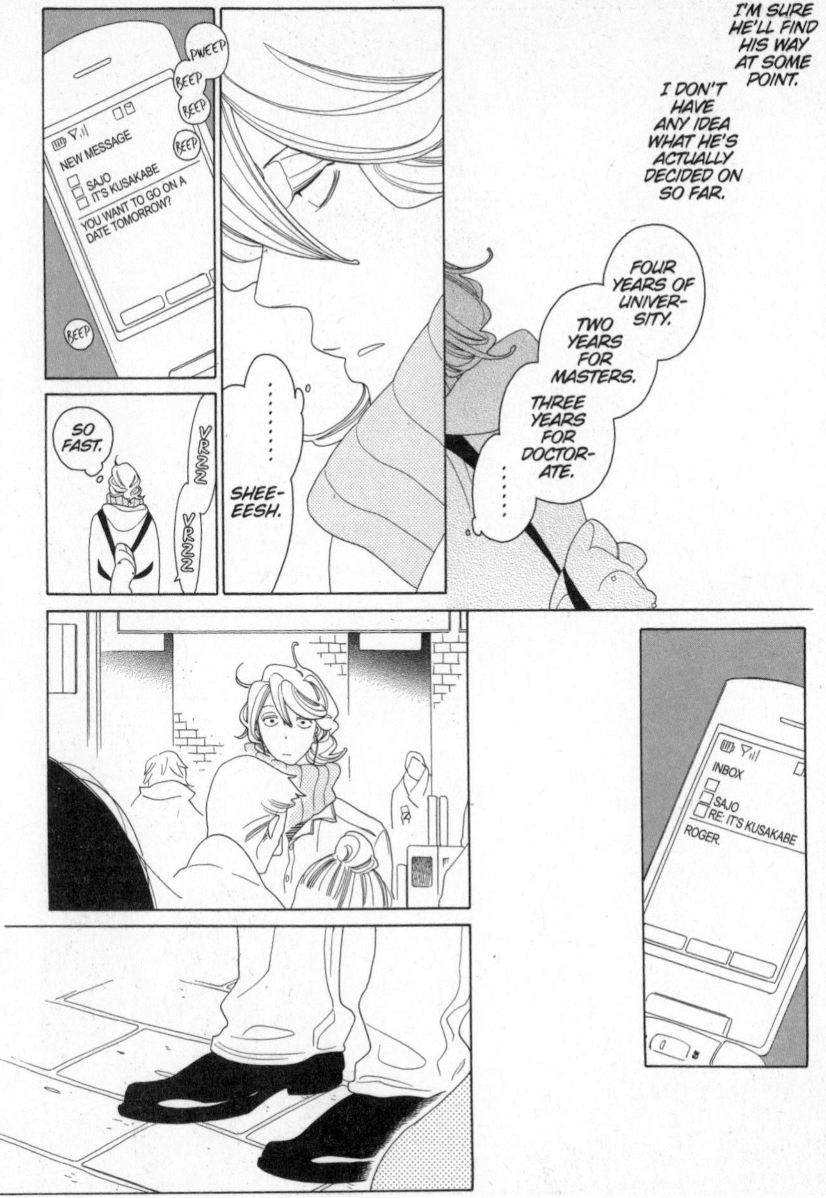
I'M SURE HE'LL FIND HIS WAY AT SOME POINT.
I DON'T HAVE ANY IDEA WHAT HE'S ACTUALLY DECIDED ON SO FAR.
FOUR YEARS OF UNIVER-SITY.
TWO YEARS FOR MASTERS.
THREE YEARS FOR DOCTOR-ATE.
......
......
SHEE-EESH.
PWEEP
BEEP
BEEP
BEEP
NEW MESSAGE
SAJO
IT'S KUSAKABE
YOU WANT TO GO ON A DATE TOMORROW?
BEEP
VRZZ
VRZZ
SO FAST.
INBOX
SAJO
RE: IT'S KUSAKABE
ROGER.

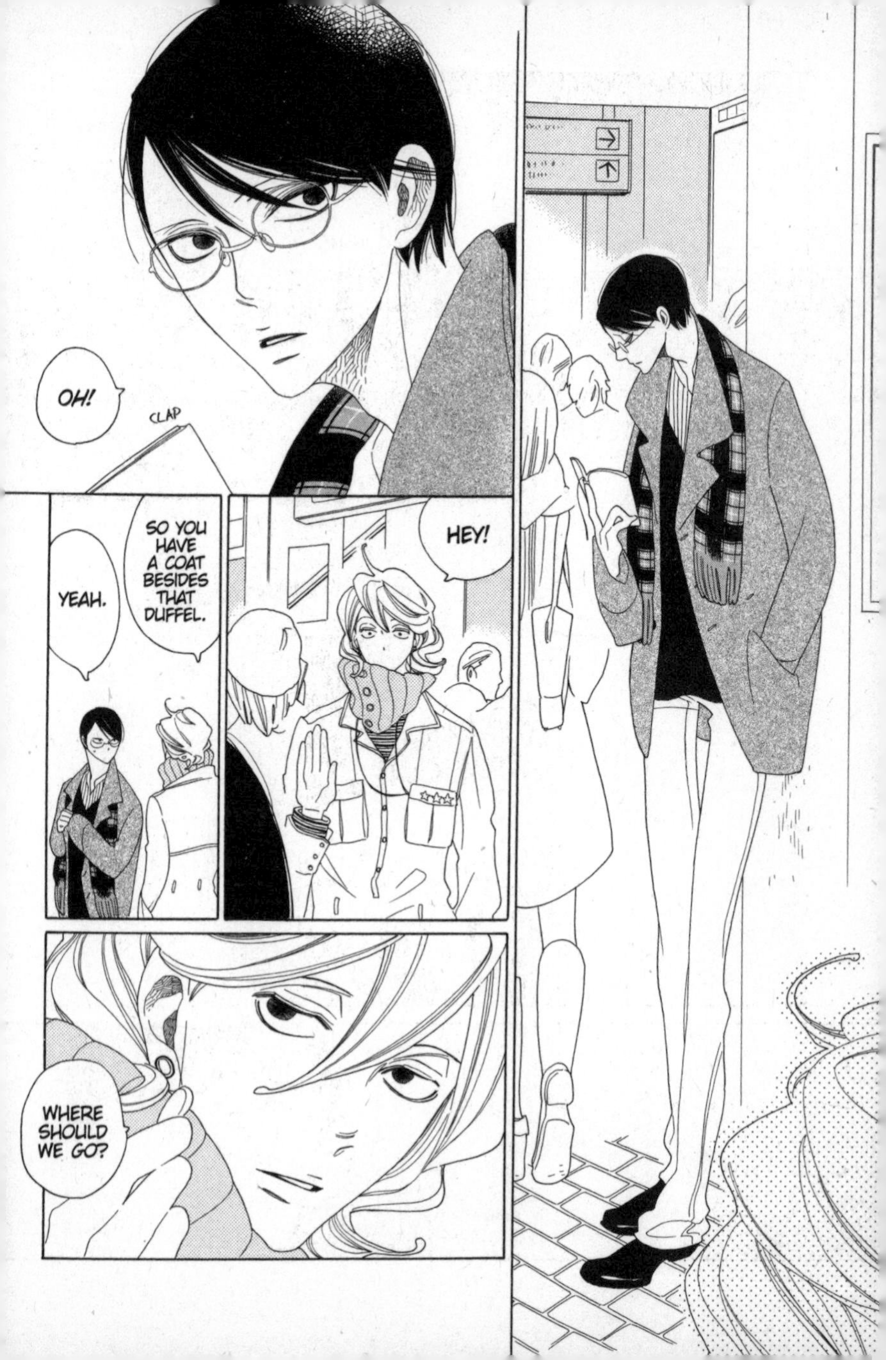
OH!
CLAP
HEY!
SO YOU HAVE A COAT BESIDES THAT DUFFEL.
YEAH.
WHERE SHOULD WE GO?

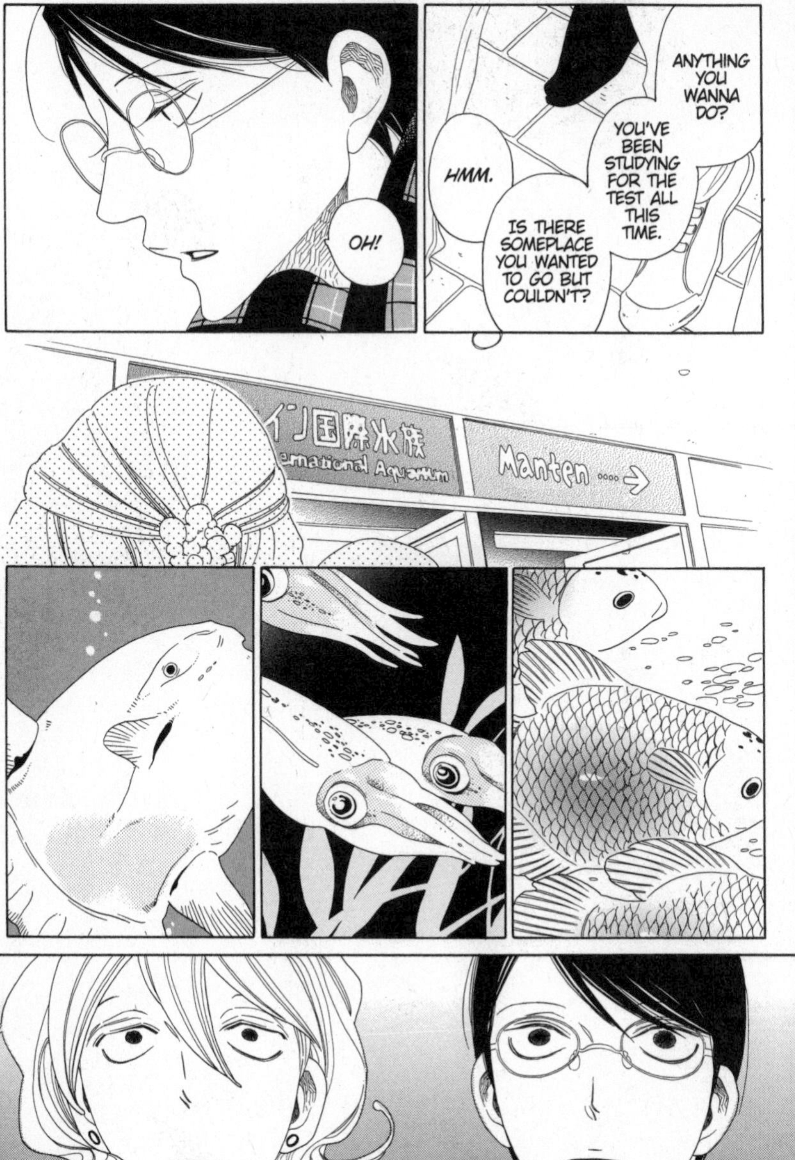
ANYTHING YOU WANNA DO?
YOU'VE BEEN STUDYING FOR THE TEST ALL THIS TIME.
IS THERE SOMEPLACE YOU WANTED TO GO BUT COULDN'T?
HMM.
OH!
ernational Aquarium
Manten

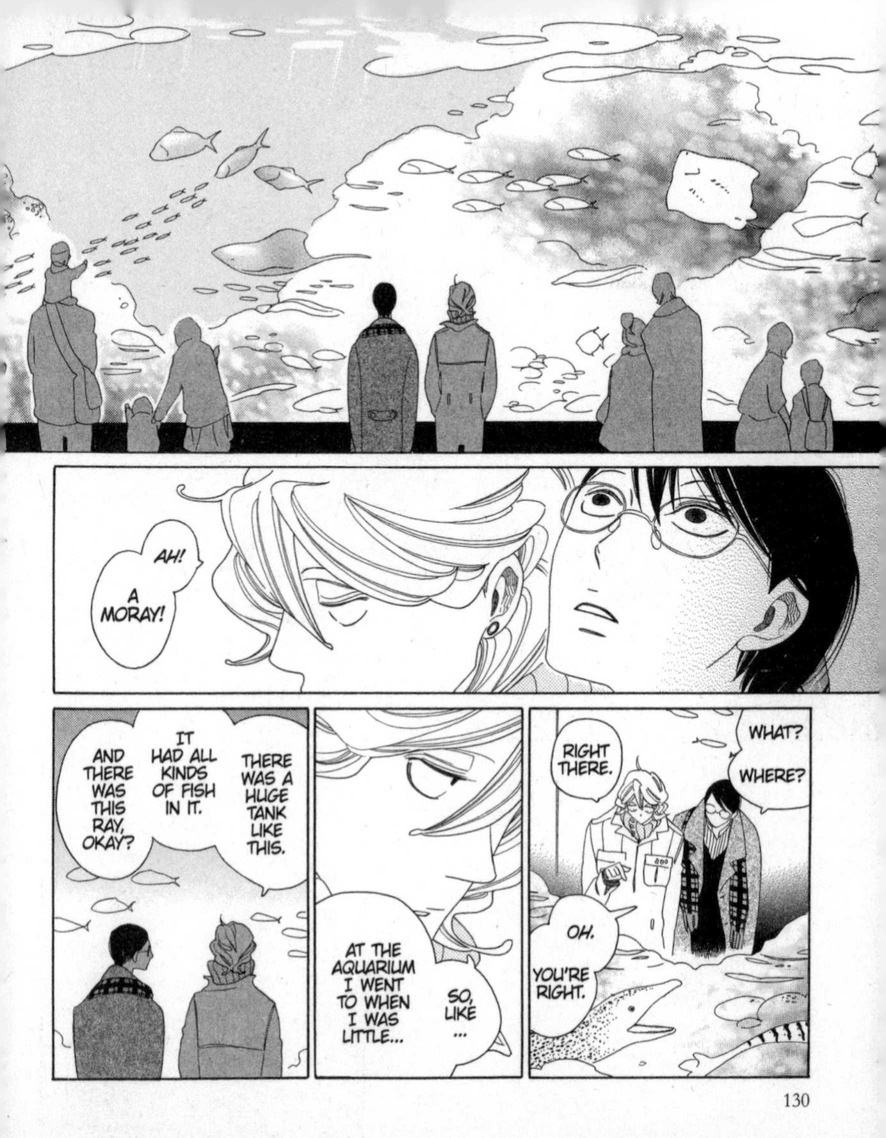
AH!
A MORAY!
WHAT?
WHERE?
RIGHT THERE.
OH.
YOU'RE RIGHT.
SO, LIKE...
AT THE AQUARIUM I WENT TO WHEN I WAS LITTLE...
THERE WAS A HUGE TANK LIKE THIS.
IT HAD ALL KINDS OF FISH IN IT.
AND THERE WAS THIS RAY, OKAY?

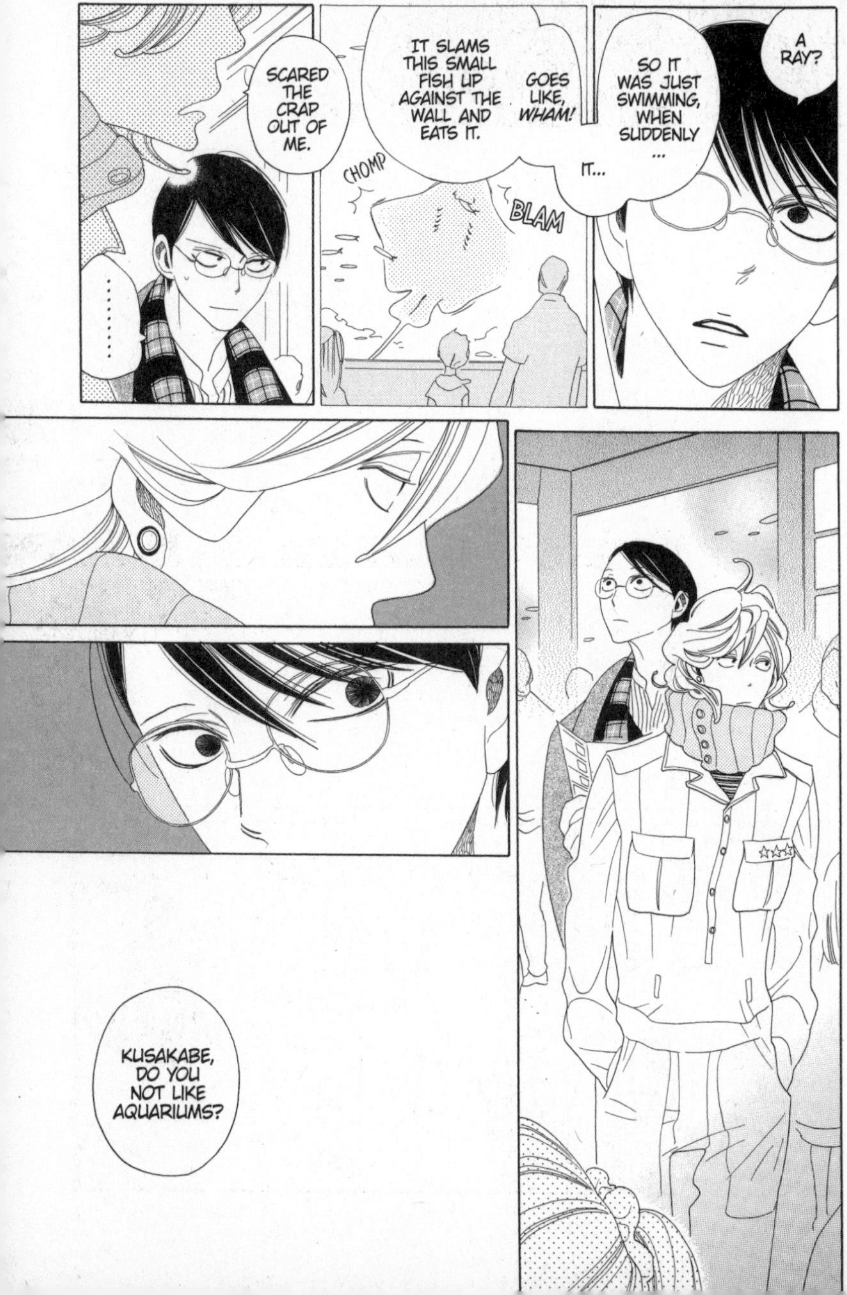
A RAY?
SO IT WAS JUST SWIMMING, WHEN SUDDENLY ...
IT...
GOES LIKE, *WHAM!*
IT SLAMS THIS SMALL FISH UP AGAINST THE WALL AND EATS IT.
BLAM
CHOMP
SCARED THE CRAP OUT OF ME.
......
KUSAKABE, DO YOU NOT LIKE AQUARIUMS?

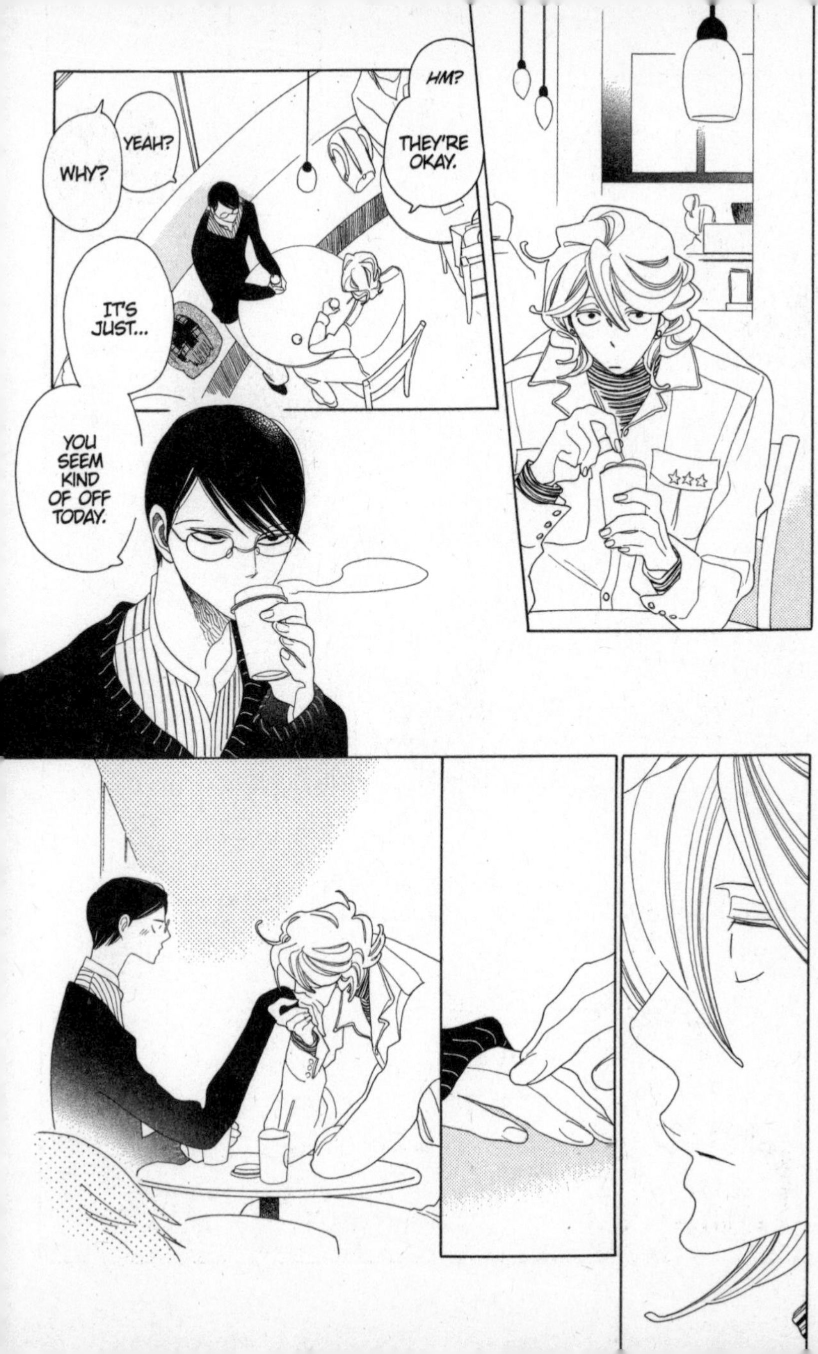
HM?
THEY'RE OKAY.
YEAH?
WHY?
IT'S JUST...
YOU SEEM KIND OF OFF TODAY.

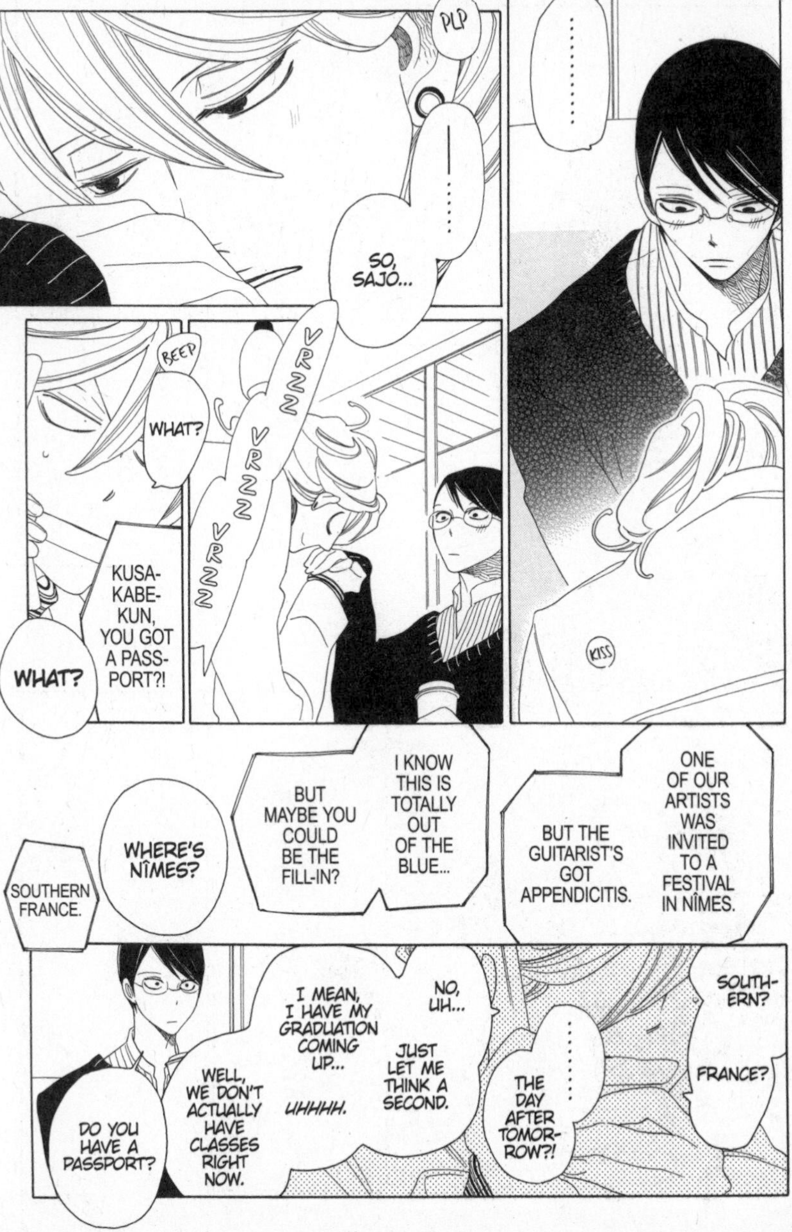
......
KISS
PLP
......
SO, SAJO...
VRZZ VRZZ VRZZ
BEEP
WHAT?
KUSA-KABE-KUN, YOU GOT A PASSPORT?!
WHAT?
ONE OF OUR ARTISTS WAS INVITED TO A FESTIVAL IN NÎMES.
BUT THE GUITARIST'S GOT APPENDICITIS.
I KNOW THIS IS TOTALLY OUT OF THE BLUE...
BUT MAYBE YOU COULD BE THE FILL-IN?
WHERE'S NÎMES?
SOUTHERN FRANCE.
SOUTHERN?
FRANCE?
......
THE DAY AFTER TOMORROW?!
NO, UH...
JUST LET ME THINK A SECOND.
I MEAN, I HAVE MY GRADUATION COMING UP...
UHHHH.
WELL, WE DON'T ACTUALLY HAVE CLASSES RIGHT NOW.
DO YOU HAVE A PASSPORT?

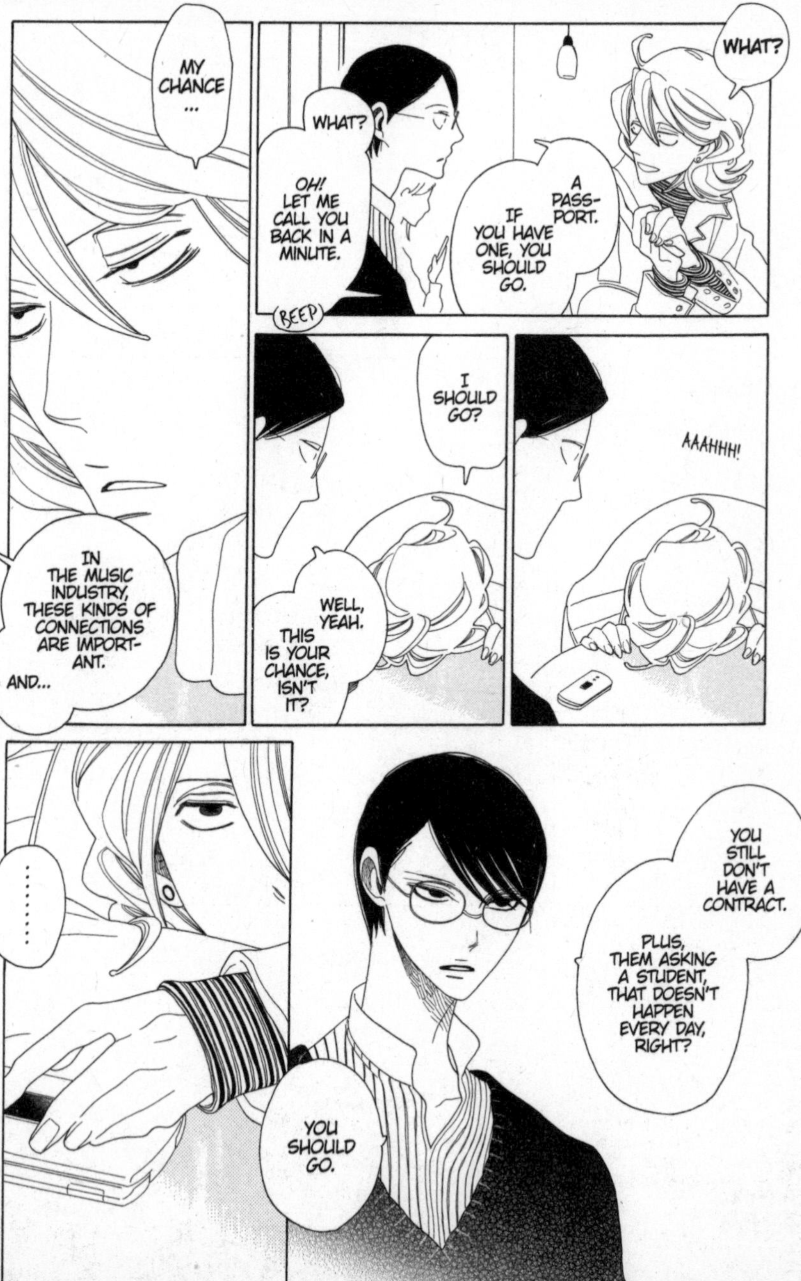
WHAT?
A PASSPORT. IF YOU HAVE ONE, YOU SHOULD GO.
WHAT?
OH! LET ME CALL YOU BACK IN A MINUTE.
BEEP
AAAHHH!
I SHOULD GO?
WELL, YEAH. THIS IS YOUR CHANCE, ISN'T IT?
MY CHANCE...
IN THE MUSIC INDUSTRY, THESE KINDS OF CONNECTIONS ARE IMPORTANT. AND...
YOU STILL DON'T HAVE A CONTRACT.
PLUS, THEM ASKING A STUDENT, THAT DOESN'T HAPPEN EVERY DAY, RIGHT?
YOU SHOULD GO.
....

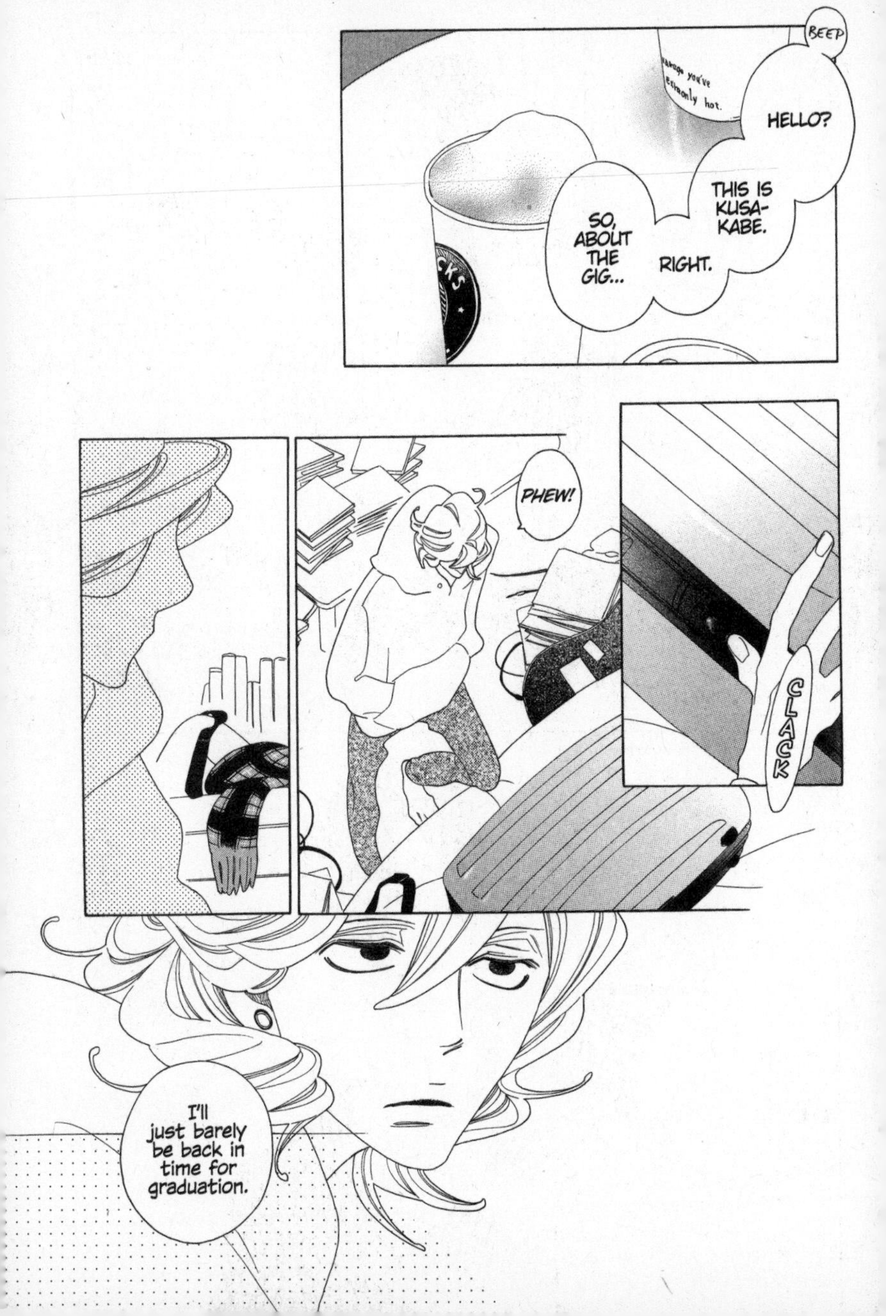
BEEP
HELLO?
THIS IS KUSA-KABE.
RIGHT.
SO, ABOUT THE GIG...
CLACK
PHEW!
I'll just barely be back in time for graduation.

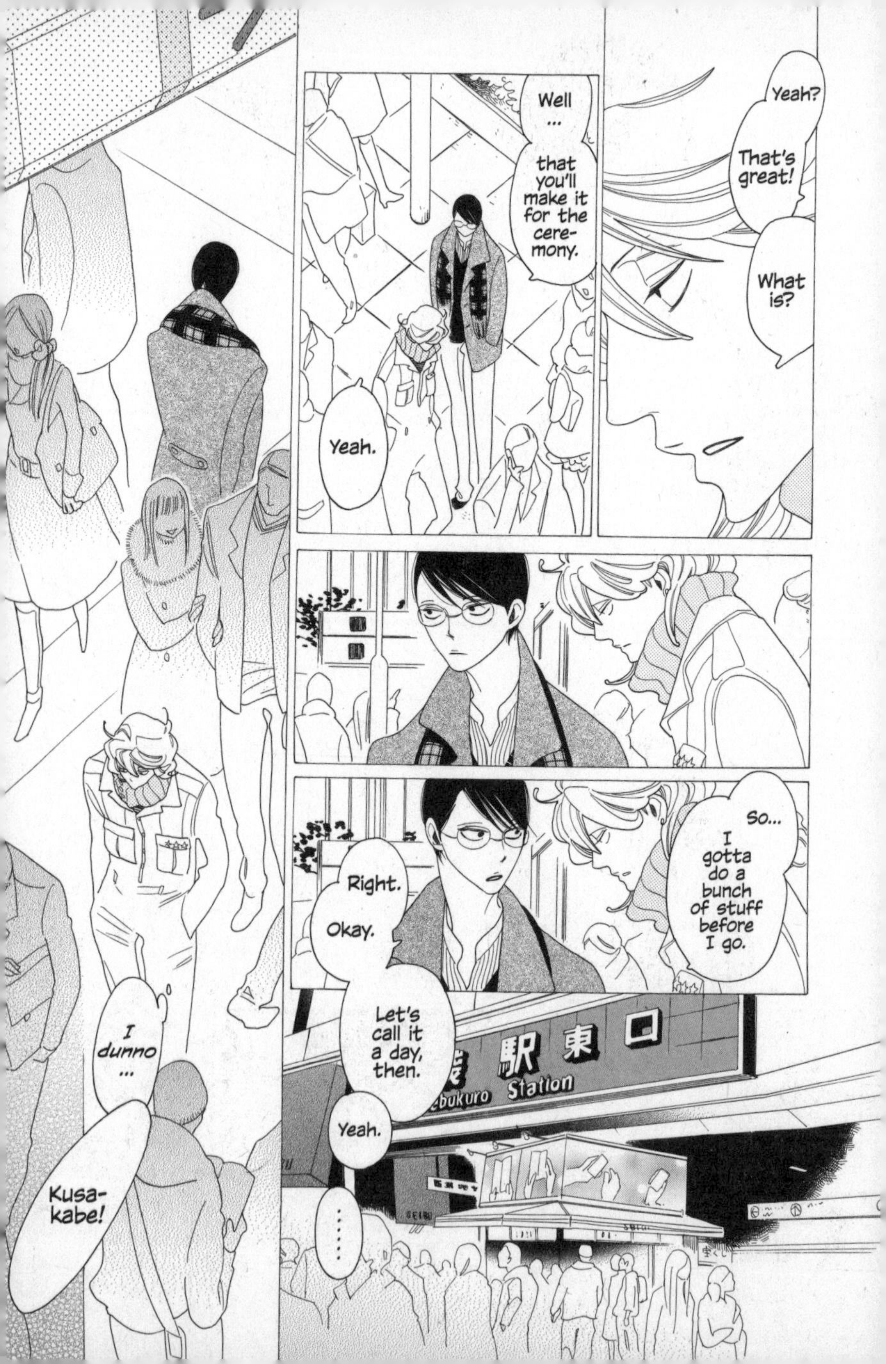
Yeah?
That's great!
What is?
Well ...
that you'll make it for the ceremony.
Yeah.
So... I gotta do a bunch of stuff before I go.
Right.
Okay.
Let's call it a day, then.
Yeah.
......
駅東口
Station
I dunno ...
Kusa-kabe!

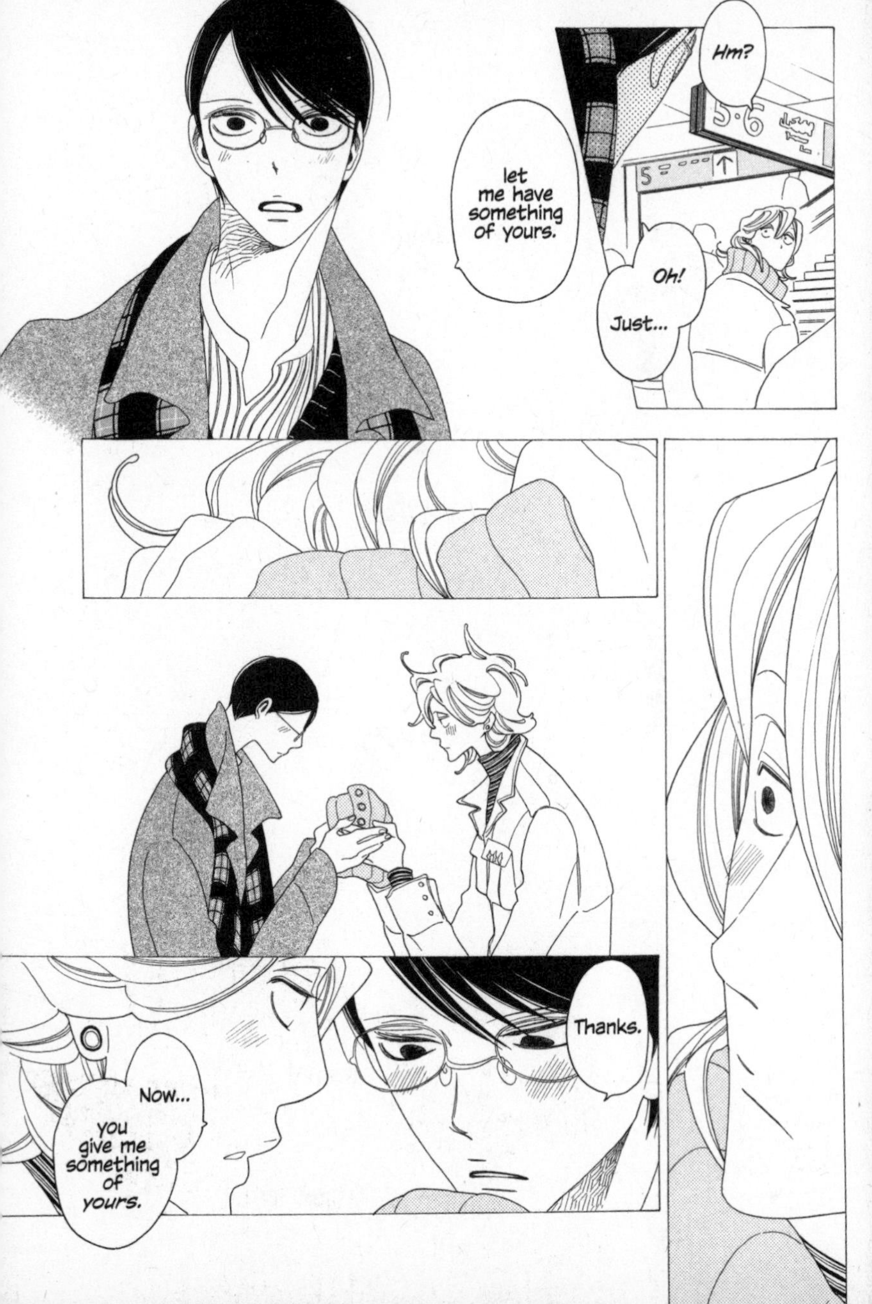
Hm?
Oh!
Just...
let me have something of yours.
Thanks.
Now... you give me something of yours.

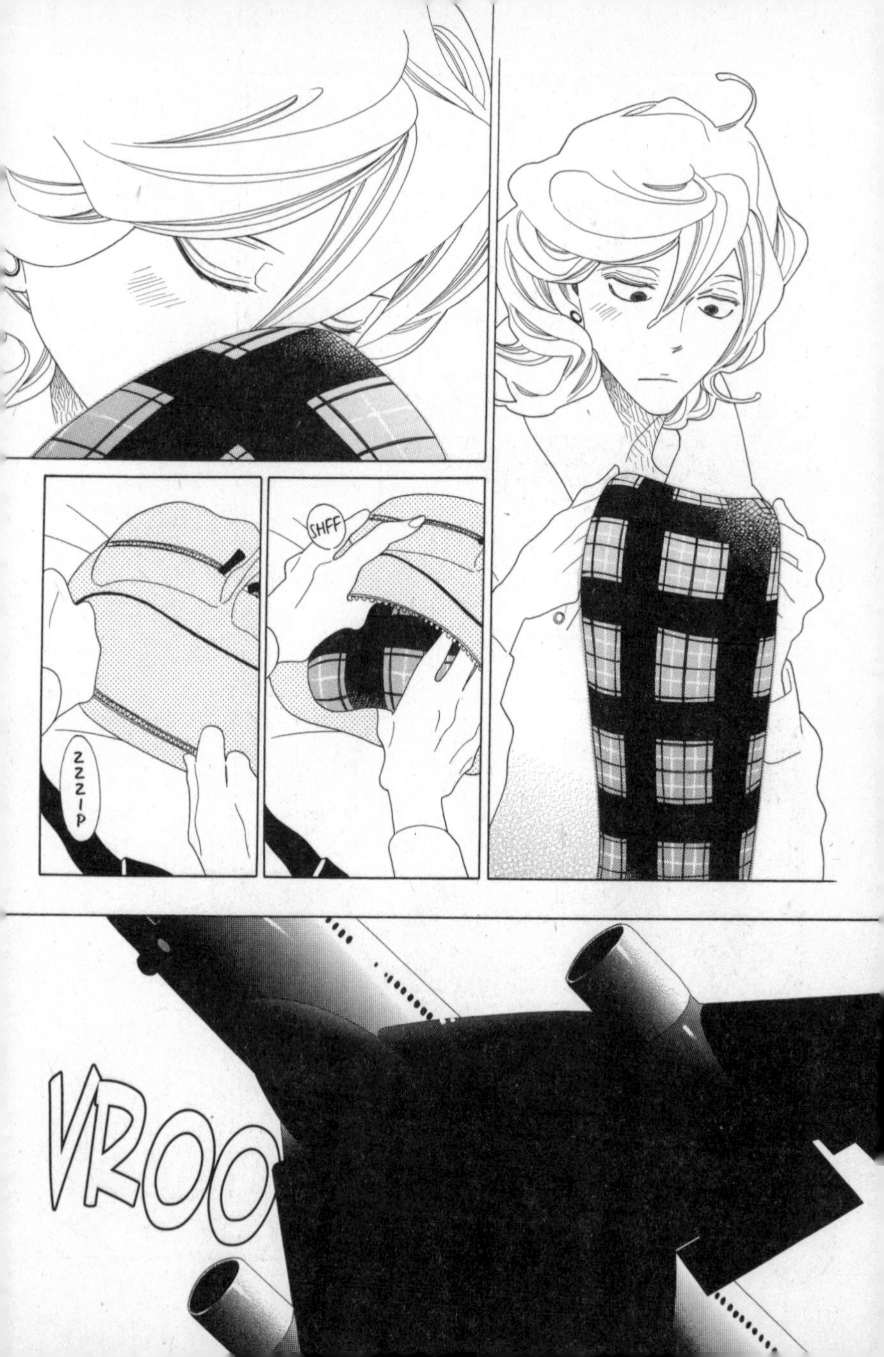
SHFF
ZZZIP
VROO

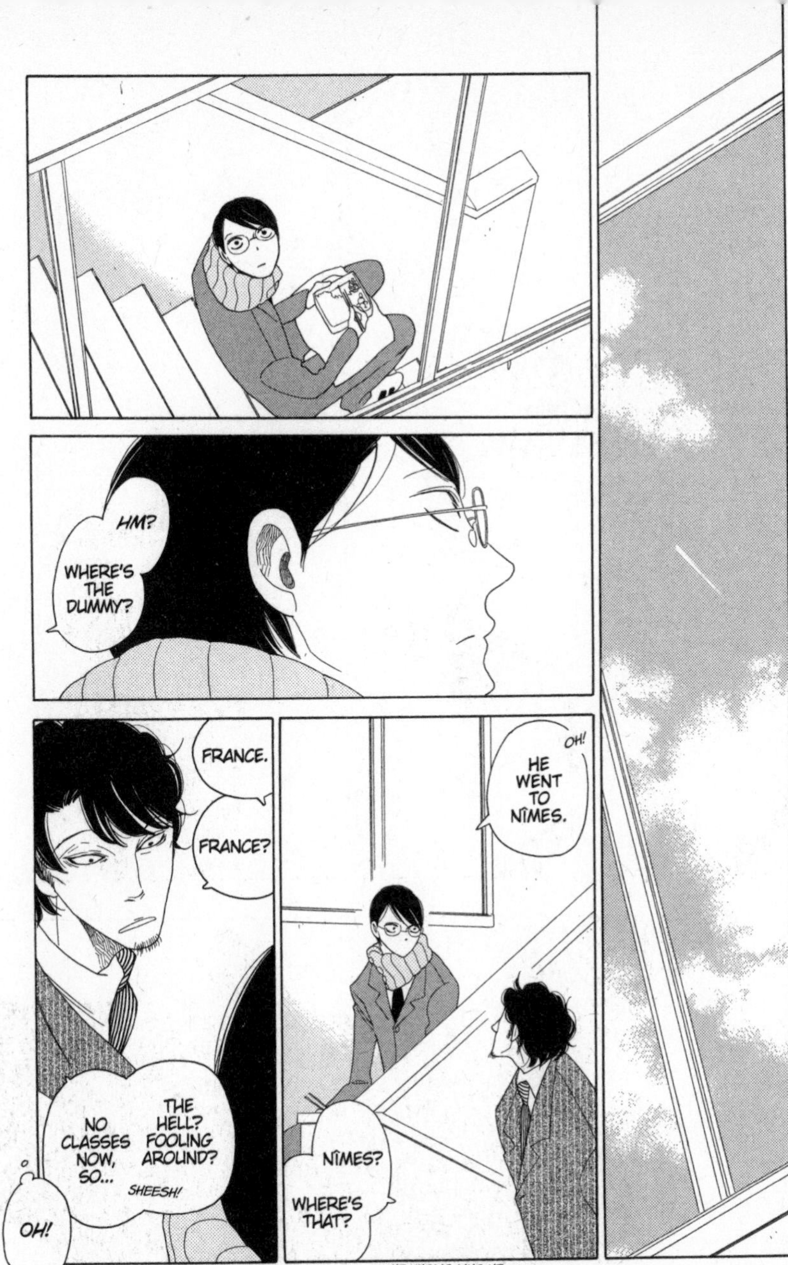
HM?
WHERE'S THE DUMMY?
OH!
HE WENT TO NÎMES.
NÎMES?
WHERE'S THAT?
FRANCE.
FRANCE?
THE HELL? FOOLING AROUND?
NO CLASSES NOW, SO...
SHEESH!
OH!

HE KNOWS WHO HE MEANT BY "THE DUMMY."

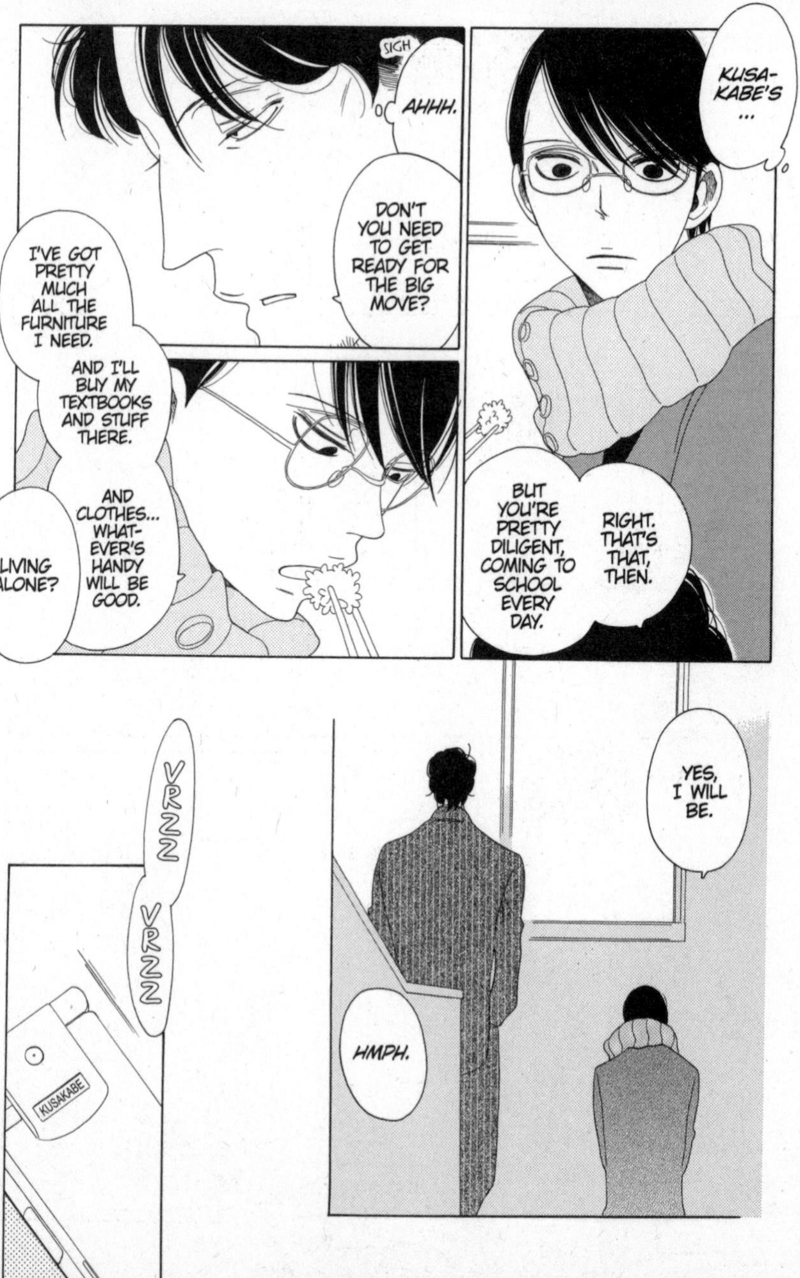
KUSA-KABE'S ...
RIGHT. THAT'S THAT, THEN.
BUT YOU'RE PRETTY DILIGENT, COMING TO SCHOOL EVERY DAY.
SIGH
AHHH.
DON'T YOU NEED TO GET READY FOR THE BIG MOVE?
I'VE GOT PRETTY MUCH ALL THE FURNITURE I NEED.
AND I'LL BUY MY TEXTBOOKS AND STUFF THERE.
AND CLOTHES... WHAT-EVER'S HANDY WILL BE GOOD.
LIVING ALONE?
YES, I WILL BE.
HMPH.
VRZZ
VRZZ
KUSAKABE

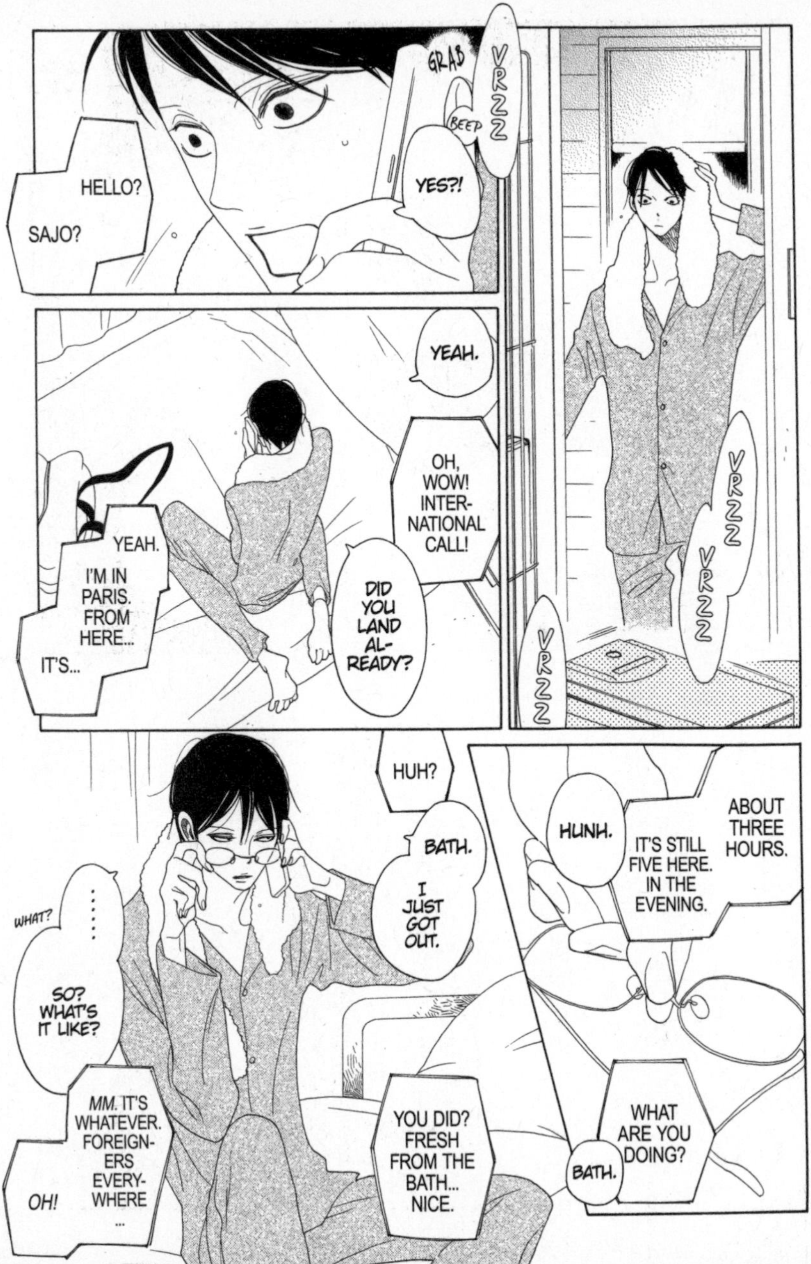
VRZZ
VRZZ
VRZZ
VRZZ
GRAB
BEEP
YES?!
HELLO?
SAJO?
YEAH.
OH, WOW! INTER-NATIONAL CALL!
DID YOU LAND AL-READY?
YEAH. I'M IN PARIS. FROM HERE... IT'S...
ABOUT THREE HOURS.
IT'S STILL FIVE HERE. IN THE EVENING.
HUNH.
WHAT ARE YOU DOING?
BATH.
HUH?
BATH. I JUST GOT OUT.
......
WHAT?
SO? WHAT'S IT LIKE?
YOU DID? FRESH FROM THE BATH... NICE.
MM. IT'S WHATEVER. FOREIGN-ERS EVERY-WHERE ...
OH!

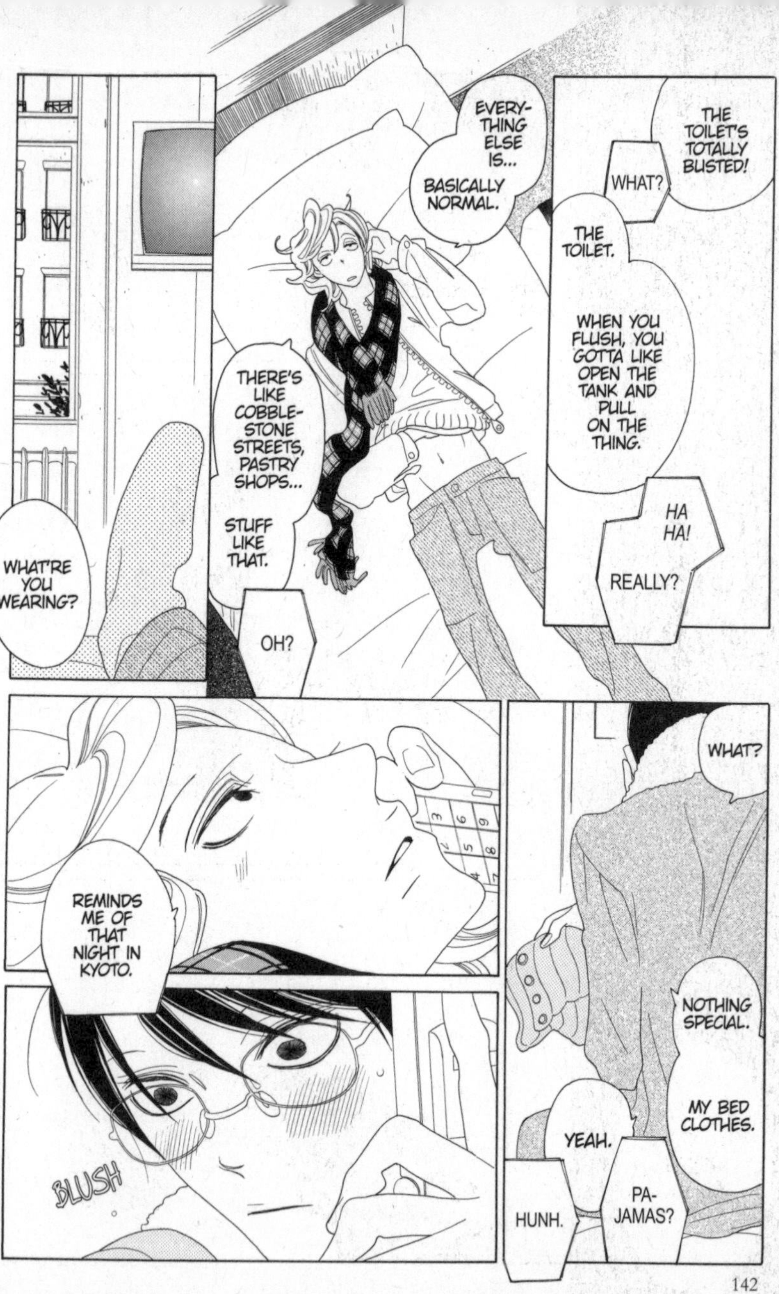
THE TOILET'S TOTALLY BUSTED!
WHAT?
THE TOILET.
WHEN YOU FLUSH, YOU GOTTA LIKE OPEN THE TANK AND PULL ON THE THING.
HA HA!
REALLY?
EVERY-THING ELSE IS...
BASICALLY NORMAL.
THERE'S LIKE COBBLE-STONE STREETS, PASTRY SHOPS...
STUFF LIKE THAT.
OH?
WHAT'RE YOU WEARING?
WHAT?
NOTHING SPECIAL.
MY BED CLOTHES.
PA-JAMAS?
YEAH.
HUNH.
REMINDS ME OF THAT NIGHT IN KYOTO.
BLUSH

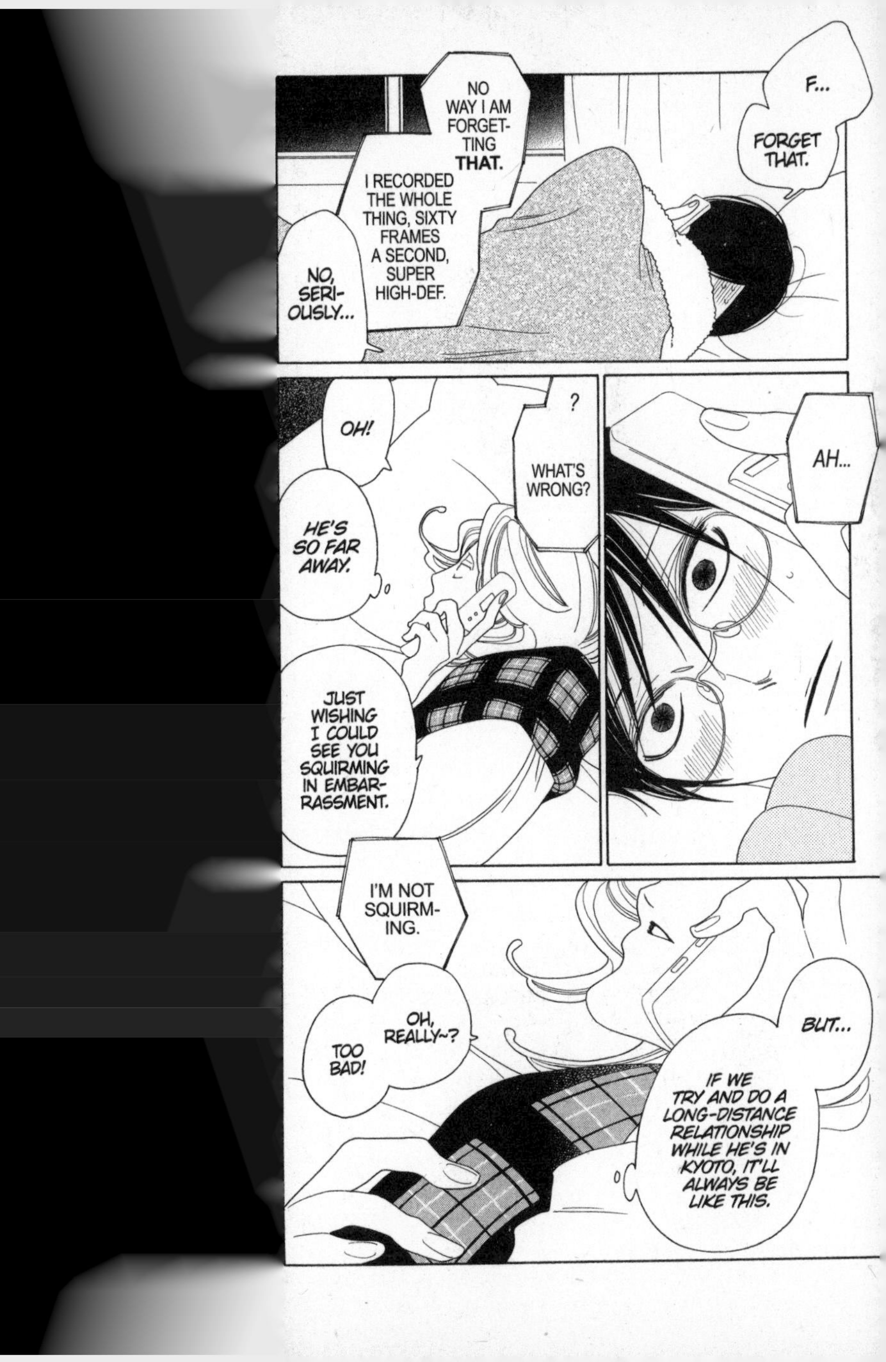
F...
FORGET THAT.
NO WAY I AM FORGETTING **THAT.**
I RECORDED THE WHOLE THING, SIXTY FRAMES A SECOND, SUPER HIGH-DEF.
NO, SERIOUSLY...
AH...
?
WHAT'S WRONG?
OH!
HE'S SO FAR AWAY.
JUST WISHING I COULD SEE YOU SQUIRMING IN EMBARRASSMENT.
I'M NOT SQUIRMING.
OH, REALLY~?
TOO BAD!
BUT...
IF WE TRY AND DO A LONG-DISTANCE RELATIONSHIP WHILE HE'S IN KYOTO, IT'LL ALWAYS BE LIKE THIS.

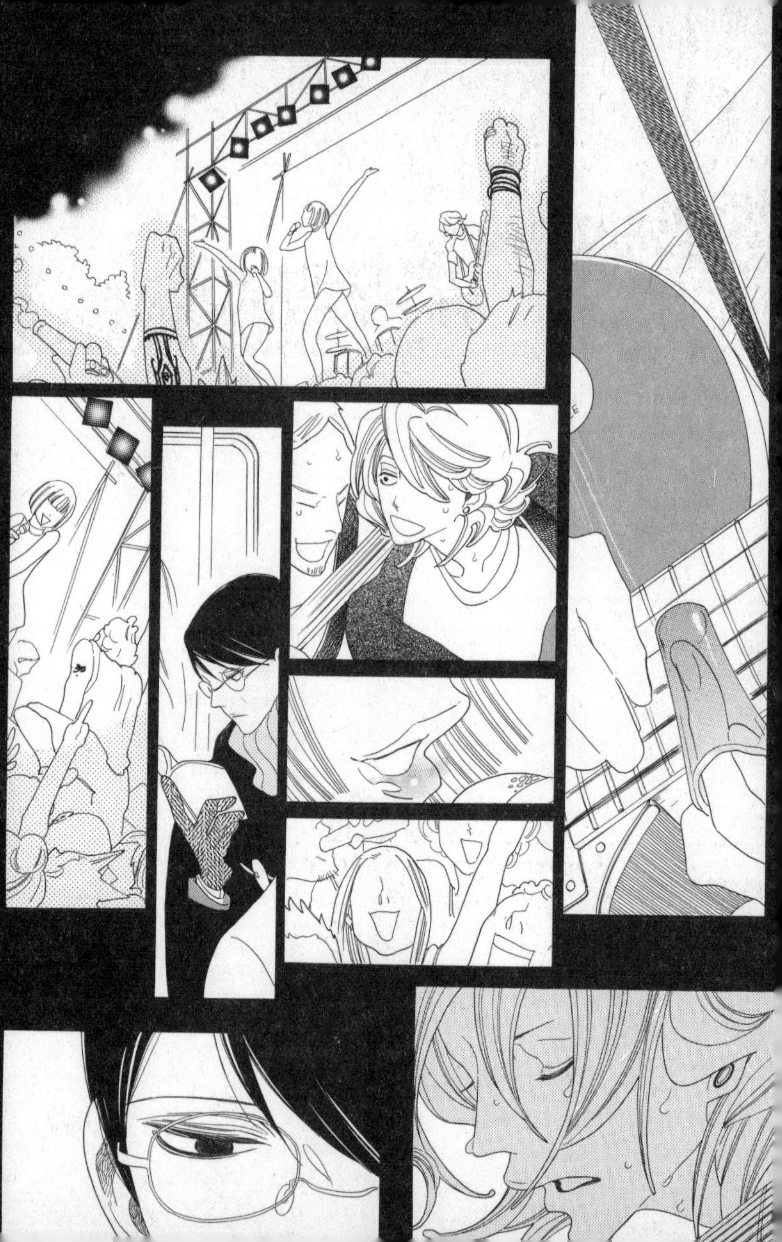

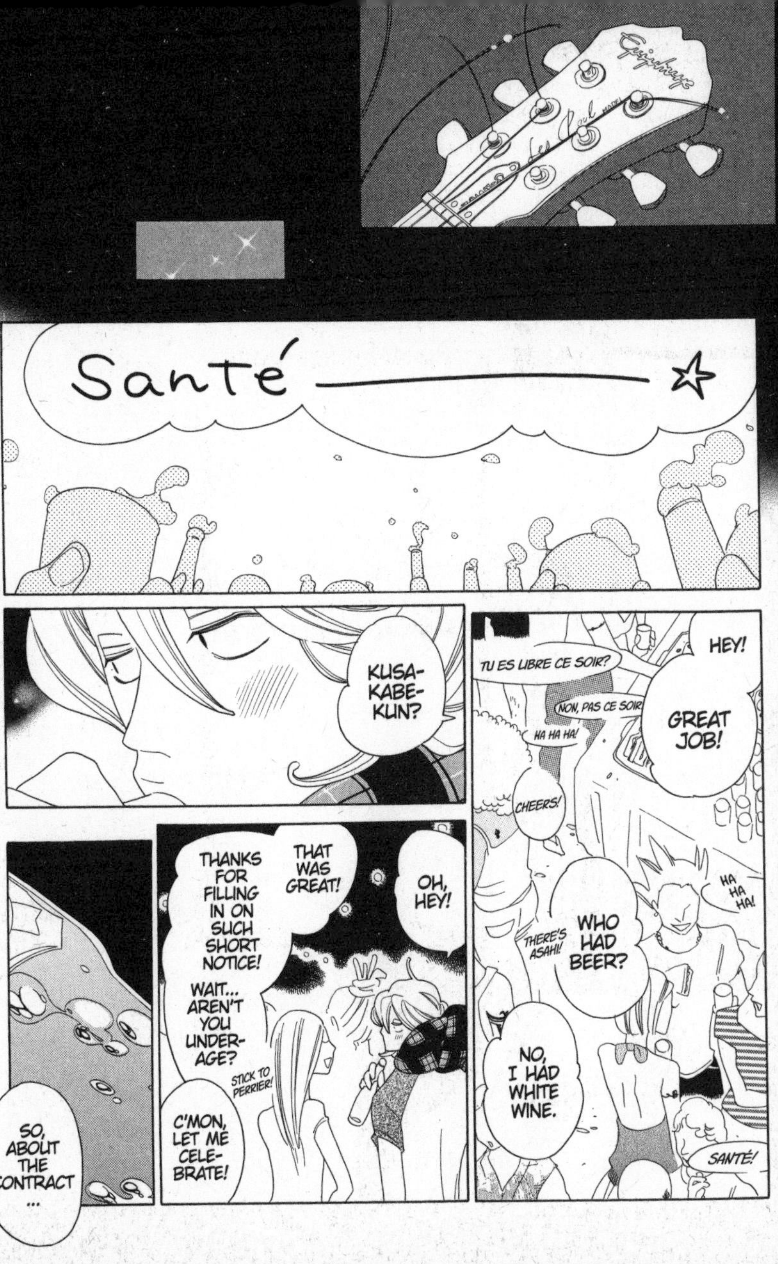
Santé
HEY! GREAT JOB!
TU ES LIBRE CE SOIR?
NON, PAS CE SOIR
HA HA HA!
CHEERS!
HA HA HA!
WHO HAD BEER?
THERE'S ASAHI!
NO, I HAD WHITE WINE.
SANTÉ!
KUSA-KABE-KUN?
OH, HEY!
THAT WAS GREAT!
THANKS FOR FILLING IN ON SUCH SHORT NOTICE!
WAIT... AREN'T YOU UNDER-AGE?
STICK TO PERRIER!
C'MON, LET ME CELE-BRATE!
SO, ABOUT THE CONTRACT...

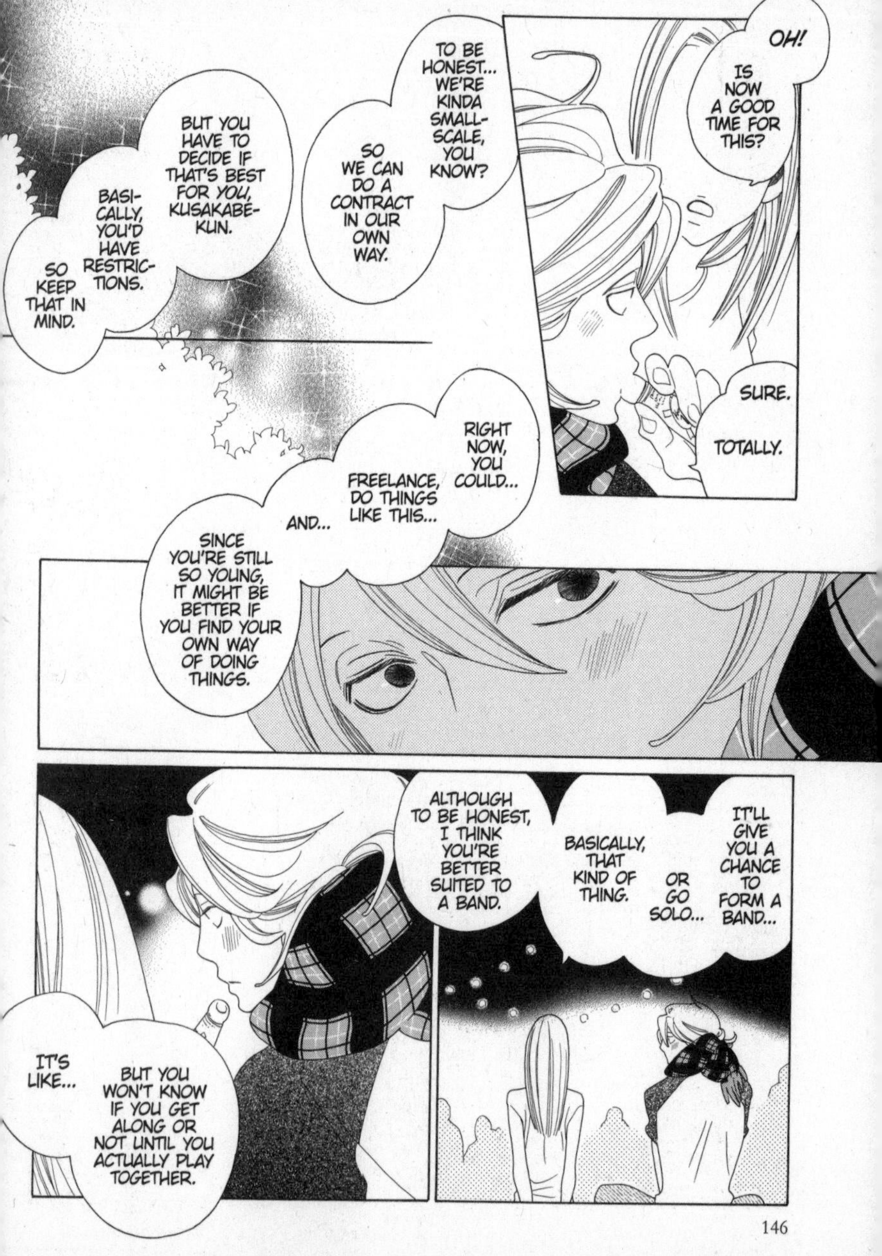
OH!
IS NOW A GOOD TIME FOR THIS?
SURE.
TOTALLY.
TO BE HONEST... WE'RE KINDA SMALL-SCALE, YOU KNOW?
SO WE CAN DO A CONTRACT IN OUR OWN WAY.
BUT YOU HAVE TO DECIDE IF THAT'S BEST FOR *YOU*, KUSAKABE-KUN.
BASICALLY, YOU'D HAVE RESTRICTIONS.
SO KEEP THAT IN MIND.
RIGHT NOW, YOU COULD...
FREELANCE, DO THINGS LIKE THIS...
AND...
SINCE YOU'RE STILL SO YOUNG, IT MIGHT BE BETTER IF YOU FIND YOUR OWN WAY OF DOING THINGS.
IT'LL GIVE YOU A CHANCE TO FORM A BAND...
OR GO SOLO...
BASICALLY, THAT KIND OF THING.
ALTHOUGH TO BE HONEST, I THINK YOU'RE BETTER SUITED TO A BAND.
BUT YOU WON'T KNOW IF YOU GET ALONG OR NOT UNTIL YOU ACTUALLY PLAY TOGETHER.
IT'S LIKE...

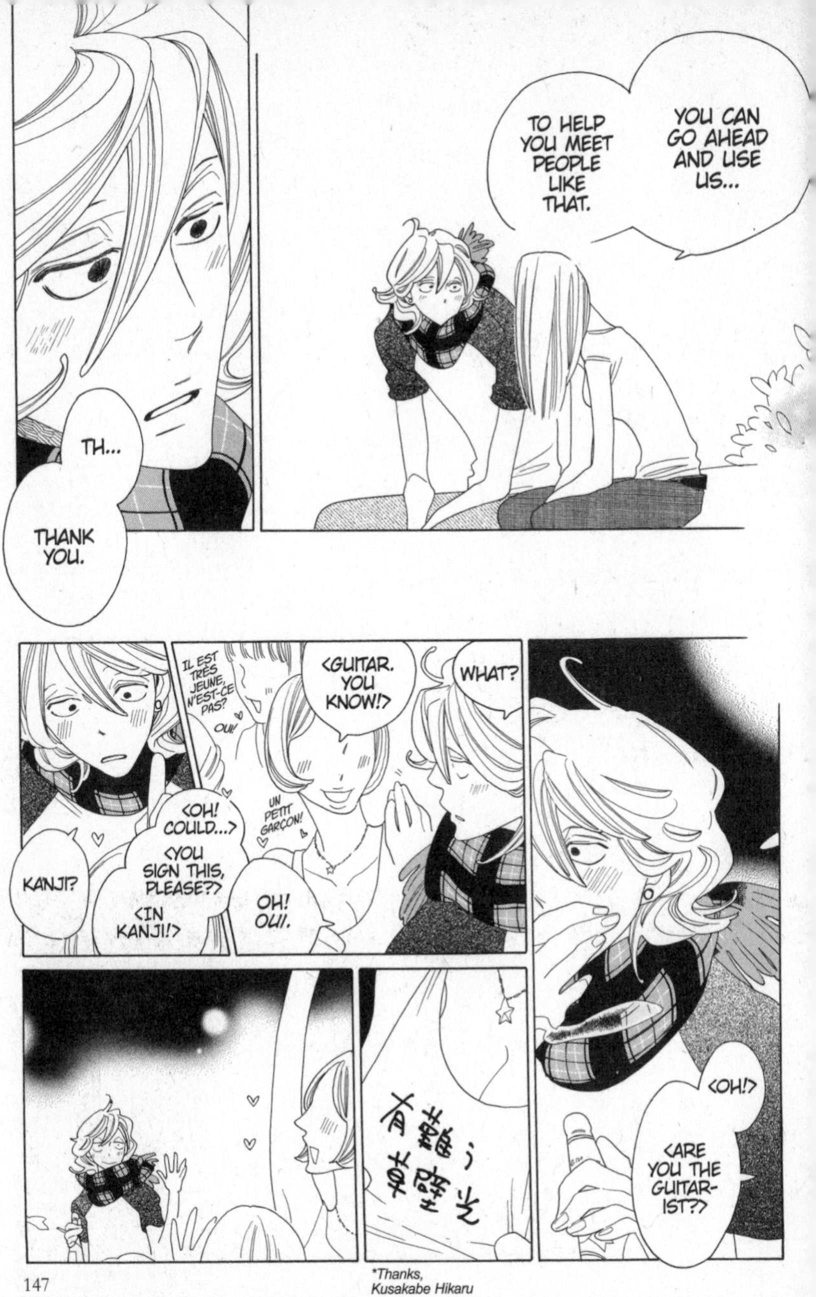
YOU CAN GO AHEAD AND USE US...
TO HELP YOU MEET PEOPLE LIKE THAT.
TH...
THANK YOU.
<OH!>
<ARE YOU THE GUITAR-IST?>
WHAT?
<GUITAR. YOU KNOW!>
IL EST TRÈS JEUNE, N'EST-CE PAS?
OUI!
UN PETIT GARÇON!
OH! OUI.
<OH! COULD...>
<YOU SIGN THIS, PLEASE?>
<IN KANJI!>
KANJI?
有難う 草壁光

*Thanks, Kusakabe Hikaru

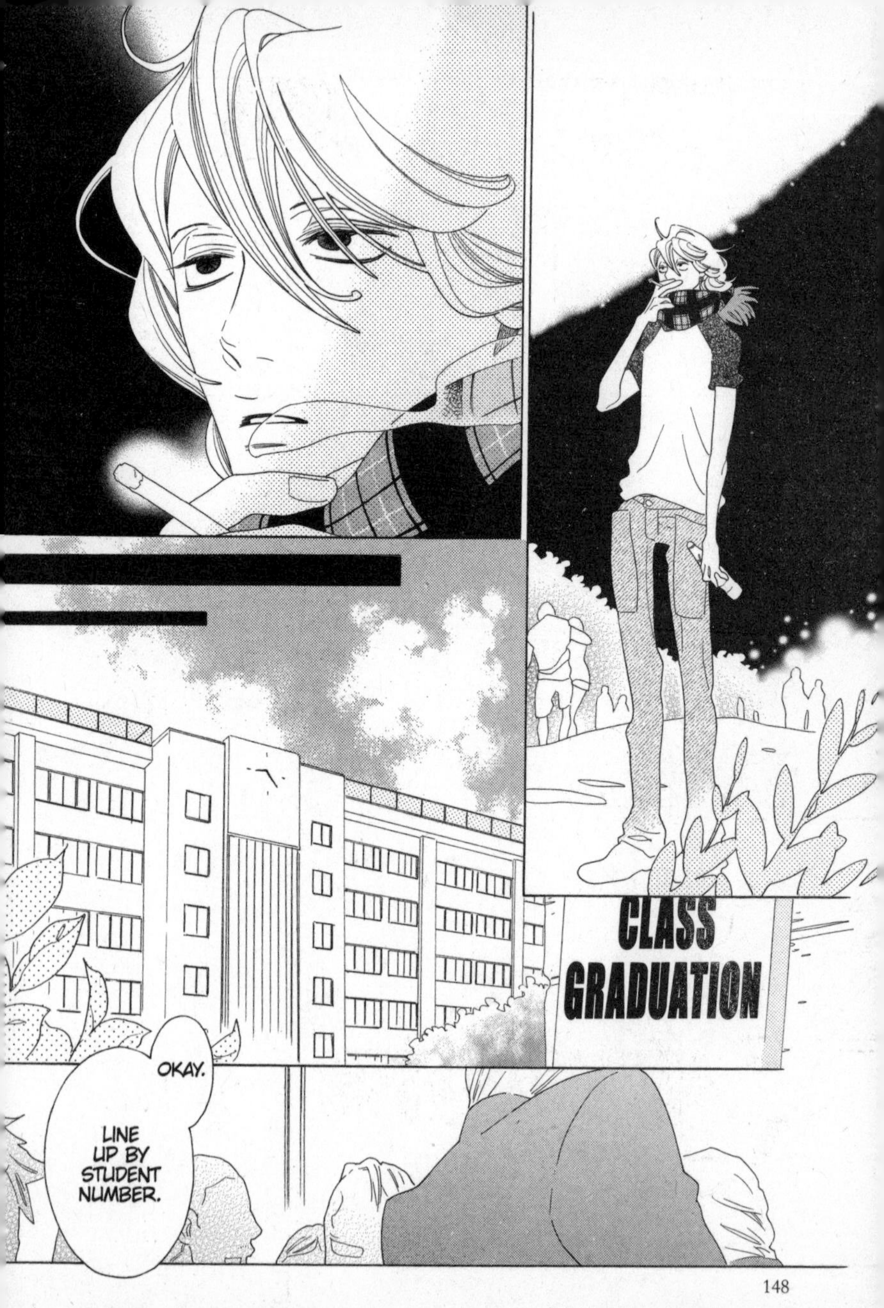
CLASS
GRADUATION
[redacted]
OKAY.
LINE UP BY STUDENT NUMBER.

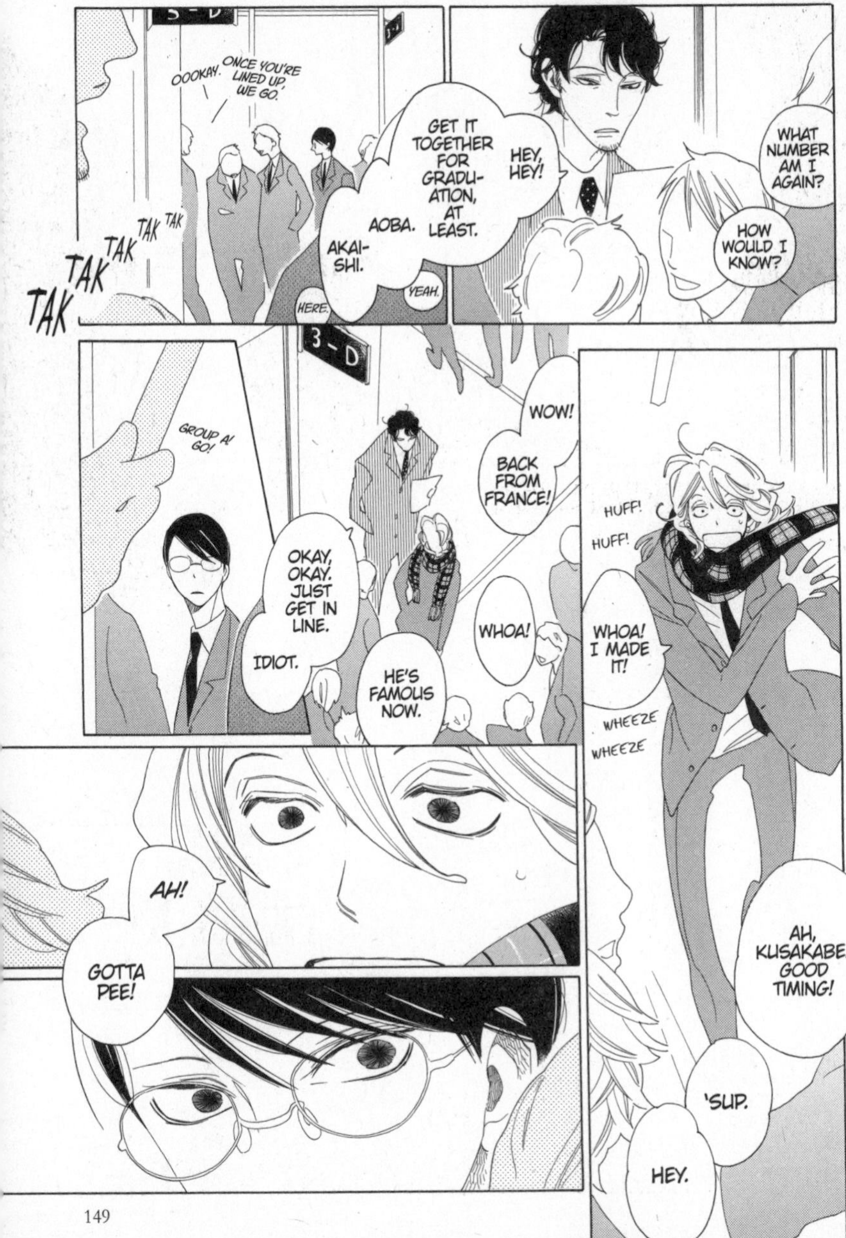
WHAT NUMBER AM I AGAIN?
HOW WOULD I KNOW?
HEY, HEY!
GET IT TOGETHER FOR GRADUATION, AT LEAST.
AOBA.
AKAI-SHI.
YEAH.
HERE.
ONCE YOU'RE LINED UP WE GO.
OOOKAY.
TAK TAK
TAK TAK
TAK
3-D
HUFF!
HUFF!
WHOA! I MADE IT!
WHEEZE
WHEEZE
AH, KUSAKABE! GOOD TIMING!
'SUP.
HEY.
WOW!
BACK FROM FRANCE!
WHOA!
HE'S FAMOUS NOW.
OKAY, OKAY. JUST GET IN LINE.
IDIOT.
GROUP A! GO!
AH!
GOTTA PEE!

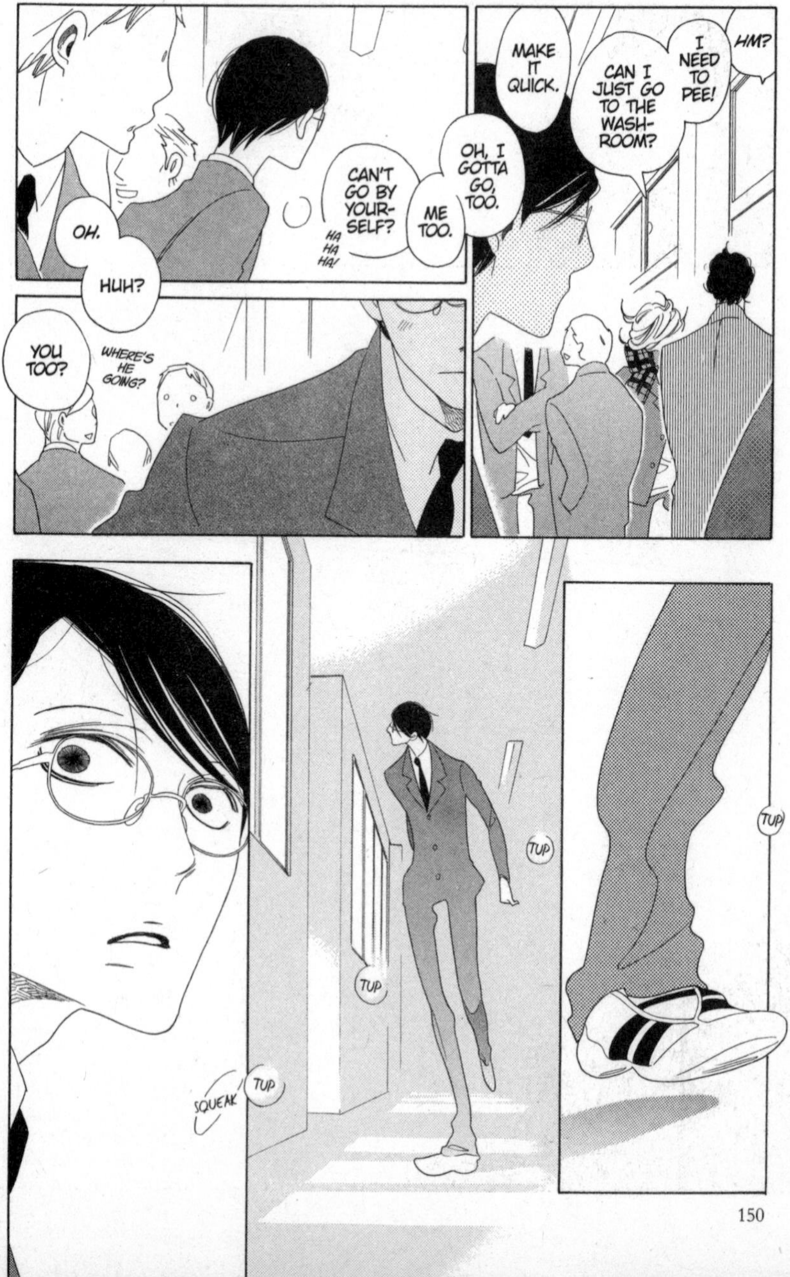
HM?
I NEED TO PEE!
CAN I JUST GO TO THE WASH-ROOM?
MAKE IT QUICK.
OH, I GOTTA GO, TOO.
ME TOO.
CAN'T GO BY YOUR-SELF?
HA HA HA!
OH.
HUH?
YOU TOO?
WHERE'S HE GOING?
TUP
TUP
TUP
TUP
SQUEAK

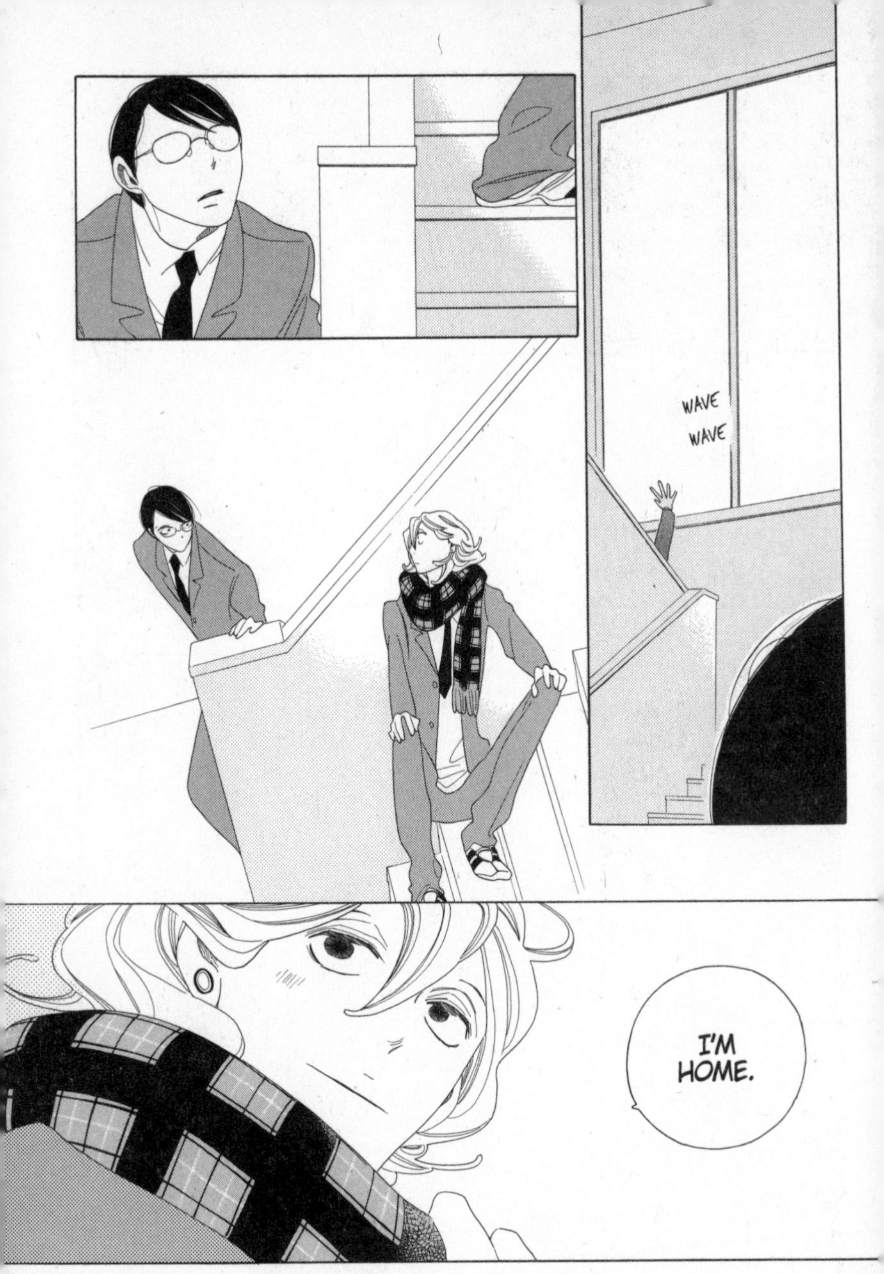
WAVE
WAVE
I'M HOME.

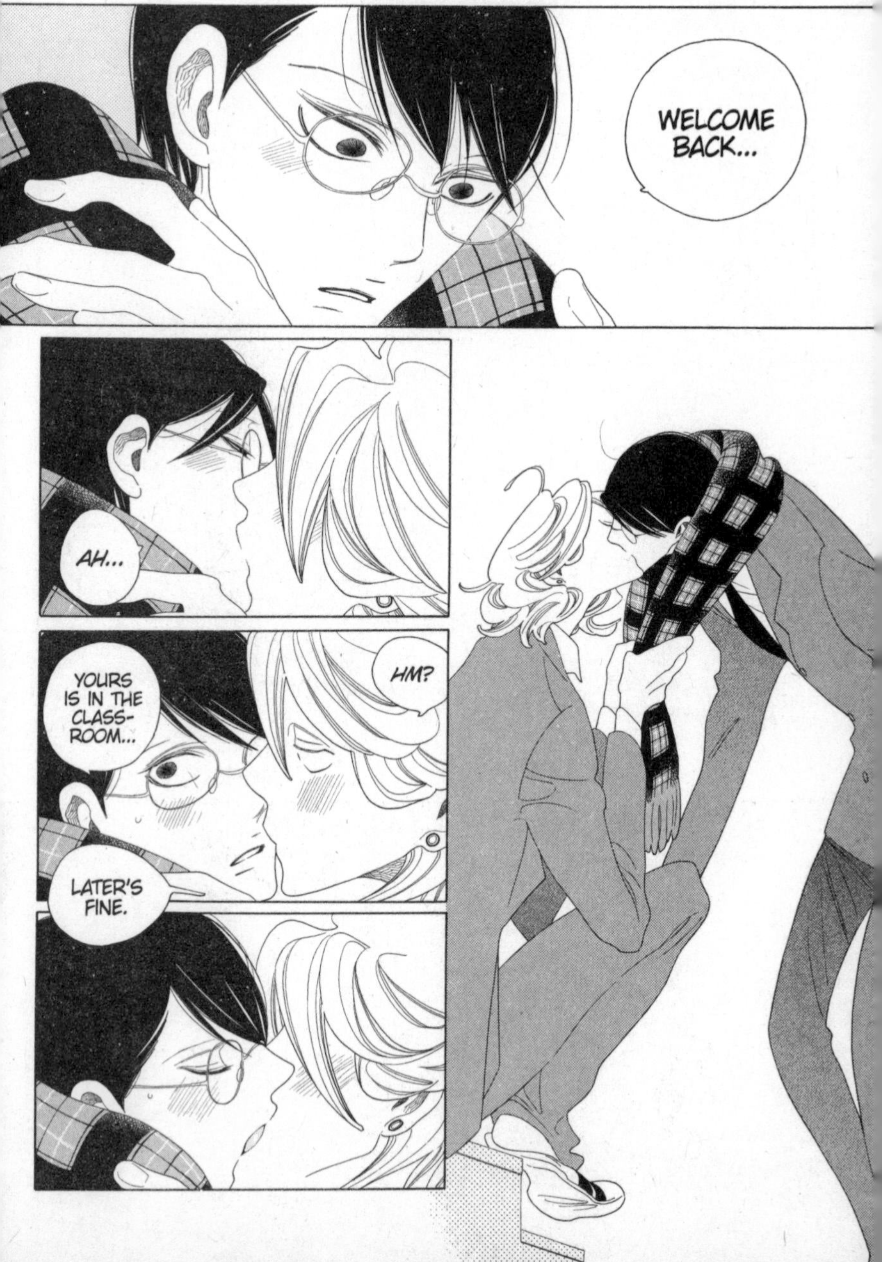
WELCOME BACK...
AH...
HM?
YOURS IS IN THE CLASS-ROOM...
LATER'S FINE.

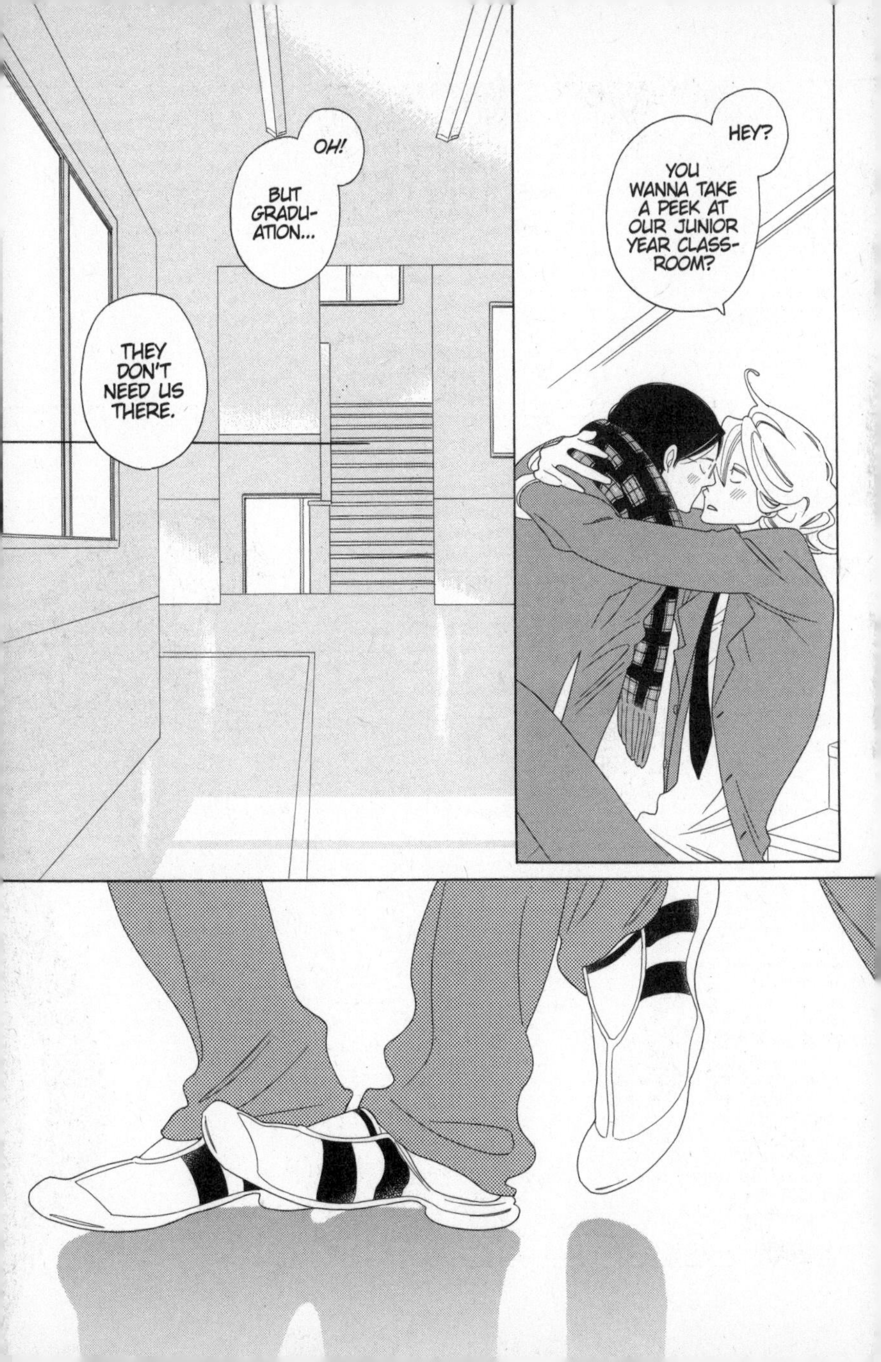
HEY?
YOU WANNA TAKE A PEEK AT OUR JUNIOR YEAR CLASSROOM?
OH!
BUT GRADUATION...
THEY DON'T NEED US THERE.

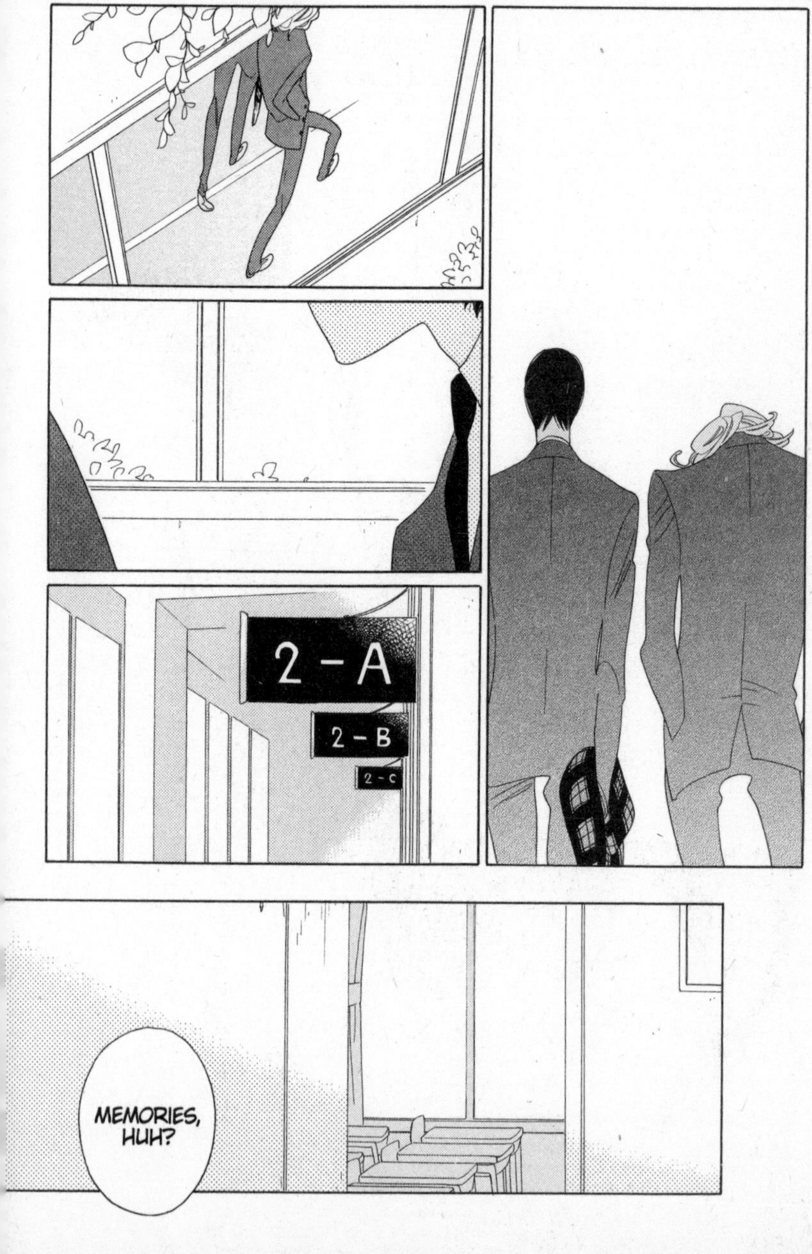
2 - A
2 - B
2 - C
MEMORIES, HUH?

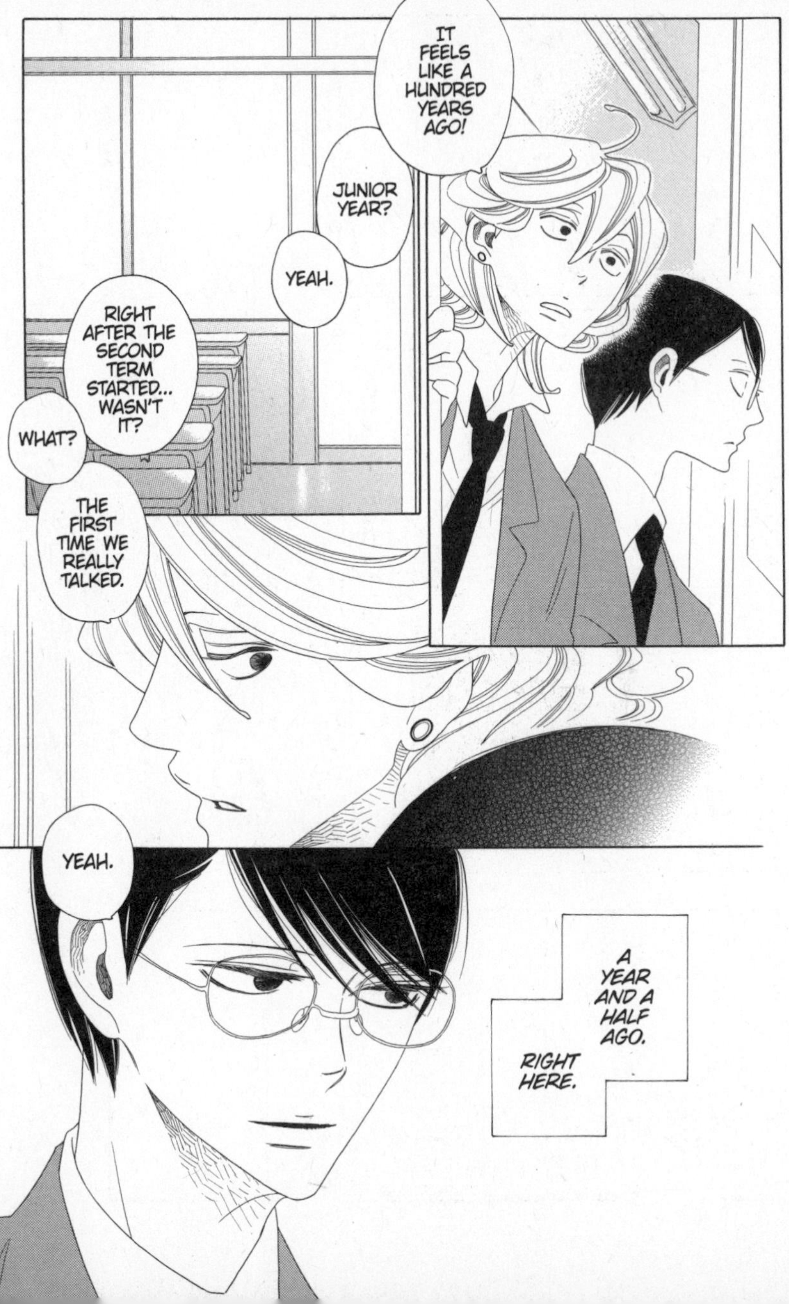
IT FEELS LIKE A HUNDRED YEARS AGO!
JUNIOR YEAR?
YEAH.
RIGHT AFTER THE SECOND TERM STARTED... WASN'T IT?
WHAT?
THE FIRST TIME WE REALLY TALKED.
YEAH.
A YEAR AND A HALF AGO.
RIGHT HERE.

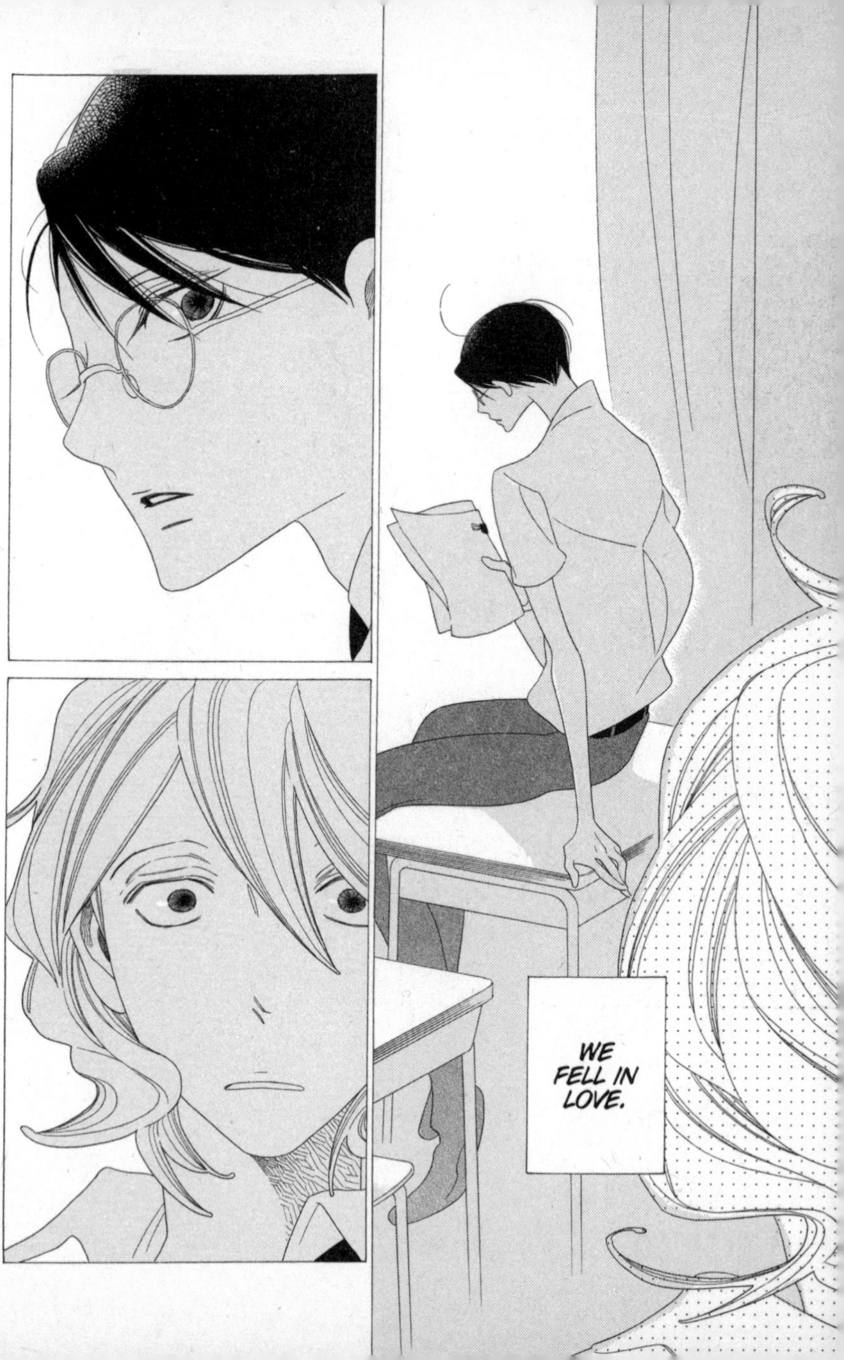
WE FELL IN LOVE.

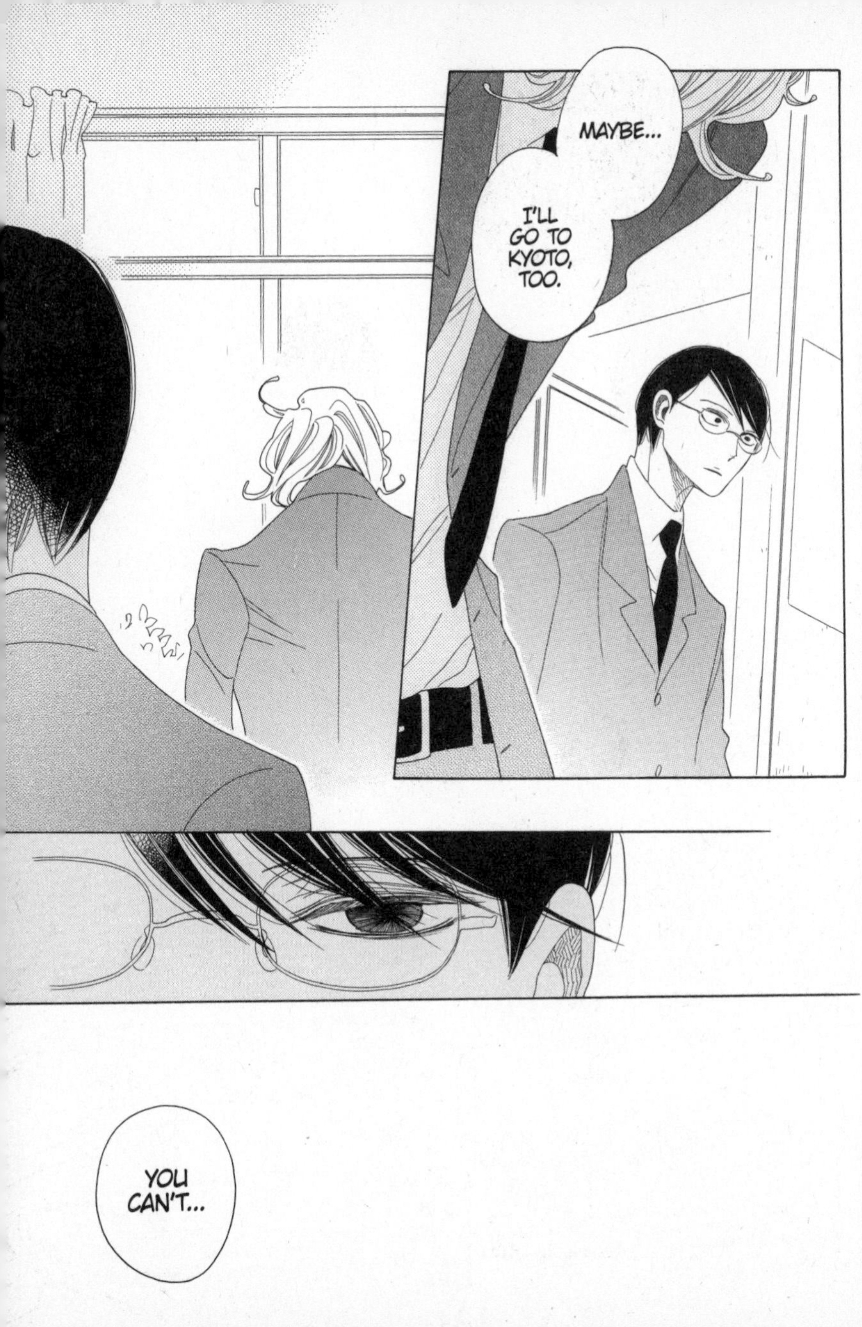
MAYBE...
I'LL GO TO KYOTO, TOO.
YOU CAN'T...

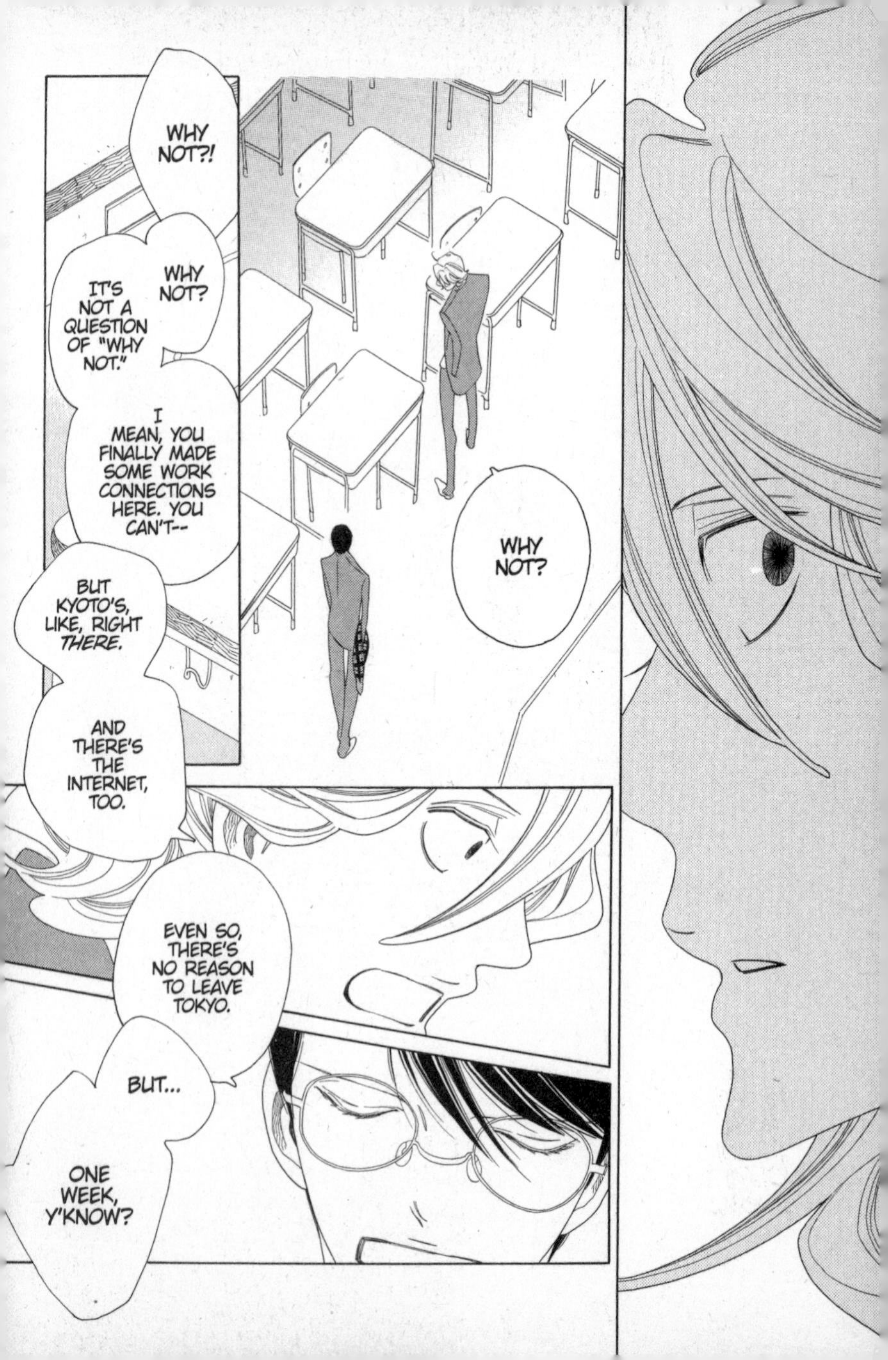

WHY NOT?!
WHY NOT? IT'S NOT A QUESTION OF "WHY NOT."
I MEAN, YOU FINALLY MADE SOME WORK CONNECTIONS HERE. YOU CAN'T--
WHY NOT?
BUT KYOTO'S, LIKE, RIGHT *THERE.*
AND THERE'S THE INTERNET, TOO.
EVEN SO, THERE'S NO REASON TO LEAVE TOKYO.
BUT...
ONE WEEK, Y'KNOW?

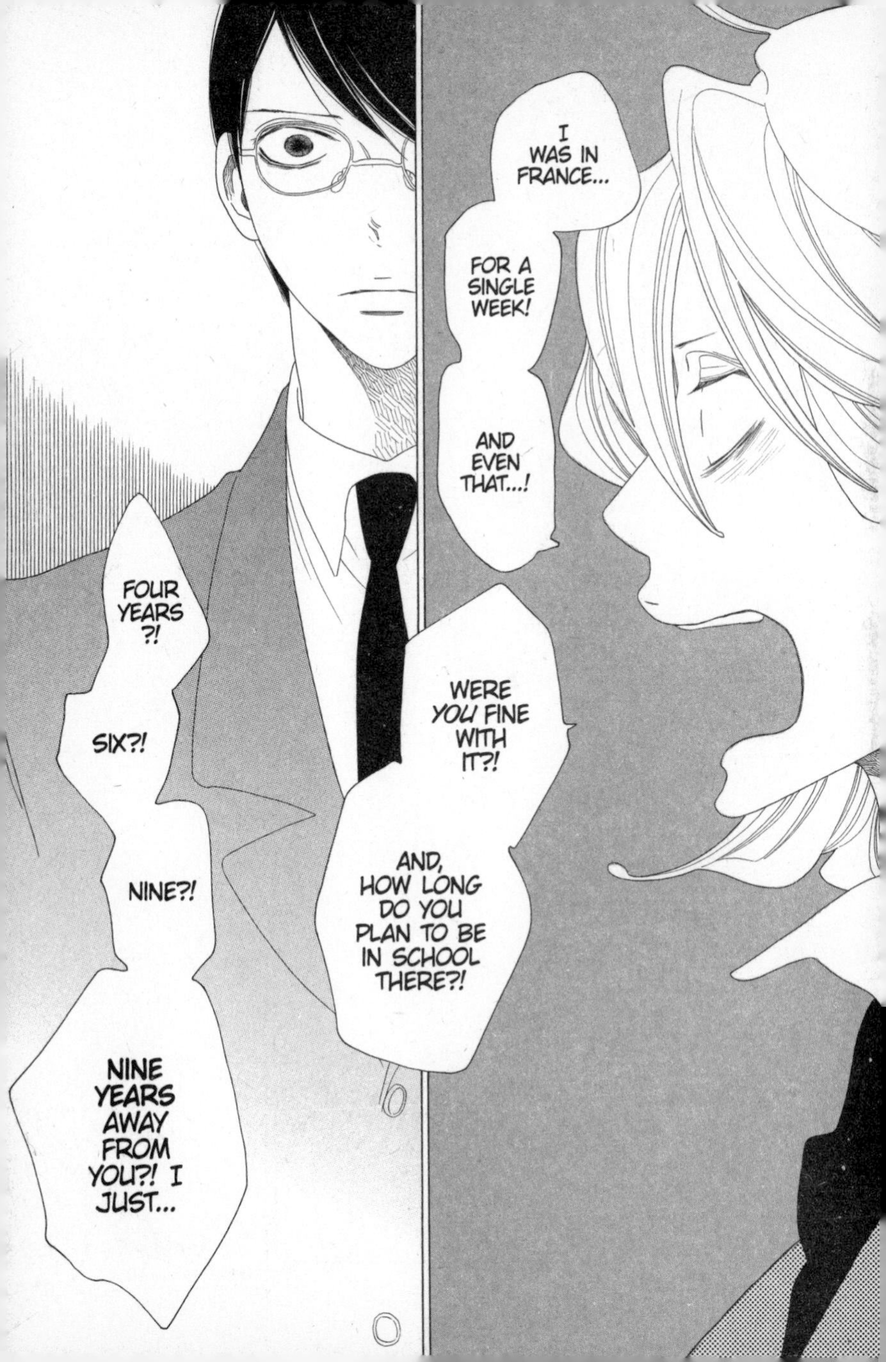
I WAS IN FRANCE...
FOR A SINGLE WEEK!
AND EVEN THAT...!
WERE *YOU* FINE WITH IT?!
AND, HOW LONG DO YOU PLAN TO BE IN SCHOOL THERE?!
FOUR YEARS ?!
SIX?!
NINE?!
NINE YEARS AWAY FROM YOU?! I JUST...

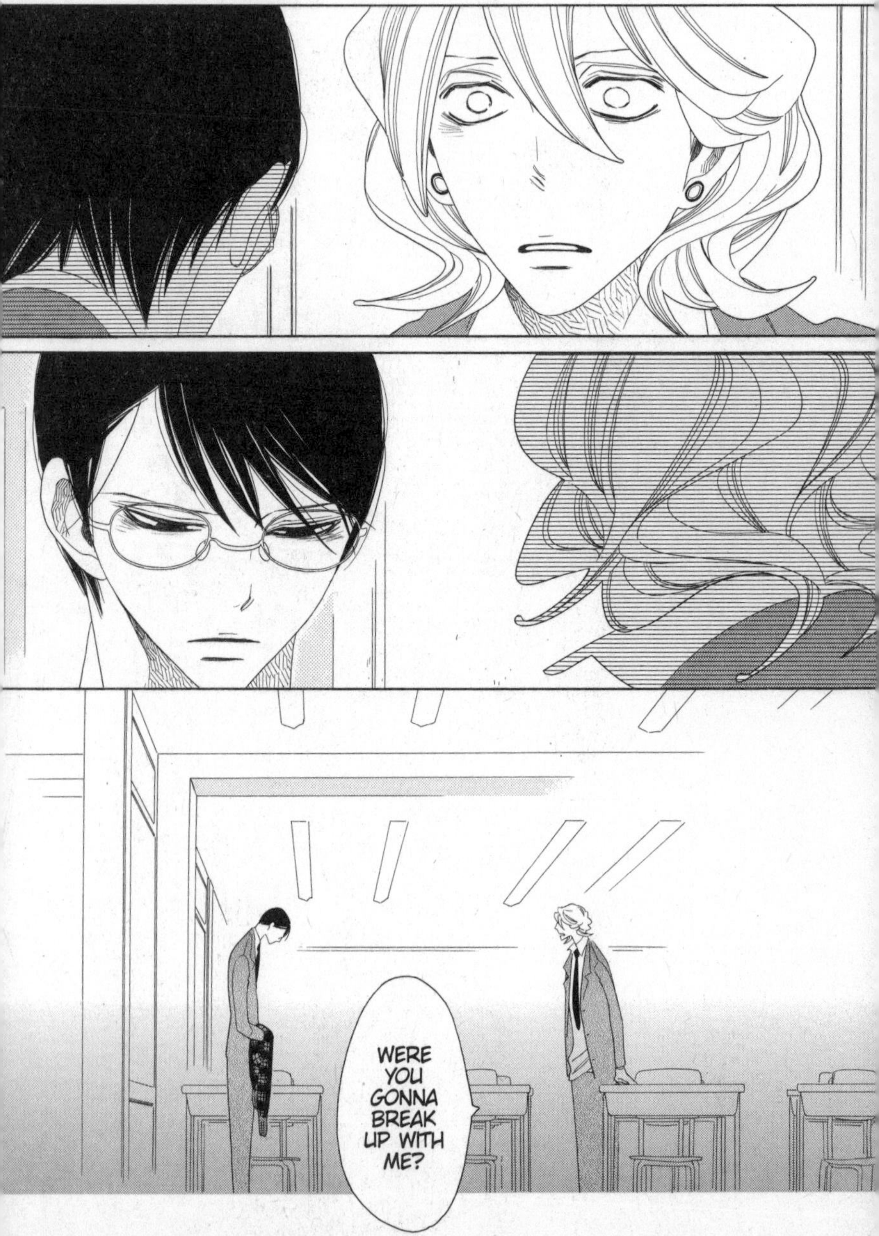
WERE YOU GONNA BREAK UP WITH ME?

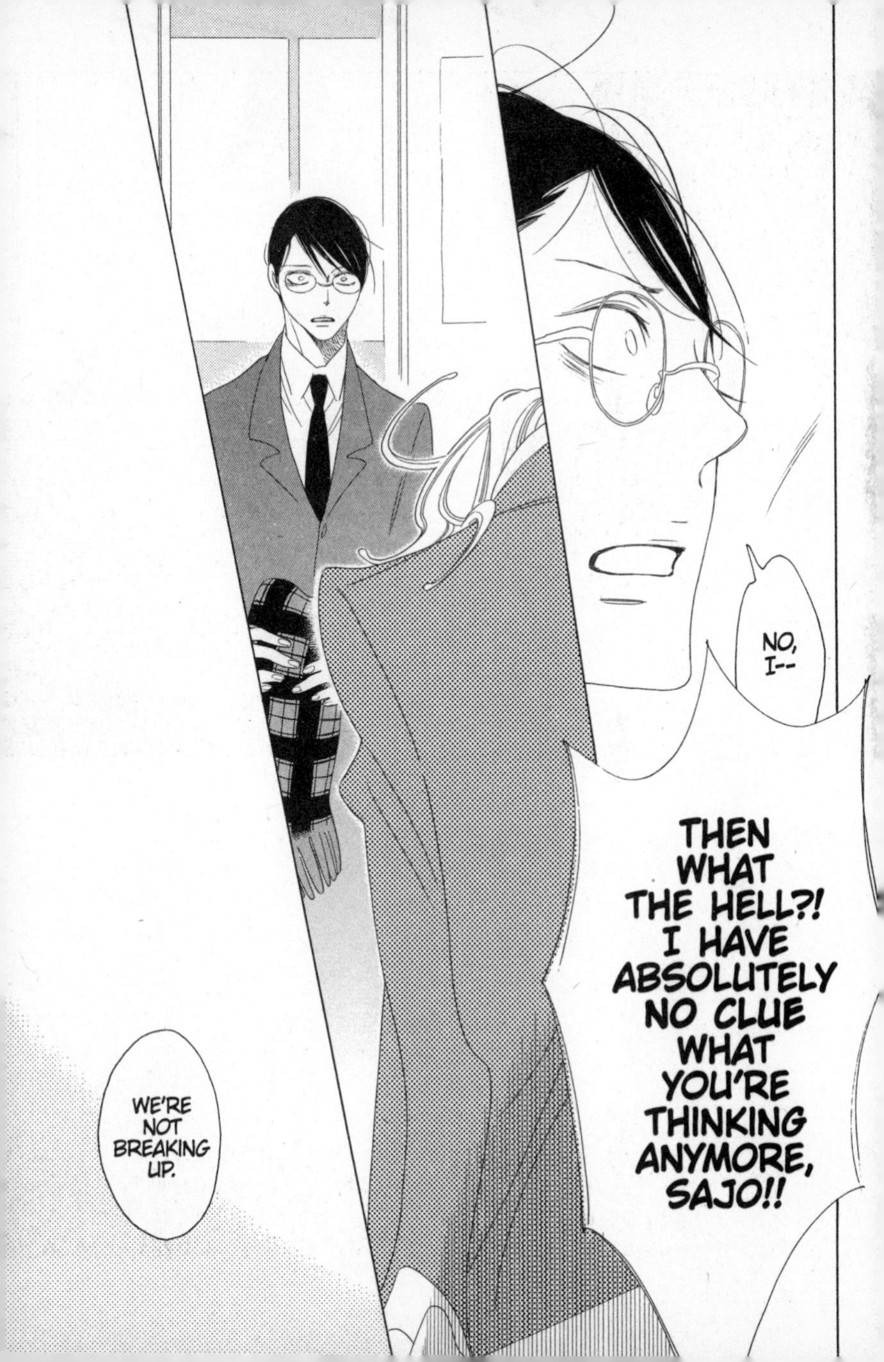
NO, I--
THEN WHAT THE HELL?! I HAVE ABSOLUTELY NO CLUE WHAT YOU'RE THINKING ANYMORE, SAJO!!
WE'RE NOT BREAKING UP.

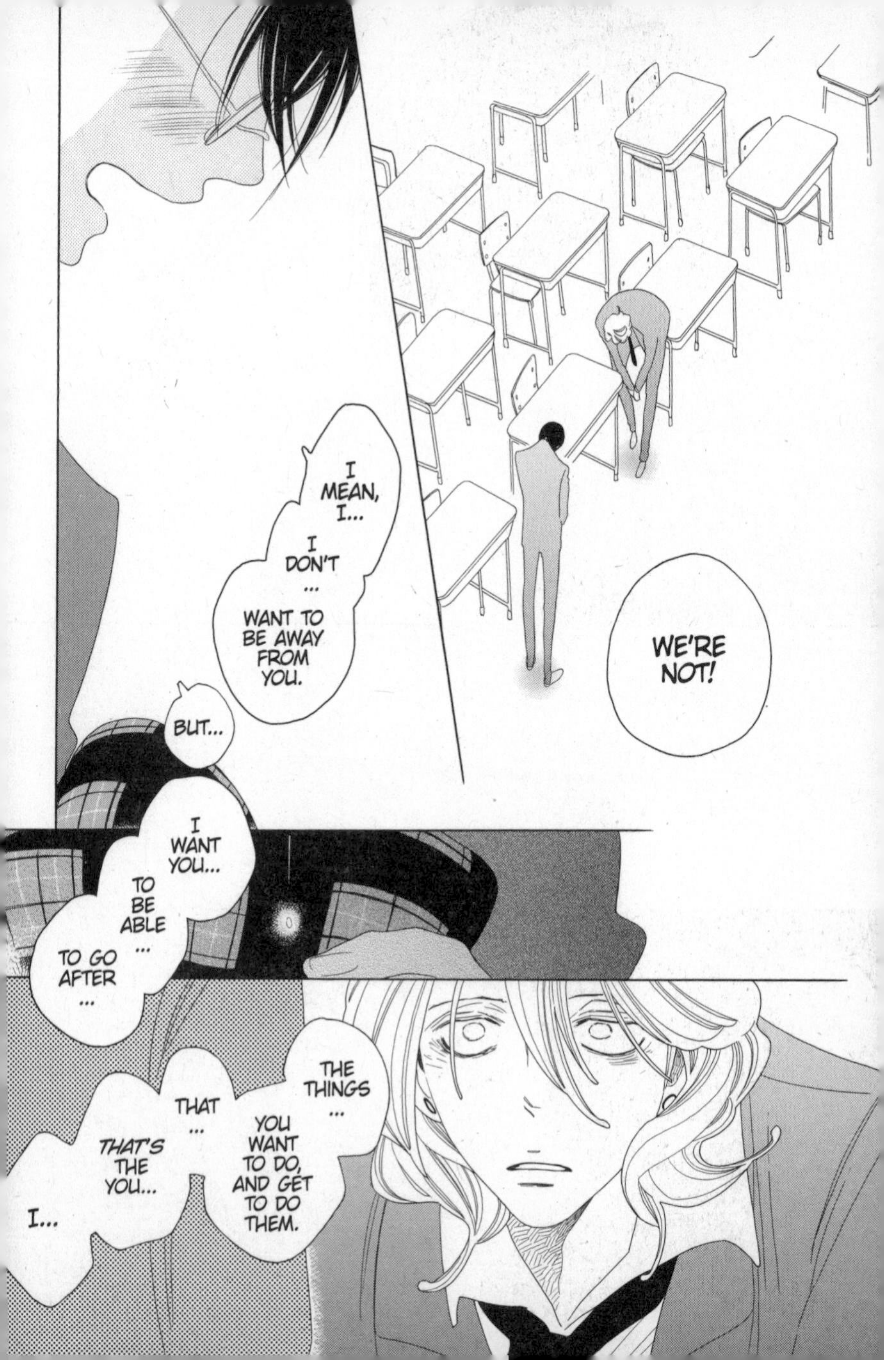
WE'RE NOT!
I MEAN, I...
I DON'T ...
WANT TO BE AWAY FROM YOU.
BUT...
I WANT YOU...
TO BE ABLE ...
TO GO AFTER ...
THE THINGS ...
YOU WANT TO DO, AND GET TO DO THEM.
THAT ...
THAT'S THE YOU...
I...

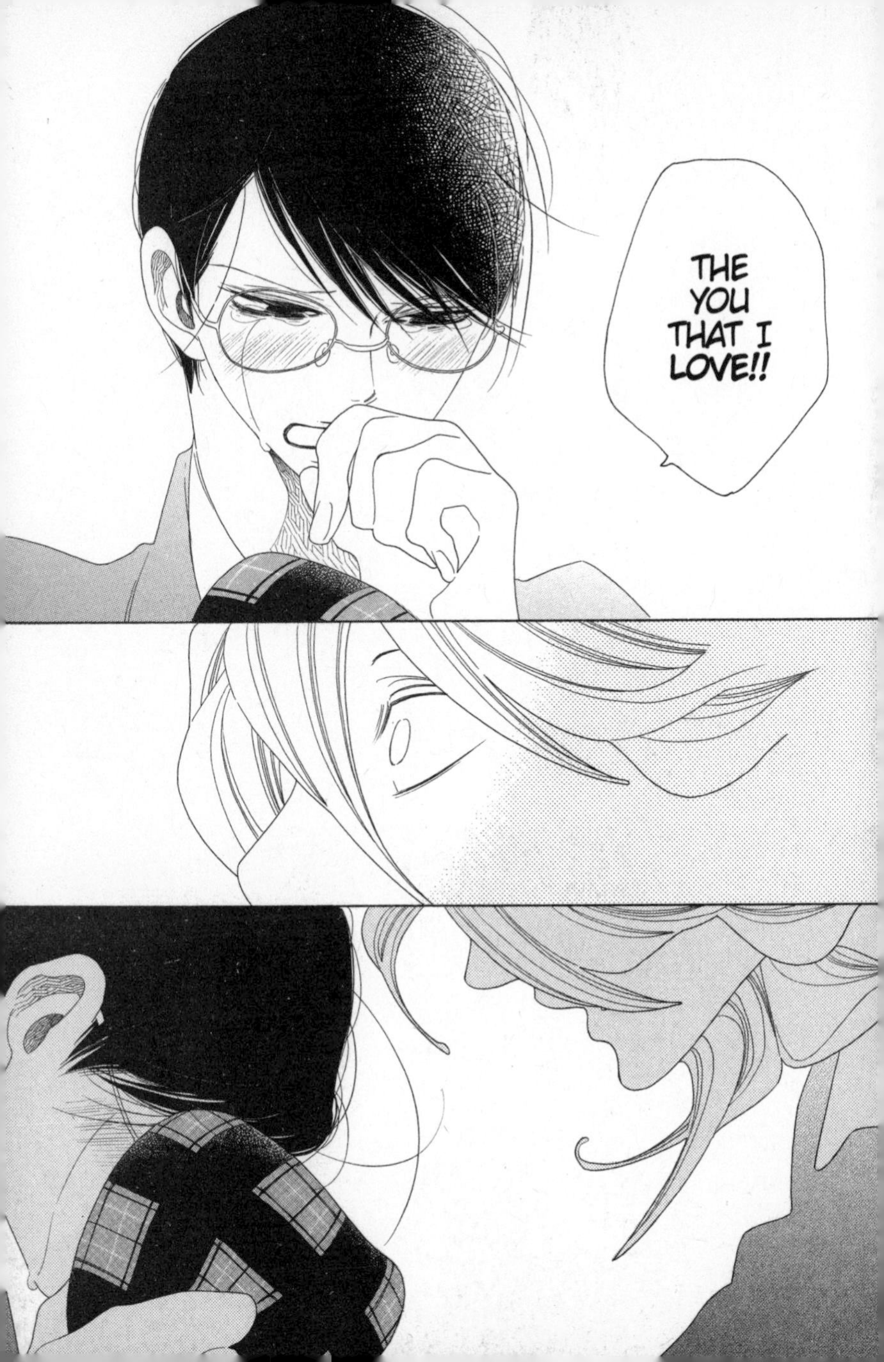
THE YOU THAT I LOVE!!

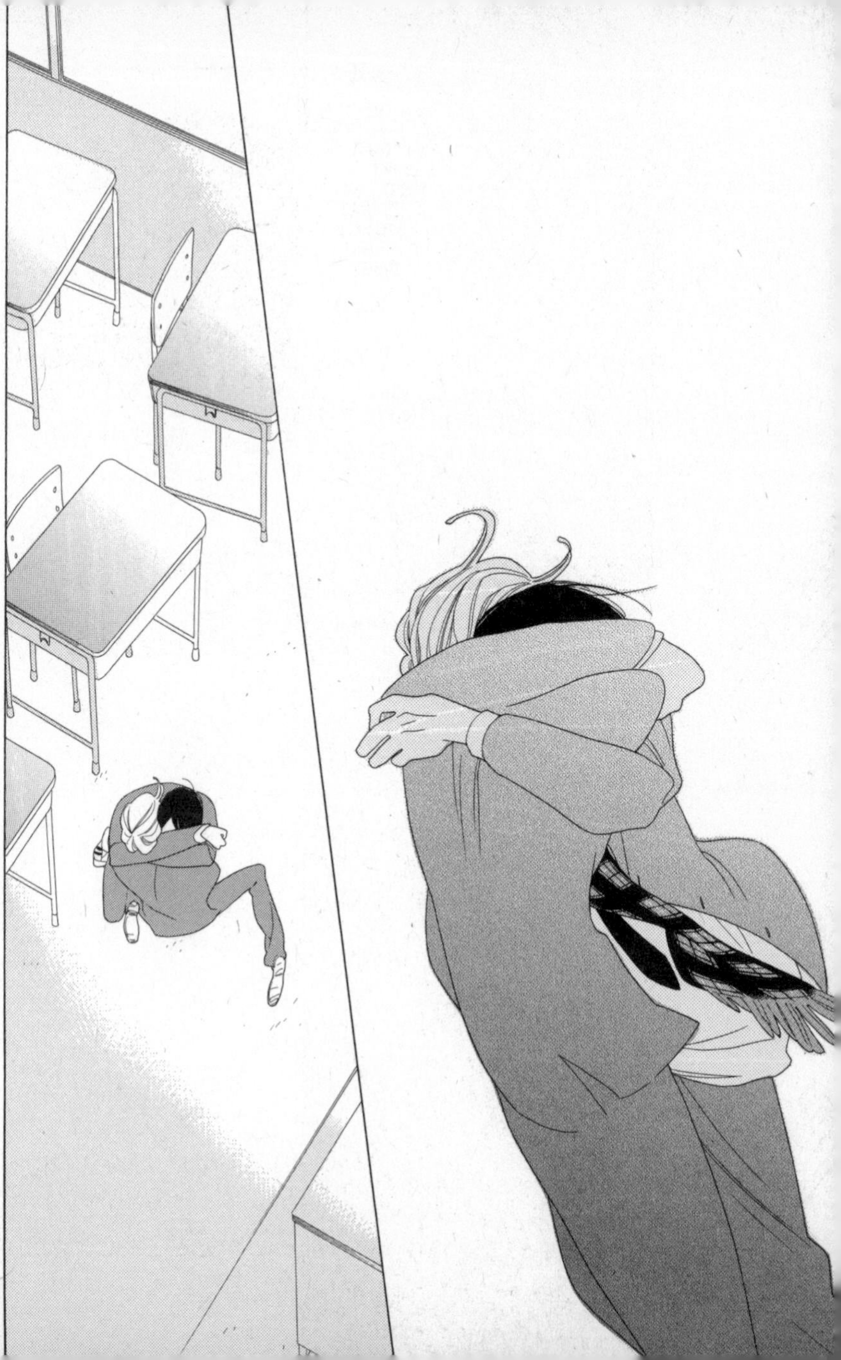

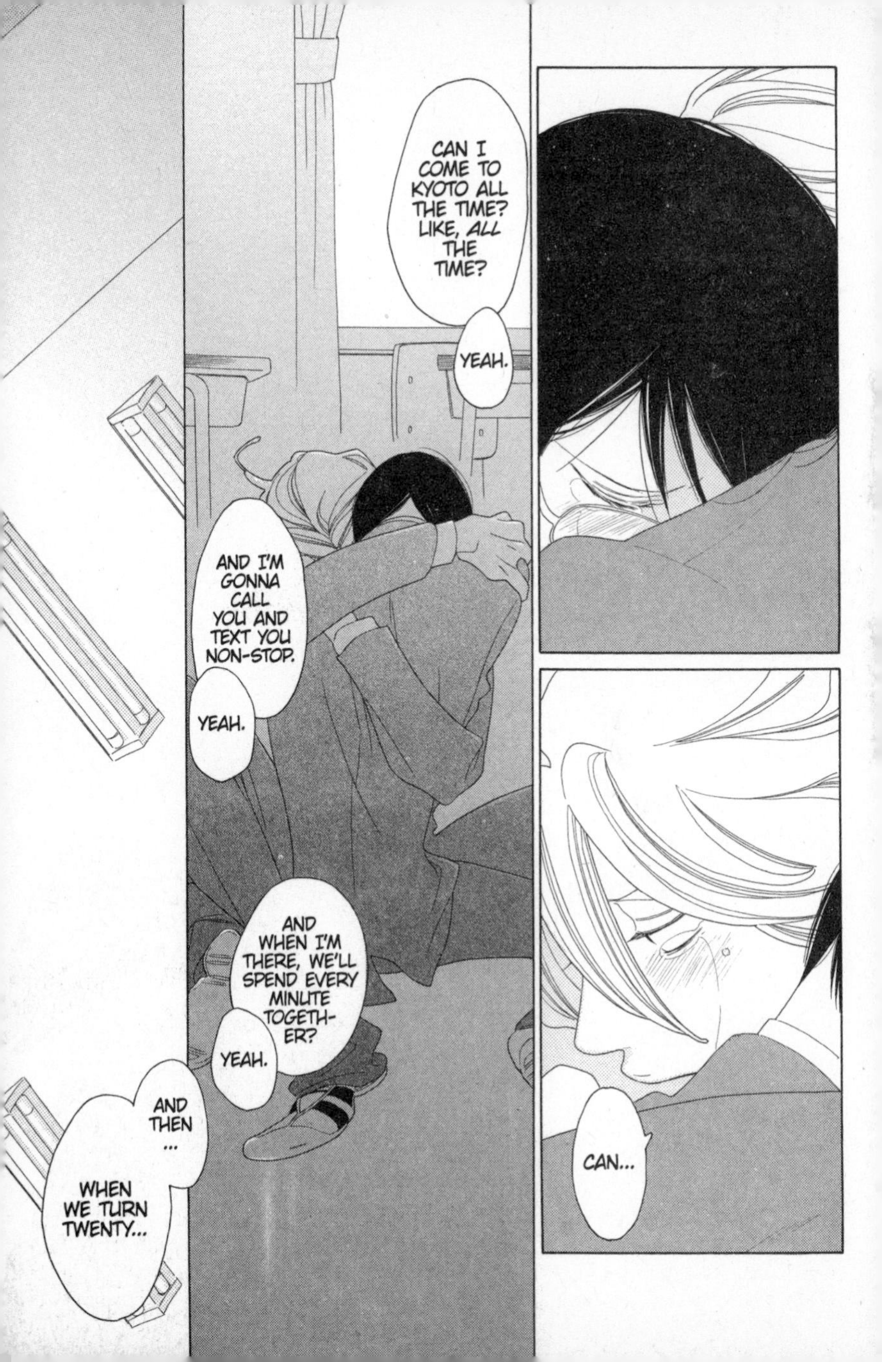
CAN...
CAN I COME TO KYOTO ALL THE TIME? LIKE, *ALL* THE TIME?
YEAH.
AND I'M GONNA CALL YOU AND TEXT YOU NON-STOP.
YEAH.
AND WHEN I'M THERE, WE'LL SPEND EVERY MINUTE TOGETH-ER?
YEAH.
AND THEN ... WHEN WE TURN TWENTY...

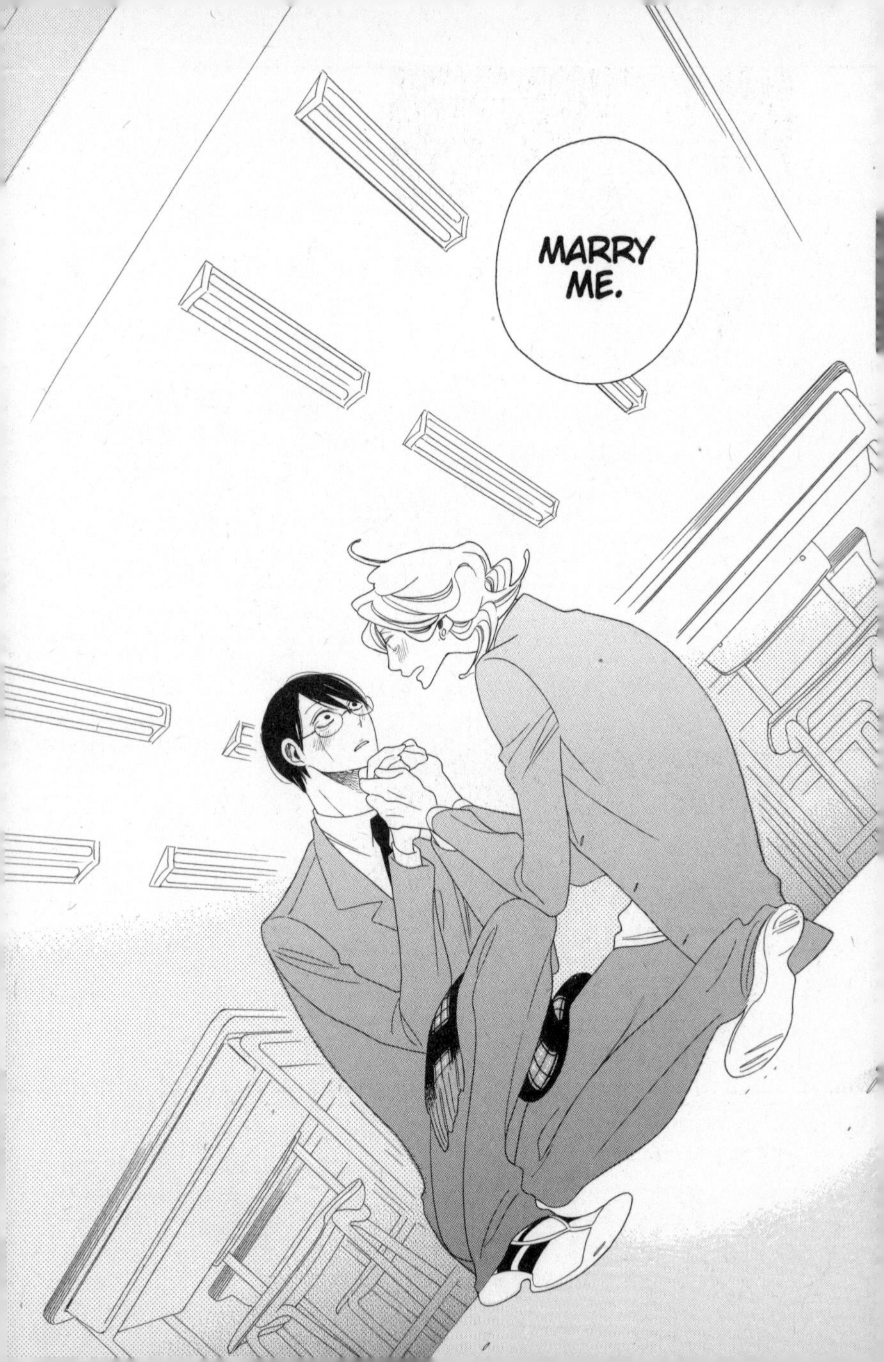
MARRY ME.

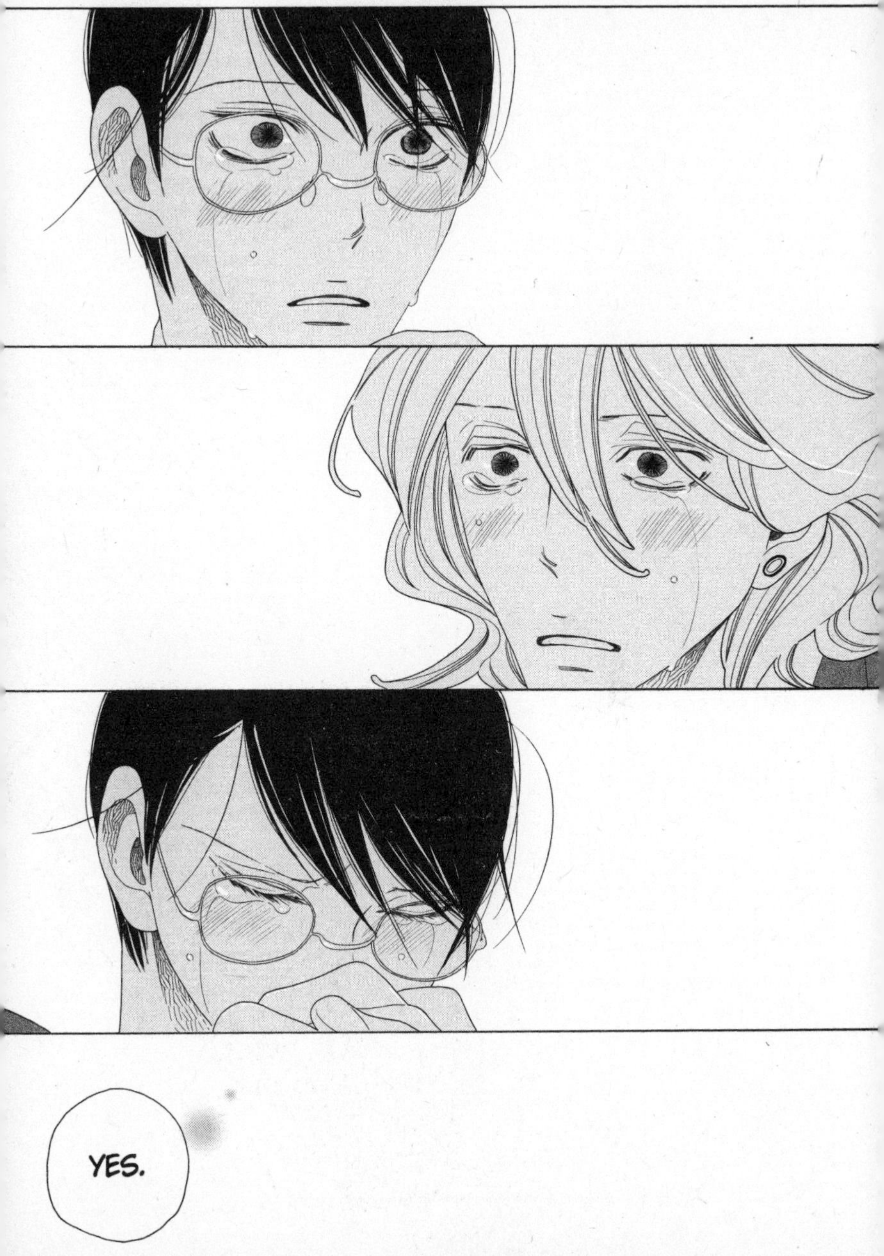
YES.

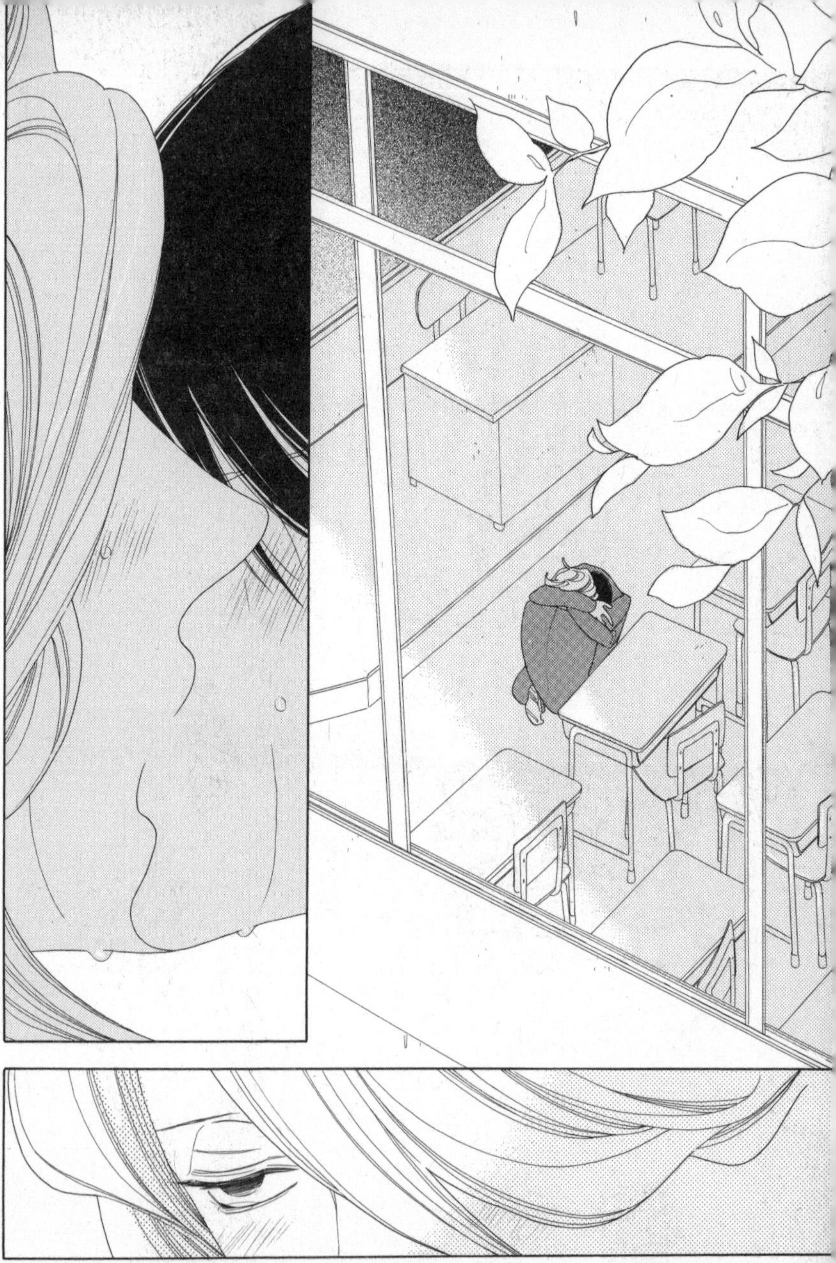

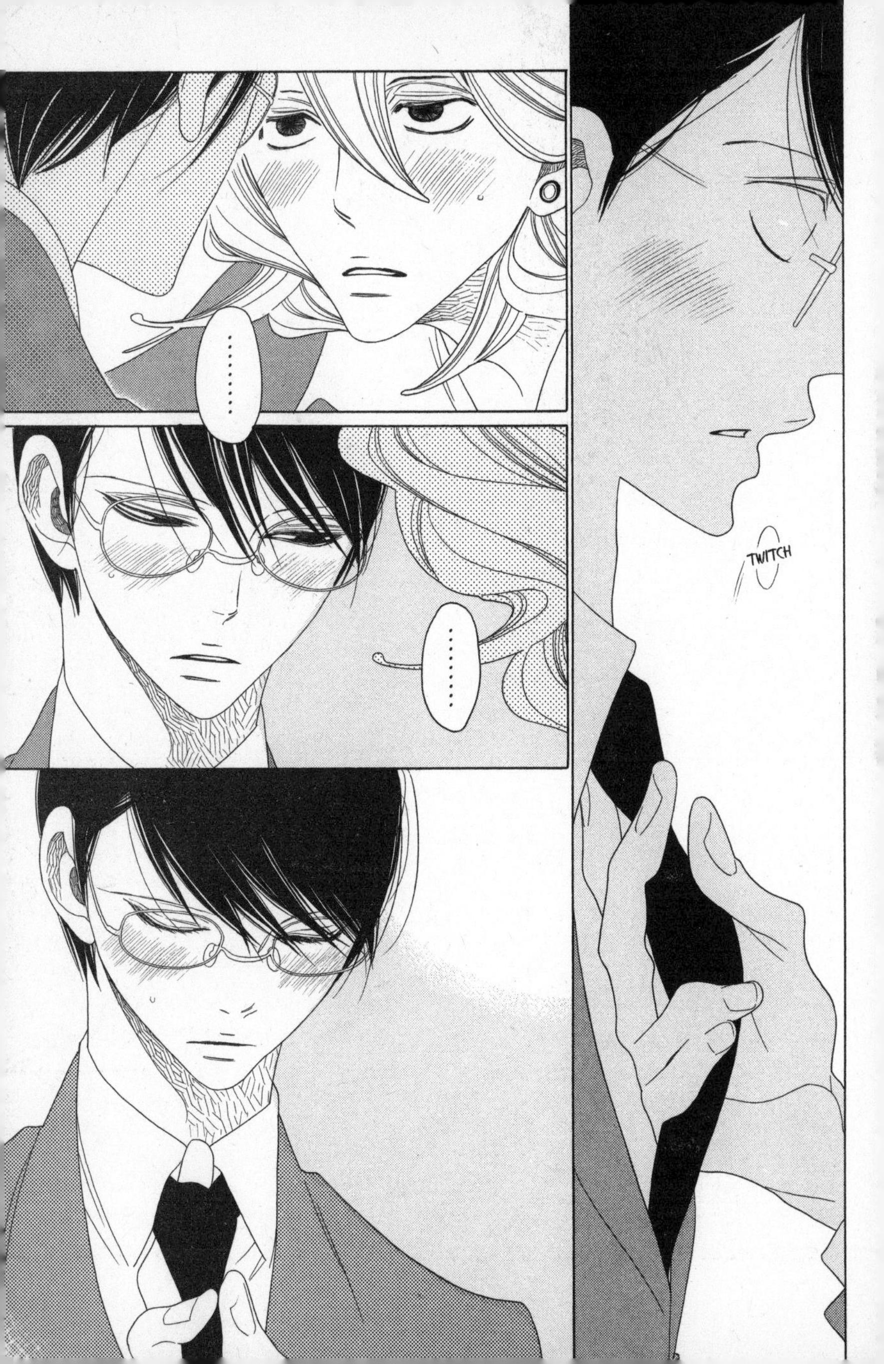
TWITCH
......
......

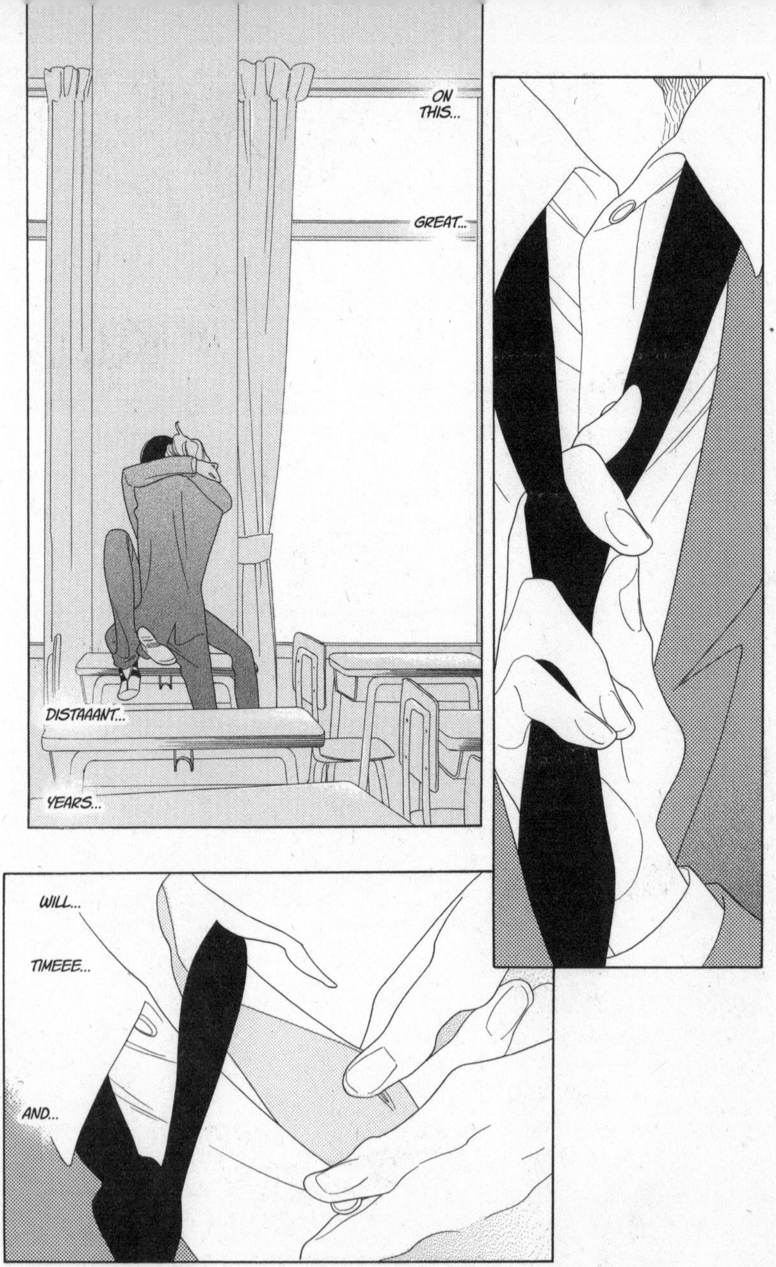
ON THIS...
GREAT...
DISTAAANT...
YEARS...
WILL...
TIMEEE...
AND...

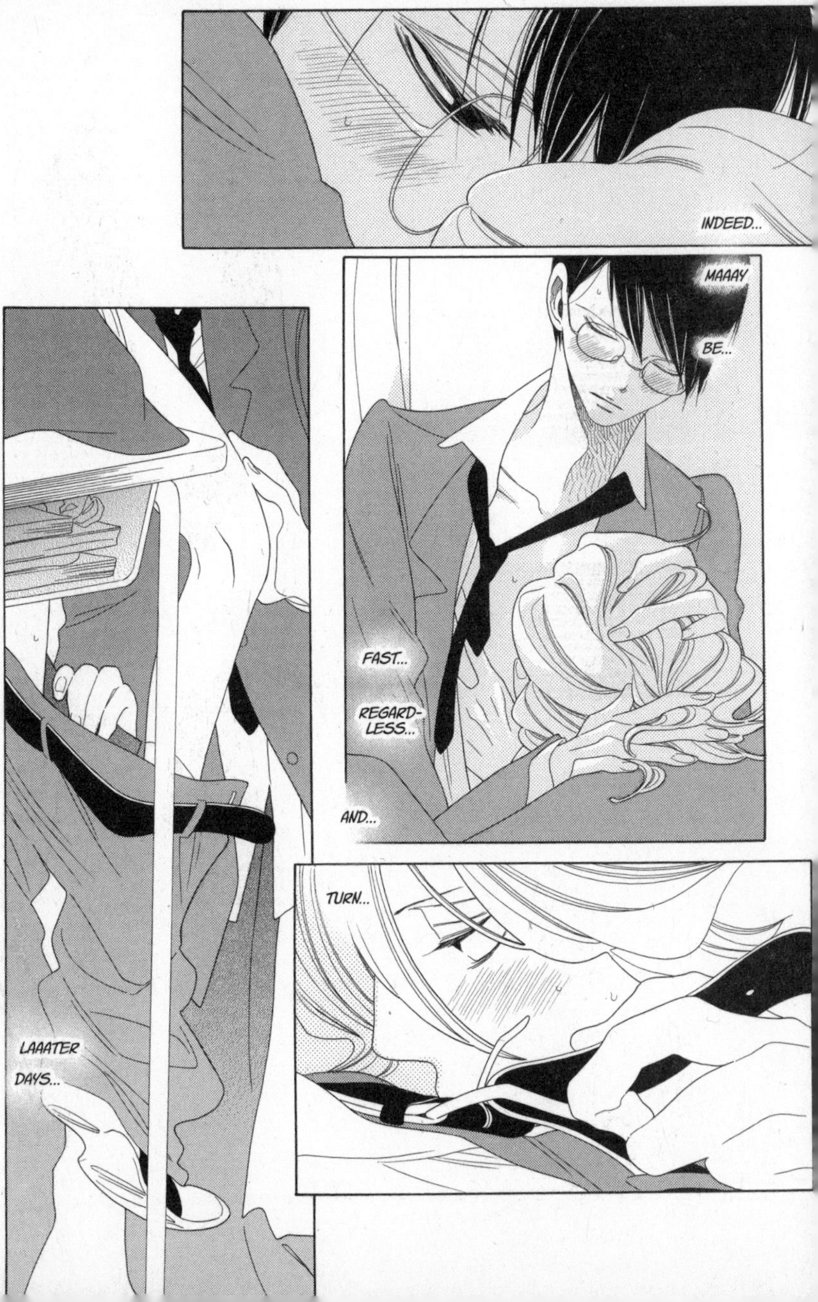
INDEED...
MAAAY
BE...
FAST...
REGARD-LESS...
AND...
TURN...
LAAATER DAYS...

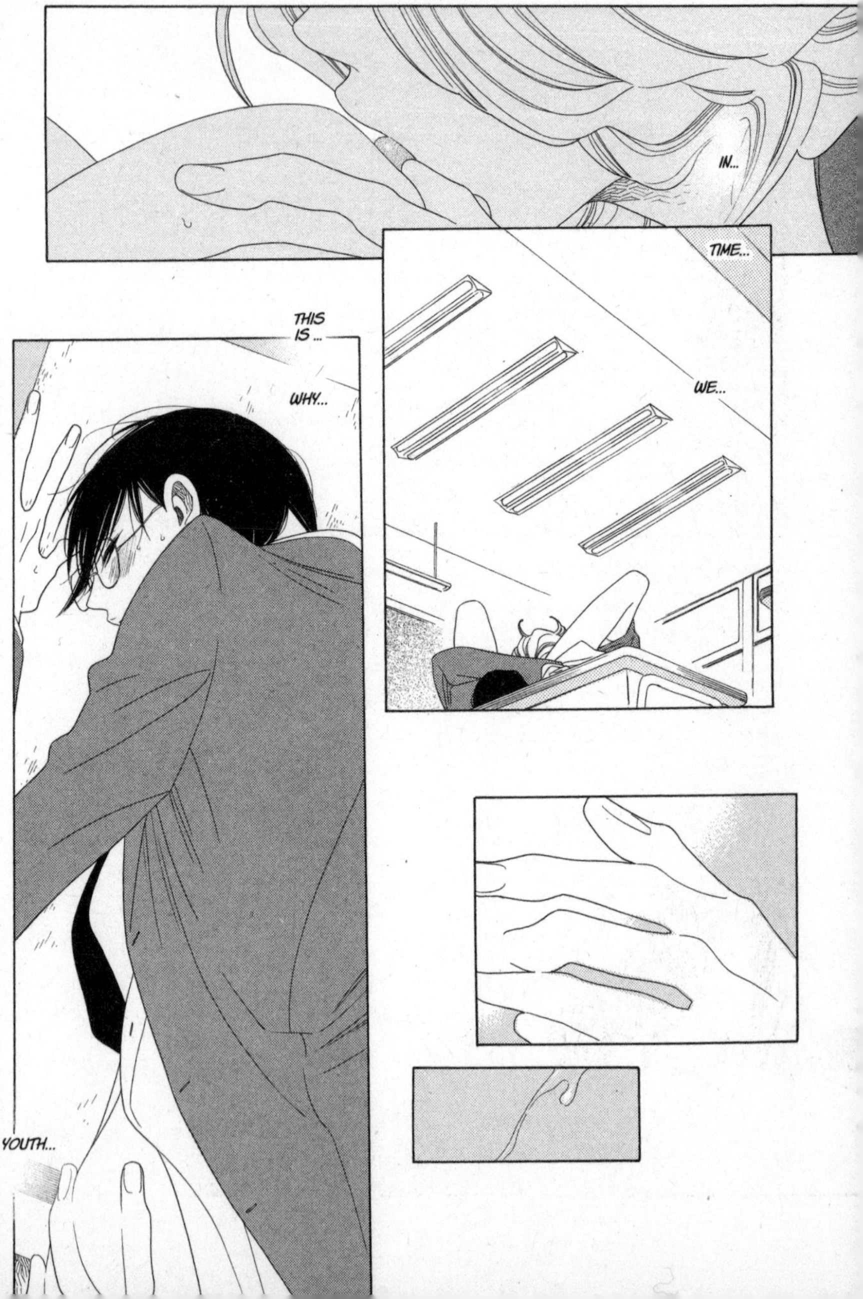
IN...
TIME...
WE...
THIS IS ...
WHY...
YOUTH...

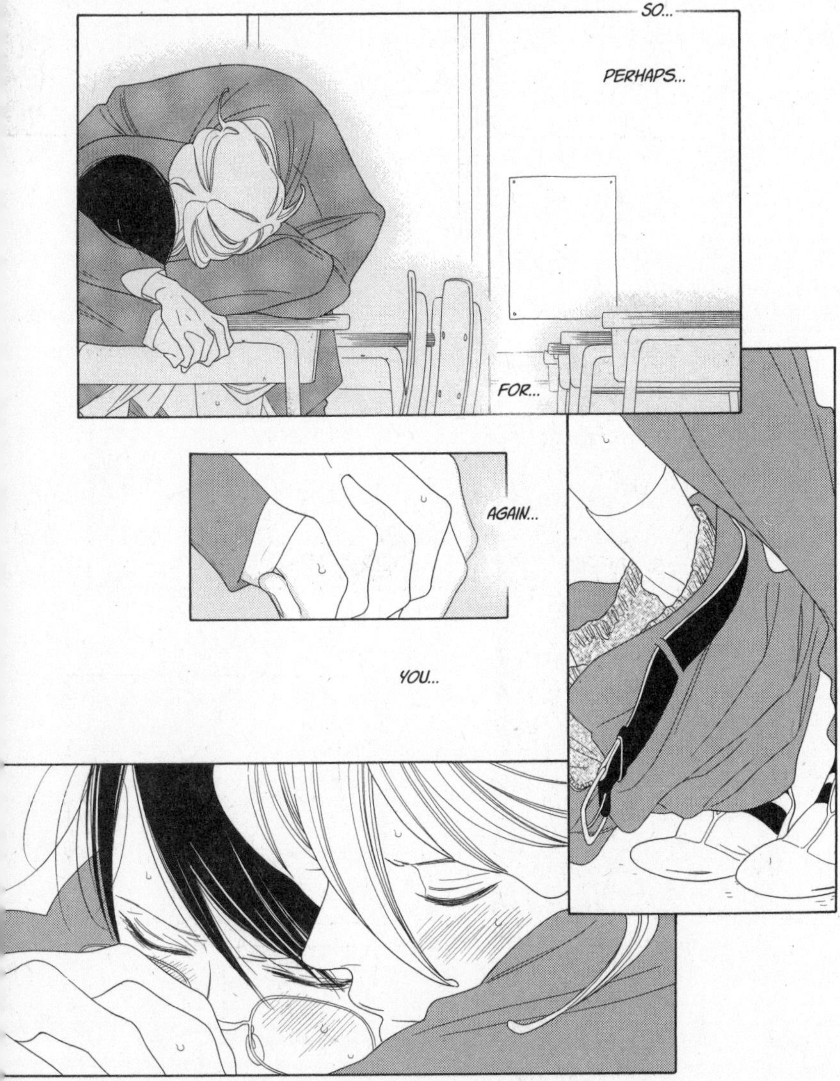
SO...
PERHAPS...
FOR...
AGAIN...
YOU...

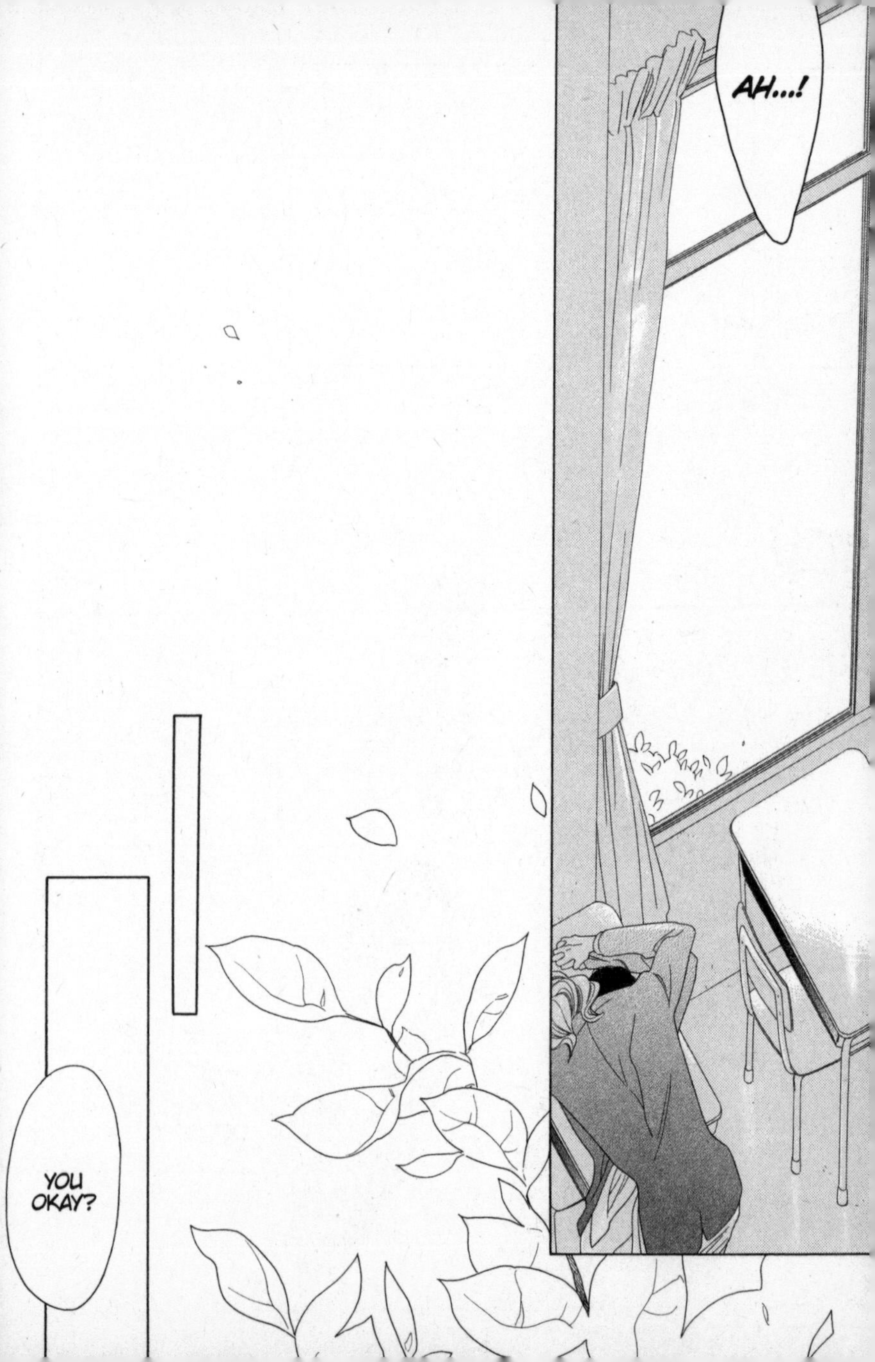
AH...!
YOU OKAY?

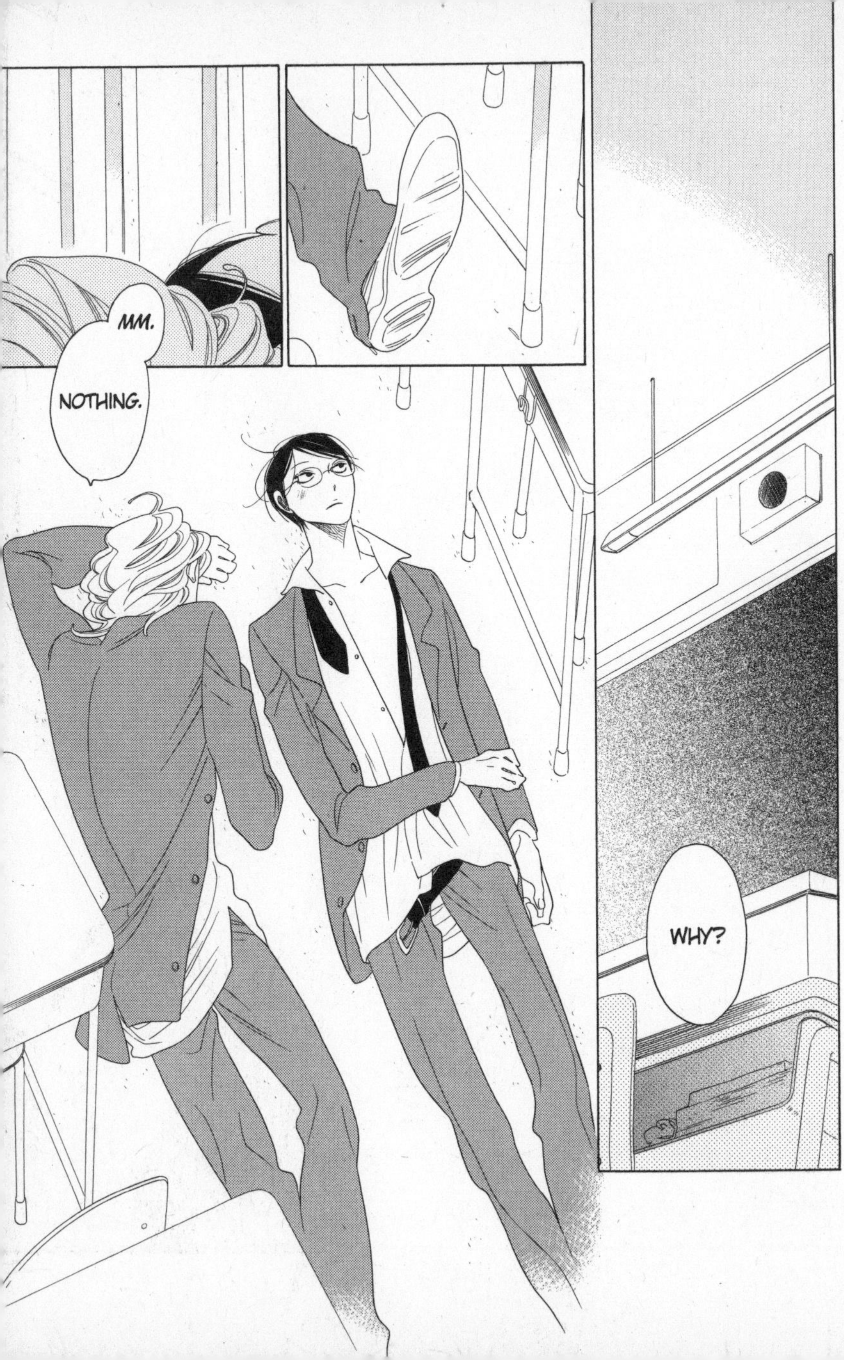
WHY?
MM.
NOTHING.

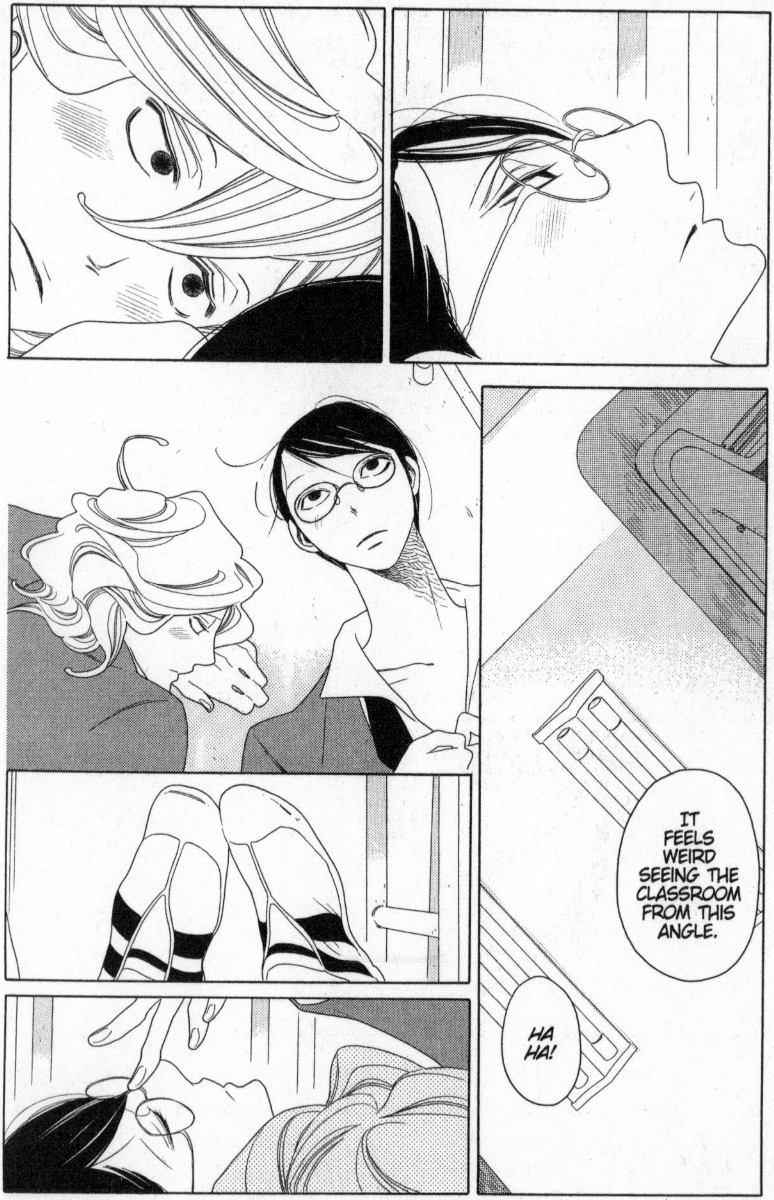
IT FEELS WEIRD SEEING THE CLASSROOM FROM THIS ANGLE.
HA HA!

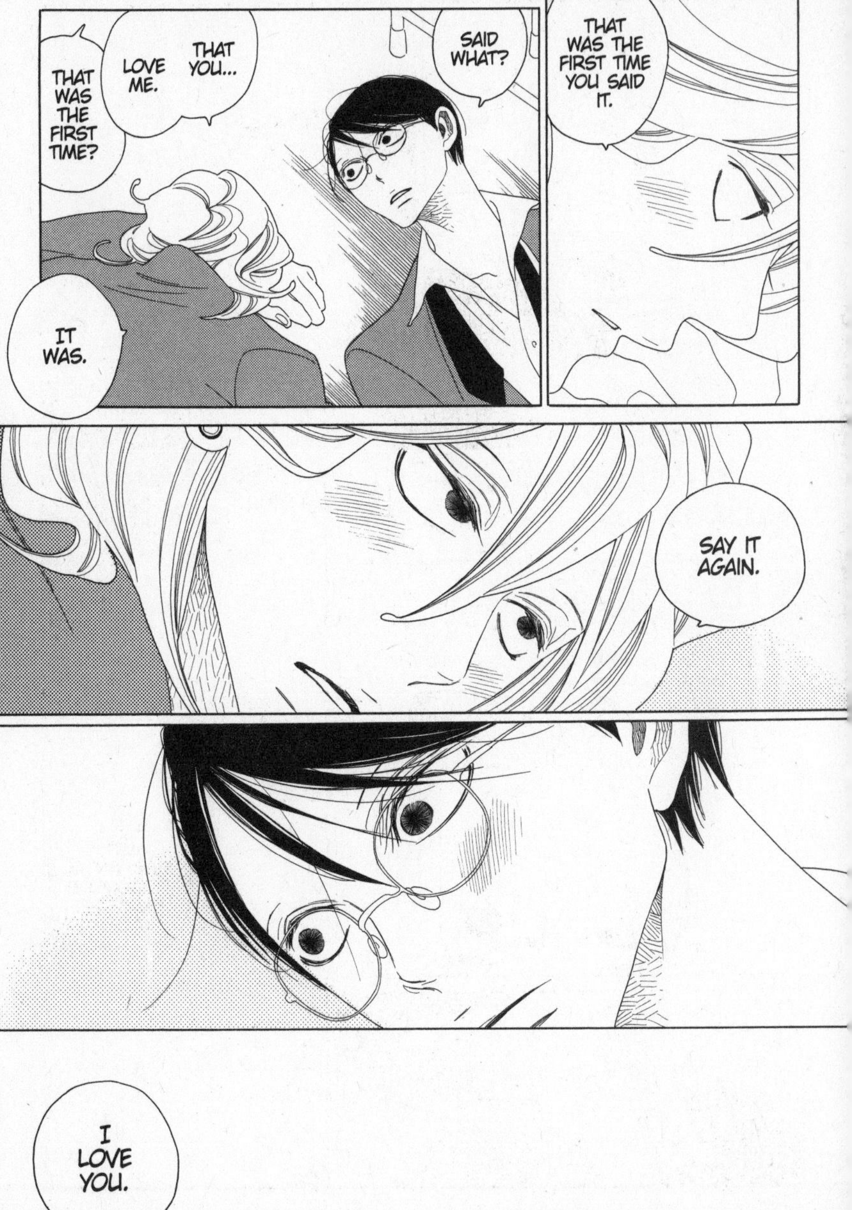
THAT WAS THE FIRST TIME YOU SAID IT.
SAID WHAT?
THAT YOU... LOVE ME.
THAT WAS THE FIRST TIME?
IT WAS.
SAY IT AGAIN.
I LOVE YOU.

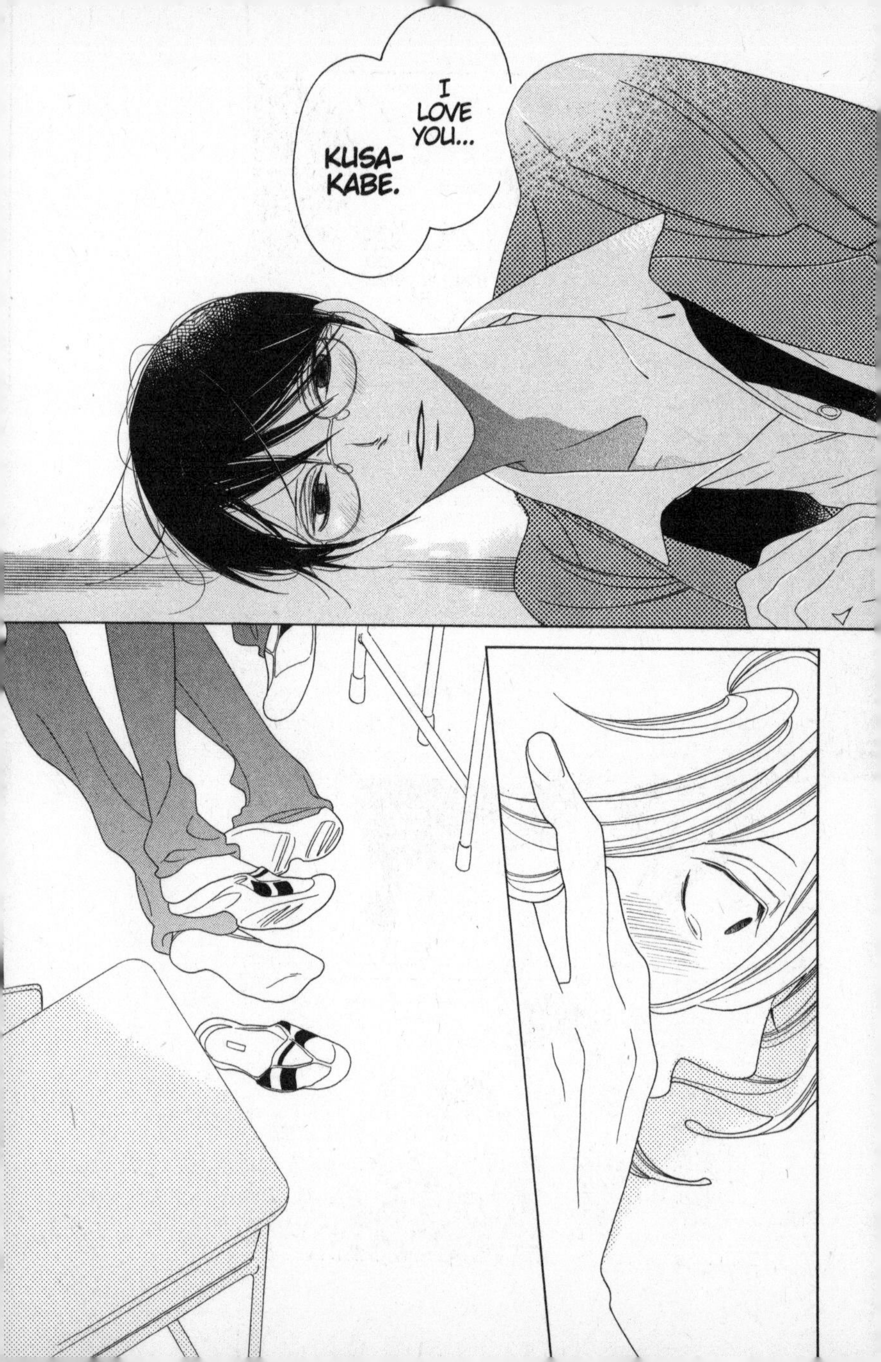
I LOVE YOU... KUSA-KABE.

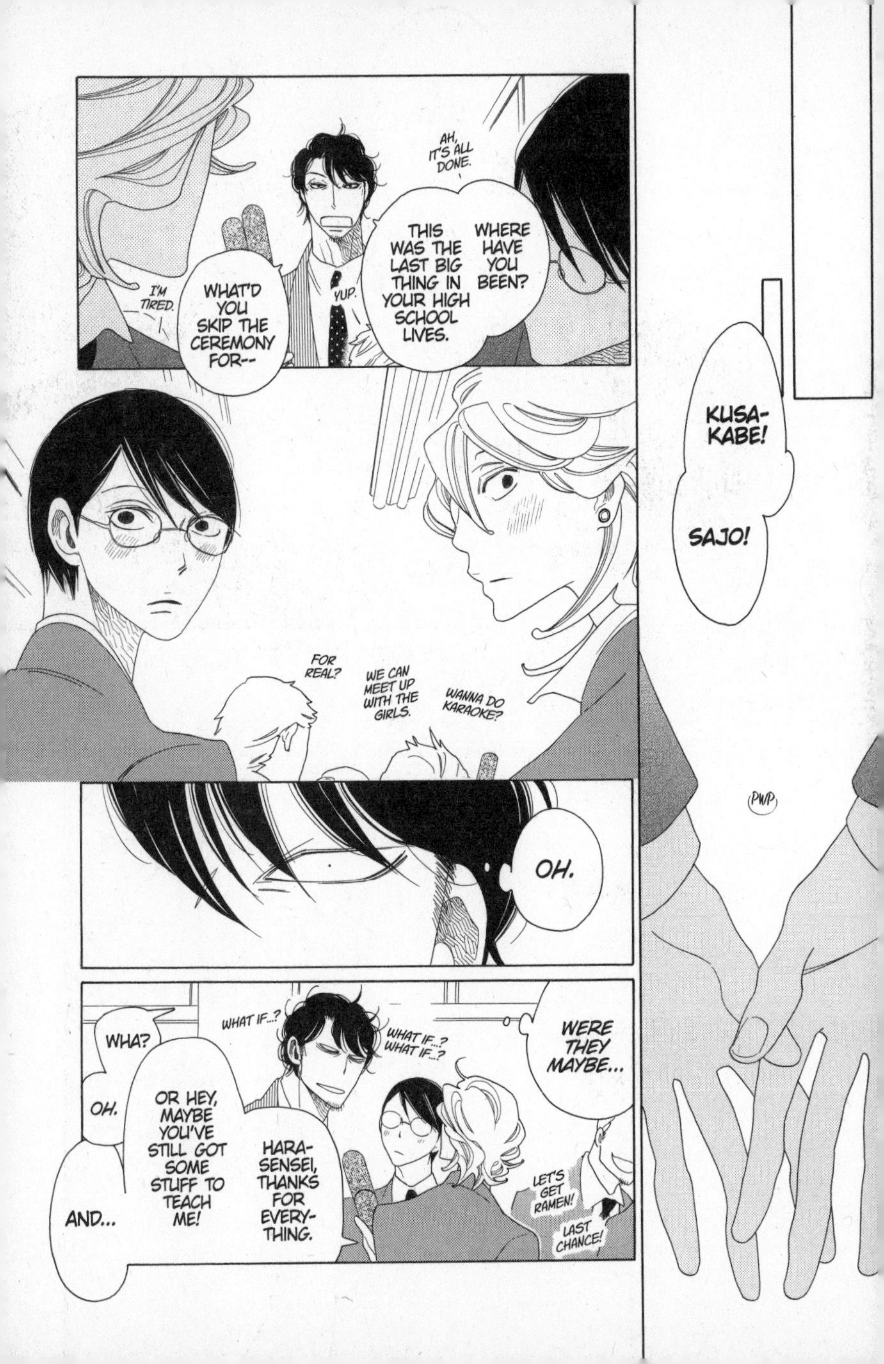
KUSA-KABE!
SAJO!
PWP
AH, IT'S ALL DONE.
WHERE HAVE YOU BEEN?
THIS WAS THE LAST BIG THING IN YOUR HIGH SCHOOL LIVES.
YUP.
WHAT'D YOU SKIP THE CEREMONY FOR--
I'M TIRED.
WANNA DO KARAOKE?
WE CAN MEET UP WITH THE GIRLS.
FOR REAL?
OH.
WERE THEY MAYBE...
WHAT IF...? WHAT IF...?
WHAT IF...?
LET'S GET RAMEN!
LAST CHANCE!
HARA-SENSEI, THANKS FOR EVERY-THING.
OR HEY, MAYBE YOU'VE STILL GOT SOME STUFF TO TEACH ME!
WHA?
OH.
AND...

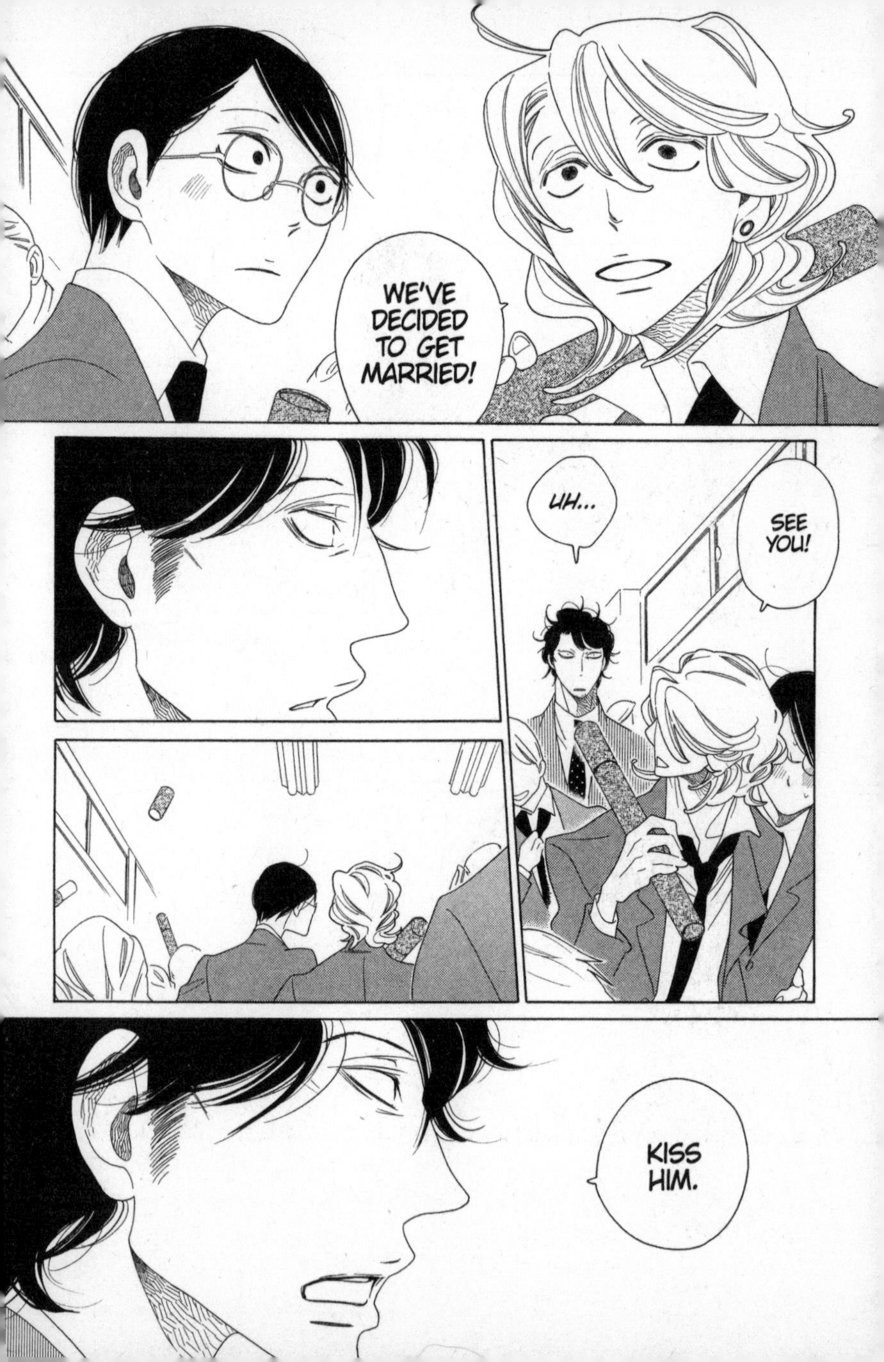
WE'VE DECIDED TO GET MARRIED!
SEE YOU!
UH...
KISS HIM.

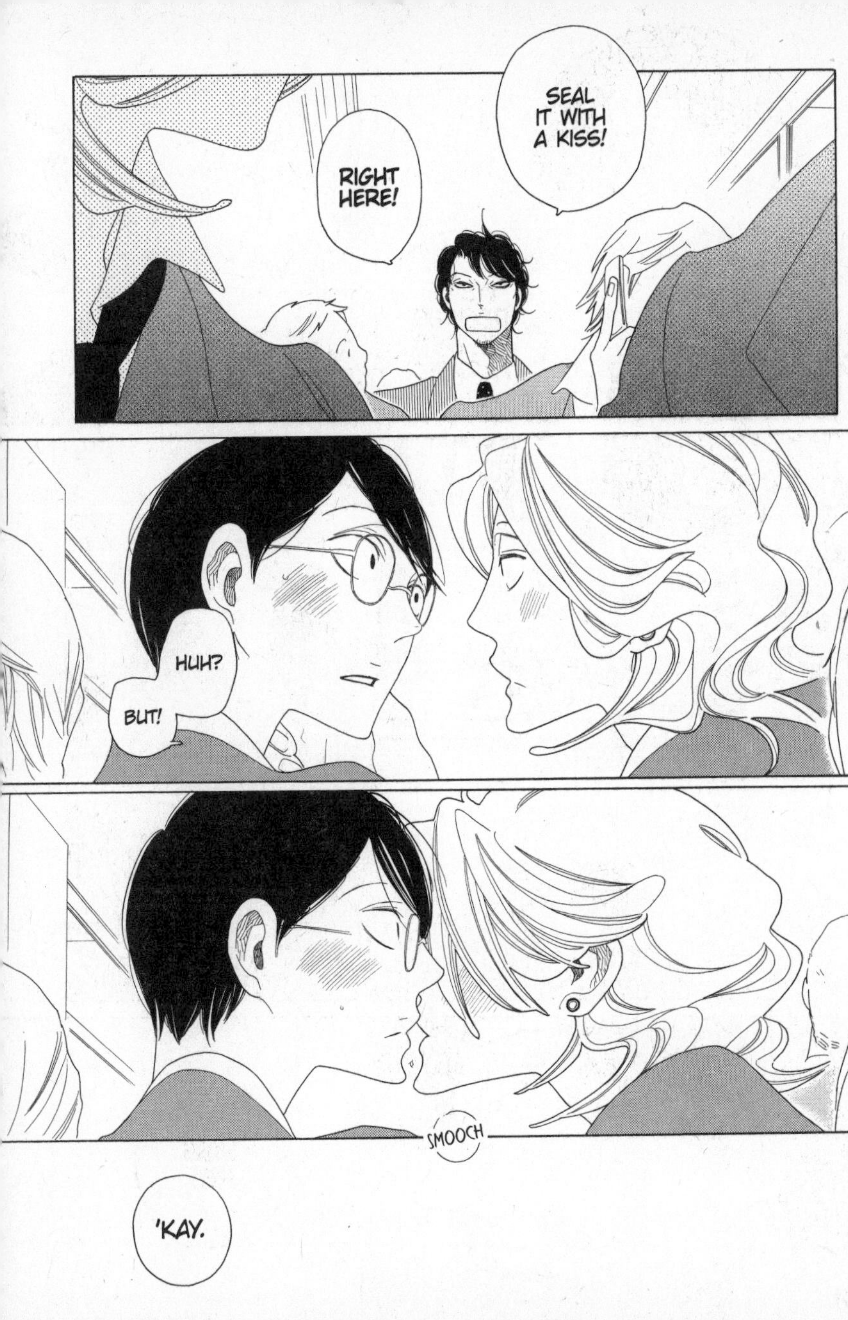
SEAL IT WITH A KISS!
RIGHT HERE!
HUH?
BUT!
SMOOCH
'KAY.

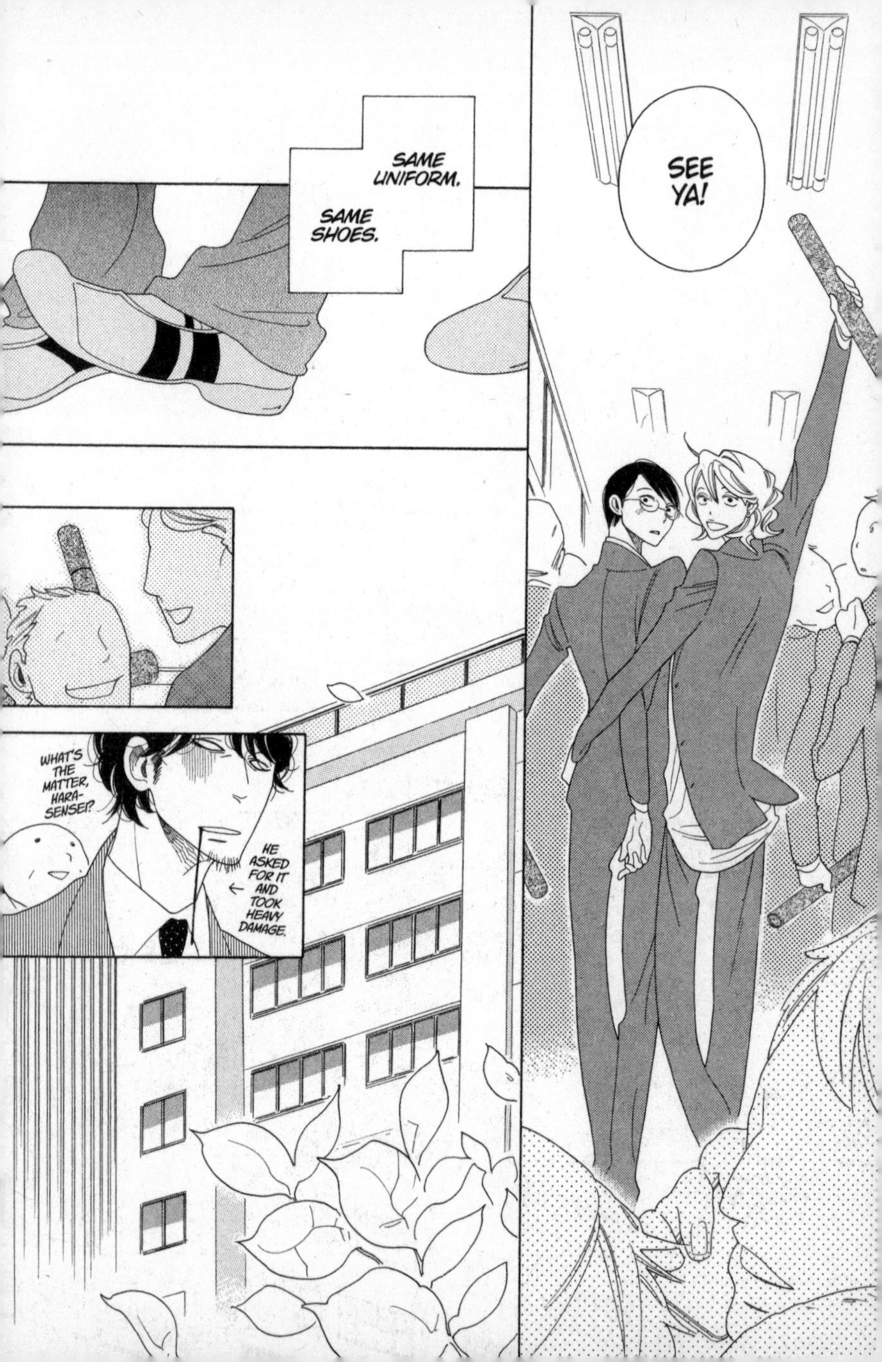
SEE YA!
SAME UNIFORM.
SAME SHOES.
WHAT'S THE MATTER, HARA-SENSEI!?
HE ASKED FOR IT AND TOOK HEAVY DAMAGE.

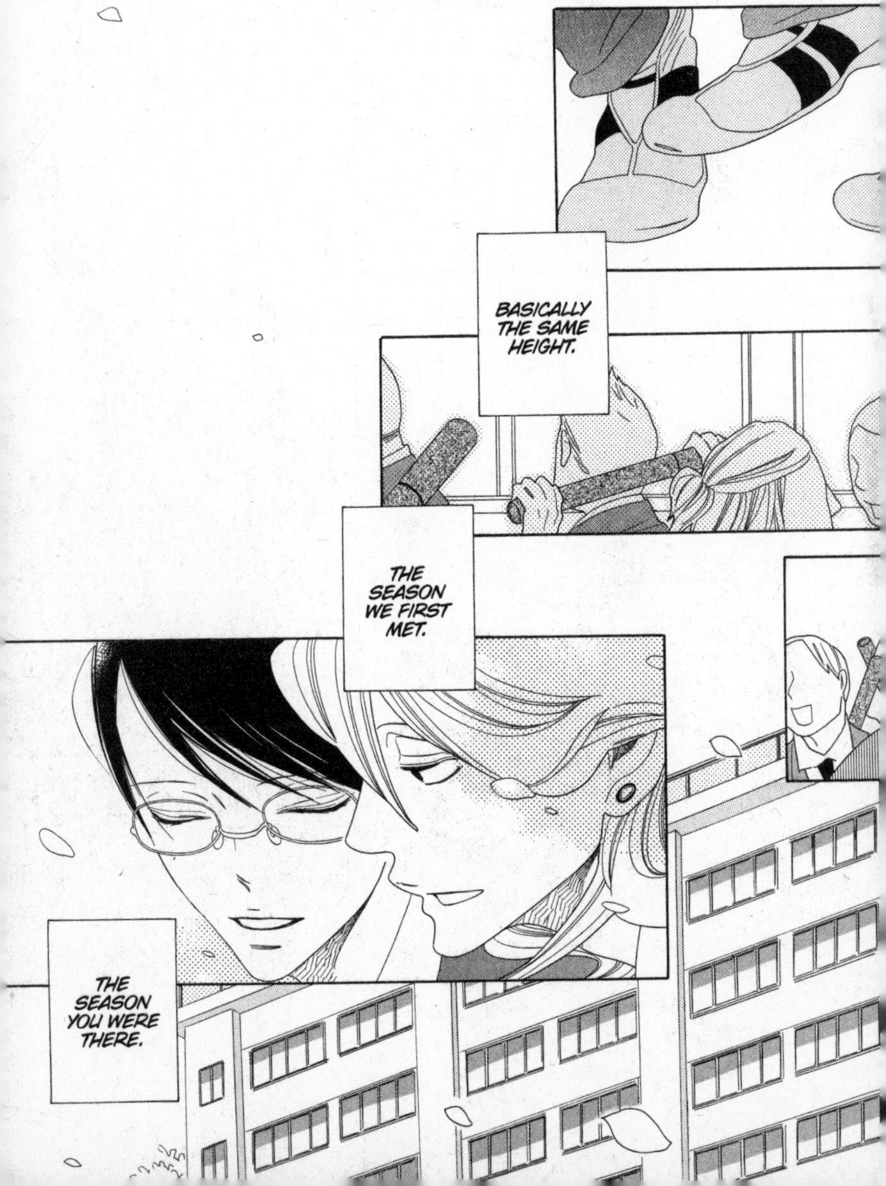
BASICALLY THE SAME HEIGHT.
THE SEASON WE FIRST MET.
THE SEASON YOU WERE THERE.

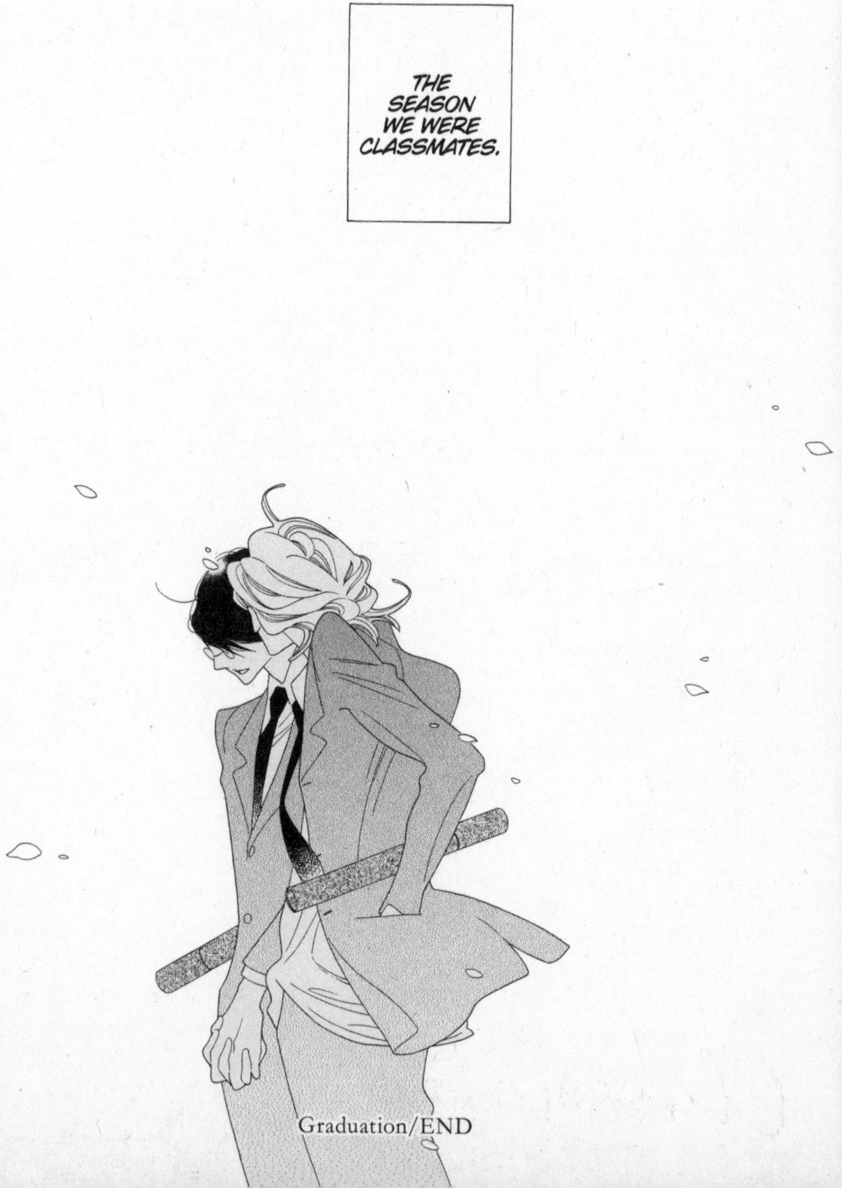
THE SEASON WE WERE CLASSMATES.
Graduation/END

Classmates

Intermission

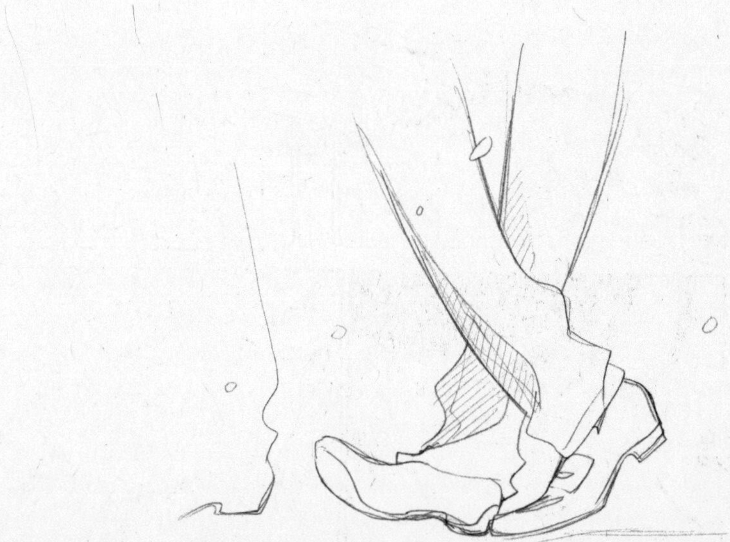

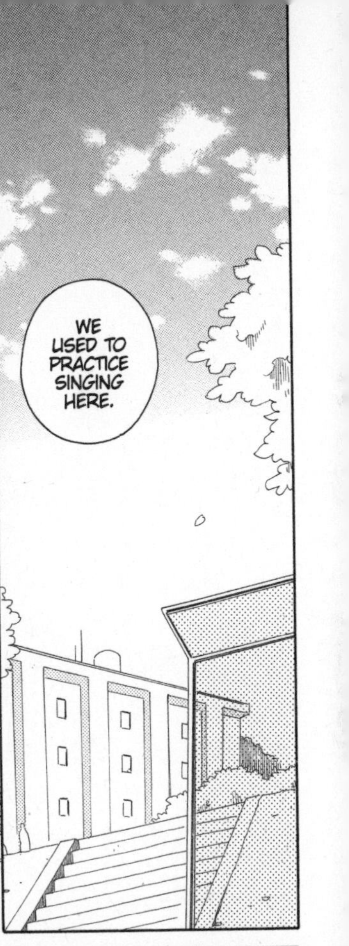
WE USED TO PRACTICE SINGING HERE.

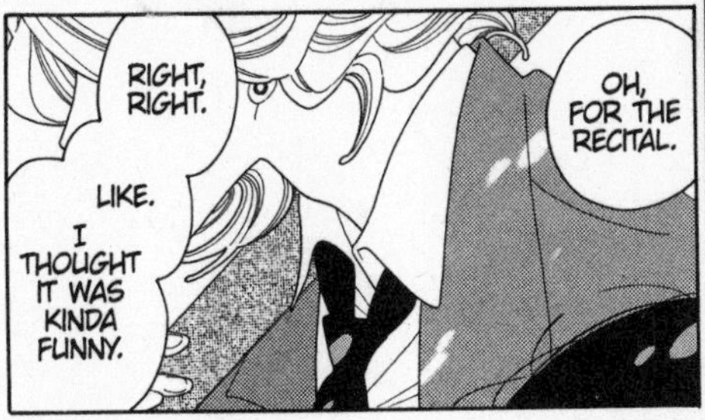
OH, FOR THE RECITAL.
RIGHT, RIGHT.
LIKE. I THOUGHT IT WAS KINDA FUNNY.

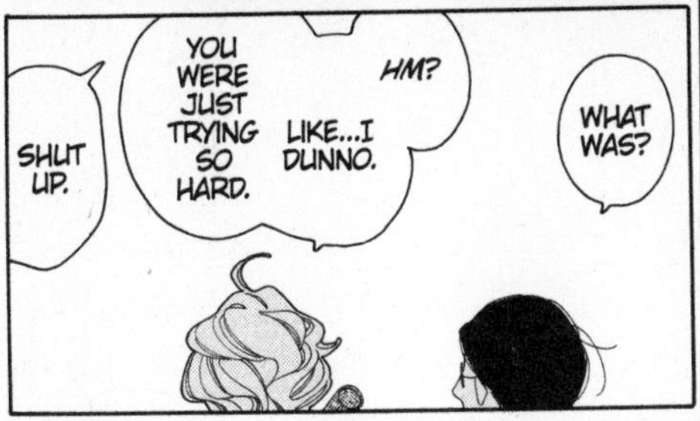
WHAT WAS?
HM?
LIKE...I DUNNO.
YOU WERE JUST TRYING SO HARD.
SHUT UP.

[After School]

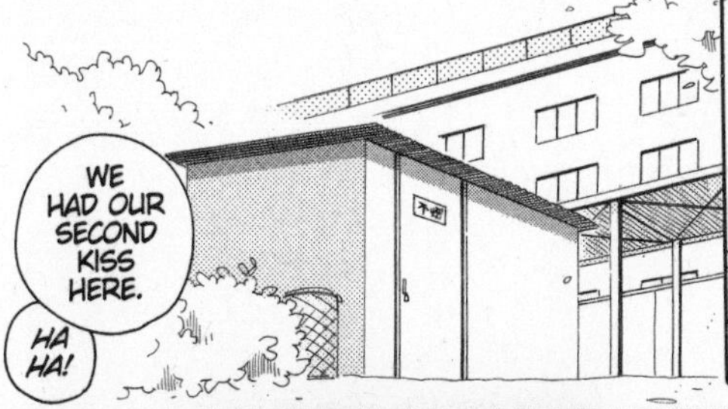
WE HAD OUR SECOND KISS HERE.
HA HA!

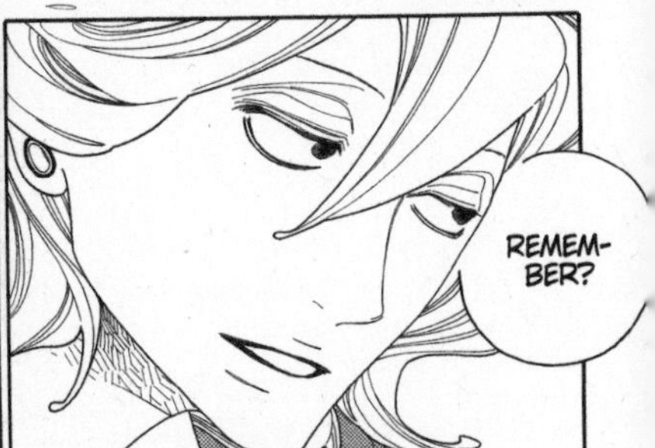
REMEMBER?

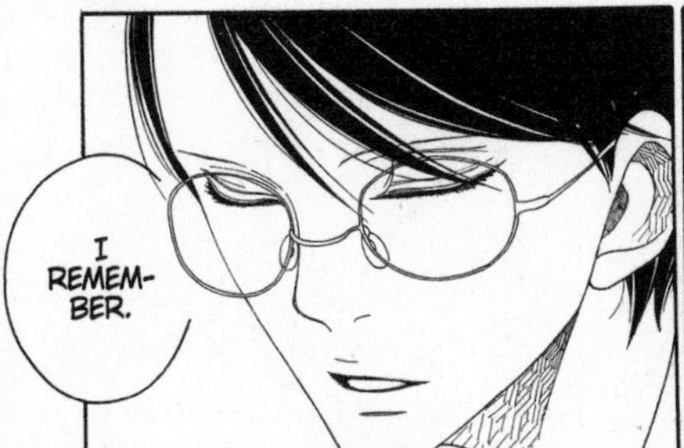
I REMEMBER.

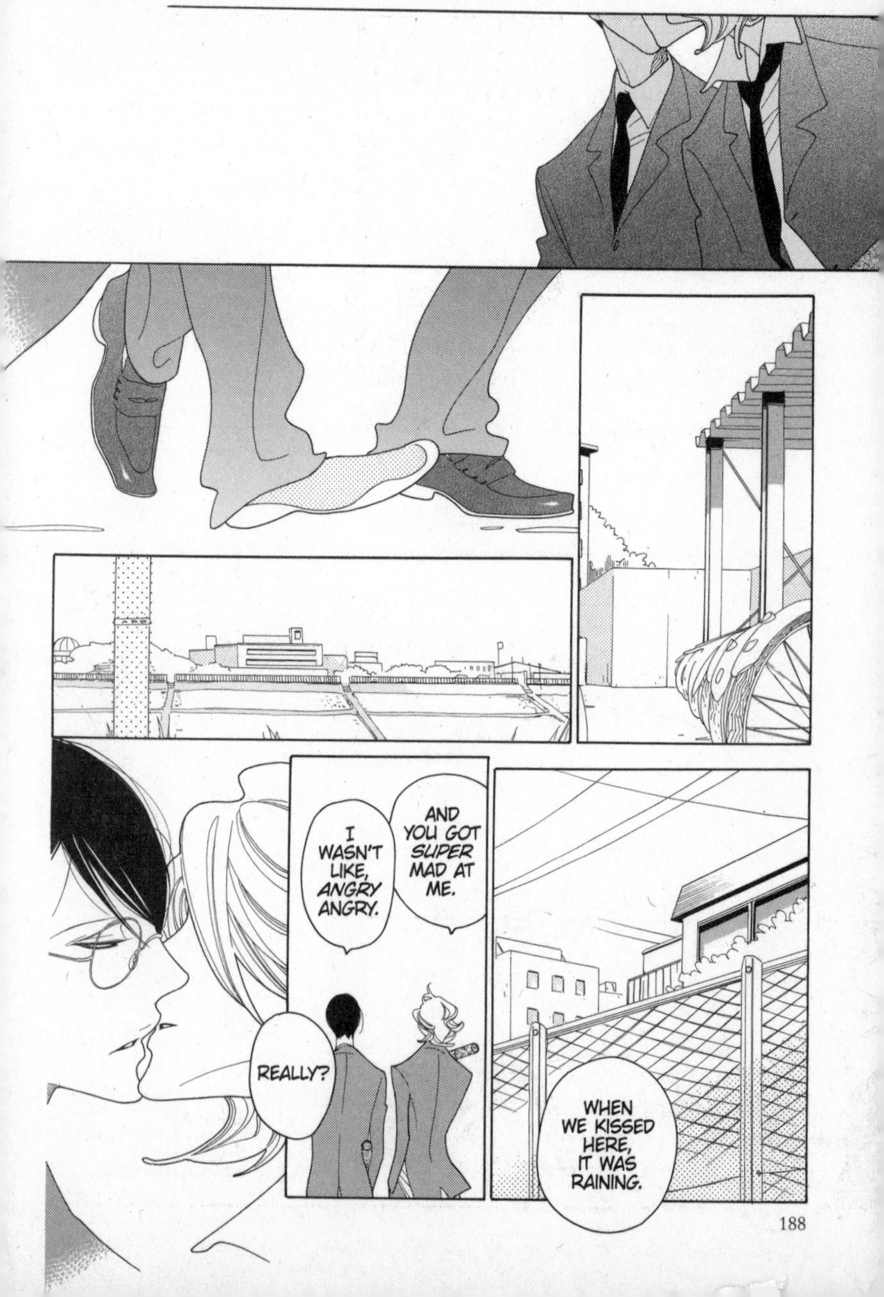
WHEN WE KISSED HERE, IT WAS RAINING.
AND YOU GOT *SUPER* MAD AT ME.
I WASN'T LIKE, *ANGRY* ANGRY.
REALLY?

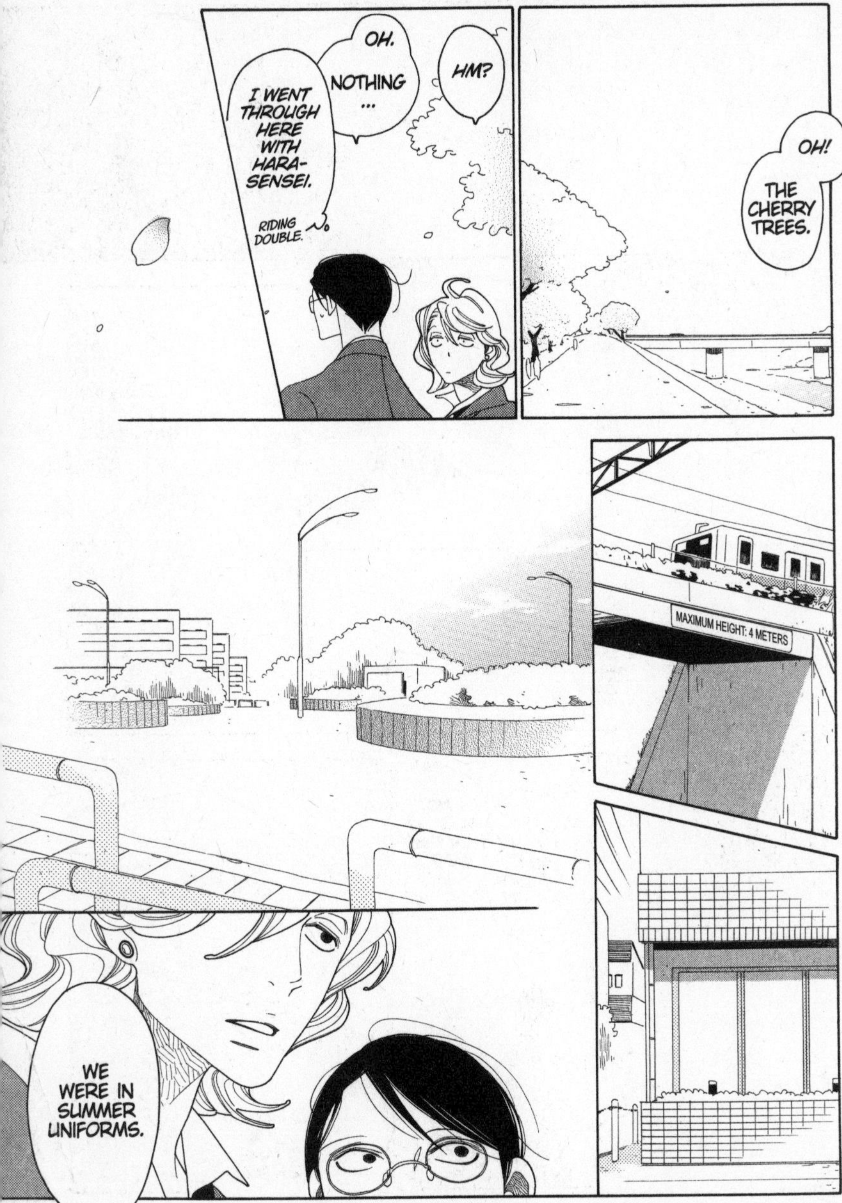
OH! THE CHERRY TREES.
HM?
OH. NOTHING ...
I WENT THROUGH HERE WITH HARA-SENSEI.
RIDING DOUBLE.
MAXIMUM HEIGHT: 4 METERS
WE WERE IN SUMMER UNIFORMS.

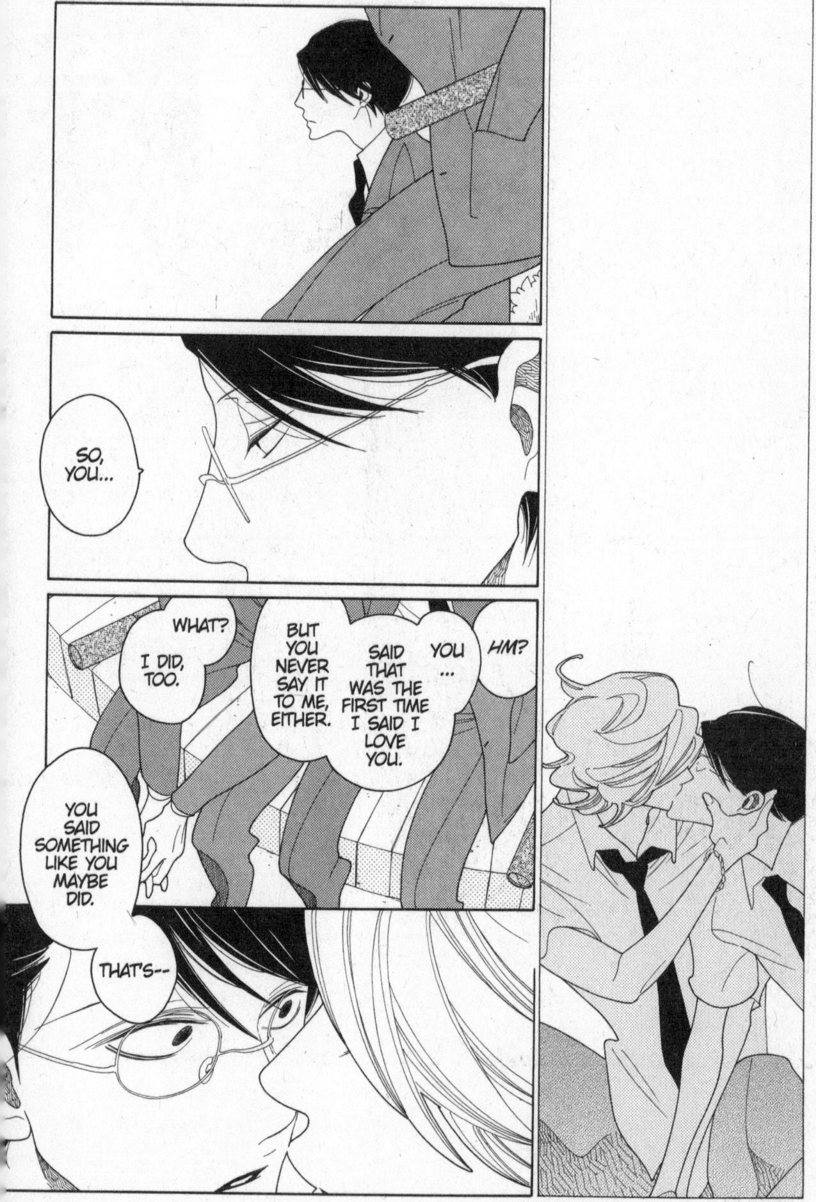
SO, YOU...
HM?
YOU ... SAID THAT WAS THE FIRST TIME I SAID I LOVE YOU.
BUT YOU NEVER SAY IT TO ME, EITHER.
WHAT?
I DID, TOO.
YOU SAID SOMETHING LIKE YOU MAYBE DID.
THAT'S--

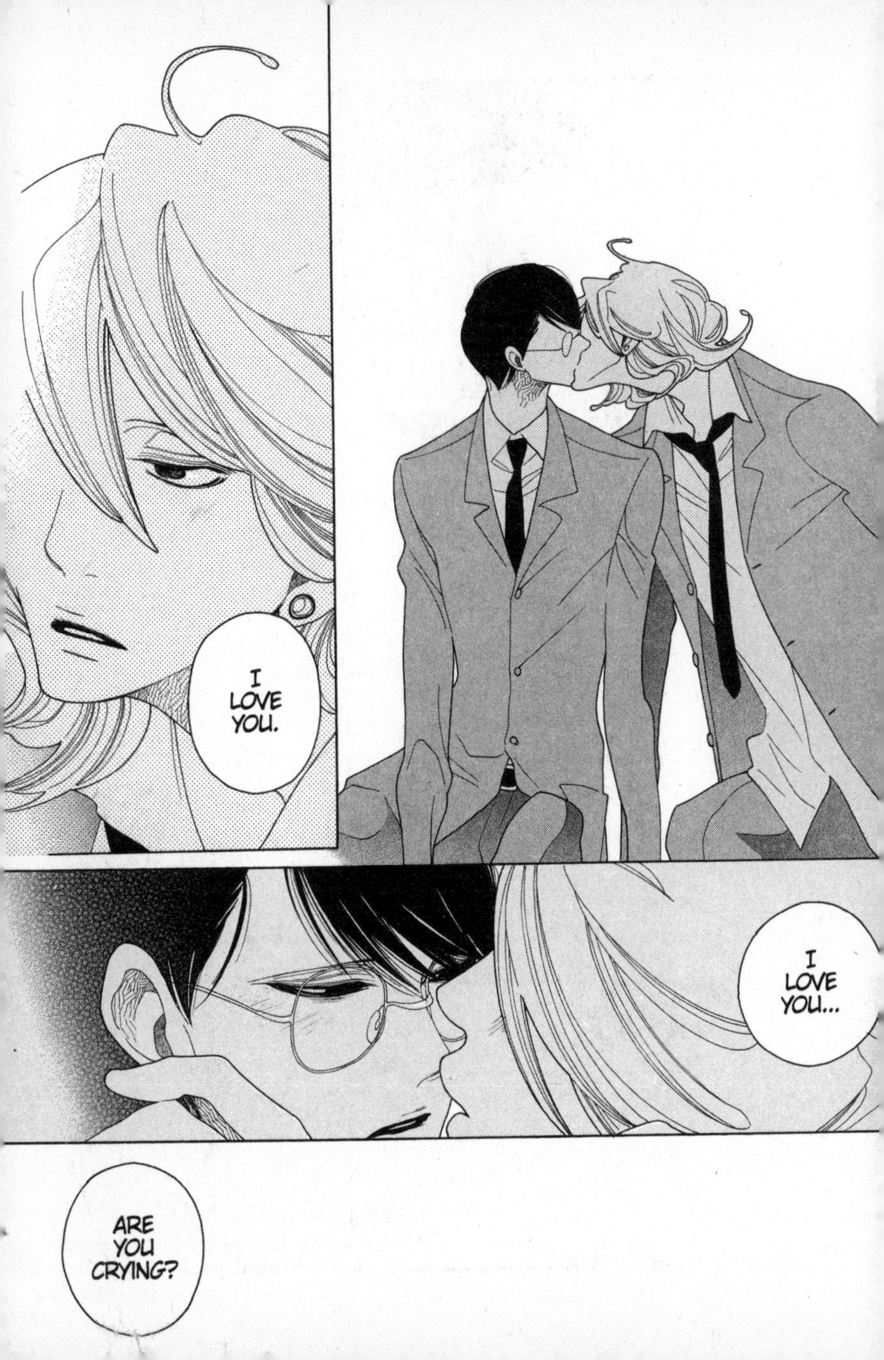
I LOVE YOU.
I LOVE YOU...
ARE YOU CRYING?

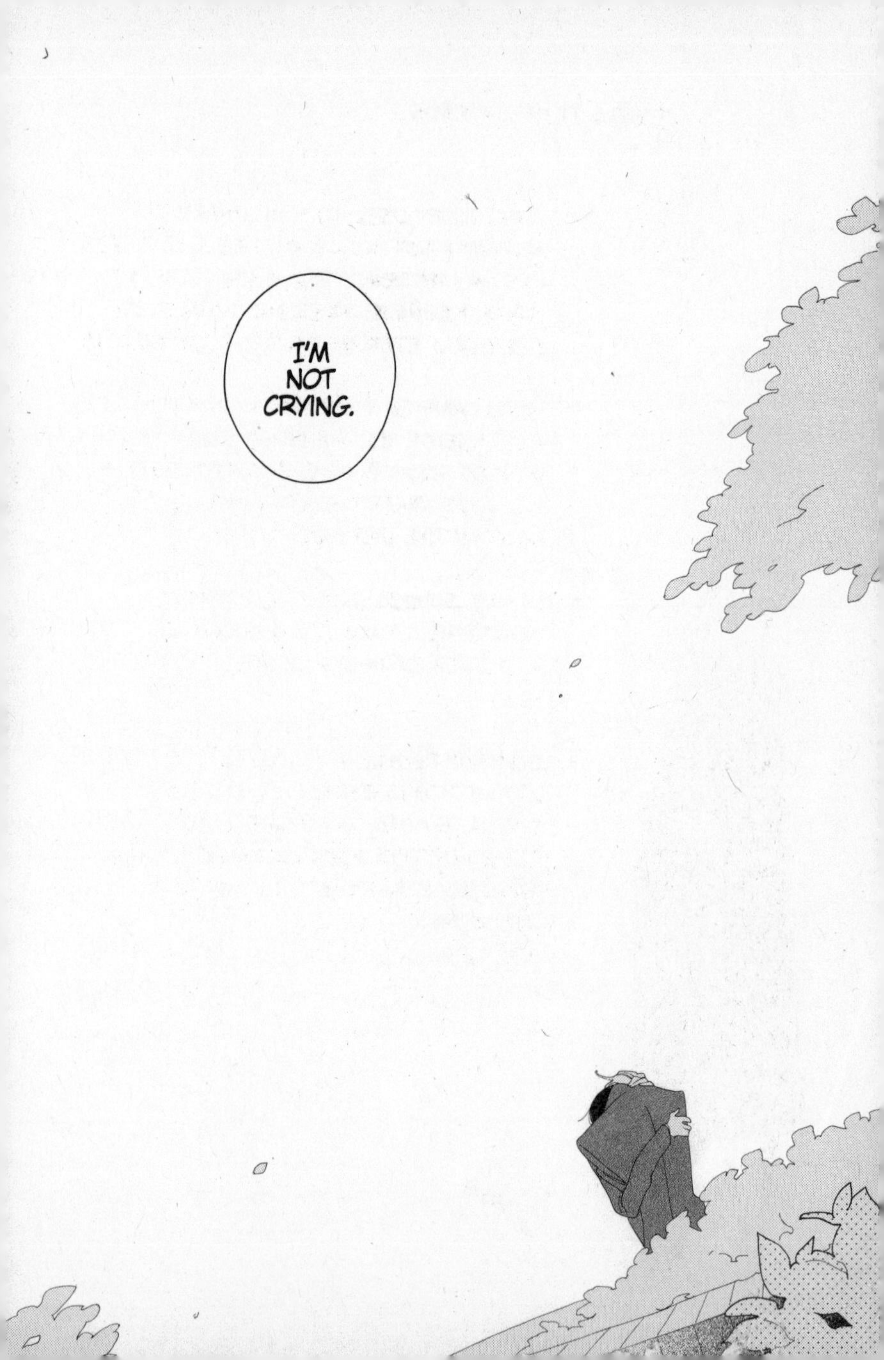
I'M NOT CRYING.

IT ENDS. IT NEVER ENDS.

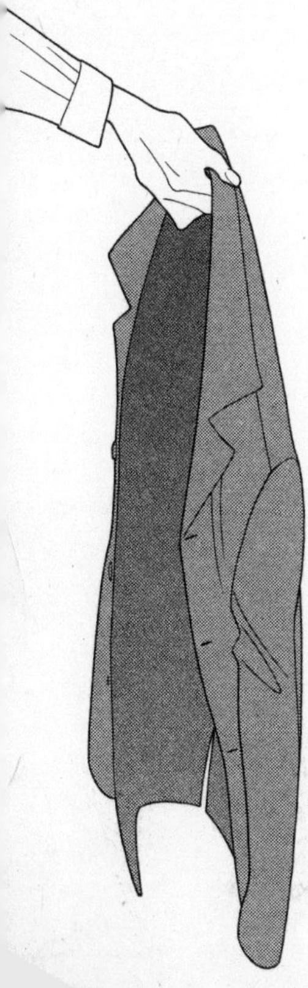

— I FEEL LIKE I USED TO RUN DOWN THE HALLWAY A LOT IN SCHOOL. I FEEL LIKE THERE WAS AN IMPATIENCE THAT MADE MY HEART STING, MAKING ME FRET AND MOAN AT MY SEEMINGLY ETERNAL HALF-PERSON STATUS.

— I ONLY WANTED TO DRAW SAJO RIHITO IN THE EXTREME OF HIS UNIFORMED LOOK. I ONLY WANTED TO DRAW THE GALLANT BEAUTY OF HIS BODY WRAPPED NEATLY IN THE RESTRICTIVE UNIFORM.

— I THINK SCHOOL DAYS ARE ACHINGLY BEAUTIFUL. I THINK IT'S A CLEAR BEAUTY, A SHOWER OF INEXPERIENCE, A REFRESHING HEAT.

— SO MANY PEOPLE HAVE HELPED ME ALONG THE WAY WITH THIS SERIES. FRIENDS, FAMILY, MY EDITOR E-MOTO-SAN, AND EVERYONE WHO PICKED UP THIS BOOK ALONG WITH YOUR FAMILIES, I PRAY THAT YOU HAVE MANY BLESSINGS.

ASUMIKO NAKAMURA

SEVEN SEAS ENTERTAINMENT PRESENTS

Classmates

story and art by **ASUMIKO NAKAMURA**   VOL. 3 Sotsu gyo sei (Spring)

TRANSLATION
Jocelyne Allen

ADAPTATION
Lillian Diaz-Przybyl

LETTERING AND RETOUCH
Ray Steeves

COVER DESIGN
KC Fabellon

PROOFREADER
Stephanie Cohen
Danielle King

EDITOR
Shannon Fay

PRODUCTION MANAGER
Lissa Pattillo

MANAGING EDITOR
Julie Davis

EDITOR-IN-CHIEF
Adam Arnold

PUBLISHER
Jason DeAngelis

SOTSU GYO SEI
© Asumiko Nakamura 2010
Originally published in Japan in 2010 by AKANESHINSHA, Tokyo.
English translation rights arranged with COMIC HOUSE, Tokyo,
through TOHAN CORPORATION, Tokyo.

Seven Seas press and purchase enquiries can be sent to Marketing Manager
Lianne Sentar at press@gomanga.com. Information regarding the distribution
and purchase of digital editions is available from Digital Manager CK Russell
at digital@gomanga.com.

Seven Seas and the Seven Seas logo are trademarks of
Seven Seas Entertainment. All rights reserved.

ISBN: 978-1-64275-068-3

Printed in Canada

First Printing: November 2019

10 9 8 7 6 5 4 3 2 1

FOLLOW US ONLINE: *www.sevenseasentertainment.com*

READING DIRECTIONS

This book reads from **right to left**, Japanese style.
If this is your first time reading manga, you start
reading from the top right panel on each page and
take it from there. If you get lost, just follow the
numbered diagram here. It may seem backwards at
first, but you'll get the hang of it! Have fun!!

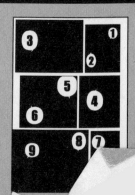